The Structure of the Japanese Language

Current Studies in Linguistics Series
Samuel Jay Keyser, general editor

The Structure of the Japanese Language

Susumu Kuno

The MIT Press   Cambridge, Massachusetts, and London, England

This book was designed by The MIT Press Design Department.
It was set in Monotype Baskerville
by Wolf Composition Co., Inc.,
printed on Finch Publisher's Offset
by Vail-Ballou Press, Inc.,
and bound in Whitman POC (No. 1776)
by Vail-Ballou Press, Inc.,
in the United States of America.

Library of Congress Cataloging in Publication Data

Kuno, Susumu, 1933–
    The structure of the Japanese language.

    (Current studies in linguistics series, no. 3)
    Bibliography: p.
    1. Japanese language—Grammar—1870–   . 2. Japanese language—Syntax.
3. Japanese language—Idioms, corrections, errors.   I. Title.
PL533.K78   495.6′5   72–11859
ISBN 0-262-11049-0

Contents

Foreword

We are pleased to present this book as the third volume in the series Current Studies in Linguistics.

As we have defined it, the series will offer book-length studies in linguistics and neighboring fields that further the exploration of man's ability to manipulate symbols. It will pursue the same editorial goals as its companion journal, *Linguistic Inquiry*, and will complement it by providing a format for in-depth studies beyond the scope of the professional article.

By publishing such studies, we hope the series will answer a need for intensive and detailed research that sheds new light on current theoretical issues and provides a new dimension for their resolution. Toward this end it will present books dealing with the widest range of languages and addressing the widest range of theoretical topics. From time to time and with the same ends in view, the series will include collections of significant articles covering single and selected subject areas and works primarily for use as textbooks.

Like *Linguistic Inquiry*, Current Studies in Linguistics will seek to present work of theoretical interest and excellence.

Samuel Jay Keyser

Preface

This book is not a comprehensive reference grammar. It does not deal with any features of Japanese that are treated more or less satisfactorily in conventional Japanese grammars. It deals only with those problems of Japanese—and just a handful of them—that are either completely ignored or erroneously treated in conventional grammars. For these features I hope that this book will give the reader a revealing account of a kind seldom found in other Japanese grammars or in grammars of any other languages.

Conventional grammars tell us when we *can* use given grammatical patterns. However, they almost invariably fail to tell us when we *cannot* use them. Many of the chapters of this book are concerned with the latter problem. They attempt to explain why some sentences that should be grammatical according to the explanations given in conventional grammars are in fact ungrammatical. In this sense, the book can be called a grammar of ungrammatical sentences.

Some chapters deal with topics that are of general interest to the linguist, regardless of whether he specializes in Japanese linguistics or not. Others deal with specific topics in Japanese of no general linguistic interest. In chapters of this type I discuss two or more patterns of similar meaning. These are the patterns with which students of Japanese most often make mistakes in choosing the appropriate forms in given contexts. No major linguistic generalizations are intended in these specific chapters, and their significance may escape a reader who has not had the crucifying experience of being able to tell that a given Japanese sentence composed by his student is ungrammatical without being able to tell why it is so.

This book can be read by three groups of people:
1. Students and teachers of Japanese with little knowledge of linguistics: Chapters 1 through 27.
2. Linguists with some knowledge of Japanese: all chapters.
3. Linguists with no knowledge of Japanese: Chapters 1, 2, 3, 8, 17 through 28.
For the convenience of individual readers, I have marked each chapter heading with an indicator showing which of the three groups will find the chapter most useful.

My research in Japanese linguistics has been supported in part by Harvard University and in part by the National Science Foundation under its grants to Harvard (GS-1934 and GS-2858). I am particularly indebted to Murray Aborn, Social Sciences Division of the NSF, for his continuing support of my work. I am also grateful to David Hays, Department of

Linguistics, State University of New York at Buffalo, for two summers, six weeks each, of peaceful research with a minimal teaching load. I am greatly indebted to Shmuel Winograd, Alan J. Hoffman, and Warren J. Plath, Mathematical Sciences Department, IBM Thomas J. Watson Research Center, for providing me with a refuge for uninterrupted research during my leave of absence from Harvard in the academic year 1971.

Many people have read the manuscripts of this book, either in part or in full, at various stages. I am grateful to Sheila Duncan, John Haig, and Frederick Damerau, who read earlier versions of the book and gave me numerous suggestions both on the linguistic aspect and on the exposition. I also wish to thank Trylla Esherick, who acted as one of my native informants on English, and who edited and typed the book through its five or six successive versions.

I have received invaluable comments on part of the book from Mineko Masamune, Kazue Campbell, James McCawley, Noriko Atatsuka, Jane Robinson, David Perlmutter, Adrian Akmajian, Bruce Fraser, John Ross, Karl V. Teeter, Paul Postal, Masatake Muraki, Masayoshi Shibatani, Emmon Bach, Charles Fillmore, and from my colleagues and students in the Department of Linguistics at Harvard. My mistakes, of course, are my own, and the people who have helped me do not necessarily agree with all I say in this book.

In my research I have relied most heavily upon the work of four scholars in Japanese linguistics. I have not had to start from scratch, but have been able to build on what these four have already accomplished. They are the following:

Shiro Hattori, to whom I owe my basic training in linguistics, and whose numerous works on general and Oriental linguistics have given me insights into the structure of Japanese. It was with great pleasure that I received the news that he was awarded the National Cultural Medal from the Japanese government in November 1971 for his contribution to research in, and teaching of, linguistics in Japan.

Anthony Alfonso, whose *Japanese Sentence Patterns* (Sophia University, Tokyo, Japan, 1966) I regard as the very best reference grammar, if not the best textbook, in existence for any language of the world.

The late Akira Mikami, whose imaginative and unique works on Japanese grammar have been the source of inspiration for my linguistic analysis. I received the news of his untimely death on September 16, 1971, with a shock and a great sense of loss.

Sige-Yuki Kuroda, whose works have laid the foundation for the analysis of Japanese in the framework of the theory of transformational grammar.

I should also hasten to thank the students at Harvard University whom I taught Japanese. Their mistakes in the use of Japanese have been responsible for many of the chapters of this book. Their mistakes were often due, not to their stupidity or carelessness, but to my own. The explanations for the use of some grammatical patterns that I and conventional grammars gave them left much room for making erroneous uses of the patterns. These mistakes, which often occurred when they tried to extend their knowledge of English to Japanese, made me realize the difference between the two languages. It was through my efforts to explain why their ungrammatical sentences were ungrammatical that I arrived at some interesting generalizations on the uses of these patterns.

Earlier versions of four chapters of this book have previously appeared elsewhere. They are:

1. Chapter 2, "*Wa* and *Ga* (Part I)—Theme, Contrast, Exhaustive Listing, and Neutral Description," in *The Bulletin of the Institute for Research in Language Teaching*, No. 289 (Summer 1969, Tokyo), pp. 17–32.

2. Chapter 3, "*Wa* and *Ga* (Part II)—Subjectivization" and Chapter 4, "*Ga* for Object Marking," in *Sciences of Language: The Journal of the Tokyo Institute for Advanced Studies of Language*, No. 2 (November 1970, Tokyo), pp. 39–72.

3. Chapter 28, "The Position of Locatives in Existential Sentences," in *Linguistic Inquiry*, Vol. 2, No. 3 (Summer 1971), pp. 333–378.

I am grateful to the editors of these journals for giving me a copyright release on the papers.

In addition, I must give special thanks to Jay Keyser, in his role as editor of the M.I.T. Press series Current Studies in Linguistics, for his encouragement and assistance.

Finally, I want to thank my wife, Yoko, whose intuition about Japanese I have relied upon greatly in my research, and without whose encouragement this book might not have seen the light.

Susumu Kuno

I
Introduction

1 †

Typological Characteristics of Japanese

This chapter has two objectives: the first is to give the reader with no previous knowledge of Japanese some idea of what kind of language Japanese is. The second is to give him a preview of what kind of problems this book is going to deal with. The standard way of accomplishing the first objective is to give a grammatical sketch of the language. Well-balanced grammatical sketches of languages, however, tend to become monotonous and boring. Therefore, I have opted here to present only representative samples of those features that make Japanese Japanese— namely, those features of Japanese which are in marked contrast to the corresponding features of English or many other Indo-European languages that the reader may be familiar with. Section 1 deals with the basic word order of Japanese and with peculiarities of Japanese attributable to, or related to, this basic word order. Section 2 deals with the problem of dele- tion of the subject, object, and other elements in the sentence. Sections 3 and 4 discuss polite and honorific expressions and adversity passives, re- spectively. Finally, Section 5 enumerates some important characteristics of Japanese that have not been touched upon in the first four sections. In the course of discussing (or simply listing) these features, I shall refer to chapters in this book in which the same problems or related topics are dealt with in detail.

1. Japanese as an SOV Language

Japanese is an SOV language—namely, a language in which the basic word order of transitive sentences is that of S(ubject)–O(bject)–V(erb). Besides Japanese, languages such as Ainu, Korean, Mongolian, Turkish, Burmese, Tamil, Hindi, and Navaho belong to this group. Except for the very rigid constraint that verbs must appear in the sentence-final position,[1] Japanese has a relatively free word order. For example,

(1) a. John ga   Mary o   but-ta.
         nominative   accusative hit-past
         particle   particle
      'John hit Mary.'

---

†This chapter should be of interest both to linguists and to students of Japanese.
[1] Of the SOV languages listed, this Verb-Final Constraint is also observed rigidly in Ainu, Korean, Mongolian, Burmese, Tamil, and Navaho, but not in Turkish and Hindi.

b.	Mary o	John ga	but-ta.
c.	*John ga	but-ta	Mary o.[2]
d.	*But-ta	John ga	Mary o.

Although (1a) represents the basic word order, (1b) is also grammatical.[3] On the other hand, (1c) and (1d) are ungrammatical because they violate the Verb-Final Constraint. The word order of (1c), namely SVO, which is unacceptable for Japanese, is the basic order of English: French, Italian, Modern Greek, Yoruba, Thai, Malay, Swedish, Finnish, Chinese, etc., are also SVO languages. The word order of (1d), namely, VSO, which is also unacceptable for Japanese, is the basic word order of languages such as Irish, Hebrew, Arabic, Chinook, and Tagabili.[4]

Although there is overwhelming evidence in Japanese that the subject precedes the object, there is some evidence that, for existential sentences such as "There are books on the table," the locative precedes the subject in the basic word order. The basic word order of existential sentences in Japanese and many other languages of the world will be examined in detail in Chapter 28 ("The Position of Locatives in Existential Sentences").

Many of the characteristics of Japanese seem to be attributable, or at least related, to the fact that Japanese is an SOV language with the strict constraint that verbs must appear at the end of the sentence. Among these characteristics are:

1. That Japanese is a postpositional (as opposed to prepositional) language
2. That Japanese is a left-branching language
3. That verb phrase deletion works backward
4. That interrogative words such as *who, which, what, when* do not have to move to the sentence-initial position

A discussion of each of these characteristics follows.

1.1 Japanese as a Postpositional Language

Japanese lacks prepositions. All case relations and other functional re-

---

[2] An asterisk is used to mark ungrammatical sentences. The symbols ?, ??, *?, *, and ** will be used to specify increasing degrees of awkwardness/unacceptability.

[3] According to a large-scale statistical study of sentence structures conducted by the National Language Research Institute, Tokyo, Japan, the ratio of frequencies of occurrences between the SOV word order and the OSV word order in Japanese is 17 to 1.

[4] Chinook is a language spoken by an American-Indian people of the north shore of the Columbia River at its mouth. Tagabili is a language spoken by a people of southern Mindanao in the Philippines.

lations that would be represented in English by prepositions, subordinating conjunctions, and coordinating conjunctions are expressed in Japanese by "particles" that are postpositional. Observe the following sentences:

(2) a. John *ga*   Mary *ni*   hon *o*   yatta.
           nom.   dat. book acc. gave
       'John gave Mary a book.'

   b. John *ga*   Mary *to*   kuruma *de* Kobe *ni* itta.
           nom.   with car   by   to went
       'John went to Kobe by car with Mary.'

There are some seventy postpositional particles, but there are no prepositional particles in Japanese. This characteristic of Japanese is shared by many other SOV languages. This fact has led Greenberg (1963) to hypothesize the following as a language universal: "With overwhelmingly greater than chance frequency, languages with normal SOV order are postpositional."[5]

There are two important matters that must be mentioned with respect to Japanese particles. First, particles are used not only to represent case relationships, or to represent the functions that are carried in English by prepositions and conjunctions, but also after sentence-final verbs to represent the speaker's attitude toward the content of the sentences. For example,

(3) a. Kore wa hon   desu *yo*.
       this   book is
       '*I am telling you that* this is a book.'

   b. Kore wa hon desu *ne*.
       '*I hope you agree that* this is a book.'

   c. Kore wa hon desu *ka*.
       '*I ask you* if this is a book.'

   d. John wa baka   *sa*.
                     foolish
       '*It goes without saying that* John is a fool.'

Second, Japanese is one of the few languages of the world that have a

---

[5] Greenberg's Language Universal 4. See Greenberg (1963, p. 79).

built-in mechanism for specifying the theme or topic of the sentence. The particle *wa* is used for this purpose. For example,

(4) John *wa* Mary ni hon o yatta.
                  to book gave
    'Speaking of John, (he) gave a book to Mary.'

What the difference in meaning between (2a) and (4) is, what other functions *wa* and *ga* have, where they can be used in what functions, and so on, will be the topics of Chapters 2 through 4. Some of the particles that are similar in meaning but different in subtle details are discussed in Chapters 4 through 8. The predictability of particles used as case markers is the topic of Chapter 27. Temporal and conditional clauses represented by particles or by use of certain inflectional forms of verbs will be compared for their similarities and differences in Chapters 11 through 16. Some subordinate clauses are tightly connected to the main clause, and some very loosely. Various degrees of subordination that exist in Japanese adverbial clauses will be discussed in Chapter 17.

1.2 Japanese as a Left-Branching Language

Genitives, adjectives, and relative clauses precede the head nouns in Japanese. For example,

(5) a. *John no* imooto ga   sinda.
              's sister   nom. died
        'John's sister has died.'

    b. John ga   *omosiroi*   hon o kaita.
              nom. interesting book   wrote
       'John has written an interesting book.'

    c. John wa *Mary ga   kaita* hon o yonda.
              theme   nom. wrote book   read
       'John read the book that Mary wrote.'

In (5a), the genitive *John no* 'John's' precedes the head noun *imooto* 'sister'. In (5b), the adjective *omosiroi* '(be) interesting' precedes the head noun *hon* 'book'. Similarly, in (5c), the relative clause *Mary ga kaita* '(that) Mary wrote' precedes the head noun *hon* 'book'.

This feature of Japanese makes it a left-branching language. What is meant by "left-branching" will become clear by observing the following sentence:

(6) a. [[[John ga　　katte-iru]ₛ neko ga　　korosita]ₛ
　　　　　　　nom. keep　　　cat　nom. killed
　　　nezumi ga　　tabeta]ₛ tiizu　wa　　kusatte-ita.
　　　rat　　nom. ate　　cheese theme rotten-was
　　　(Literal word order) [[[John keeps] cat killed] rat ate] cheese was
　　　rotten.'

　 b. 'The cheese that the rat that the cat that John keeps killed ate
　　　was rotten.'

Example (6a) is a perfectly grammatical and intelligible sentence, while
its English translation (6b) is almost totally unintelligible. Sentence (6a)
has roughly the syntactic structure shown in (7). This sentence has three

(7)

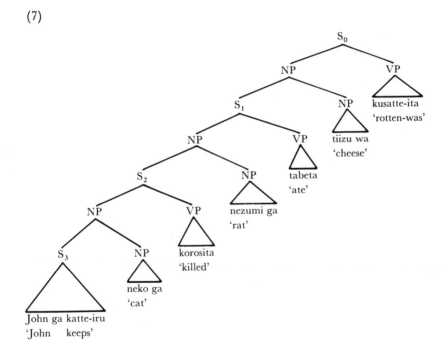

embedded left-branching clauses, namely, S_1, S_2, and S_3.[6] This is not the upper limit to the depth of left-branching clauses in Japanese. One can easily construct sentences with many more embedded left-branching clauses. This is why Japanese is called a left-branching language. On the other hand, English is basically a right-branching language. For example, (8a) is a perfectly normal sentence, with no difficulty in comprehension; it has the structure shown in diagram (8b).

(8) a. John owned a cat that killed a rat that ate cheese that was rotten.

b.

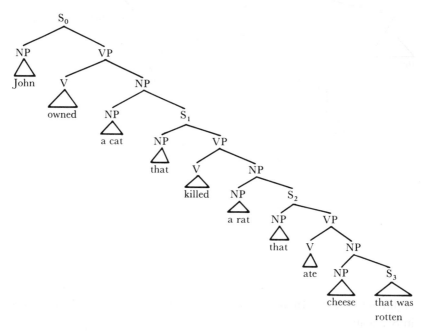

From the diagram it is clear that neither left-branching nor right-branching, extended arbitrarily far, impairs comprehension. Why is it, then, that (6b) is almost totally unintelligible? The difference between (6b), on

[6] The symbol S in this book will be used in two senses, according to traditional practice. When phrase structures of the type of (6) or (7) are involved, S represents a sentence or clause. When word order is under discussion, as in SOV, SVO, and VSO, S represents the subject. Since contexts for the two uses of S are sufficiently clear, no ambiguity will result.

the one hand, and (6a) and (8), on the other, is that the former involves self-embedding. A structure of category A is self-embedded if it is preceded and followed by nonnull strings B and C, and if BAC is also of category A, namely, if we have $[BAC]_A$. Observe the representation of the structure

(9)

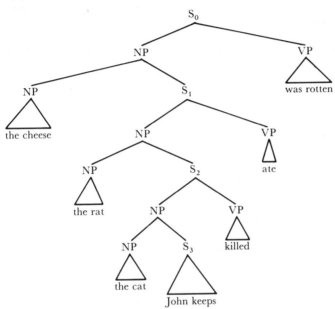

of (6b) given in (9). In the diagram, S_3 (that is, *John keeps*) is self-embedded in S_2, as in

(10) $[$the cat S_3 killed$]_{S_2}$

Furthermore, S_2 (that is, *the cat that John keeps killed*) is self-embedded in S_1, as in

(11) $[$the rat S_2 ate$]_{S_1}$

And S_1, in turn, is self-embedded in S_0. It is the layer of self-embedded structures that impairs comprehension.[7]

[7] This observation is due to Chomsky (1961).

Are there relative clause constructions in Japanese that involve deep self-embedding? The answer, of course, is affirmative, although no such constructions have been discussed in the literature. Consider the following examples:

(12) a. John ga tegami o yonda.
            letter   read
      'John read the letter.'

   b. John ga [Mary ga syoonen ni kaita] tegami o yonda.
                   boy   to wrote letter   read
      'John read the letter that Mary wrote to the boy.'

   c. John ga [Mary ga [Jane ga aisite-iru] syoonen ni kaita]
                         loving-is boy   to wrote
      tegami o yonda.
      letter   read
      'John read the letter that Mary wrote to the boy that Jane loved.'

Sentence (12c) is as difficult for the Japanese speakers to comprehend as (6b) is for the English speakers. Incidentally, note that the English translation of (12c) involves right-branching, and not self-embedding, and therefore causes no difficulty in comprehension.

1.3 Direction of Verb Phase Deletion
In English, there is a process of deleting all but the first n identical verbs or verb phrases in coordinated sentences.[8] For example,

(13) a.   John hit Mary, Bill hit Jane, and Tom hit Martha.

   b.   John hit Mary, Bill Jane, and Tom Martha.

   c.   *John Mary, Bill Jane, and Tom hit Martha.

---

[8] Deletion of verb phrases leaving auxiliaries behind (to be referred to as "nontensed verb deletion") is an entirely different process, and has a broader applicability. For example,

(i) a.   John will do it if he can do it.
    b.   *John will do it if he. (verb phrase deletion)
    c.   John will do it if he can. (nontensed verb deletion)

(ii) a.   John came.   Mary did not come.
     b.   John came.   *Mary not.   } (verb phrase deletion)
                        *Not Mary.   }
     c.   John came.   Mary didn't. (nontensed verb deletion)

I shall use the notation *SVO SO* to refer to the pattern of (13b). In other SVO languages, also, verb phrase deletion in coordinated sentences works forward. For example,

(14) a. Jean a   frappé Marie, Jacques a frappé Jeanne, et Antoine a
              has hit
          frappé Michelle.

     b. Jean a frappé Marie, Jacques Jeanne, et Antoine Michelle.

     c. *Jean Marie, Jacques Jeanne, et Antoine a frappé Michelle.

On the other hand, in Japanese, verb phrase deletion in coordinated sentences works backward; namely, it deletes all but the last of *n* identical verbs. Observe the following examples:

(15) a. John ga Mary o but-i,   Bill ga Jane o but-i,   Tom ga Martha o
                          hit-and   hit-and
          butta.
          hit

     b. *John ga Mary o but-i, Bill ga Jane o, Tom ga Martha o.

     c. John ga Mary o, Bill ga Jane o, Tom ga Martha o butta.

I shall use the notation *SO SOV* to refer to the pattern of (15c).

   Example (15c) may appear very unusual to the English speakers, but the same pattern manifests itself in English also. For example, observe the following:

(16) a. Yesterday John came, and today Mary came.

     b. Yesterday John came, and today Mary. (forward deletion)

     c. Yesterday John, and today Mary, came. (backward deletion)

(17) a. John feebly protested, and Mary vehemently protested.

     b. John feebly protested, and Mary vehemently. (forward deletion)

     c. John feebly, and Mary vehemently, protested. (backward deletion)

From (13), (16), and (17), one can tentatively hypothesize that forward deletion in English applies rather freely (subject to constraints that do not concern us here), while backward deletion applies only when the common verb appears at the end of each conjoined clause.

Now, observe the phenomenon of verb phrase deletion in German. German is an SVO language, and in main clauses the same pattern of verb phrase deletion is obtained as in English:

(18) a.   Johann schlug Maria, und Peter schlug Anna.
            hit   and   hit
      b.   Johann schlug Maria, und Peter Anna.
      c.   *Johann Maria, und Peter schlug Anna.

In subordinate clauses in German, verbs must appear at the clause-final position. Here, verb phrase deletion works either forward or backward, showing that the same hypothesis that we have set up for English applies to German also.

(19) a.   Wilhelm sagt, dass Johann Maria schlug und Peter Anna
                says   that   hit
         schlug.
         hit
         'William says that John hit Mary and Peter hit Anna.'
      b.   *Wilhelm sagt, dass Johann schlug Maria und Peter schlug Anna.
      c.   Wilhelm sagt, dass Johann Maria schlug und Peter Anna. (forward deletion)
      d.   Wilhelm sagt, dass Johann Maria und Peter Anna schlug. (backward deletion)

Why is it, then, that verb phrase deletion does not work forward in Japanese? In (15a) the common verb appears at the end of each of the conjoined clauses, just as in (16), (17), and (19), and therefore if the same principles of verb phrase deletion that are applicable to English and German are also applicable to Japanese, example (15b) should be grammatical. Is it the case that the principles of verb phrase deletion in Japanese are totally different from those in English and German?

It seems that Japanese shares the same principles, but (15b) is ungrammatical because Japanese is a rigid SOV language. Namely, all clauses in Japanese must end with verbs, and since (15b) ends with a noun phrase (that is, *Martha o*), it violates this condition. It is not the case that all SOV languages are strict SOV languages. For example, Persian and Amharic are predominantly SOV. However, there are sentence patterns in these languages that end with nonverbal elements. In Persian, *John went to home*, in that word order, as well as *John to home went*, is grammatical. In Amharic, interrogative questions such as *where is the hotel* end with the subject at the sentence-final position. In these languages, both *SOV SO* and *SO SOV* patterns are acceptable; namely, both forward and backward verb phrase deletions apply to *SOV SOV*.

To recapitulate, verb phrase deletion in coordinated clauses applies forward rather freely (but subject to certain constraints that do not concern us here). On the other hand, verb phrase deletion applies backward only when the common verb phrase appears in clause-final positions. Japanese appears to be an exception to the former principle, but only superficially so. Forward deletion does not apply to Japanese because it is a rigid SOV language, and all clauses must end with verbs.

1.4 Position of Interrogative Words

Questions are expressed in Japanese by adding the interrogative particle *ka* at the end of the sentence. For example,

(20) a. Kore wa hon   desu.
          this   book is
          'This is a book.'
      b. Kore wa hon desu *ka*.
          'Is this a book?'

The fact that the interrogative particle in Japanese appears at the sentence-final position does not seem to be accidental. Greenberg[9] observes that postpositional languages (which many SOV languages are; see Section 1.1) generally use the sentence-final particle, and prepositional languages the sentence-initial particle, if a particle is used for formation of questions.

In Japanese, the interrogative words such as *dare* 'who', *dore* 'which', *nani* 'what' in *wh*-questions do not have to be preposed to sentence-initial positions. Observe the following examples:

(21) a. John ga *dare o* butta ka siranai.
              who   hit   know-not
          'I don't know whom John hit.'
      b. *Dare o* John ga butta ka siranai.

In (21a) the interrogative word *dare* 'who' stays in its second position in

---

[9] This is Greenberg's Language Universal 9: "With well more than chance frequency, when question particles or affixes are specified in position by reference to the sentence as a whole, if initial, such elements are found in prepositional languages, and if final, in postpositional." See Greenberg (1963, p. 81).

the sentence, without undergoing preposing. In (21b), which is also grammatical, *dare o* appears in the sentence-initial position, but this word order
is a marked one in that *dare o* is emphasized just as *Mary o* of (22b) is
emphasized.

(22) a. John ga Mary o butta.
                      hit
         'John hit Mary.'
      b. Mary o John ga butta.

This characteristic stands in marked contrast with that of English, in which
interrogative words must be preposed:

(23) a. *Whom* did John hit?
      b. *John hit *whom?*

Example (23b) is ungrammatical unless it is an echo question. Greenberg
observes:[10] "If a language has dominant order VSO in declarative sentences, it always puts interrogative words or phrases first in interrogative
word questions; if it has dominant order SOV in declarative sentences,
there is never such an invariant rule."[11]

   In English, in which interrogative words must be preposed to the sentence-initial position, there are questions that are semantically plausible
but syntactically implausible. For example, observe the following:

(24) a. John believed that Mary did not like *someone.*
      b. *Whom* did John believe that Mary did not like?

(25) a. John believed the claim that Mary did not like *someone.*
      b. **Whom* did John believe the claim that Mary did not like?

(26) a. John took away the book that Mary gave to *someone.*
      b. **Whom* did John take away the book that Mary gave to?

Ross (1967) has observed that what makes (24b) grammatical and (25b)
ungrammatical is that in the former *that Mary did not like someone* is a simple
noun clause, while in the latter *the claim that Mary did not like someone* is a
complex noun phrase. A complex noun phrase, according to Ross, is a
noun phrase that has the structure of [NP S], where NP contains a lexical

[10] Greenberg's Language Universal 12. See Greenberg (1963, p. 83).
[11] Bach (1971) has proposed an interesting account of why the interrogative words in
wh-questions are never preposed in sentence-initial positions in SOV languages.

noun. His generalization is that nothing can be moved out of a complex NP. The Complex NP Constraint, as it is called, seems to be in operation not only in *wh*-questions but also in other transformations that involve movements. For example,

(27) Relative Clause Formation
      a. This is the man that John believed that Mary did not like.
      b. *This is the man that John believed the claim that Mary did not like.

(28) Topic Formation
      a. This man, John believed that Mary did not like.
      b. *This man, John believed the claim that Mary did not like.

(29) Cleft Sentence Formation
      a. It is this man that John believed that Mary did not like.
      b. *It is this man that John believed the claim that Mary did not like.

Now, note that interrogative sentences in Japanese corresponding to (24b), (25b), and (26b) are all grammatical:

(30) a. John wa, Mary ga *dare o* kiratte-iru to   sinzite-ita ka?
                    whom hating-is   that   believing-was
        'Whom did John believe that Mary hated?'
      b. John wa, Mary ga *dare o* kiratte-iru to-yuu syutyoo o
                    whom hating-is   that   claim
        sinzite-ita ka?
        believing-was
        '(Lit.) Whom did John believe the claim that Mary hated?'
      c. John wa, Mary ga *dare*   *ni* ageta hon o toriageta ka?
                    whom to gave book took-away
        '(Lit.) Whom did John take away the book that Mary gave to?'

Some more examples of the same type follow:

(31) a. Mary ga *dare*   *ni* ageta hon ga omosirokatta ka?
              whom to gave book   interesting-was
        '(Lit.) Whom was the book that Mary gave to interesting?'
      b. Mary ga *dare o* kiratte-iru koto ga akiraka ka?
               whom hating-is fact that certain
        '(Lit.) Whom is the fact that Mary hates (him) clear?'

These are the sentences for which there are no appropriate English translations.

Similarly, an interrogative word may appear as part of the coordinate structure. For example,

(32) a. [Mary to   *dare*] ni aimasita ka?
              and who to met
         '(Lit.) *[Mary and who] did you meet? *Who did you meet Mary and?'

   b. [Hon to   *nani*] o kaimasita ka?
        book and what   bought
        '(Lit.) *[Books and what] did you buy? *What did you buy books and?'

Note that the English equivalents are ungrammatical. That the Japanese sentences in (30), (31), and (32) are grammatical is undoubtedly due to the fact that interrogative words such as *dare* 'who', *dore* 'which', *nani* 'what' are not moved to the sentence-initial position in Japanese *wh*-questions.

2. Ellipsis

In English and many other languages, such as French and German, there is a very strong structural pressure that there be overt subjects for finite verbs, that transitive verbs have overt objects, and that subjects appear at the sentence-initial position. This results in abundant use of pronouns. Consider the following English examples:

(33) a.   Since John came, *I* went to see *him*.
           *Since John came, went to see.

   b.   If John can, *he* will do it.
        If *he* can, John will do it.
        *If can, John will do it.
        *If John can, will do it.

   c.   *It* is certain that Mary is a fool.
        *Is certain that Mary is a fool.

   d.   *It* is raining.
        *Is raining.

Examples (33a) and (33b) show that personal pronouns cannot be deleted;

examples (33c) and (33d) show that English sometimes uses dummy subjects to retain the subject-verb pattern.

In Japanese, sentences can have their subjects missing, and transitive
verbs can have their objects missing. For example,

(34) a. John ga kita   node, ai ni itta.
             came since see to went
        'Since John came, (I) went to see (him).'

     b. John ga deki-reba suru desyoo.
             can-if   do   will
        'If John can, (he) will do (it).'

This is, no doubt, related to the fact that word order is rather free in
Japanese except for the verb-final constraint. In normal sentences, subjects appear sentence-initially, but when some other elements in the sentence are emphasized, they can be placed rather freely to the left of the
subject. For example, observe the following sentences, all of which are
grammatical:

(35) a. John ga Mary ni hon o yatta.
                      to book gave
        'John gave Mary a book.'

     b. John ga hon o Mary ni yatta.
        'John gave a book to Mary.'

     c. Mary ni John ga hon o yatta.
        'To Mary John gave a book.'

     d. Mary ni hon o John ga yatta.
        '(Lit.) To Mary, a book John gave.'

     e. Hon o John ga Mary ni yatta.
        'A book, John gave to Mary.'

     f. Hon o Mary ni John ga yatta.
        '(Lit.) A book, to Mary John gave.'

Japanese lacks authentic third person pronouns. In colloquial speech,
in which there are many levels of first person and second person pronouns
used, no third person pronouns are used. Where English would use *he,
she, it, they,* Japanese would either (i) have no overt forms, (ii) have attribute nouns such as titles, or (iii) have full-fledged noun phrases. Ex-

amples of type (i) have been given in (34). Examples of types (ii) and (iii) follow:

(36) a. Tanaka-sensei   ga irassyat-tara,   *sensei*   ni tanomoo.
            teacher   come-have-when teacher to ask
      'When Teacher Tanaka has come, (I) will ask the teacher.'
    b. Tanaka-sensei ga irassyat-tara, *Tanaka-sensei* ni tanomoo.
      'When Teacher Tanaka has come, I will ask Teacher Tanaka.'
    c. Tanaka ga kitara, *aitu*   ni tanomoo.
                          that-guy
      'When Tanaka has come, I will ask (lit.) that guy.'

In the speech and writing of educated Japanese, on the other hand, what can be called third person pronouns do appear. They are *kare* 'he', *kanozyo* 'she', *kare-ra* 'they', and *kanozyo-ra* 'they (female)'. However, these are forms originally derived from demonstrative pronouns. For example, *kare* once meant 'that-there', *kanozyo* 'that-there woman'. On the other hand, since these forms display peculiarities that are very similar to those of English personal pronouns, they could justifiably be called pronouns.

It is not clear at present when subjects, objects, and other elements of sentences can be deleted and when they must not be deleted. A great deal depends upon how unambiguously the missing elements can be supplied. For example, (37a) can never be realized as (37b).

(37) a. John ga Mary o but-i,   Mary ga John o hikkaita.
                      hit-and   scratched
      'John hit Mary, and Mary scratched John.'
    b. *John ga Mary o but-i, hikkaita.

Example (37b) would be grammatical if it were intended to mean "John hit, and scratched, Mary." On the other hand, consider example (37c).

(37) c. Mary ga kita   toki   ai ni kita.
                  came when see to came

This sentence can mean either 'When Mary came, (I) came to see (her)', or 'When Mary came, (she) came to see (me).' Exact conditions for the acceptability and unacceptability of such deletions await further studies.

3. Polite and Honorific Expressions
Japanese is well known for its richness in grammatical and lexical means for distinguishing various levels of politeness and various levels of respect-

fulness. There are four levels of sentence styles with respect to politeness: informal, polite, superpolite, and formal writing.[12] Observe the following examples:

(38) a. Informal   Kore wa hon *da.*
                           this   book is
                           'This is a book.'

      b. Polite   Kore wa hon *des-u.*
                                          be-present

      c. Superpolite   Kore wa hon *de   gozai-mas-u.*
                                          being be-polite-present

      d. Formal writing   Kore wa hon *de   ar-u.*
                                          being be-present

(39) a. Informal   Kore wa *omosiro-i.*
                           this   interesting-present
                           'This is interesting.'

      b. Polite   Kore wa *omosiro-i desu.*

      c. Superpolite   Kore wa *omosiroo gozai-mas-u.*

      d. Formal writing   (same as Informal)

(40) a. Informal   John ga doa o *ake-ru.*
                                        door   open-present
                           'John opens the door.'

      b. Polite   John ga doa o *ake-mas-u.*
                                        open-polite-present

      c. Superpolite   (missing)

      d. Formal writing   (same as Informal)

These are productive patterns and apply to all copulative, adjectival, and verb expressions in Japanese.

The preceding four levels of style have nothing to do with the level of respect, which is on a different plane. They are dependent upon how close the speaker is justified to feel toward the hearer and, in this regard, are somewhat analogous to the use of first names in addressing others in English. The informal style can be used among friends, but, for example, a student can never use (38a) when he is talking to his teacher.

12 The following accounts of polite and honorific expressions are based on Mikami (1970).

Differences in politeness and level of respect have their reflection not only in verbal paradigms but also in use of different vocabularies, as shown in (47) and (48).

		'yes'	'I'	'be'	'do'
(47)	a. Informal	un	ore/boku	ar-u	su-ru
	b. Polite	ee	boku/watakusi	ar-i-mas-u	si-mas-u
	c. Superpolite	hai	watakusi	gozai-mas-u	itas-i-mas-u
	d. Formal writing	sikari	watakusi	ar-u	su-ru

		'come'	'go'	'die'
(48)	a. Plain	ku-ru	ik-u	sin-u
	b. Respect for subject	oide ni nar-u (*o-ki ni nar-u)	o-ik-i ni nar-u	nakunar-u
	c. Respect for object		mair-u o-ik-i su-ru	

Japanese has a very rich vocabulary of giving and receiving verbs. Which one of these verbs is to be used in which context is determined by (i) the speaker's respect for the subject, and (ii) the relative positions of the subject and the object in social status. This problem will be the topic of Chapter 9 ("Giving and Receiving Verbs").

4. Adversity Passives
In English, only transitive sentences have corresponding passives. For example,

(49) a. John beat Mary.
        Mary was beaten by John.
   b. Rain fell.
        *(It) was fallen by rain.

In Japanese, on the other hand, intransitive verbs can appear in passive constructions. For example,

(50) a. Ame ga hut-ta.
        rain   fall-past
        'Rain fell.'

      b. John ga ame ni hur-are-ta.
                rain by fall-passive-past
                '(Lit.) John was fallen by rain.'

(51) a. Tuma ga sin-da.
        wife   die-past
        'The wife died.'

      b. John ga tuma ni sin-are-ta.
                wife by die-passive-past
                '(Lit.) John was died by his wife.'

(52) a. Kodomo ga asa-hayaku   oki-ta.
        child   morning-early get-up-ed
        'The children got up early in the morning.'

      b. John ga kodomo ni asa-hayaku   oki-rare-ta.
                child   by early-morning get-up-passive-ed
                '(Lit.) John was gotten up early in the morning by the children.'

Verbs such as *hur-u* 'to fall', *sin-u* 'to die', and *oki-ru* 'to get up' are strictly intransitive and cannot take either direct or indirect objects under any circumstances. Still they can be followed by the passive morpheme *rare/are*, as shown. Note that this passive morpheme that appears in these peculiar passive sentences is the same as the one that appears in ordinary passive sentences such as

(53) a. John wa sensei   ni sikar-are-ta.
                teacher by scold-passive-ed
        'John was scolded by the teacher.'

      b. John wa Mary ni izime-rare-ta.
                   by bully-around-passive-ed
        'John was bullied around by Mary.'

Of the same nature as (50)–(52) are the following passive sentences:

(54) a. Sensei ga kodomo o sikat-ta.
        teacher child   scold-ed
        'The teacher scolded the child.'

      b. John ga sensei   ni kodomo o sikar-are-ta.
                teacher by child   scold-passive
                '(Lit.) John was scolded his child by the teacher.'

(55) a. Mary ga piano o hi-ita.

                play-ed

    'Mary played the piano.'

   b. John ga Mary ni piano o hik-are-ta.

    '(Lit.) John was played the piano by Mary.'

What is peculiar syntactically about (50), (51), (52) and (54), (55) is that these passive sentences have one extra noun phrase compared to the corresponding active sentences. What is peculiar semantically about these passives is that they mean that the subject of the main sentence is adversely affected. For example, (50b) means that John was adversely affected by rain falling or that, to John's chagrin, it rained. Similarly, (55b) means that John was adversely affected by Mary's playing the piano and thus implies that he was annoyed by the sound.

There are some apparent counterexamples to this semantic analysis, such as

(56)   Boku wa kodomo o sensei   ni home-rare-ta.

       I   child   teacher by praise-passive-ed

      '(Lit.) I was adversely affected by the teacher's praising my child.'

Obviously, the speaker was not really adversely affected by the teacher's praising his child. However, it seems that this sentence is a reflection of the traditional Japanese attitude, probably extinct by this time and remaining only fossilized in expressions such as this one, that modesty is a virtue and that one should not boast about his or his family's merit. Apparently the expression in (56) used to mean that the speaker was embarrassed (thus adversely affected) by the teacher's praising his child, thus giving the speaker the pretense that he was not really bragging about his child. This connotation of embarrassment is almost nonexistent at present, but is probably responsible for the origin of this expression.

How pure passives and adversity passives in Japanese are derived and how they are related to causative sentences will be discussed in Chapter 25 ("The Reflexive Pronoun and the Passive and Causative Constructions").

5. Some Other Characteristics of Japanese

In the preceding sections, I have discussed characteristics of Japanese related to (i) word order, (ii) deletion, (iii) polite and honorific expressions, and (iv) adversity passives. There are many other interesting features of

Japanese that I shall not examine in detail. Some of them will be simply enumerated in the sections that follow.

5.1 Relative Pronouns

Japanese lacks relative pronouns. Relative clauses precede their head nouns directly, without being preceded or followed by relative pronouns or conjunctions. For example,

(57) *Mary ga kaku* tegami wa omosiroi.
　　　　　　write letter　　interesting is
　　'Letters that Mary writes are interesting.'

Other peculiarities of Japanese relative clauses will be discussed in detail in Chapters 20 ("Relative Clauses") and 21 ("Themes and Relative Clauses").

5.2 Classifiers

As in Chinese, Japanese has a rich system of classifiers, with each classifier related to a class of nouns. For example,

(58)　a.　is-*satu* no hon 'one book'[13]
　　　　　one-volume book
　　　　　ni-*satu* no hon 'two books'
　　　　　two-volume book

　　　b.　ip-*pon* no ki 'one tree'
　　　　　one-stick tree
　　　　　ni-*hon* no ki 'two trees'
　　　　　two-stick tree

　　　c.　ip-*pai* no mizu 'a cup of water'
　　　　　one-cup water
　　　　　ni-*hai* no mizu 'two cups of water'
　　　　　two-cup water

[13] The *no* in these examples is not the genitive particle *no* but the attributive form of the copula *da*, which appears in
(i) John wa gakusei *da*.
　　　　　　student is
　　'John is a student.'
(ii) gakusei *no* John
　　 student is
　　'John, who is a student'
Thus (58a) literally means 'book which is one', and 'books which are two'.

    d. ip-*piki* no inu 'one dog'
       one-head dog
       ni-*hiki* no inu 'two dogs'
       two-head dog

Numerals and numeral-classifier combinations are basically adverbial. For example,

(59) a. Hon o *is-satu* katta.
       book one-vol. bought
       'I bought a book (lit.) one-volume-ly.'

    b. Ringo o *hitotu* tabeta.
       apple one ate
       '(I) ate an apple (lit.) one-ly.'

    c. Ringo o *takusan* tabeta.
       apple many ate
       '(I) ate apples (lit.) many-ly.'

5.3 Number

Nouns are not usually marked with respect to number. For example,

(60) Boku wa otooto ga aru.
     I brother have
    'I have (lit.) brother.'

This can mean either 'I have a brother' or 'I have brothers'. For human beings the plural suffix -*tati* can be used, as in *kodomo-tati* 'children', *gakusei-tati* 'students'. However, the basic function of -*tati* is not that of the English plural morpheme -*s*, but that of 'and others, and the likes'. For example, *John-tati* means, not 'Johns' (two or more people bearing the name John), but 'John and others'. Japanese also lacks what can be called definite and indefinite articles (*the* and *a* in English).

5.4 Demonstratives

Demonstrative pronouns, adjectives, and adverbs have a quadruple system, as shown in (61). These pronouns can be used not only in referring to objects that the speaker and the hearer can see and point to but also in referring to objects that are not visible but have been referred to previously in the conversations. The latter usage of the demonstrative words will be examined in detail in Chapter 24 ("The Anaphoric Use of *Kore, Sore,* and *Are*").

		pronoun	adjective	place
(61)	a. Nearer to the speaker	kore	kono	koko
	b. Nearer to the hearer	sore	sono	soko
	c. Far from both the speaker and the hearer	are	ano	asoko
	d. Interrogative	dore	dono	doko

5.5 Use of "Self"

The Japanese reflexive pronoun *zibun* 'self' is used for all persons and genders (that is, as "myself, yourself, himself, herself," etc.). It cannot be used for other than higher animals. Although (62) is ungrammatical in English, its counterpart with the reflexive *zibun* is grammatical in Japanese.

(62) *John told Mary that she should respect himself (=John).

This does not mean that *zibun* 'self' can be used freely. Example (63) cannot be realized in Japanese with *zibun* in the place of *him*.

(63) John died instantaneously when Mary shot him (=John).

This peculiar behavior of *zibun* will be explained in comparison with the English pronouns and reflexives in Chapters 25 ("The Reflexive Pronoun and the Passive and Causative Constructions") and 26 ("The Reflexive Pronoun and Internal Feeling").

5.6 Inflection of Verbs

Verbs do not inflect with respect to person and number. They inflect in the manner shown in (64).

(64)	a. Present (or nonpast)	tabe-ru	hanas-u	'eat, speak'
	b. Perfect (or past)	tabe-ta	hanas-ita	'ate, spoke'
	c. Imperative	tabe-ro tabe-yo	hanas-e	'Eat, Speak.'
	d. Cohortative	tabe-yoo	hanas-oo	'Let's eat, speak.'

e. Continuative	tabe	hanas-i	'eating, speaking'
f. Gerundive	tabe-te	hanas-ite	'eat-and, speak-and'
g. Conditional	tabe-reba	hanas-eba	'if . . . eat, speak'
h. Perfect conditional	tabe-tara	hanas-itara	'if . . . have eaten, spoken'
i. Perfect suppositional	tabe-taroo	hanas-itaroo	'(I suppose) . . . '

5.7 Inflection of Adjectives

Adjectives can constitute predicates without being accompanied by copulas. As shown in (65), they inflect in a manner similar to verbs.

(65)			
a. Present	aka-i	'is red'
b. Perfect	aka-kat-ta	'was red'
c. Suppositional	aka-kar-oo	'I suppose . . . is red'
d. Continuative	aka-ku	'redly'
e. Gerundive	aka-kute-te	'is red and'
f. Conditional	aka-ke-reba	'if . . . is red'
g. Perfect conditional	aka-kat-tara	'if . . . was (has been) red'
h. Perfect suppositional	aka-kat-taroo	'I suppose . . . was red'

5.8 Nominal Adjectives

There is a class of words called nominal adjectives. They are adjectival in meaning, but they do not inflect. They share certain characteristics with nouns. For example,

(66) a. Kore wa hon   da.
         this   book is
         'This is a book.'

     b. Kore wa hen   da.
         this   strange is
         'This is strange.'

(67) a. Kore wa hon de,   are mo hon da.
         this   book is-and that also book is
         Kore wa hon, are mo hon da.
         'This is a book, and that, too, is a book.'

    b. Kore wa hen de, are mo hen da.
        Kore wa hen, are mo hen da.
        'This is strange, and that, too, is strange.'

(68) a. *Kore wa hon da ka?
         Kore wa hon ka?
         'Is this a book?'

    b. *Kore wa hen da ka?
        Kore wa hen ka?
        'Is this strange?'

In these examples, *hon* 'book' is a noun, and *hen* 'strange' is a nominal adjective. Copulas after nouns and nominal adjectives can be deleted in certain contexts, as in (67), or must be deleted in certain other contexts, as in (68). At the same time, nominal adjectives are not real nouns; they cannot be used as subjects and objects of sentences and cannot be modified by adjectives.

5.9 Action Verbs with *Yar-u* and *Kure-ru*

Action verbs are often followed by *yar-u* 'give' and *kure-ru* 'give (to the speaker)'. In the former compounds, the actions represented by the main verbs are understood to be a favor given by the subjects. In the latter, actions represented by the main verbs are understood to be a favor received by the speaker. For example,

(69) a. John ga Mary ni hon o yon-de *yar*-u.
                          to book read-ing give-present
        'John gives Mary the favor of reading a book.'

    b. John ga hon o yon-de   *kure*-ru.
                  book read-ing give
       'John gives me the favor of reading a book.'

5.10 Action Verbs with *Ku-ru* and *Ik-u*

Action verbs are often followed by *ku-ru* 'come' and *ik-u* 'go'. In the former compounds, actions are taken to be toward the place of the speaker;

in the latter, they are taken to be away from the place of the speaker. For example,

(70) a. John ga kaet-te   *ki*-ta.
                 return-ing came
             '(Lit.) John came returning. John returned (to the speaker's place).'
     b. John ga kaet-te   *it*-ta.
                 return-ing went
             '(Lit.) John went returning. John returned (away from the speaker).'

(71) a. John ga hon o kat-te   *ki*-ta.
                 book buy-ing came
             '(Lit.) John came buying books. John bought books and came to the speaker.'
     b. John ga hon o kat-te   *it*-ta.
                 book buy-ing went
             '(Lit.) John went buying books. John bought books (at the speaker's place) and went away.'

5.11 Verbs Representing States

Verbs, with only a few exceptions, represent actions, and not states. In order to refer to the present state, action verbs must be followed by *i-ru* 'be in the state of'. For example, *aisu-ru* 'to love', *sum-u* 'to live', *sir-u* 'to know' in Japanese are all action verbs, although their English equivalents can represent states. Therefore, for representing the state such as "John loves Mary," "John lives in Tokyo," and "John knows the answer," the *i-ru* 'be in the state of' form must be used.

(72) a. John wa Mary o aisi-te i-ru.
                       lov-ing is
             'John loves Mary.'
     b. John wa Tokyo ni sun-de i-ru.
                       in liv-ing is
             'John lives in Tokyo.'
     c. John wa kotae o sit-te   i-ru.
                       answer knowing is
             'John knows the answer.'

Even the passive of *aisu-ru* 'to love' represents an action and must be followed by *i-ru* if the present state is being referred to:

(73) Mary wa John ni ais-are-te   i-ru.
                    by love-passive-ing is
      'Mary is loved by John.'

We shall go into details of action verbals and state verbals in Chapter 10 ("Stative and Nonstative Verbals").

5.12 Transitive Constructions

In colloquial Japanese, transitive constructions, with few exceptions, require higher animals as their subjects. Thus the following sentences are all ungrammatical:

(74) a. *Zidoosya-ziko ga teen-ager o korosita.
              traffic accident   killed
          'A traffic accident killed a teen-ager.'

      b. *Taihuu ga mado   o kowasita.
              typhoon   window broke
          'A typhoon broke glass windows.'

      c. *Tibusu ga oozei no hito o sin-ase-ta.
              typhus   many   people die-cause-d
          'Typhus has caused many people to die.'

Intransitive constructions are used instead:

(75) a. Zidoosya-ziko de, teen-ager ga sinda.
              traffic-accident in   died
          'A teen-ager died in a traffic accident.'

      b. Taihuu de mado   ga kowareta.
              typhoon by window   broke
          'Because of a typhoon, windows broke.'

      c. Tibusu de, takusan no hito   ga sinda.
              typhus by many   people   died
          'Because of typhus, many people have died.'

5.13 Tense in Subordinate Clauses

The present and perfect tenses in subordinate clauses in Japanese display interesting peculiarities. For example, (76) means that John closed the book that he *was* reading.

(76) a. John wa *yon-de*   *i-ru* hon o tozita.
               read-ing is   book   closed
       'John closed the book that (he) (lit.) *is reading*.'

On the other hand, (77) is ungrammatical.

(77) *John wa Mary ga sono toki *yon-de*   *i-ru* hon o toriageta.
                     that time read-ing is   book   took away
       'John took away the book that Mary (lit.) *is reading* at that time.'

The perfect tense *yon-de i-ta* 'was reading' must be used instead. In what contexts the present tense can be used when referring to past time and in what contexts it cannot be used will be discussed in Chapter 22 ("Tense in Relative Clauses").

Similarly, (78a) and (78b) are both roughly translatable as 'If John comes, I will leave' but are different in subtle details because in (78a) the perfect conditional is used, while in (78b) the present tense plus *nara* 'if' is used.

(78) a. John ga ki-tara, kaeru.
          come-if return

    b. John ga ku-ru-nara,   kaeru.
          come-present-if

This problem will be examined in detail in Chapters 13 ("Assertive *Nara* Clauses") and 14 ("Perfective *Tara* Clauses").

5.14 Embedded Clauses and Verb Phrases

Japanese is rich in grammatical patterns for embedding clauses and verb phrases. For example,

(79) a. *-i*:   kak-*i*   hazimeru
                write-gerundive begin
                'begin to write'

    b. *-te*:   tabe-*te*   miru
                eat-continuative try
                'try to eat'

    c. *-yoo to*:   tabe-*yoo to*   suru
                eat   let's that do
                'try to eat, be about to eat'

    d. -*to*:   John ga baka   da *to*   omou.
                              foolish is that think
                        '(I) think that John is a fool.'

    e. -*koto*:   John ga sinda *koto* o sitta.
                              died that got-to-know
                        'I got to know that John died.'

    f. -*no*:   John ga naku *no* o kiita.
                              cry   that heard
                        'I heard John cry.'

The difference of meaning between *to*, *koto*, and *no* will be discussed in Chapter 18 ("*Koto, No,* and *To*").

The same *no* appears in the peculiar pattern *no da* (informal), *no desu* (polite), and *no de aru* (formal writing), which is extensively used in giving some kind of explanation meaning 'it is that . . .'. In formal speech, even *no de aru no de aru* 'it is that it is that . . .' appears. Where this *no da/ desu/ de aru* construction can be used and what it means will be discussed in Chapter 19 ("*No Desu* 'It Is That'").

5.15 Negative Questions

It is usually said that in answering negative questions such as "Are you not hungry?" *yes* in Japanese means "No, I am not hungry," and *no* means "Yes, I am hungry." This is partly correct and partly incorrect. When *yes* is used for yes and when it is used for no, when *no* is used for no and when it is used for yes, will be examined in Chapter 23 ("Yes and No").

5.16 Subjectless Expressions and *X Wa Y Da* Patterns

There are subjectless expressions of the following type:

(80) a. Ame da.
          rain is
          'It is raining! It has started raining!'

      b. John da.
          'John has come. John is here. It is John, etc.'

The *X wa Y da* 'Speaking of *X*, *X* is *Y*' pattern is highly ambiguous.

(81) a. Boku wa unagi da.

    I   eel   is

    'I am an eel. I am for eating eels. I will order eels, etc.'

  b. Boku wa Red Sox da.

    'I will back the Red Sox. I am a team member of the Red Sox, etc.'

  c. Boku wa Tokyo da.

    'I am from Tokyo, I am for going to Tokyo, I am going to Tokyo, etc.'

5.17 Multiple Subject Constructions

Japanese has double-subject and triple-subject constructions. For example,

(82) a. *Bunmeikoku no dansei no heikinzyumyoo*   ga mizikai.

    civilized   's male 's average-life-span   short-is
    countries

    'The average life-span of males of civilized countries is short.'

  b. *Bunmeikoku no dansei* ga *heikinzyumyoo* ga mizikai.

  c. *Bunmeikoku* ga *dansei* ga *heikinzyumyoo* ga mizikai.

Example (82a) is a single-subject construction meaning 'The average life-span of males of civilized countries is short.' Example (82b) is a double-subject construction, meaning 'Males of civilized countries (have the characteristic that) their average life-span is short.' Example (82c) is a triple-subject construction meaning 'Civilized countries (have the characteristic that) males (have the characteristic that) their average life-span is short.' How these double-subject and triple-subject constructions are formed in Japanese will be the topic of Chapter 3 (*"Wa* and *Ga* (Part II)— Subjectivization") of this book.

I hope that these fragmentary descriptions of some features of Japanese have given the reader with no previous knowledge of Japanese an idea of what the language is like and how different it is from English. A fuller picture of the language can be obtained by reading Miller (1967), Martin (1962), Jorden (1962), or Alfonso (1966). In the succeeding chapters, I shall examine in more detail some of the features touched upon in this chapter.

II
Particles

2 [†]

Wa and *Ga* (Part I)—Theme, Contrast, Exhaustive Listing, and Neutral Description

1. The Uses of *Wa* and *Ga*

The distinction in meaning between *wa* and *ga* is a problem that perpetually troubles both students and instructors of Japanese. For example, what is the difference in meaning between (1a) and (1b) or between (2a) and (2b)?

(1) a. John *wa* gakusei desu.
　　　　　　student　is
　　　'John is a student.'

    b. John *ga* gakusei desu.

(2) a. Ame *wa* hutte　imasu ga ...
　　　rain　　falling is　　but
　　　'It is raining, but ...'

    b. Ame *ga* hutte imasu.

Conventional grammars state that in (1a) *gakusei* 'student' is emphasized, while in (1b) *John* is emphasized. Then, why is there a reading of (2b) in which there is no emphasis on *ame* 'rain'? Similarly, why is the only possible reading of (2a) one in which *ame* is contrasted with something else, while (1a) allows a reading in which *John* is not contrasted with anyone else? Likewise, why are the (b) sentences that follow ungrammatical, while (a) sentences are grammatical?

(3) a.　Dare *ga* kimasita ka?
　　　　Who　　came　　interrogative
　　　　　　　　　　　　particle

　　　　'Who came?'

    b.　*Dare *wa* kimasita ka?

(4) a.　Dareka　　*ga* kimasita.
　　　　Someone　　came
　　　　'Someone has come'

    b.　*Dareka *wa* kimasita.

†This chapter is for all readers.

(5) a.   Oozei no[1] hito   ga party ni kimasita.
      many   people   came
      'Many people came to the party.'

    b. *Oozei no hito *wa* party in kimasita.

In this chapter I shall attempt to answer all these questions by examining various uses of *wa* and *ga*, pinpointing their meanings, and defining the restrictions of their distributions.

    There are two different uses of *wa* and three of *ga*. They are enumerated with brief explanations in (6):

(6) a. *wa* for the theme of a sentence: "Speaking of . . . , talking about . . ."
      Example:
      John *wa* gakusei desu.
                student is
      'Speaking of John, he is a student.'

    b. *wa* for contrasts: "X . . . , but . . . , as for X . . . "
      Example:
      Ame *wa* hutte   imasu ga . . .
      rain   falling is   but
      'It is raining, but . . . '

    c. *ga* for neutral descriptions of actions or temporary states
      Example:
      Ame *ga* hutte   imasu.
      rain   falling is
      'It is raining.'

    d. *ga* for exhaustive listing.[2] "X (and only X) . . . " "It is X that . . . "
      Example:
      John *ga* gakusei desu.
                student is
      '(Of all the people under discussion) John (and only John) is a student.' 'It is John who is a student.'

    e. *ga* for object marking

---

[1] *No* is the attributive form of the copula. *Oozei no hito* can be literally translated as 'people who are many'.

[2] The distinction between the *ga* for neutral descriptions of actions or temporary states and the *ga* for exhaustive listing was first pointed out by Sige-Yuki Kuroda (1965a).

Example:
Boku wa Mary *ga* suki   desu.
I   fond of am
'I like Mary.'

These uses will henceforth be referred to as thematic *wa*, contrastive *wa*, descriptive *ga*, exhaustive-listing *ga*, and objective *ga*. Since I shall discuss the objective *ga* separately in Chapter 4 of this book, only the first four will be considered in this chapter.

2. The Nature of Themes

Before discussing the thematic *wa*, it is necessary to examine the nature of themes. It seems that only objects and concepts that have been mentioned and recorded in the registry of the present discourse can become themes of sentences. Nouns of unique reference in this universe of discourse, such as *the sun, the moon, my wife, my children,* seem to be in the permanent registry. Once their entry in the registry is established, they do not have to be reentered for each discourse. Objects of some specific reference are added to the registry of the current discourse the first time they are mentioned: "a man I saw yesterday," "Americans whom I know," etc. Only after this entry in the registry is accomplished can they become themes of sentences. Now, observe the following sentences:

(7) a. Speaking of *the man* that she met, he was a hardworking accountant.
   b. *Speaking of a man that she met, he was a hardworking accountant.
   c. A man that she met in the park came to see her.

The man that she met in (7a) has some specific referent in the universe of discourse, but he also has already been referred to, so that listeners know what the speaker is talking about. Such a noun phrase will henceforth be referred to as an *anaphoric noun phrase*.[3] The antecedent of an anaphoric

---

[3] What I have called *anaphoric* here is sometimes called *definite* because anaphoric noun phrases usually contain the definite article *the*. However, I have chosen to reserve the term *definite* for referring to the syntactic feature that determines the presence or absence of *the*.

The term *specific* requires some explanation also. Observe the following sentences:

(i) Mary wants to marry a doctor. He is a specialist in brain surgery.
(ii) Mary wants to marry a doctor, although she does not have anyone in mind at present.   *Continued overleaf*

noun phrase may be within the same sentence, in the temporary registry (as is the case in (7a)), or in the permanent registry (as is the case with *the sun, my wife*, etc.). We can say that (7a) is grammatical because the theme is an anaphoric noun phrase. Compare this with *a man that she met* in (7b). This noun phrase also has a specific referent in the speaker's universe of discourse, but it is not anaphoric; that is, probably this is the first time that the speaker has mentioned him (hence the use of the indefinite article *a*), and therefore it has not yet been entered into the temporary registry of the present discourse. This distinction between anaphoric and nonanaphoric noun phrases, both with specific reference, will become clear by examining the following sentences:

(8) a. *Speaking of *three boys who came to the party*, they did not behave themselves.

   b. Three boys came to the party. Speaking of *the three boys*, they did not behave themselves.

Both *three boys who came to the party* of (8a) and *the three boys* of (8b) have the same referents in the universe of discourse. The difference between these two sentences is that in (8a) the speaker *talks about* the three boys for the first time without previously establishing their registry entry, while in (8b) he first establishes their registry entry and then *talks about* the three boys. Hence (8a) is ungrammatical and (8b) is grammatical.

   What determines whether a specific noun phrase can become a topic or not depends on whether the noun phrase is anaphoric and not whether it is definite. There are specific noun phrases that are definite and are not anaphoric. For example, in (9), the noun phrase *man who killed Robert Kennedy* is preceded by *the*, not because it is anaphoric, but because there is only one person who killed Robert Kennedy.

(9) I know *the man who killed Robert Kennedy*.

The indefinite noun phrase *a doctor* can have either some *specific* referent, as in (i), or can be used without any specific referent, as in (ii), in the sense of 'any doctor, if there is one'. In the former case the existence of *a doctor that Mary wants to marry* is presupposed by the speaker, while in the latter there is no such presupposition. *A doctor* in (i) and (ii) are called *specific* and *nonspecific*, respectively. Similarly, the following is ambiguous with respect to the specificity or nonspecificity of *a doctor*:

(iii) A doctor was sought.

See Kuno (1970).

The use of the indefinite article *a* would mean that there is more than one person who killed Robert Kennedy and that the speaker knows one of them. Now, assume that the speaker has been talking about President Kennedy with the hearer and that the speaker knows that the hearer does not know that Robert Kennedy was killed by an assassin. In such a situation, the speaker cannot introduce a new topic by saying:

(10) Speaking of the man who killed Robert Kennedy, he does not seem to have been involved in any conspiracy.

The reason seems to be that *the man who killed Robert Kennedy* in this context is definite, but is not anaphoric, and thus violates the condition that the topic of a sentence be anaphoric. The speaker could use (10) for dramatic effect. In either case, the use of (10) would be a departure from the normal use of topics.

   Generic noun phrases—that is, noun phrases that refer to classes such as *man* (human beings in general), *Americans* (Americans in general, all Americans, any American), and *the linguist* (linguists in general, all linguists, any linguist)—can also become topics of sentences. For example,

(11) a. Speaking of *man*, he is mortal. (man in general)
     b. Speaking of *cats*, they are sneaky, malicious animals. (cats in general, all cats)
     c. Speaking of *the Japanese*, they are hardworking people. (the Japanese in general)

The italicized noun phrases in (11) are generic noun phrases; that is, they refer to classes, and not to some arbitrary members of the classes. Generic noun phrases seem to be in the permanent registry of discourse, and do not have to be reentered into the temporary registry for each discourse. In the sense that they are permanently stored in the registry of discourse, generic noun phrases are also anaphoric. The speaker of the sentences in (11) assumes that the hearer has heard about the classes of objects called *man*, *cats*, and *the Japanese*. If the speaker knows that the hearer has never heard of a certain class of objects that he is going to talk about, he cannot use the generic noun phrase for the class as the topic of a sentence. For example, if he assumes that the hearer does not know what *etas* 'social outcasts' are, he cannot start a discourse with

(12) Speaking of *etas* in Japan, they are still socially discriminated against in the countryside.

He will have to establish an entry for *etas* in the hearer's registry of discourse by introductory statements such as

(13) In Japan, there is a class, called *eta*, of social outcasts.

Only after statement (13) has been made can the speaker use the *eta* as the topic of a sentence as in (12).

Similarly, if the speaker knows that the hearer is not aware of the fact that beavers live in Canada, he will not ordinarily use *the beaver(s) in Canada* as the topic of a sentence.

(14) Speaking of the beavers in Canada,[4] they have a longer life-span than the beavers in the States.

[4] Generic noun phrases with postpositional modifiers can take the "*the* + plural" form, while those with no postpositional modifiers cannot. Observe the following:

(i) a. A beaver builds dams.
   b. Beavers build dams.
   c. The beaver builds dams.
   d. *The beavers build dams.

(ii) a. The beaver in Canada builds dams.
   b. The beavers in Canada build dams.

(iii) a. The women who are old cannot work.
   b. *The old women cannot work.

(iv) a. The boys who are red-haired have quick tempers.
   b. *The red-haired boys have quick tempers.

Example (i-d) is ungrammatical because *the beavers* is not followed by any postpositional modifier, while (ii-b) is grammatical because it is followed by the postpositional modifier *in Canada*. Examples (iii-a) and (iv-a), with postpositional relative clauses, are grammatical, while (iii-b) and (iv-b), with the adjectives preposed, are ungrammatical. This phenomenon lends strong support to the contention that the definite article *the* for generic noun phrases is transformationally derived, and is not in the deep structure.

As the subclass represented by a generic noun phrase containing restrictive modifiers gets smaller, it becomes difficult to use the "*the* + singular noun" form in the generic sense. Example (ii-a) is grammatical in the generic sense, but the following sentences are not:

(iii) c. *The woman who is old cannot work.
   d. *The old woman cannot work.

(iv) c. *The boy who is red-haired has a quick temper.
   d. *The red-haired boy has a quick temper.

According to John Haig, to whom this observation is due, the sentences in (iii) and (iv) would be grammatical in the contexts in which *the woman who is old/the old woman* and *the*

I have mentioned that topics in English must be anaphoric. When anaphoric noun phrases are quantified, as in *many Americans* (that is, many of the Americans in general) and *many of the Americans that I associated with*, some speakers of English find it difficult to use them as topics.

(15) a.   Many Americans tend to be apathetic about politics.

     b.   ?Speaking of many Americans, they tend to be apathetic about politics.

     c.   Many of the Americans that I associated with came to the party.

     d.   ?Speaking of many of the Americans that I associated with, they came to the party.

Compare these sentences with the following:

(15) e.   Many Americans that I associated with came to the party.

     f.   *Speaking of many Americans that I associated with, they came to the party.

Example (15f) is totally ungrammatical because *many Americans that I associated with* is neither generic nor anaphoric. Examples (15b) and (15d),

---

boy who is red-haired/the red-haired boy are used as well-defined class names, as in an ecological study of some population. For example, the sentences in (iv) would be grammatical if they were preceded by

(v) In this village, there are two kinds of boys—the boy who is red-haired (or the red-haired boy) and the boy who is blond-haired (or the blond-haired boy).

Similarly, in example (vi) *the chicken on his farm* can have only the specific interpretation—that is, some specific chicken on his farm—and not the generic interpretation.

(vi) The chicken on his farm is healthy.

However, observe the following:

(vii) a. The student she teaches becomes a competent linguist.

     b. The boy she dates is a boy she likes.

     c. The disciple of *X*'s becomes a competent linguist.

These sentences are grammatical in the generic sense—for example, (vii-a) means

(vii) d. All students that she teaches become competent linguists.

However, there is a subtle difference in meaning between (vii-a) and (vii-d). The former implies that she teaches one student at a time, while the latter does not have such an implication. The same applies to (vii-b) and (vii-c). On the other hand, sentence (vi) is ungrammatical in the generic sense because a farm ordinarily has more than one chicken at the same time.

in which quantified noun phrases are anaphoric (generic in the case of (15b)), are not acceptable to many speakers. They would say, instead:

(16) a. Speaking of Americans, many tend to be apathetic about politics.

   b. Speaking of the Americans that I associated with, many came to the party.[5]

3. Thematic and Contrastive *Wa*

The themes of Japanese sentences, as in English sentences, must be either generic or anaphoric. Observe the following sentences:

(17) a. *Kuzira wa* honyuu-doobutu desu.
         whale   mammal   is
         'Speaking of whales, they are mammals. A whale is a mammal.'

   b. *John wa* watakusi no tomodati desu.
              I   's friend   is
         'Speaking of John, he is my friend.'

   c. *Hutari wa* party ni kimasita.
         two   to came
         'Speaking of the two persons, they came to the party.'

---

[5] Native speakers' judgment on the grammaticality of (15b) and (15d) varies considerably. For some speakers, both are acceptable. For some others, for a reason that I cannot identify, (15d) is acceptable, but (15b) is not.

It goes without saying that quantifiers preceded by determiners can appear in topics with no difficulty.

(i) Speaking of the *many* girl friends that he had, they were very devoted to him.

In connection with what has been said, observe that a generic noun phrase used as a theme cannot be preceded by an indefinite article.

(ii) a. The beaver builds dams.
   b. Beavers build dams.
   c. A beaver builds dams.

(iii) a. Speaking of the beaver, it builds dams.
   b. Speaking of beavers, they build dams.
   c. *Speaking of a beaver, it builds dams.

If the indefinite article *a* for generic noun phrases is to be regarded as derived from *any*, as is proposed by Perlmutter (1971b), the fact that (iii-c) is ungrammatical will be an automatic consequence of the fact that the following is ungrammatical:

(iv) *Speaking of any beaver, it builds dams.

(18) a. **Oozei no hito wa* party ni kimasita.
        many   people
        'Speaking of many people, they came to the party.'

   b. **Omosiroi   hito wa* party ni kimasita.
        interesting people
        *'Speaking of interesting people, they came to the party.'

   c. **Dareka wa* byooki desu.
        somebody sick   is
        *'Speaking of somebody, he is sick.'

Both (17a) and (17b) are grammatical because *kuzira* 'whale' and *John* in these sentences are generic and anaphoric noun phrases, respectively. Example (17c) is grammatical only when *hutari* is taken as meaning '*the two people (under discussion)*'. The sentence would be ungrammatical if it meant 'the people who came to the party numbered two', that is, if *hutari* was taken as two people with no anaphoric reference. On the other hand, the sentences in (18) are ungrammatical because *oozei no hito* 'many people', *omosiroi hito* 'interesting people', and *dareka* 'somebody' are noun phrases of specific but nonanaphoric reference and their referents have not been entered into the registry of the present discourse. Similarly, the reason that (2a) cannot be interpreted as 'Speaking of rain, it is falling' is that *ame* 'rain' in this context is neither generic nor anaphoric. If it were, grammatical sentences with the thematic interpretation would be the result.

(19) a. **Ame wa* hutte imasu.
        rain   falling is
        'Speaking of rain, it is falling.'

   b. Asa   hayaku ame ga huri   dasita ... Yoru ni
      morning early   rain   falling started   night-ly
      natte   mo *ame wa* hutte ita.
      becoming even rain   falling was
      Anaphoric: 'It started raining early in the morning ...
      (Lit.) Speaking of *the rain*, it was still falling even when it became night.'

   c. *Kyoo no ame wa* zuibun hidoi.
      today 's rain   very   violent
      Anaphoric—unique reference: 'Today's rain is very violent.'

d. *Ame wa* sora karu huru.

    rain   sky   from fall

    Generic: 'Speaking of the rain (in general), it falls from the sky.'

In Japanese, the *NP no Quantifier* construction can enter into the theme rather freely. Observe the following sentences:

(20) a. Gakusei no ooku wa dokusin desu.

       students   many   single   are

       'Many of the students are single.'

    b. Ooku no gakusei wa dokusin desu.

       many   students   single   are

       'Many students are single.'

    c. Amerika-zin no daibubun wa se ga   takai.

       Americans   's   most part   stature are high

       'Most of the Americans are tall.'

    d. Daibubun no Amerika-zin wa se ga   takai.

       most part 's Americans   stature are high

       'Most Americans are tall.'

    e. Subete no ningen wa   byoodoo desu.[6]

       all   human-beings equal   are

       'All human beings are equal.'

I have mentioned that the themes of Japanese sentences must be anaphoric. The contrastive *wa*, on the other hand, can place nonanaphoric noun phrases in contrast. Consider the following sentences:

(21) a. *Ame wa hutte   imasu.

       rain   falling is

       'Speaking of rain, it is falling.'

    b. *Ame wa* hutte   imasu ga, taisita   koto wa arimasen.[7]

       rain   falling is   but serious matter   not exist

       'It is raining, but it is not much.'

---

[6] Because of the idiosyncrasy of *subete*, *ningen no subete* does not ordinarily mean 'all human beings', but means 'all about human beings'.

[7] Minoru Nakau (personal communication) has pointed out to me the following interesting sentence:

(i) Ame *wa* hutte   imasu ga, kasa   wa motte   ikimasen.

    rain   falling is   but umbrella   having don't got

    'The rain is falling, but I am not taking my umbrella with me.'

    c. **Oozei no hito* wa party ni kimasita.
        many   people   to came
        'Speaking of many people, they came to the party.'

    d. *Oozei no hito* wa party ni kimasita ga, *omosiroi*
        many   people   to came   but interesting
        hito wa hitori   mo   imasen desita.
        people one person even was not
        'Many people came to the party indeed, but there was none who
        was interesting.'

Since generic and anaphoric noun phrases can be followed either by the thematic *wa* or by the contrastive *wa*, ambiguous sentences should result. That this is indeed the case can be seen in (22).

(22) a. John wa sono hon o yonda
          the book read
      'Speaking of John, he read the book.'

     b. John wa sono hon o yonda ga Mary wa yomanakatta.
          the book read   did not read
      'John read the book, but Mary didn't.'

While noun phrases preceding the thematic *wa* do not receive prominent intonation, those preceding the contrasting *wa* do.

Assume that no mention has been made in the previous conversation of the rain that is falling now. Since *ame* here does not pertain to rain in general, and also since it is not anaphoric, it cannot be the theme of the sentence according to my analysis. On the other hand, *ame* here is not contrasted with *yuki* 'snow', *mizore* 'sleet', or *hyoo* 'hail'. Neither is it the case that it is in contrast with *kasa* 'umbrella'. It seems that Japanese allows transpositions of contrastive *wa*. Sentence (i) is synonymous with

(ii) Ame ga hutte *wa* imasu ga, kasa   o motte *wa* ikimasen.
    rain   falling   is   but umbrella taking   go-not

In (ii) the fact that it is raining is contrasted with the speaker's determination not to take an umbrella with him. Transpositions of contrasting words are not peculiar to Japanese. English displays a similar characteristic. For example,

(iii) a. He can speak not only Chinese but also Japanese and Korean.

      b. He can not only speak Chinese but also Japanese and Korean.

(iv) a. He teaches, not Chinese, but Korean.

      b. He doesn't teach Chinese, but Korean.

It is not clear to me, however, under what conditions such transpositions are permissible in Japanese.

The following sentence will make the distinction between the thematic *wa* and the contrastive *wa* clearer:

(23) Watakusi ga sitte iru hito wa party ni kimasen desita.
     I   know   people   did not come
     a. 'Speaking of the persons whom I know, they did not come to the party.'
     b. '(People came to the party, but) there was none whom I know.'

Watakusi ga sitte iru hito 'people whom I know' is ambiguous: it can mean either one or more persons whom the speaker knows, whom he has already talked about, or some persons whom the speaker knows, whom he probably has not talked about. If the first meaning is the correct one, *wa* in (23) can be regarded as thematic *wa*, and therefore the interpretation given in (23a) results. Thus (23), in this interpretation, is a statement about Mr. A, Mr. B, . . . Mr. Z, whom the speaker knows, and it proposes that they did not come to the party. On the other hand, if *watakusi ga sitte iru hito* 'people whom I know' is taken as nonanaphoric, *wa* of (23) cannot be thematic; it must be contrastive. Therefore the interpretation given in (23b) results. Example (23) in this interpretation does not have a theme: it is not a statement about Mr. A, Mr. B, . . . Mr. Z, that is, persons whom the speaker knows. *Watakusi ga sitte iru hito* 'people whom I know' is presented in this sentence in contrast to *watakusi ga siranai hito* 'people whom I don't know'.

A given sentence can have only one thematic *wa*: if there is more than one occurrence of *wa* in a sentence, only the first can be thematic: all the rest (and probably the first one also) are contrastive. Examine the following:

(24) a. Watakusi wa tabako wa suimasu.
        I   cigarette   smoke
        'Speaking of myself, I dó smoke.'

     b. Watakusi wa tabako wa suimasen.
        I   cigarette   smoke-not
        'Speaking of myself, I don't smóke.'

     c. Watakusi wa tabako wa suimasu ga   sake wa nomimasen.
        I   cigarette   smoke   but wine   drink-not
        'Speaking of myself, I do smoke, but I don't drink.'

    d. Watakusi wa syuumatu ni wa hon wa yomimasu.
       I   weekend on   book   read
       'Speaking of myself, I do read bóoks on the wéekend.'

    e. Watakusi wa syuumatu ni wa hon wa yomimasen.
       I   weekend on   book   read-not.
       'Speaking of myself, I don't read bóoks on the wéekend.'

    f. Watakusi wa syuumatu ni wa hon wa yomimasu ga benkyoo wa
       I   weekend on   book   read   but study
       simasen.
       do-not
       'Speaking of myself, I read bóoks on the wéekend, but I don't do
       any studying.'

Sentences (24a) and (24d) are definitely contrastive. These two sentences
sound incomplete in isolation: the hearer expects to be given some statement that contrasts something with smoking or reading. Thus the con-
cluding remark of each of (24c) and (24f) makes (24a) and (24d) natural
and smooth. On the other hand, (24b) and (24e), with the negative instead
of the affirmative predicate of (24a) and (24d), are perfectly natural in
isolation although the contrastive nature of smoking and reading is still
quite clear. This seems to be due to the fact that nonlinguistic environments are usually positive and that the negative sentences such as (24b)
and (24e) are contrastive with such positive environments.[8] For example,
Watakusi wa tabako wa suimasen 'As for me, I don't smoke' contrasts with
the positive environment of the other party's offering a cigar to the speaker
expecting that he will smoke. This predicts that if a nonlinguistic environment happens to be a negative one, positive sentences such as (24a) and
(24d) will be natural, and it is indeed the case. Suppose, for example,
someone is passing out "It's a boy" cigars. He knows that the speaker
doesn't smoke cigarettes, and so he doesn't offer him a cigar. Then the
speaker can request a cigar with (24a), which will have the connotation
"Contrary to your expectation, I do smoke cigars."

4. Descriptive and Exhaustive-Listing *Ga*
With regard to the descriptive and exhaustive-listing *ga*, only the subject
of action verbs, existential verbs, and adjectives/nominal adjectives that

---

[8] This observation is due to John Haig.

action verbs } *+ descriptive ga*
existential v
adj

represent changing states can be followed by the descriptive *ga*,[9] while there are no such restrictions in the case of exhaustive-listing *ga*.[10] First, consider the following sentences:

(25) a. John ga asoko   ni tatte   iru.
              that-place at standing is
        'John is standing there.'

     b. Tegami ga kita.
        letter   came
        'Mail has come.'

     c. Ame ga hutte iru.
        rain   falling is
        'It is raining.'

(26) a. Tukue no ue ni hon ga aru.
        table   's top on book   is
        'There is a book on the table.'

     b. Oya, asoko ni John ga iru.
        Oh   there at   is
        'Oh, John is there.'

(27) a. Sora ga akai.
        sky   is-red
        'Look! The sky is red.'

     d. Atama ga itai.
        head   is-aching
        '(Lit.) Head aches. I have a headache.'

     c. Te   ga tumetai.
        hand   cold
        'My hands are cold.'

actions

neutral description

existence/ons
neutral descriptions

adj: changing states
neutral description
on current temporary state

The verbs in (25) represent actions, and therefore the sentences in (25) are all neutral descriptions of some actions. The verbs in (26) represent existence, and therefore these sentences also receive the neutral-description interpretation. Because the adjectives in (27) all represent changing states, the sentences in (27) are neutral descriptions on current temporary states.

[9] This condition will be slightly relaxed later in this chapter.
[10] As has been mentioned before, this condition for the distribution of the descriptive and the exhaustive-listing uses of *ga* is due to Kuroda's insightful observations (Kuroda, 1965a).

Sentences of neutral description present an objectively observable action, existence, or temporary state as a new event.

The following sentences all have predicates that represent states:

(28) a. John ga gakusei desu.

　　　　　　　　student is

　　　　　　'(Of all the people we are talking about) John (and only John) is a student; it is John who is a student.'[11]

　　 b. Saru　　 ga ningen no senzo　　 desu.

　　　　 monkey　　 man　 's ancestor is

　　　　 'It is the monkey that is the ancestor of man.'

　　 c. John ga nihongo o sitte　　 iru.

　　　　　　　　Japanese　 knowing is

　　　　 'John (and only John) knows Japanese.'

　　 d. John ga nihongo　ga dekiru.

　　　　　　　　Japanese　　 can

　　　　 'John (and only John) can speak Japanese.'

---

[11] The English cleft-sentence construction "It is *X* that . . . " is used to give an exhaustive answer and is similar to the Japanese exhaustive *ga* in this respect. The cleft-sentence construction does not seem to require that *X* be definite. Observe the following sentences:

It was $\left\{ {a \atop the} \right\}$ *boy* that Mary met in the park that came to the party.

It was $\left\{ {a \atop the} \right\}$ *seven-year-old boy* who won the abacus competition.

However, *X* must be such that it can enter into the "*X* and only *X*" construction.

{ *Many people and only many people came to the party.
{ *It was many people that came to the party.

{ *Twó bóys and only twó bóys came to the party.
{ *It was twó bóys that came to the party.

{ Twó boys and only twó boys came to the party.
{ It was twó boys that came to the party.

The same applies to the exhaustive-listing *ga* construction in Japanese. Observe this sentence:

Oozei no hito ga gakusei desu.
many　　 people student is
'Many people are students.'

It is perfectly grammatical, but it does not mean 'Many people and only many people are students.' This problem will be discussed later in this chapter.

    e. Boku ga osusi ga tabetai.

       I   sushi   want

      'I (and only I) want to eat sushi.'

The sentences in (28) are awkward, if not ungrammatical, out of context. They require contexts that solicit exhaustive listings such as

(29) a. Dare ga gakusei desu ka?

      who   student is

      'Who is a student?'

    b. Nani ga ningen no senzo   desu ka?

      what   man   's ancestor is

      'What is the ancestor of mankind?'

    c. Dare ga nihongo o sitte   iru ka?

      who   Japanese knowing is

      'Who knows Japanese?'

If John, Mary, Tom, the speaker, and the hearer are in the current universe of discourse, and if John and Tom are students but the others are not, then (28a) would not constitute a correct answer to (29a). Sentence (29a) requires as an answer an exhaustive list of people who are students—as a matter of fact, this seems to be why *ga*, and not *wa*, is used after interrogative pronouns. Therefore the correct answer to (29a) in our assumed universe of discourse would be

(30) a. John to   Tom ga gakusei desu.

         and   student are

      'John and Tom are students.'

If the hearer knew that both John and Tom are students and nonetheless answered with (28a), he would be telling a lie. The hearer could reply:

(30) b. John wa gakusei desu ga . . .

               student is   but

      'John is a student, but . . . '

Then he implies that he knows that John is a student but that he does not know whether the rest are students or not. Under such a circumstance the hearer could not give (28a) as an answer because (28a) implies that only John is a student and that all the rest are nonstudents.

    When action verbs, existential verbs, and adjectives of changing states are in the predicates, sentences with *ga* marking their subjects can poten-

tially be ambiguous. When stative verbs and adjectives and nominals of
more or less permanent states are in the predicates, only the exhaustive-
listing interpretation of *ga* results.

(31) a. John ga sinda.   (neutral description)
     died
   'John died.'

  b. Dare ga sinda ka? John ga sinda.   (exhaustive listing)
    who died   died
   'Who died? It is John who died.' (That is, John and only John
   died.)

(32) a. Sora ga aoi.   (neutral description)
    sky blue
   'Look! The sky is blue.'

  b. Sora ga aoi.   (exhaustive listing)
   'It is the sky that is blue.'

(33) a. John ga kita.   (neutral description)
   'John came.'

  b. John ga kita.   (exhaustive listing)
   'It was John who came.'

(34) a. *Saru ga ningen no senzo desu. (neutral description)
    monkey man 's ancestor is
   'Look! A monkey is the ancestor of mankind.'

  b. Saru ga ningen no senzo desu.   (exhaustive listing)
   'It is the monkey that is the ancestor of mankind.'

(35) a. *Tokyo ga ookii.   (neutral description)
        is big
   'Look! Tokyo is big.'

  b. Tokyo ga ookii.   (exhaustive listing)
   'It is Tokyo that is big.'

(36) a. *John ga nihongo ga dekiru.   (neutral description)
       Japanese can
   'John can speak Japanese.'

  b. John ga nihongo ga dekiru.   (exhaustive listing)
   'John (and only John) can speak Japanese.'

In the preceding, all the (a) sentences are meant to represent the use of *ga* for neutral description. Note that (34a), (35a), and (36a) are ungrammatical in this intended interpretation because their predicates represent stable states. The (b) sentences are meant to represent the use of *ga* for exhaustive listing. For them to be fully grammatical and natural, it is necessary to supply appropriate contexts such as the one shown in (31b).

It is not the case that NP-*ga* subjects can always receive the neutral-description interpretation if their predicates represent action, existence, or changing state. Observe the following examples:

(37) a. Kinoo,   John ga kimasita. *Appearance toward*
          yesterday   came   *speaker*
          'Yesterday, John came (to see me).' *NOT neutral*
                                               Movement away
    b. ?Kinoo,   John ga Boston ni ikimasita. *from speaker*
          yesterday   to went
          'Yesterday, John went to Boston.'   *not neutral*
                                               description

(38) a. John ga asoko ni imasu.
                  there at is
          '(Look!) John is over there.'

    b. ?John ga Boston ni imasu.
                       in is
          'John is in Boston.'

(39) a. *Boku ga Boston ni ikimasita.
          I   to went
          'I went to Boston.'

    b. *Boku ga koko ni imasu.
          I   here am
          'I am here.'

In the preceding, the symbols ? and * are used, not to mark the ungrammaticality of the sentences, but to indicate the fact that they are not readily amenable to the neutral-description interpretation. They are acceptable as sentences of exhaustive-listing interpretation.

Sentences that indicate the existence or coming into existence of something at the place of the speaker seem most readily amenable to the neutral-description interpretation. Example (37a) is a perfectly natural sentence because it describes John's appearance toward the speaker. On the other hand, it is difficult to assign the neutral-description interpretation to (37b) because John's movement is away from the speaker. Similarly, (38a) is a natural sentence because it describes John's existence at the place of the speaker, while (38b) is awkward as a sentence of neutral description because John is somewhere else. It also seems that the speaker is not allowed to look at his own action or existence objectively and to describe it as if it were a new event. This seems to be why it is next to impossible to interpret sentences with the first person subject, such as (39a) and (39b), as sentences of neutral description. They almost invariably receive the exhaustive-listing interpretation.

   Ga is used for marking the object of stative verbals, that is, a handful of transitive verbs (such as *dekiru* 'be able to', *wakaru* 'understand', *iru* 'need'), all transitive adjectives (such as *hosii* 'wants', *tabetai* 'be anxious to eat'), and all transitive nominal adjectives (such as *suki* 'be fond of', *nigate* 'be bad at'). Note that the objective *ga* does not have the exhaustive-listing connotation. For example, consider these sentences:

(40) a. John wa eigo   ga dekiru.
            English   can

   b. Boku wa okane ga hosii.
       I   money   want

   c. John wa Mary ga suki   desu.
                         fond of is

   d. John ga Mary ga suki   desu.
                         fond of is

   e. Boku ni wa nihongo ga nigate desu.
       I   to   Japanese   bad at am

They have the following meanings:

(41) a. Speaking of John, he can speak English.

   b. Speaking of myself, I want money.

   c. Speaking of John, he likes Mary.

   d. John (and only John) likes Mary.

   e. As for me, I am not good at Japanese.

They do not have the following meanings:

(42) a. Speaking of John, he can speak English (and only English).

   b. Speaking of myself, I want money (and only money).

   c. Speaking of John, he likes Mary (and only Mary).

   d. John (and only John) likes Mary (and only Mary).

   e. As for me, I am not good at Japanese (and only Japanese).

The preceding examples suggest that the *ga* for object marking is of a nature entirely different from that of subject marking.

The distinction between the thematic *wa* and the descriptive *ga* and the exhaustive-listing *ga* becomes neutralized in subordinate clauses. All three are realized as *ga*, as shown in the following:

(43) a. Anata wa John (*ga*) nihongo ga dekiru koto o sitte imasu ka.
       you   (*wa) Japanese can that knowing are
       'Do you know that John can speak Japanese?'

   b. John (*ga*) suki na ko wa Mary desu.
          (*wa) fond-of is girl is
       'The girl that John likes is Mary.'

The foregoing sentences do not respectively have the interpretation 'that John and only John can ...' and 'The girl that John and only John likes ...'. However, the contrastive *wa* can appear in subordinate clauses.

(44) a. Anata wa, kinoo no party ni *John wa* kitta (ga Mary wa
       you   yesterday 's   to   came but
       konakatta) koto o sitte imasu ka.
       came-not that knowing are
       'Do you know that *John* came (but *Mary* did not come) to yesterday's party?'

   b. *John wa* suki da ga *Bill wa* kirai na ko wa Mary
             fond-of is but   hateful-of is girl
       desu.
       is
       'The girl whom John likes but whom Bill dislikes is Mary.'

It goes without saying that (43b) and (44b) are ambiguous: *John ga, John wa*, and *Bill wa* in these sentences can be the object of the nominal adjective *suki* 'fond of'. In this interpretation they mean 'The girl who likes John is Mary' and 'The girl who likes John but dislikes Bill is Mary.'

5. *Ga* after Quantified Noun Phrases

In the foregoing, I have discussed the neutral-description and exhaustive-listing *ga*, maintaining that only the subjects of action and existential verbs and adjectives/nominal adjectives that represent changing states can be followed by the descriptive *ga*. This statement requires some qualification. First, observe the following sentences:

(45) a. John ga kanemoti desu.
             rich   is
      'John (and only John) is rich.'

    b. Kono kuni   de wa, minna ga kanemoti desu.
       this   country in   all   rich   are
      'In this country, all are rich.'

Unquestionably (45a) is an example of the exhaustive-listing usage of *ga*. It means that among the people in the present universe of discourse, John and only John is rich. On the other hand, (45b) does not seem to have the exhaustive-listing connotation. It does not mean that all are rich (and no one else is). It is a neutral description of the wealth of the people in the country under discussion. According to the constraint on the descriptive *ga* given earlier, (45b) as a neutral description should be ungrammatical because *kanemoti desu* 'are rich' does not represent a changing state. However, it is a perfectly grammatical sentence, requiring no special context. Similarly, observe the following:

(46) San-nin   ga kanemoti desu.
     three persons   rich   are

    a. 'The three (that we have been talking about) and only they are rich.'

    b. 'There are three who are rich.'

The sentence is ambiguous. Of course, a part of the difference in meanings can be attributed to the fact that in one interpretation *san-nin* is an anaphoric noun phrase representing three persons uniquely identifiable in the present universe of discourse, while in the second interpretation it is not anaphoric at all. However, this alone cannot account for the fact that in the first interpretation *ga* has the exhaustive-listing sense, while in the second it does not. Example (46) in the second sense is a neutral description with no exhaustive-listing connotation.

The generalization seems to be that when the subject contains a numeral or a quantifier, it can be followed by the descriptive *ga* even if its predicate represents a stable state.

(47) a. Watakusi no class de wa, go-nin   ga otoko de,
        I   of   in five-persons   male and
        roku-nin   ga onna   desu.
        six-persons   female are
        'In my class, five are boys and six are girls.'

     b. Amerika-zin no ooku ga kanemoti desu.
        Americans   many   rich   are
        'Many of the Americans are rich.'

     c. Daibubun no gakusei ga dokusin desu.
        most   students   single are
        'Most students are single.'

     d. Gakusei no daibubun ga dokusin desu.
        'Most of the students are single.'

     e. Subete no gakusei ga dokusin desu.
        all   students   single   are
        'All students are single.'

This phenomenon is not peculiar to Japanese. In English and in many other languages, as a general rule, a specific but nonanaphoric noun phrase cannot become the subject of a predicate that denotes a more or less stable state.[12] For example,

(48) a. *A boy was tall.

     b. *A man that she met was a hardworking accountant.

However, when the subject contains a stressed numeral or quantifier, we obtain a grammatical sentence.

[12] See Perlmutter (1971b).

(49) a. Óne boy was tall.   Compare: *Ǎ bóy was tall.

　　　b. Twǒ boys were tall.   Compare: *Twǒ bóys were tall.

　　　c. Áll boys were tall.   Compare: *Alľ bóys were tall.[13]

There is a parallelism between the Japanese and English usages. In English, when *stressed* numerals and quantifiers are not found in the subjects of stative predicates, ungrammatical sentences result. In Japanese, when numerals and quantifiers are not found in the subjects of stative predicates, sentences of only the exhaustive-listing *ga* interpretation result. On the other hand, when they are found in the subjects, grammatical sentences result in English, and sentences of the descriptive *ga* (and probably of the exhaustive-listing *ga* as well) interpretation result in Japanese.

6. Summary of *Wa* and *Ga* Uses

The uses of *wa* and *ga* discussed in this chapter are summarized here:

Wa:

(i)　　*Wa* is either *thematic* or *contrastive*.

　　　a. Thematic:
　　　　John wa gakusei desu.
　　　　　　　　 student is
　　　　'John is a student.'

　　　b. Contrastive:
　　　　Ame wa hutte　imasu ga ...
　　　　rain　　falling is　　but
　　　　'Rain is falling, but ... '

(ii)　Themes must be anaphoric or generic. Nonanaphoric nongeneric themes result in ungrammaticality.

　　　Oozei no hito　　*wa* party ni kimasita.
　　　many　people　　　　to came
　　　'Many people came to the party.'

[13] The starred sentences in (48) and (49) are acceptable in a peculiar context when *boy(s)* is contrasted with, say, *girls*. For example,

Speaker A:　No one under ten is tall in this group.

Speaker B:　Óne six-year-old boy is tall.
　　　　　　 One six-year-old bóy is tall.
　　　　　　 A six-year-old bóy is tall.

(iii) On the other hand, nonanaphoric nongeneric noun phrases can be contrasted. Thus

Oozei no hito   *wa* party ni kimasita ga,
many   people   to came   but
omosiroi   *hito*   *wa* kimasen desita.
interesting people   came-not
'Many people came to the party, but there was none who was interesting.'

Ga:

(iv) *Ga* marks the subject of the sentence in either *neutral description* or *exhaustive listing*.

    a. Neutral description:
      John ga kita.
             came
      'John came.'

    b. Exhaustive listing:
      John ga gakusei desu.
             student is
      'John and only John is a student. It is John who is a student.'

(v) If the predicate represents an action, existence, or temporary state, the subject with *ga* is ambiguous between neutral description and exhaustive listing.

John ga kita.

    a. Neutral description:
      'John came.'

    b. Exhaustive listing:
      'It was John who came.'

(vi) If the predicate represents a stable state, the subject with *ga* can receive only the exhaustive-listing interpretation.

John ga gakusei desu.
               student is

    a. Neutral description:
      nonexistent

    b. Exhaustive listing:
      'It is John who is a student.'

(vii) However, when the subject contains a numeral or quantifier, the neutral-description interpretation is possible even with a stative predicate.

Gakusei no daibubun ga dokusin desu.
student 's most   single is

Neutral description:
'Most of the students are single.'

(viii) *Ga* also marks the *object* of stative transitive verbals:

John wa *eigo*   *ga* dekiru.
          English   can
'John can (speak) English.'

3[†]

Wa and *Ga* (Part II)—Subjectivization

1. Introduction

The theme (NP-*wa*) of Japanese sentences has received two different treatments in the framework of the generative theory of transformational grammar. Some[1] claim that the theme does not exist as such in the deep structure but that it is produced by the process of attaching *wa* to some major constituent in the sentence and preposing the "constituent+*wa*" to the beginning of the sentence. To them, sentence (1) has the deep structure corresponding to (2a).

(1) Kono hon   *wa* John ga yonda.
    this   book   read
    'Speaking of this book, John has read it.'

(2) a. [John] [kono hon] [yonda]+*wa*.
            this   book read

This is realized as (1) by the following intermediate stages:

(2) b. [John]-ga [kono hon]-o [yonda]+*wa*. (subject and object
                                     marking)

    c. [John]-ga [kono hon]-o-*wa* [yonda]. (*wa* attachment)

    d. [Kono hon]-o-*wa* [John]-ga [yonda]. (theme preposing)

    e. [Kono hon]-*wa* [John]-ga [yonda]. (deletion of particles before
                                          other particles)

Others, on the basis of sentences such as (3), claim that themes must be in the deep structure as such.

(3) Sakana *wa* tai   ga oisii.
    fish   red snapper   delicious-is
    'Speaking of fish, red snapper is the most delicious.'

To them, (1) is derived from the deep structure corresponding to (4),

---

[†]This chapter is basically for students and teachers of Japanese and for the linguists who are interested in the double- and triple-subject constructions in Japanese.
[1] For example, see Kuroda (1965a).

which is realized as (1) via the deletion of the identical noun phrase in the main clause.

(4) [Kono hon]$_{theme}$ John kono hon yonda.

On the other hand, it has been generally believed that the NP-*ga*, whether it is that of neutral description or of exhaustive listing, is in the subject position in the deep structure. In this chapter I shall clarify in what contexts the NP-*ga* assumes the connotation of exhaustive listing, and show that certain uses of the exhaustive-listing NP-*ga* must be derived, as is the case with the theme, either by a movement transformation or, alternatively, by placing it as a special phrase in the deep structure.

2. Interpretation of NP-*Ga*

English allows the exhaustive-listing interpretation not only of the subject but also of the other parts of the sentence depending upon where the stress is placed.

(5) a. Jóhn likes Mary = It is John who likes Mary/Only John likes Mary.

b. John likes Máry = It is Mary whom John likes/John likes only Mary.

c. *Jóhn likes Máry = Only John likes only Mary.

Example (5c) shows that only one major constituent in a given sentence can receive the exhaustive-listing interpretation. Generally speaking, this is true also for Japanese.

(6) a. Jóhn ga Mary ni okane o yatta.
                      money   gave
    = It was John who gave the money to Mary.

b. John ga Máry ni okane o yatta.
    = It was to Mary that John gave the money.

c. John ga Mary ni okáne o yatta.
    = It was the money that John gave to Mary.

However, when the *ga* that can receive only the exhaustive-listing interpretation is present in a sentence, it takes precedence, and no other elements can be given the exhaustive-listing interpretation.

(7) John ga mainiti   gakkoo ni iku.
          every-day school   go
    'John (and only John) goes to school every day.'

Since the predicate of (7) represents a habitual action, *John ga* can receive only the exhaustive-listing interpretation, and (8) in the specified interpretation is ungrammatical.

(8) *John *ga* mainiti gakkóo ni iku.
    'It is to school that John (and only John) goes every day.'

That (9) can mean only 'It is John who likes Mary', and not 'It is Mary that John likes', therefore, is a corollary of the preceding generalization.

(9) John *ga* Mary *ga* suki da.

    Now, observe the following sentences:

(10) a. Kono class[2] *wa* dansei *ga* yoku dekiru.
           this   male   well are-able
           'Speaking of this class, the boys do well (at studies).'

     b. Kono class *wa* John *ga* yoku dekiru.
           'Speaking of this class, John does well (at studies).'

Kuroda[3] has observed that (10a) is ambiguous: it can mean (i) 'Speaking of this class, boys and only boys do well' (exhaustive-listing interpretation on *dansei ga* implying that the girls don't do well); and (ii) 'As for this class, the boys do well' (neutral-description interpretation on *dansei ga*). What (10a) represents in its second interpretation is that in some classes boys do well in their studies, and in some other classes they do poorly, and that 'this class' can be characterized as a class in which the boys do well. The sentence does not say anything about the girls in the class. It

---

[2] The word "class" is used here in the sense of Japanese *kurasu*. It means, not 'course meetings' but 'a body of around thirty students in the same year'. They take courses together, and once a student is put in, say, Class *X*, he is identified as a member of that class (and of no other "classes") during that school year.

[3] Personal communication (October 1969). Mikami (1963, pp. 32–33) has also observed that sentences such as (i) in isolation give the impression that there is something missing, and they are often realized with themes, as in (ii).

(i) Dansei ga yoku dekiru. 'The boys do well in their studies.'

(ii) Kono class wa dansei ga yoku dekiru. 'Speaking of this class, the boys do well.'

Mikami seems to have been aware of the phenomenon under discussion.

might be that the girls in this class do even better than the boys. This is what is meant by saying that *ga* in interpretation (ii) is of neutral description.

On the other hand, (10b) can receive only the exhaustive-listing interpretation: 'In this class, John is the only person who does well.' Similarly, (11a) is ambiguous between exhaustive listing and neutral description with respect to the interpretation of *dansei ga*, while (11b) has only one interpretation, that is, the one that gives the exhaustive-listing reading to *Tokyo ga*.

(11) a. Nihon *wa* dansei *ga* tanmei   desu.
        Japan   male   short-life-span are
        'As for Japan, men have a short life-span.'
     b. Nihon *wa* Tokyo *ga* sumi-yoi.
                            easy-to-live-in
        'As for Japan, Tokyo is comfortable to live in.'

Observe that the themeless version of (10a) and (11a) can receive only the exhaustive-listing interpretation.

(10) a'. Kono class no dansei *ga* yoku dekiru.
          this   's male   well are-able
          'It is the boys in this class that do well.'

(11) a'. Nihon no dansei *ga* tanmei   desu.
          Japan 's male   short-life-span are
          'It is men in Japan that have a short life-span.'

This observation may suggest that the NP-*wa*, which appears in (10a) and (11a), optionally neutralizes the exhaustive-listing *ga* that follows, and turns it into the *ga* of neutral description. That is, in (10a'), the *dansei ga* 'men' receives only the exhaustive-listing interpretation because its predicate, *yoku dekiru* 'do well', represents a state, while the *dansei ga* of (10a) can receive both the exhaustive-listing and neutral-description interpretations because the previously mentioned condition has been neutralized by the presence of an NP-*wa* (*Nihon wa*) at the beginning of the sentence. According to this suggestion, (10b) and (11b) are unambiguous because the neutral-description interpretation of these sentences, although claimed to be syntactically possible, is semantically implausible. That is, semantically, it would not make sense to say, "As for this class, in contrast to other classes, John does well" unless more than one student with the name 'John' is being compared, or unless John belongs to more than one class and his performance in this class is contrasted with that in his other classes. However, the following examples show that this explanation does not seem to hold:

(12) Nihongo wa *John ga* heta   desu.
Japanese   bad-at is
'As for Japanese, it is John who is bad at it.'

(13) Atama wa *John ga* warui.
head   is-wrong
'(Lit.) As for the head, it is John who is weak.'

(14) Dansei wa *kono class ga* yoku dekiru.
male   this class   well are-able
'(Lit.) As for men, it is this class that does well.'

(15) Dansei wa *Nihon ga* tanmei   desu.[4]
male   short-life-span are
'(Lit.) As for men, Japan has a short life-span.'

All these sentences have, unambiguously, the exhaustive-listing interpretation on the italicized NP-*ga*, and it is not possible to assign the neutral-description interpretation to them, although semantically it should be possible. For example, there should be nothing wrong semantically with using (12) in the context "As for Japanese, John is bad at it, but as for other languages, he is not bad at them." Therefore, the explanation must be sought elsewhere.

---

[4] Examples (12)–(15) involve a word-order inversion, as well as changes in particles, from the more ordinary

(12') John wa nihongo ga heta   desu.
Japanese   bad-at is
'John is bad at Japanese.'

(13') John wa atama ga warui.
head   is-wrong
'John is weak in the head.'

(14') Kono class wa dansei ga yoku dekiru.
this   male   well are-able
'As for this class, the boys do well.'

(15') Nihon wa dansei ga tanmei   desu.
Japan   male   short-life-span are
'As for Japan, men have a short life-span.'

All of these have ambiguous readings of the NP-*ga* between exhaustive listing and neutral description.

First note that, corresponding to some of the *NP-wa NP-ga* . . . sentences that we have been using as examples, there are *NP-ga NP-ga* . . . sentences. For example,

(16) a. Kono class *wa* dansei *ga* yoku dekiru (= 10a)
      this   male   well are-able
      'Speaking of this class, the boys do well.'
      (*dansei ga*: exhaustive listing and neutral description)

    b. Kono class *ga* dansei *ga* yoku dekiru.
      'It is this class that the boys do well in.'
      (*dansei ga*: neutral description)

(17) a. Nihon *wa* dansei *ga* tanmei   desu. (= 11a)
      Japan   male   short-life-span are
      'Speaking of Japan, men have a short life-span.'
      (*dansei ga*: exhaustive listing and neutral description)

    b. Nihon *ga* dansei *ga* tanmei desu.
      'It is Japan that men have a short life-span in.'
      (*dansei ga*: neutral description)

As has been noted, (16a) and (17a) have ambiguous readings with respect to whether *dansei ga* receives the interpretation of exhaustive listing or neutral description. On the other hand, (16b) and (17b) are unambiguous, and *dansei ga* can receive only the neutral-description interpretation. The latter fact seems to be consistent with the observation previously made (see example (8)) that when the *ga* that can receive only the exhaustive-listing interpretation is present in a sentence, it takes precedence, and that no other elements can be given the exhaustive-listing interpretation. The preceding generalization seems to work from left to right in a sentence, so that when there is more than one NP-*ga* in a sentence that can potentially receive the exhaustive-listing interpretation, the leftmost one takes precedence, and the rest are interpretable only as neutral description.

It is not the case, however, that all *NP-wa NP-ga* . . . sentences have corresponding *NP-ga NP-ga* . . . sentences. Observe the following:

(18) a.   Kono class *wa* John *ga* yoku dekiru. (= 10b)
       this   well is-able
       'Speaking of this class, it is John who does well.'
       (*John ga*: exhaustive listing)

b. *Kono class *ga* John *ga* yoku dekiru.
   'It is this class that John does well in.'

(19) a.   Nihon *wa* Tokyo *ga* sumi-yoi. (= 11b)
          'Speaking of Japan, Tokyo is easy to live in.'
          (*Tokyo ga*: exhaustive listing)

     b.   *Nihon *ga* Tokyo *ga* sumi-yoi.
          '(Lit.) It is Japan that Tokyo is easy to live in.'

(20) a.   Nihongo *wa* John *ga* heta   desu. (= 12)
          Japanese   bad-at is
          'As for Japanese, it is John who is bad at it.'
          (*John ga*: exhaustive listing)

     b.   *Nihongo *ga* John *ga* heta desu.
          'It is Japanese that John is bad at.'

Note that when the *NP-wa NP-ga* ... sentences have ambiguous readings, as in (16a) and (17a), the corresponding *NP-ga NP-ga* ... sentences are grammatical, as shown in (16b) and (17b), while when the *NP-wa NP-ga* ... sentences have only the exhaustive-listing interpretation, as in (18a), (19a), and (20a), the corresponding *NP-ga NP-ga* ... sentences are ungrammatical. Or, conversely, when an *NP-ga NP-ga* ... sentence is grammatical, the corresponding *NP-wa NP-ga* ... sentence can receive an ambiguous interpretation, and when an *NP-ga NP-ga* ... sentence is ungrammatical, the corresponding *NP-wa NP-ga* ... sentence can receive only the exhaustive-listing interpretation.

3. Distribution of Multiple-Subject Constructions
Before explaining the phenomena observed here, we must consider under what circumstances NP-*ga* appears where it is not ordinarily expected to appear. The source of (16b) and (17b) seems to be

(21) Kono class *no* dansei ga yoku dekiru.
     this   's male   well are-able
     'This class's boys (and only they) do well.'

(22) Nihon *no* dansei ga tanmei   desu.
     Japan 's male   short-life-span are
     'Men of Japan (and only they) have a short life-span.'

Similarly,

(23) a. John *no* otoosan ga sinda.
                  's father   died
        (i) 'John's father died.'
        (ii) 'It is John's father that has died.'

    b. John *ga* otoosan ga sinda.
        'It is John whose father died.'

(24) a. Yama   *no* ki   ga kirei   desu.
          mountain 's trees   pretty are
        (i) 'It is trees in the mountains that are pretty.'
        (ii) '(Look!) The trees in the mountains are pretty.'

    b. Yama *ga* ki ga kirei desu.[5]
        (i) 'It is the mountains that trees are pretty in.'
        (ii) '(Look!) The mountains—their trees are pretty.'

---

[5] The word *kirei* 'pretty' can be used both for describing a more or less stable state and for depicting the current state. For example,

(i) Sora ga kirei desu.
    sky   pretty is

This is ambiguous between (a) 'Out of all the things that we have been talking about, the sky and only the sky is pretty,' and (b) 'Oh, look! The sky is pretty!' In the latter usage, the sentence is often followed by *ne* 'isn't it.' On the other hand, observe this sentence:

(ii) Nihon no ki   ga kirei   desu.
     Japan 's trees   pretty are

It can receive only the interpretation of exhaustive listing because it is usually taken as a generic statement meaning '(Of all the things under discussion) it is the trees in Japan that are pretty.' This is because statements of neutral description require that the referent of the subject be something that the speaker can observe and point to. One can call the portion of the sky that he can see *sora* 'the sky', and those trees on the mountains that he can see *yama no ki* 'the trees in the mountains'—hence the grammaticality of (24a) and of (i). On the other hand, one cannot refer to the Japanese trees that he is looking at as *Nihon no ki* 'the trees in Japan'—hence the ungrammaticality of (ii). He can, of course, say

(iii) Nihon no ki *wa* kirei desu.
      'Speaking of Japanese trees, they are pretty.'

However, *Nihon no ki* in this sentence is used, not to refer to the trees that one is looking at at present, but as a generic noun phrase meaning 'the trees in Japan in general'.

(25) a. John *no* kodomo ga sensei   ni sikarareta.
            's child   teacher by was-scolded
        (i) 'John's child was scolded by the teacher.'
        (ii) 'It is John's child that was scolded by the teacher.'

    b. John *ga* kodomo ga sensei ni sikarareta.[6]
       'John—his child was scolded by the teacher.'

On the other hand, if NP-*no* is in the middle of a sentence, and not at
the leftmost position, we get ungrammatical sentences:

(26) a. Sensei   ga John *no* kodomo o sikatta.
          teacher   's child   scolded
          'The teacher scolded John's child.'

    b. John *no* kodomo o sensei ga sikatta.
        'John's child, the teacher scolded.'

    c. *John *ga* sensei ga kodomo o sikatta.
        'John—the teacher scolded his child.'

On the basis of this observation, let us tentatively assume that there is a
transformational process, which I shall call Subjectivization, that makes
the leftmost NP-*no* of a sentence its new subject. Note that this transformation applies to sentences that maintain their basic word order, that is,
before (26a) is changed to (26b) by the Scrambling Rule. This process
can be applied iteratively as shown in the following example:

(27) a. Bunmeikoku no dansei no heikin-zyumyoo ga mizikai.
          civilized   's male 's average life-span   is-short
          countries
          'It is the average life-span of men of civilized countries that is
          short.'

---

[6] The ordinary adversity-passive construction is preferred:

John ga kodomo *o* sensei   ni sikarareta.
            child   teacher by was-scolded
'To John's chagrin, his son was scolded by the teacher.'

However, I can accept (25b) as grammatical. Even to those speakers who do not accept
(25b) as grammatical, the difference in degree of grammaticality between (25b) and (26c)
that follows should be obvious.

b. Apply Subjectivization to *bunmeikoku no dansei* 'men of civilized countries':
Bunmeikoku no dansei *ga* heikin-zyumyoo *ga* mizikai.
'It is men of civilized countries that the average life-span is short in.'

c. Apply Subjectivization to *bunmeikoku* 'civilized countries' of (b):
Bunmeikoku *ga* dansei *ga* heikin-zyumyoo ga mizikai.
'It is civilized countries that men—their average life-span is short in.'

On the other hand, if we had applied Subjectivization to *bunmeikoku* 'civilized countries' of (a), we would obtain

(27) d. Bunmeikoku *ga* dansei no heikin-zyumyoo *ga* mizikai.
'It is civilized countries that men's average life-span is short in.'

It goes without saying that in all these examples, only the newly formed first NP-*ga* can receive the exhaustive-listing interpretation.

4. Derivation of Multiple-Subject Constructions
I am now ready to present a set of ordered rules to account for the phenomena under discussion in this chapter.

(28) a. *Subjectivization* (tentative formulation) [optional]:
Change the sentence-initial NP-*no* to NP-*ga*, and make it the new subject of the sentence.

b. *Marking for Exhaustive Listing* [obligatory for the matrix sentence]:
If the predicate of a sentence represents a state or a habitual/generic action, and if the sentence-initial NP-*ga* does not contain a numeral or quantifier, mark that NP-*ga* as [+exhaustive listing].

c. *Thematization* [optional]:
Add *wa* to an *NP+particle*, and prepose the *NP+particle* *+wa* to the beginning of the sentence.[7]

---

[7] It is not clear what types of NP's can be made themes and what types cannot be. What is clear, however, is that Thematization has a much wider scope than Subjectivization. For example,

(i) Sensei ga *John no* kodomo o sikatta.
teacher   's child   scolded
*John ga sensei ga kodomo o sikatta.
John wa sensei ga kodomo o sikatta.
'The teacher scolded John's child.'   (*Continued overleaf*)

The preceding analysis is based on the view that the exhaustive-listing interpretation of (29) is no different from that of (30) because of a general rule of Japanese which says that any major constituent can receive a prominent stress (unless there is already one) and can receive the exhaustive-listing interpretation.

(29) *Jóhn ga* kita.
    'John came.'
(30) John ga *hón o* yonda.
    'John read the bóok.'

On the other hand, the analysis claims that the exhaustive-listing reading of (31) is something special and should be dealt with differently from (29) and (30).

(31) *Inu ga* doobutu desu.
    dog   animal   is
    'The dog (and only the dog) is an animal.'

Now let us examine how these rules can account for some of the crucial examples previously mentioned. First, observe the following derivation:

(32) a. Kono class no dansei yoku dekiru. (deep structure)
        this   's male well are-able
        'This class's boys do well.'

    b. Kono class no dansei *ga* yoku dekiru. (Subject Marking)

If we do not apply Subjectivization to (32b), the application of the obligatory marking for exhaustive listing yields

(32) c. *Kono class no dansei ga* [+exhaustive] *yoku dekiru.*
        'It is the boys of this class that do well.'

This in itself is a grammatical sentence. If we thematize *kono class no* of (32c), we obtain

(32) d. *Kono class wa* [+theme] *dansei ga* [+exhaustive] *yoku dekiru.*
        'Speaking of this class, the boys (and not the girls) do well.'

This derivation accounts for one reading of (10a).

(ii) John wa *kono hon o* yonda.
          this book read
    **Kono hon ga* John ga yonda.
    Kono hon wa John ga yonda.
    'John read this book.'

On the other hand, if we apply Subjectivization to (32b), we obtain

(32) e. *Kono class ga* dansei ga yoku dekiru.

This, in turn, undergoes the obligatory marking for exhaustive listing, yielding

(32) f. *Kono class ga* [+exhaustive] dansei ga yoku dekiru.
      'It is this class that the boys do well in.'

If we thematize *kono class ga* of the preceding sentence, we obtain

(32) g. *Kono class wa* [+theme] dansei ga yoku dekiru.
      'Speaking of this class, the boys do well.'

Note that *dansei ga* in the preceding sentence is not marked as [+exhaustive], thus allowing the neutral-description interpretation. This accounts for the second reading of (10a).

To return to (32f), if Thematization is applied, not to *kono class ga*, but to *dansei ga*, the following sentence is obtained:

(32) h. *Dansei wa* [+theme] *kono class ga* [+exhaustive] yoku dekiru.
      'Speaking of the boys, this class (and only this class) does well.'

Observe that, in this sentence, *kono class ga* receives the interpretation of exhaustive listing, which is the only possible interpretation for the sentence.

On the other hand, assume that we have the following deep structure:

(33) a. Kono class no John yoku dekiru.
      this   's   well is-able
      'John, who is in this class, does well.'

After application of Subject Marking, we obtain

(33) b. Kono class no John *ga* yoku dekiru.

Now, for some reason[8] *kono class no*, although it is the sentence-initial

---

[8] It seems that when the NP-*no* of "NP-*no* NP" phrases is a nonrestrictive modifier of the second NP, and not a restrictive one, it cannot undergo Subjectivization. In (33), *kono class no John* means, not 'the John who is in this class (and not other Johns)', but 'John, who is in this class'. In this sense, *kono class no* is nonrestrictive. On the other hand, in (32), *kono class no dansei* means 'the boys who are in this class', and thus *kono class no* plays a role of a restrictive modifier of *dansei*. Similarly,

(*Continued overleaf*)

NP-*no*, cannot undergo Subjectivization. Therefore, we cannot get

(33) c. **Kono class ga* John ga yoku dekiru.

Therefore, the following derivation is ruled out:

(33) d. **Kono class ga* [+exhaustive] John ga yoku dekiru. (Marking for Exhaustive Listing)

(33) e. **Kono class wa* [+theme] John ga yoku dekiru. (Thematization)

Hence, there is no possibility of obtaining the interpretation in which *ga* of *John ga* is of neutral description. In (33b), Marking for Exhaustive Listing is obligatorily applied to *kono class no John ga*, resulting in

(33) f. *Kono class no John ga* [+exhaustive] yoku dekiru.
'It is John, who is in this class, that does well.'

If Thematization is applied to *kono class no* of the preceding sentence, we obtain

(33) g. *Kono class wa* [+theme] *John ga* [+exhaustive] yoku dekiru.
'Speaking of this class, John and only John does well.'

In this sentence *John ga* receives the interpretation of exhaustive listing. If Thematization is applied to *kono class no John ga* of (33f), we obtain

(33) h. *Kono class no John wa* [+theme] yoku dekiru.
'Speaking of John, who is in this class, he does well.'

The ambiguity of (24b) can be explained in the following manner. It has, as its deep structure,

(34) a. Yama   no ki   kirei   desu.
        mountain 's trees pretty are
        'The trees in the mountains are pretty.'

(i)   Sooridaizin   no Ikeda-si ga sinda.
      prime-minister   Mr. died
      'Mr. Ikeda, (who is) Prime Minister, has died.'

(ii) *Sooridaizin ga Ikeda-si ga sinda.

No in this example is the attributive form of the copula *da*. It is not altogether clear what other types of sentence-initial NP-*no* can or cannot undergo Subjectivization. What is definitely clear is that the semantic relationship between the first and the second NP plays a decisive role here.

After the application of Subject Marking, we obtain

(34) b. Yama no ki *ga* kirei desu.

Now, assume that we do not apply Subjectivization to *yama no*. If *kirei desu* is taken as representing a generic statement, (34b) undergoes the obligatory application of Marking for Exhaustive Listing, resulting in

(34) c. *Yama no ki ga* [+exhaustive] kirei desu.
       'It is the trees of mountains which are pretty.'

Sentence (34c) can further undergo Thematization either of *yama no ki ga* or of *yama no*:

(34) d. *Yama no ki wa* [+theme] kirei desu.
       'Speaking of the trees of mountains, they are pretty.'

   e. *Yama wa* [+theme] *ki ga* [+exhaustive] kirei desu.
       'Speaking of mountains, it is the trees that are pretty.'

On the other hand, *kirei desu* of (34b) can be taken as representing the current temporary state. In that case, Marking for Exhaustive Listing does not apply. Thus, we obtain

(34) f. Yama no ki ga kirei desu (ne).
       'Look! The trees of that mountain are pretty (aren't they).'

Sentence (34f) can further undergo Thematization either of *yama no ki ga* or *yama no*, resulting in

(34) g. *Yama no ki wa* [+theme] kirei desu (ne).
       'Speaking of the trees of that mountain, they are pretty (aren't they).'

   h. *Yama wa* [+theme] ki ga kirei desu (ne).
       'Speaking of that mountain, the trees are pretty (aren't they).'

In sentence (34b), if we do apply Subjectivization, we obtain

(34) i. Yama *ga* ki ga kirei desu.

Now again, depending upon whether *kirei desu* represents a generic statement or not, the marking of *yama ga* for exhaustive listing is or is not applied.

(34) j. *Yama ga* [+exhaustive] ki ga kirei desu.
'It is mountains that trees are pretty in.'

   k. Yama ga ki ga kirei desu (ne).
'That mountain—its trees are pretty (aren't they).'

Thematization can be applied to *yama ga* of the preceding sentence, yielding

(34) l. *Yama wa* [+theme] ki ga kirei desu.
'Speaking of mountains, their trees are pretty.' (generic statement)

   m. *Yama wa* [+theme] ki ga kirei desu (ne).[9]
'Speaking of that mountain, the trees are pretty (aren't they).'

I have mentioned that Subjectivization applies to the sentence-initial NP-*no*. There are apparent counterexamples to this rule:

(35) a. New York *ga* koosoo-kentiku   ga ooi.[10]
                 high-rise-building   are-many
'It is New York that there are many high-rise buildings in.'

---

[9] This has an unpleasant consequence in that *Yama wa ki ga kirei desu (ne)* with *ki ga* as neutral description has two different derivations: one as shown here, and the other as shown for (34h). Sentence (34m) is different from (34h) in that it has gone through one additional stage—that is, the changing of *yama no* to *yama ga*. A similar phenomenon can be observed in

(i)   *John ga* [+exhaustive] nihongo ga nigate da.
                        Japanese   bad-at is
"John is bad at Japanese."

(ii) (Thematization):
John wa [+theme] nihongo ga nigate da.

(iii) a. (*Ga/ni* change):
John ni nihongo ga nigate da.

   b. (Thematization):
John ni wa nihongo ga nigate da.

   c. (Particle Deletion):
John wa [+theme] nihongo ga nigate da.

As shown above, *John wa nihongo ga nigate da* can be derived either directly from (i) as shown in (ii) or through three steps as shown in (iii). I do not have any answer at present as to how this problem of multiple derivations for unambiguous sentences can be avoided when *wa* is involved.

[10] This example is due to Kuroda (personal communication, October 1969).

b. New York *ga* koosoo-kentiku ga takusan aru.
                                     many   exist
'It is New York that many high-rise buildings exist in.'

c. New York *ga* koosoo-kentiku ga takusan tatte-iru.
                                     many   standing-exist
'It is New York that many high-rise buildings exist standing in.'

Note that *New York ga* in the preceding sentences cannot be derived from *New York no* as shown in (35d).

(35) d. *New York *no* koosoo-kentiku ga ooi.
      '(Lit.) New York's high-rise buildings are many.'

However, we have, for example,

(36) a. New York *ni* koosoo-kentiku ga takusan aru.
                in
      'In New York there are many high-rise buildings.'

b. New York *ni* koosoo-kentiku ga takusan tatte-iru.
      'In New York there are many high-rise buildings standing.'

If (36) is the source for (35), it should be noted that this *NP-ni→NP-ga* change,[11] that is, the subjectivization of locative NP-*ni*, seems to be restricted to cases involving existential statements.

(37) a. Gakusei ga New York *ni* itta.
         student   to went
         'The students went to New York.'

b. New York *ni* gakusei ga itta.
               to students   went
      'The students went to New York.'

c. *New York *ga* gakusei ga itta.
      'It is New York that the students went to.'

Note that (37a), where we have a directional particle *ni* 'to' instead of

---

[11] This change, which is regarded here as a process of subjectivization, should not be confused with the *NP-ga→NP-ni* change, to be discussed in the next chapter.

John *ga* nihongo *ga* nigate desu.
John *ni* nihongo *ga* nigate desu.
'John is bad at Japanese.'

locative *ni* 'in, at', is not an existential statement. Although (37b) is grammatical, (37c) is not possible. If we assume that existential sentences such as those shown in (36) have the basic word order *Locative + NP (something)-ga + Exist*, but that nonexistential sentences with locatives such as (37a) have the basic word order *NP-ga Location-ni Exist*, then we can account for the grammaticality of (35) and the ungrammaticality of (37c) by assuming that Subjectivization applies only to sentencė-initial NP-*no/ni*. *New York ni* of (37b) would not undergo Subjectivization because, at the time of the application of the rule, *New York ni* would not be in the sentence-initial position, but would appear after *gakusei ga*, as in (37a). It seems that this hypothesis that existential sentences in Japanese have locatives in the sentence-initial position can be supported by other evidence in the language and can also be shown to hold for many other languages of the world.[12]

---

[12] I shall return to this topic in Chapter 28 of this book. Although the analysis presented in this chapter seems to account for the majority of the double-subject and triple-subject constructions in Japanese, it is not free from counterexamples. One class of counterexamples involves *no hoo* ' . . . 's side' as the first "subject." For example,

(i) a. Boku wa *John to*   sitasii.
         I   with friendly-am
         'I am on friendly terms with John.'

     b. **John ga* boku wa sitasii.

     c. *John no hoo ga* boku wa sitasii.

(ii) a. Boku wa *Tokyo ni* ikitai.
         I   to go-want
         'I want to go to Tokyo.'

     b. **Tokyo ga* boku wa ikitai.

     c. *Tokyo no hoo ga* boku wa ikitai.

The ungrammaticality of the (b) sentences is predictable. Namely, *John to* 'with John' and *Tokyo ni* 'to Tokyo' are not the sentence-initial NP-*no/ni* and therefore cannot undergo Subjectivization. What is mysterious is that these sentences become grammatical if *no hoo* ' . . . 's side ' is added. I have no explanation, at present, for the grammaticality (or for the derivational source) of the (c) sentences.

4†

Ga for Object Marking

1. Constructions with *Ga* Marking the Object

It is usually said that *ga* marks the subject, and *o* the object, of a sentence. For example, in (1), *John* is the subject, and *hon* the object, of the sentence.

(1) John *ga* asoko   de hon   o yonde   imasu.
           that-place at book   reading is
   'John is reading a book there.'

However, in certain constructions, *ga* appears where *o* is expected. For example,

(2) a. Watakusi wa eigo   *ga* hanas-e-ru.
      I   English   speak-can
      'I can speak English.'

    b. Watakusi wa okane   *ga* hosii.
      I   money   want
      'I want money.'

    c. Watakusi wa Mary *ga* suki   da.
      I   fond-of am
      'I like Mary.'

In conventional Japanese grammars, *eigo*, *okane*, and *Mary* in the preceding sentences are said to be the subject. For example, Martin (1962, p. 44) states that "The particle *ga* shows the SUBJECT. In *Eiga ga suki desu* 'I like movies' the particle *ga* shows that *eiga* 'movies' is the subject of *suki desu* 'are liked'." Also note the following quotation from Jorden (1962, p. 100): "-*Tai* words have one special characteristic: the direct object (followed by particle *o*) of a verbal often becomes the subject (followed by particle *ga*) of the adjectival -*tai* derivative. Thus, *shinbun o kaimasu* 'I am going to buy a newspaper, but ...' but: *shinbun ga kaitai n desu ga ...* 'I want to buy a newspaper, but ...'." However, if *eiga* and *shinbun* are the subjects of *suki desu* and *kaitai*, respectively, what can *watakusi* and *dare* be in the following sentences?

†This chapter is mainly for students and teachers of Japanese.

(3) a. Dare *ga* eiga   *ga* suki   desu ka?
     who   movie   fond-of is
     'Who likes movies?'

  b. Watakusi *ga* eiga   *ga* suki   desu.
     I   movie   fond-of am
     'I like movies.'

If we accept the analysis that says that *eiga* is the subject of *suki desu*, then we have to say that (3a) and (3b) have two subjects: *watakusi/dare*, on the one hand, and *eiga*, on the other hand. This would be a very peculiar analysis, to say the least.

It would not do to regard (3a) and (3b) as double-subject sentences of the same type as those discussed in the previous chapter. For example,

(4) Bunmeikoku   *ga* dansei no heikin-zyumyoo *ga* mizikai.
   civilized countries   male 's average-life-span   short-is
   'It is the civilized countries that males' average life-span is short in.'

This sentence clearly has double subjects: *bunmeikoku* 'civilized countries' and *dansei no heikin-zyumyoo* 'average life-span of males.' However, one of the characteristics of these double-subject constructions is that we obtain a nonelliptical sentence even without the first subject.

(5) Dansei no heikin-zyumyoo ga mizikai.
   male 's average-life-span   short-is
   'It is males' average life-span that is short.'

On the other hand, the deletion of the first NP-*ga* from (3a) and (3b) would result in elliptical sentences:

(6) a. Eiga   ga suki   desu.
     movie   fond-of is
     '(I am, he is, etc.) fond of movies.'

  b. Okane ga hosii.
     money   want
     '(I) want money.'

Furthermore, for (4) there is a corresponding single-subject sentence, namely,

(7) Bunmeikoku   *no* dansei no heikin-zyumyoo ga mizikai.
   civilized country 's male 's average-life-span   short-is
   'It is the average life-span of males of civilized countries that is short.'

However, it is not the case for (3a) and (3b).

(8) a. *Watakusi *no/ni* eiga ga suki desu.
I movie fond-of is
'I am fond of movies.'

b. *Watakusi *no/ni* okane ga hosii.
I money want
'I want money.'

In what follows, I shall show that *ga* is used not only for marking the subject but also for marking the object of all transitive adjectives and nominal adjectives (*keiyoo-doosi*) and of a certain class of transitive verbs. I shall further show that these verbals which take *ga* for object marking have the common semantic characteristic that they represent, not actions, but states. Since it is inherent in the nature of adjectives and nominal adjectives to represent states, this generalization automatically accounts for the fact that all transitive adjectives and nominal adjectives take *ga* for object marking.

2. Semantic Classification of Verbals Used with Object-Marking *Ga*

Transitive adjectives and nominal adjectives can be classified in the following semantic categories:

(9) Competence: *zyoozu* 'good at', *nigate* 'bad at', *heta* 'bad at', *tokui* 'good at, proud of', *umai* 'good at'.

a. Dare ga eigo *ga zyoozu* desu ka?
who English good-at is
'Who is good at English?'

b. Boku ga nihongo *ga nigate/heta* na koto wa minna
I Japanese bad-at am fact-that everyone
yoku sitte imasu.
well know
'Everyone knows well that I am bad at Japanese.'

c. Dare ga nihongo *ga umai* desu ka?
who Japanese good-at is
'Who is good at Japanese?'

    d. John wa hito   o damasu koto *ga umai.*
               others   deceive to   good-at
      'John is good at deceiving others.'

(10) Adjectives and Nominal Adjectives of Feeling: *suki* 'fond of', *kirai* 'hateful of', *hosii* 'want', *kowai* 'be fearful of'

    a. John ga Mary *ga suki/kirai*   na koto   wa yoku
                      fond-of/hateful-of is fact-that   well
      sitte   imasu.
      know
      'I know very well that John likes/dislikes Mary.'

    b. Boku wa Mary *ga kowai.*
      I   am-fearful-of
      'I am afraid of Mary.'

    c. Boku wa okane *ga hosii.*
      I   money   want
      'I want money.'

    d. Kimi wa nanigo   *ga tokui*   desu ka?
      you   what-language   good-at   are
      'What language are you good at?'

    e. Boku wa oyogu koto *ga suki*   da.
      I   swim   to   fond-of am
      'I like swimming.'

(11) *-Tai* Derivatives: *yomitai* 'want to read', *tabetai* 'want to eat', etc. Although *ga* is preferred, *o* can be used for marking objects.

    a. Boku wa eiga $\begin{Bmatrix} ga \\ o \end{Bmatrix}$ *mitai.*
      I   movie   see-want
      'I am anxious to see movies.'

    b. Boku ga osusi $\begin{Bmatrix} ga \\ o \end{Bmatrix}$ *tabe-tai*   koto   o, nando   ittara
      I   sushi   eat-want fact-that   how-often if-I-said
      wakaru   no desu ka?
      understand that is
      'How many times is it that I have to tell you that I am anxious to eat sushi?

Incidentally, *tai* derivatives 'be anxious to' and *kowai* 'be fearful of', *hosii* 'want', *tokui da* 'be good at', and several others constitute the small class of verbals in Japanese which require that their subject be in the first person if they are used in isolated affirmative sentences. Consider the following:

(12) a. *Boku* wa eiga   ga mitai.
         I   movie   want-see
         'I am anxious to see movies.'

    b. *John wa eiga ga mitai.
         'John is anxious to see movies.'

    c. *Kimi* wa eiga ga mitai?
         you
         'Are you anxious to see movies?'

    d. *John wa eiga ga mitai?
         'Is John anxious to see movies?'

(13) a. *Boku* wa okane ga hosii.
         I   money   want
         'I want money.'

    b. *John wa okane ga hosii.
         'John wants money.'

    c. *Kimi* wa okane ga hosii?
         you
         'Do you want money?'

    d. *John wa okane ga hosii?
         'Does John want money?'

Examples (12) and (13) show that *mitai* 'be anxious to see' and *hosii* 'want' require that their subject be the first person in affirmative sentences and that it be the second person in interrogative sentences. These verbals represent an internal feeling. The speaker has no basis for making an affirmative judgment on the second or third person's internal feeling. He can express only his own internal feeling. Hence, only the first person subject is allowed in (12) and (13) in affirmative sentences. The speaker can ask about the internal feeling of the hearer, but not about the internal feeling of some third person. He cannot ask the hearer about his (the speaker's) own feeling, either. Hence, only the second person is allowed for questions. Because the phenomenon under discussion is much more complex than has been implied when subordinate clauses are involved, when certain final particles follow these verbals, or when they appear in narratives, I shall leave this problem for future discussions[1] and proceed to the more central matter of *ga* for object marking.

Now, when the subject is a second or third person, *garu* forms are used instead. Observe the following sentences:

(14) a. John wa eiga $\begin{Bmatrix} o \\ *ga \end{Bmatrix}$ *mi-ta* -*gatta*.
      movie   see-want-showed a sign of
     'John showed a sign of being anxious to see movies.'

   b. John wa okane $\begin{Bmatrix} o \\ *ga \end{Bmatrix}$ *hosi* -*gatta*.
       money   want-showed a sign of
     'John showed a sign of wanting money.'

Garu means 'to show a sign of, to behave like -*ing*', and it changes verbals of internal feeling into those of outward manifestation of internal feeling. Note that *mitagaru* 'show a sign of being anxious to see' and *hosigaru* 'show a sign of wanting', both of which represent actions, can no longer take *ga* for object marking. This can be accounted for automatically by the generalization that action verbals take *o* and state verbals *ga* for object marking, since *mitai* 'be anxious to see' and *hosii* 'want' are state verbals while *mitagaru* and *hosigaru* are action verbals.

There are only a small number of transitive verbals that take *ga* for object marking. They fall into the following semantic categories:

(15) Competence: *dekiru* and *re/rare* forms
   a. Dare ga nihongo *ga dekiru* ka?
     who   Japanese   can
     'Who can (speak) Japanese?'

   b. Dare ga nihongo o hanasu koto *ga dekiru* ka?
     who   Japanese speak to   can
     'Who can speak Japanese?'

   c. Dare ga nihongo $\begin{Bmatrix} ga \\ o \end{Bmatrix}$ *hanas-e-ru* ka?
     who   Japanese   speak-can
     'Who can speak Japanese?'

---

[1] See Kuroda (1971) for some interesting discussions on this subject.

d. Amerika de wa oisii   osusi *ga tabe-rare*-nai.
   America in   delicious sushi   eat-can-not
   '(We) cannot eat good sushi in America.'

Observe that the noun clause *nihongo o hanasu koto* 'to speak Japanese' is the object of *dekiru* in (15b).[2] Note also that *re/rare* forms can take *o* for object marking, although *ga* is usually preferred. This, together with the observation made for the *-tai* derivatives, leads to the generalization that the *ga/o* alternative is allowable only when *stative* derivatives are involved. If the noun phrase is taken to be the object of the derivatives as a whole, which are stative by assumption, *ga* is used as the object case marker. On the other hand, if the noun phrase is taken to be the object of only the verb stems, which are action verbs, then *o* is used for marking the object.

(16) Nonintentional Perception: *wakaru* 'understand', *kikoeru* 'hear', *mieru* 'see'

a. Anata wa nihongo *ga wakarimasu* ka?
   you   Japanese   understand
   'Do you understand Japanese?'

b. John ga nihongo *ga wakaranai*   kara, eigo
                     Japanese   not-understand since English
   de hanasimasyoo.
   in let's speak
   'Let's speak in English because John does not understand Japanese.'

c. Anata ga kono oto   *ga kikoenai* no wa   toozen desu.
   you   this sound   not-hear fact-that natural is
   'It is natural that you should not hear this sound.'

d. Anata ga kokuban   no zi   *ga mienai* no wa
   you   blackboard 's letters   not-see fact-that
   toozen desu.
   natural is
   'It is natural that you should not see what is written on the blackboard.'

---

[2] Note that *nihongo* 'Japanese' is followed by *ga* in (15a), but by *o* in (15b). This is because it is the object of a state verb *dekiru* 'can' in the former, but not in the latter, where it is the object of *hanasu* 'speak'.

Compare the preceding with *siru* 'get to know', *kiku* 'listen to', and *miru* 'look at', all of which are action verbs:

(17) a. Watakusi wa kono koto *o* kyoo hazimete   sitta.
      I   this thing today for-the-first-time got-to-know
      'I got to know this for the first time today.'

   b. Watakusi wa sono ongaku *o kiita*.
      I   the music   listened-to
      'I listened to the music.'

   c. Watakusi wa sono e   *o mita*.
      I   the picture looked-at
      'I looked at the picture.'

While *wakaru* 'understand' is a state verb, *siru* is an action verb. *Siru* is ordinarily translated as 'to know', but this is a mistranslation. It means 'to get to know'. This is why we cannot say *Watakusi wa sore o sirimasu*, implying 'I know it'.[3] We must say *Watakusi wa sore o sitte-imasu*. In the negative form, however, *sitte-inai* is usually realized as *siranai*. Therefore, *Watakusi wa sore o siranai* is used for 'I don't know it'. Anyway, since *siru* is an action verb, it takes *o* for object marking, in contrast to *wakaru*, a state verb, which takes *ga* for object marking.

(18) Possession, Need: *aru* 'have', *iru* 'need'

   a. Anata ga okane *ga aru* koto wa minna   ga sitte   imasu.
      you   money   have fact-that everyone   knowing is
      'Everyone knows that you have money.'

   b. Anata ga okane *ga nai*   koto wa minna   ga sitte   imasu.
      you   money   not-have that   everyone knowing is
      'Everyone knows that you don't have any money.'

   c. Watakusi wa okane *ga iru*.
      I   money   need
      'I need money.'

Note that *nai* in (18b) is a form derived from **aranai* 'not have'. Conventional grammars say that *aru* and *nai* are intransitive verbs meaning 'to exist' and 'not to exist', respectively, implying that *okane* 'money' is the subject of these verbs in (18). This explanation fails for two reasons:

[3] This matter will be discussed more systematically in Chapter 10 ("Stative and Non-stative Verbals").

First, if *okane* were the subject of *aru/nai*, then what would *anata* 'you' be? Second, *aru/nai* of this usage behaves differently from *aru/nai* of 'to exist'. Observe the following sentences:

(19) a. *Heya ni kodomo ga *aru*.
     room in children
     'There are children in the room.'

  b. Heya ni kodomo ga *iru*.

(20) a. Heya ni teeburu *ga aru*.
     room   table
     'There is a table in the room.'

  b. *Heya ni teeburu ga *iru*.

(21) a. *Heya ni kodomo ga *nai*.
     room   children
     'There are no children in the room.'

  b. Heya ni kodomo ga *inai*.

These sentences show that when the subject of "there are, there exist" is an animate noun, *aru* cannot be used and that *iru* is used instead. Now observe the following sentences:

(22) a. Boku wa kodomo ga *aru/nai*.
     I   children
     'I have/don't have children.'

  b. Boku wa kodomo ga *iru/inai*.

In (22a), *aru* is used with animate *kodomo*. What this implies is that (22a) is of a construction different from that of (19), (20), and (21). If *kodomo* is regarded as the object of transitive verb *aru* 'to have',[4] as is proposed in this study, this phenomenon can be automatically accounted for. *Aru* 'to have', like most other verbs, does not change forms regardless of whether it has an animate subject or not. In (22a), *boku* is the subject of *aru*. Since *aru* 'to have' is a state verb, its object is marked, not by *o*, but by *ga*.

[4] It is not surprising that the verb *aru*, which originally meant 'to exist', has come to be used in the sense 'to have'. There are many languages in which the *be* verb and the *have* verb interchange. For example: "There *is* a flower in the vase" and "The vase *has* a flower in it." In French the verb *avoir* 'to have' is used in the *y avoir* construction: "Il *a* un livre" (He has a book) and "Il *y a* un livre sur la table" (There is a book on the table).

Hence, *kodomo ga* in (22a). In (22b), on the other hand, *kodomo* is the subject of *iru/inai* 'to exist/not exist'. *Boku wa* is probably a contraction of *boku ni wa*. Therefore, (22b) can be literally translated as 'As for me, there are (are no) children'.

3. *Ga/Ni* Conversion

I have shown that all transitive adjectives and nominal adjectives, as well as verbs of competence, nonintentional perception, possession, and need, take NP-*ga* as their objects.[5] I have also pointed out that all these verbals can be characterized semantically as representing states rather than actions. What this implies is that, given a verb and its semantic content, we can predict to some extent whether it takes *o* or *ga* for object marking.

When we have NP_1 *ga* NP_2 *ga Verbal* constructions, NP_1 *ga* can change to NP_1 *ni* in many instances.[6] Observe the following sentences:

(23) a. Dare *ga* kore *ga* dekiru ka?
who   this   can
'Who can do this?'

    b. Dare *ni* kore *ga* dekiru ka?

(24) a. Dare *ga* kono uta *ga* utaeru ka?
who   this song   sing-can
'Who can sing this song?'

    b. Dare *ni* kono uta *ga* utaeru ka?

(25) a. Dare *ga* kono uta *o* utaeru ka?
who   this song   sing-can
'Who can sing this song?'

    b. *Dare *ni* kono uta *o* utaeru ka?

(26) a. Dare *ga* sugu   nemuremasu ka?
who   immediately sleep-can
'Who can fall asleep immediately?'

    b. *Dare *ni* sugu nemuremasu ka?

---

[5] I shall discuss in Chapter 27 ("Case Marking in Japanese") how these occurrences of *ga* and *o* can be predicted on the basis of the semantic features of verbals and on the basis of the deep structures in which the verbals can appear.

[6] This analysis is originally due to Inoue (1966). However, her analysis of what I regard as *ga* for object marking is entirely different from mine.

Sentences (23) and (24) are examples that show this NP_1 *ga* NP_2 *ga* → NP_1 *ni* NP_2 *ga* change. Examples (25b) and (26b) are ungrammatical because, although *re/rare* forms can potentially undergo this change, (25a) and (26a) do not fulfill the required *ga . . . ga* pattern. More examples follow:

(27) a. Dare $\begin{Bmatrix} ga \\ ni \end{Bmatrix}$ nihongo *ga* wakaranai   ka?
        who   Japanese   understand-not
        'Who does not understand Japanese?'

   b. John $\begin{Bmatrix} ga \\ ni \end{Bmatrix}$ nihongo *ga* wakaranai   kara, eigo   de
        Japanese   understand-not since English in
        hanasimasyoo.
        let's speak
        'Let's speak in English because John doesn't understand Japanese.'

   c. Anata $\begin{Bmatrix} ga \\ ni \end{Bmatrix}$ kono oto   *ga* kikoenai no wa toozen desu.
        you   this sound   not-hear that   natural is
        'It is natural that you should not hear this sound.'

   d. Anata $\begin{Bmatrix} ga \\ ni \end{Bmatrix}$ kokuban   no zi   *ga* mienai no wa
        you   blackboard 's letters   not-see that
        toozen desu.
        natural is
        'It is natural that you should not see the letters written on the blackboard.'

   e. Anata $\begin{Bmatrix} ga \\ ni \end{Bmatrix}$ okane *ga* aru   koto wa minna   *ga* sitte   imasu.
        you   money   have that   everyone   knowing is
        'Everyone knows that you have money.'

   f. Dare $\begin{Bmatrix} ga \\ *ni \end{Bmatrix}$ okane *ga* iru   no   desu ka.
        you   money   need that is
        'Who is it that needs money?'

Sentence (27f) shows that *iru* 'to need' is an exception to this optional change. That this is a strictly idiosyncratic phenomenon can be seen from the following examples:

(28) a. Dare $\begin{Bmatrix} ga \\ *ni \end{Bmatrix}$ eigo   *ga* zyoozu desu ka.
        who   English   good-at is
        'Who is good at English?'

b. Boku $\left\{\begin{array}{c} ga \\ *ni \end{array}\right\}$ nihongo *ga* heta   na koto...
   I   Japanese   bad-at am that
   'That I am bad at Japanese...'

c. John $\left\{\begin{array}{c} ga \\ *ni \end{array}\right\}$ Mary *ga* suki/kirai   na koto...
                            fond-of/hateful-of
   'That John likes/dislikes Mary...'

d. Boku $\left\{\begin{array}{c} ga \\ ni \end{array}\right\}$ nihongo *ga* nigate na koto...
                        bad-at
   'That I am bad at Japanese...'

e. Boku $\left\{\begin{array}{c} ga \\ *ni \end{array}\right\}$ eiga   *ga* mitai   koto...
                  movie   see-want that
   'That I want to see movies...'

4. Verbals Taking *Ga* for Object Marking

The following is a more or less exhaustive list of Japanese verbals that take *ga* for object marking. In the list, (1st) indicates that an entry to which it is attached can take only the first person subject in ordinary constructions; (*koto*)/(*no*) indicates that the entry can take a noun clause object ending with *koto* and *no* as its object; (*ni*) shows that the entry cannot undergo *ga*/*ni* alternations; (obj=higher animal), (obj=human), etc., indicate that the entry can take as its object only higher animals or humans, respectively.

(29) *Verbs*

-reru/rareru   'to be able to'
aru/nai   'to have'
dekiru   'to be able to' (koto)
iru   'to need' (*ni)
kikoeru   'to hear'
mieru   'to see'
wakaru   'to understand'

(30) *Adjectives*

-tai   'to be anxious to' (1st), (*ni)
arigatai   'to be grateful for' (1st), (koto/no)
hazukasii   'to be bashful of, be ashamed of' (1st), (*ni),
              (koto/no)
hosii   'to want' (1st), (*ni)

    itosii   'to think tenderly of' (1st), (*ni), (obj=human)
    kawaii   'to hold dear' (1st), (*ni), (obj=higher animal)
    kutiosii   'to be regretful of' (1st), (*ni), (koto/no)
    mazui   'to be bad at' (*ni), (koto/no)
    natukasii   'to miss, to feel yearning for' (1st), (*ni), (koto/no)
    netamasii   'to be jealous of' (1st), (*ni), (koto/no)
    nikurasii   'to be hateful of' (1st), (*ni), (obj=higher animal)
    omosiroi   'to be interested in' (1st), (koto/no)
    osorosii   'to be afraid of, to be fearful of' (1st), (koto/no)
    tanosii   'to enjoy' (1st), (koto/no)
    tumaranai   'to be disinterested in' (1st), (koto/no)
    umai   'to be good at' (*ni), (koto/no)
    urayamasii   'to be envious of' (1st), (*ni), (koto/no)

(31) *Nominal Adjectives*
    heta   'to be bad at' (*ni), (koto/no)
    hituyoo   'to need' (koto)
    kanoo   'to be able to' (koto)
    kirai   'to dislike' (*ni), (koto/no)
    konnan   'to be difficult at' (koto/no)
    nigate   'to be bad at' (koto/no)
    suki   'to be fond of' (*ni), (koto/no)
    tokui   'to be good at' (*ni), (koto/no)
    yooi   'to be easy' (koto/no)
    zannen   'to regret' (*ni), (koto/no)
    zyoozu   'to be good at' (*ni), (koto/no)

5. Dual Nature of Some Object-*Ga* Verbs

I have proposed in this chapter, first, that *okane ga* and *Mary ga* of (32) are not the subject, but the object of the verbals *hosii* and *suki da* and, second, that all stative verbals that are transitive (and no action verbals) take *ga* for object marking.

(32) a. Watakusi wa *okane ga* hosii.
      I   money want
     'I want money.'

    b. Watakusi wa *Mary ga* suki   da.
      I   fond-of am
     'I am fond of Mary.'

The second of the two proposals is original with me, but the first is not. For example, see Tokieda (1941, 1950) and Tamura (1969).

Tokieda (1941) notes that verbals such as *hosii* 'want' and *suki da* 'be fond of' represent subjective feelings of their subjects toward certain objects. They do not represent attributes of *okane* 'money' or *Mary*. On the other hand, in (33), *omosiroi* 'interesting' can be taken as representing not only the subject's subjective feeling but also an attribute of the plot of the story.

(33) *Watakusi* wa *kono hon   no suzi* ga omosiroi.
     I   this book 's plot   interesting-am
     'I am fond of (find interesting) the plot of this book.'

Thus, in (34), *kono hon no suzi* can be regarded as the subject of *omosiroi*.

(34) *Kono hon   no suzi* ga omosiroi.
     this book 's plot   interesting-is
     'It is the plot of this story that is interesting.'

In that interpretation, *omosiroi* no longer represents any subjective feeling but is a property of the plot of the story.

The foregoing explanation by Tokieda seems to account for the dual nature of some of the verbals that I have discussed in this chapter. Stative verbals that are transitive and represent only the subjective feelings (or competence, etc.) of the grammatical subject yield elliptical sentences when their subject is missing. For example,

(6) a. Eiga   ga suki   da.
      movie   fond-of is
      '(*I* am, *he* is, etc.) fond of movies.'

    b. Okane ga hosii.
      money   want
      '(*I*) want money.'

(35) a. Gohan ga tabe-ta-i.
      meal   eat-want
      '(*I*) want to eat.'

    b. Nihongo ga hanas-e-ru.
      Japanese   speak-can
      '(*I, he*, etc.) can speak Japanese.'

These all sound highly elliptical. On the other hand, stative verbals that can represent both the subjective feelings of the subject and the objective attributes (or properties) of the object do not yield elliptical sentences when their subjects are missing. For example,

(36) a. Hen   na oto   ga kikoeru.
        strange is sound   ⎰ hear
                            ⎱ audible-is
      'A strange sound is audible.'

   b. Yama   ga mieru.
      mountain   ⎰ see
                     ⎱ visible-is
      'A mountain is visible.'

   c. Kono inu wa kowai.
      this   dog   ⎰ fear
                     ⎱ fearful-is

      'This dog is fearful.'

These sentences are, in fact, ambiguous. They can be intransitive sentences, as translated here, with the verbals representing the objective attributes of their subjects *hen na oto* 'strange sound', *yama* 'mountain', and *kono inu* 'this dog'. Alternatively, they can be transitive sentences, with the speaker as the understood subject. In the latter interpretation, the sentences mean 'I hear a strange sound', 'I see a mountain', and 'I am afraid of this dog'. Note that in these interpretations the verbals no longer represent the objective attributes of *hen na oto* 'strange sound', *yama* 'mountain', and *kono inu* 'this dog' but indicate instead the subjective feeling (or the competence) of the speaker toward these objects.

6. Stative Verbs That Cannot Take *Ga*
It was mentioned that the *-tai* derivatives and *re/rare* potential forms can take either *ga* or *o* for object marking. For example,

(37) a. Boku wa eiga   *ga/o* mitai.
        I   movie   see-want
      'I want to see a movie.'

   b. Dare ga nihongo *ga/o* hanaseru ka?
      who   Japanese   speak-can
      'Who can speak Japanese?'

It is not the case, however, that this option is allowed for all verbs in their *-tai* derivatives and potential forms. Tamura (1969) notes that (38b) is grammatical, but (38a) is extremely awkward.

(38) a. ??Syoka   *ga* koonyuusitai.
           bookcase   buy-want
           'I want to buy a bookcase.'

     b.   Syoka *o* koonyuusitai.

Compare (38) with the following:

(39) a. Syoka   *ga* kaitai.
         bookcase   buy-want
         'I want to buy a bookcase.'

     b. Syoka *o* kaitai.

Both *koonyuusuru* and *kau* mean 'to buy'. The former is a verb of Sino-Japanese origin, while *kau* is of Japanese origin.

The potential form of *suru* 'do' is *dekiru* 'can (do)'. Therefore, the Sino-Japanese verbs form their potential derivatives by adding *dekiru* to their nominal stems. Tamura observes the following interesting phenomenon:

(40) a.   Syoka   *ga* kaeru.
          bookcase   buy-can
          '(I) can buy a bookcase.'

     b.   Syoka *o* kaeru.

(41) a. ??Syoka *ga* koonyuu-dekiru.
                buy   can
           'I can buy a bookcase.'

     b.   Syoka *o* koonyuu-dekiru.

(42) a.   Tennis *ga* dekiru.
          'I can play tennis.'

     b. ??Tennis *o* dekiru.

It seems that the use of *ga* for object marking, which is purely of Japanese origin, is not compatible in style with verbs of Sino-Japanese origin,[7] most

---

[7] Note that all stative verbs are of purely Japanese origin. The Sino-Japanese verbs are all nonstative because they are formed by adding *suru* 'do' (which represents an action, not a state) to Sino-Japanese nouns.

of which have a rather formal or literary flavor. Hence, low acceptability results when the desiderative and potential derivatives of the Sino-Japanese verbs appear in the *NP-ga NP-ga* pattern.[8] The result is the extreme awkwardness of (38a) and (41a). Example (41b) is grammatical because *koonyuu* 'buying', in spite of the fact that its verbal ending *suru* 'do' has disappeared, still has a verbal force. Thus, *syoka* 'bookcase' can be regarded as the object of the action verb *koonyuu* 'buy', and not of the stative *koonyuu-dekiru* 'can buy'. On the other hand, (42b) is ungrammatical because *suru* of *tennis o suru* '(lit.) to do tennis, to play tennis' has completely disappeared, leaving no action verb that can take *o* for object marking. Since *dekiru* itself is stative, it must take *ga* for object marking. Note, as has been mentioned previously, that the *ga/o* alternative is allowable only when we have stative *derivatives*.

---

[8] Those Sino-Japanese verbs such as *benkyoosuru* 'to study' which have completely lost the literary flavor can appear in the *NP-ga NP-ga* pattern. For example,

(i) Nihongo ⎰*ga*⎱ benkyoositai.
     Japanese ⎱ *o* ⎰ study-want
     'I want to study Japanese.'

(ii) Nihongo ⎰*ga*⎱ benkyoo-dekiru.
     Japanese ⎱ *o* ⎰ study-can
     'I can study Japanese.'

5†

Place Particles *O, Ni,* and *De*

In English, there is a small class of motion verbs that can take an object for specifying where the motion takes place. For example,

(1) a. I climbed the slope.

　　b. I crossed the intersection.

　　c. I walked the distance in two hours.

　　d. I swam the distance in two hours.

In Japanese, too, some verbs of motion take NP-*o* as their object. The sentences in (1) can be translated into Japanese as

(2) a. Watakusi wa sono saka　*o* nobotta.
　　　I　　　　　　the　slope　climbed

　　b. Watakusi wa koosaten　　*o* watatta.
　　　I　　　　　　intersection　crossed

　　c. Watakusi wa nizikan　　de sono kyori　　*o* aruita.
　　　I　　　　　　two-hours in the　distance　walked
　　　Watakusi wa sono kyori　　*o* aruku no ni nizikan　　kakatta.
　　　I　　　　　　the　distance　walk　to for two-hours spent

　　d. Watakusi wa nizikan　　de sono kyori　　*o* oyoida.
　　　I　　　　　　two-hours in the　distance　swam
　　　Watakusi wa sono kyori　　*o* oyogu no ni nizikan　　kakatta.
　　　I　　　　　　the　distance　swim　to for two-hours spent

More examples of the same type follow:

(3) a. yama o oriru　　'to climb down the mountain'

　　b. miti o aruku　　'to walk along the street'

　　c. sora o tobu　　'to fly through the sky'

　　d. rooka o hasiru　　'to run along the hallway'

　　e. yama-miti o iku　　'to go along the mountain path'

　　f. yuka o hau　　'to crawl on the floor'

†This chapter is mainly for students and teachers of Japanese.

  g. saka o korogaru 'to roll down the slope'

  h. miti o yokogiru 'to cross the street'

  i. saka o kudaru 'to go down the slope'

Some of these verbs can also be preceded by *ni* and/or *de* phrases. In many cases, the difference in meaning is very clear. For example, observe the following:

(4) a. yama *o* oriru 'to climb down the mountain'

  b. yama *ni* oriru 'to descend on the mountain (from a helicopter or by parachute)'

(5) a. kawa *o* kudaru 'to go down the stream (for some distance)'

  b. kawa *ni* kudaru 'to go down to the stream (probably from the mountain ridge)'

(6) a. miti *o* aruku 'to walk along the street'

  b. miti *ni* aruku 'to walk to the street'

  c. miti *de* aruku 'to walk on the street (probably back and forth, and across)'

(7) a. sora *o* tobu 'to fly through the sky'

  b. sora *ni* tobu 'to fly to the sky'

  c. sora *de* tobu 'to fly in the sky'

As the foregoing examples show, *o, ni,* and *de* correspond to the following distinct meanings:

NP-*o*: indicates that the motion designated by the verb takes place covering the entire dimension (or the major portion thereof) of the NP continuously and unidirectionally.

NP-*ni*: indicates that the NP is the goal of the motion designated by the verb.

NP-*de*: indicates that the motion designated by the verb takes place in a location or locations within the dimension of the NP not necessarily continuously or unidirectionally.

For instance, consider the following examples:

(8) a. kawa *o* oyogu 'to swim across the river, or to swim up the stream or down the stream for some distance'

b. kawa *de* oyogu   'to swim in the river, probably not across the
                        river, and probably in a small area of the river'

(9) a. rooka *o* hasiru   'to run along the hallway for some distance'

b. rooka *ni* hasiru   'to run to the hallway, probably from inside
                        a room'

c. rooka *de* hasiru   'to run in the hallway, not necessarily along
                        the hallway for some distance'

For some verbs, it is not easy to distinguish the difference in meaning
between the NP-*o*, NP-*ni*, and NP-*de* forms. If one asks native speakers of
Japanese what the difference in meaning is between (10a) and (10b), they
will very likely be unable to tell the difference.

(10) a. yama *o*   noboru
        mountain climb

b. yama *ni* noboru

On the basis of the observations presented here, we can guess that (10a)
indicates motion (that is, climbing), covering the whole dimension of the
mountain (*yama*), while (10b) indicates that *yama* is the goal of the movement. We can verify or disprove this extrapolation by observing how *o*
noboru and *ni noboru* behave in contexts that allow only the dimensional
movement or the goal-directed movement interpretation.

First, assume that one has gotten to the top of a mountain by a helicopter. Under such circumstances, the mountain is the goal of "climbing", and it is not the case that the movement of climbing has covered the
whole dimension of the mountain. Therefore, according to the hypothesis,
yama ni should be acceptable, but not *yama o*. It is indeed the case, as
shown in (11):

(11) a. Helicopter de   yama *ni* nobotta.
                  by-means-of
         '(Lit.) I climbed (to the top of) the mountain by helicopter.'

b. *Helicopter de yama *o* nobotta.

Next, assume that one has climbed to the top of a mountain by car.
Under such circumstances, not only is the mountain the goal of climbing,
but the motion of climbing has also covered the whole dimension of the

mountain. Therefore, we expect that both *yama ni* and *yama o* should be acceptable. Example (12) shows that this is indeed the case:

(12) a. Jeep de yama *ni* nobotta.
   'I climbed the mountain by jeep.'

  b. Jeep de yama *o* nobotta.

Observe that what is called *yama* in (12b) is the whole dimension of the slope starting at the foot of the mountain and leading to the top, while what is called *yama* in (12a) is the top of the mountain. Compare this with words such as *saka* 'slope' and *kaidan* 'stairway'. The top of a *saka* or a *kaidan* is not called *saka* or *kaidan*, respectively. Therefore, we can expect that *ni noboru* is unacceptable for these words, and this prediction is verified by the following examples:

(13) a. Saka *o* yukkuri nobotta.
   slope slowly climbed
   'I climbed up the slope slowly.'

  b. *Saka *ni* nobotta.
   slope climbed
   'I climbed to the top of the slope.'

(14) a. Kaidan *o* ippo-ippo nobotta.
   stairway step-by-step climbed
   'I went up the stairs step by step.'

  b. *Kaidan *ni* nobotta.
   stairway climbed
   'I climbed to the top of the stairway.'

We can construct contexts in which (13b) and (14b) could become acceptable, as shown in (15). Observe that *noboru* no longer represents the process of climbing up a slope step by step. It now means the process of placing oneself in a position higher than he was originally.

(15) a. Mati no yakei o miru tame ni saka *ni* nobotta.
   city 's night-view see in-order-to slope climbed
   'I went up to (some point in) the slope in order to see the night view of the city.'

   b. Heya no syasin   o toru tame ni   kaidan *ni* nobotta.
      room 's picture   take in-order-to stairway climbed
      'I stepped up on a step of the stairway in order to take a picture
      of the room.'

A similar distinction in meaning is observed in the following pair of
sentences, also:

(16) a. Hasigo *o* nobotta.
        'I climbed up the ladder (step by step).'

     b. Hasigo *ni* nobotta.
        'I stood on a step of the ladder.'

   The following is a list of verbs that can take NP-*o* as their object:

(17) *agaru*, kaidan o   'to climb up (the stairs)'
     aruki-mawaru, mati o   'to walk around (the town)'
     aruku, miti o   'to walk along (the street)'
     hasiri-mawaru, undoozyoo o   'to run around (the playground)'
     hasiru, miti o   'to run along (the street)'
     hau, yuka o   'to crawl on (the floor)'
     iku, oodoori o   'to go along (the main street)'
     kaeru, oodoori o   'to go back along (the main street)'
     korogaru, saka o   'to roll down (the slope)'
     kudaru, yamamiti o/kawa o   'to climb down (the mountain path)/
                                to go down (the river)'
     kuru, oodoori o   'to come along (the main street)'
     magaru, kado o   'to turn (the corner)' Compare: kado de 'to
                             turn at (the corner)'
     mawaru, genkan o   'to go around (the front porch)'
     meguru, meisyo o   'to make a tour of (noted places)'
     modoru, miti o   'to retrace (one's path)'
     nagareru, kawa o   'to flow down (the river)'
     nigeru, hukuro-kozi o   'to run away along (blind alleys)'
     noboru, yama o   'to climb (the mountain)'
     oriru, yama o   'to climb down (the mountain)'
     otiru, kaidan o   'to fall down (the stairs)'
     oyogu, kawa o   'to swim across/down/up (the river)'

samayou, yama o   'to wander about over (the mountain)'   Compare: *yama de* 'to wander about on (the mountain)'

suberu, saka o   'to slide down (the slope)'

sugiru, eki o   'to pass by (the station)'

susumu, miti o   'to proceed along (the street)'

tadayou, umi o   'to drift over (the sea)'

tobi-mawaru, sora o   'to fly around through (the sky)'

tobu, sora o   'to fly through (the sky)'

tooru, miti o   'to pass along (the street)'

watari-aruku, seken o   'to wander through (the world)'

wataru, miti o/kawa o   'to cross (the street/the river)'

yokogiru, miti o   'to cross (the street)'

6†

To Au and *Ni Au*

A large number of verbals in Japanese can take both *to* 'and, with' and *ni* 'to' as particles for marking their object NP's. For example,

(1) a. John ga Mary *to*   atta.
                    with met

   b. John ga Mary *ni* atta.
                    to met

Both sentences may be translated roughly as 'John met Mary.' *Niru* 'to get to be similar', *onazi* 'to be identical', *soodansuru* 'to consult', *akusyusuru* 'to shake hands', *seppunsuru* 'to kiss', *butukaru* 'to collide', and so on, belong to the same category. The objective of this chapter is to elucidate the subtle difference in meaning between (1a) and (1b).

When a proposition represented in *X ga Y to V* is true, then propositions represented in *Y ga X to V*, [*X to Y*] *ga V*, and [*Y to X*] *ga V* are also true. Observe the following:

(2) a. John ga Mary to   kekkonsita.
                    with married
      'John married Mary.'

   b. Mary ga John to kekkonsita.
      'Mary married John.'

   c. [John to   Mary] ga kekkonsita.
          and   married
      'John and Mary married.'

   d. [Mary to John] ga kekkonsita.
      'Mary and John married.'

If proposition (2a) is true, then propositions (2b), (2c), and (2d) are all true.[1] This characteristic of *Y ga X to V* constructions is not restricted to

---

†This chapter is mainly for students and teachers of Japanese.
[1] Discussions on the language-universal nature of this characteristic are found in Lakoff and Peters (1969). The nature of coordinated noun phrases in Japanese such as (2c) and (2d) will be examined more fully in Chapter 8.

verbals such as *kekkonsuru* 'to marry', *au* 'to meet', *niru* 'to get to be similar' which have something to do with relations. Consider the following set of sentences:

(3) a. John ga Mary to   benkyoosita.[2]
                     with studied
       'John studied with Mary.'

    b. Mary ga John to benkyoosita.
       'Mary studied with John.'

    c. [John to   Mary] ga benkyoosita.
             and   studied
       'John and Mary studied.'

    d. [Mary to John] ga benkyoosita.
       'Mary and John studied.'

In (3), also, if proposition (a) is true, then propositions (b), (c), and (d) are equally true.

Now, compare the following two sentences:

(4) a. John ga Mary *to*   renaisite iru.
                     with in-love   is
       'John is in love with Mary.'

    b. John ga Mary *ni* renaisite iru.
                     to in-love   is
       '(Lit.) John is in love to Mary.'

Sentence (4a) has the *X ga Y to V* pattern and therefore implies that Mary is also in love with John. On the other hand, (4b) does not necessarily mean that Mary is. Sentences (4b) and (4c) are not synonymous.

(4) c. Mary ga John ni renaisite iru.
                    to in-love   is
       '(Lit.) Mary is in love to John.'

In other words, (4a) represents a reciprocal love and (4b) a unidirectional one. The same difference exists between (5a) and (5b).

---

[2] Note in (i) that *ni* cannot be used in place of *to*.

(i) *John ga Mary *ni* benkyoosita.
    'John studied (lit.) to Mary.'

(5) a. John wa sono mondai ni-tuite,   Mary *to*   soodansita.
       the   problem with-regard-to   with consulted
    'John consulted with Mary on the problem.'

   b. John wa sono mondai ni-tuite,   Mary *ni* soodansita.
       the   problem with-regard-to   to consulted
    '(Lit.) John consulted to Mary on the problem.'

In (5a) John and Mary consulted each other, while in (5b) the consulta-
tion was unidirectional from John to Mary: in other words, Mary probably did not ask John's opinions, although John certainly asked Mary's.

It is now clear where the difference lies in the meanings of (1a) and
(1b). In (1a) the encounter was reciprocal. It implies that both John and
Mary came intentionally or unintentionally all the way to the common
meeting place. On the other hand, example (1b) says that the encounter
was unidirectional. Mary was there at the common meeting place, and
John came, intentionally or unintentionally, all the way to meet her. The
difference can be schematized as shown in (6).

(6) a. John ga Mary *to*   atta.
                   with met
      John→(encounter)←Mary.

   b. John ga Mary *ni* atta.
                 to met
      John→(encounter) Mary.

The distinction is not necessarily physical but psychological. Mary, as well
as John, might have been rambling along the street. But the speaker,
when he uses (1b) instead of (1a), psychologically evaluates this encounter
as if Mary had already been at the place of the encounter and only John
had been moving.

For this reason, if we have an NP whose referent is psychologically not
considered to be moving, we should be able to use NP *ni*, but not NP *to*.
Now, observe the following sentences:

(7) a. Watakusi wa Mary *to*   ai   ni Harvard Square ni itta.
       I   with meet to   to went
    'I went to Harvard Square to see Mary.'

   b. Watakusi wa Mary *ni* ai   ni Harvard Square ni itta.
                      to meet to   to went

(8) a. ?Watakusi wa sensei *to*   ai   ni Harvard Square ni itta.
    I   teacher with meet to   to went
    'I went to Harvard Square to see the teacher.'

    b. Watakusi wa sensei *ni* ai   ni Harvard Square ni itta.
    I   teacher to meet to   to went
    'I went to Harvard Square to see the teacher.'

Sentence (8a) is not ungrammatical but is rarely used. It would imply that the common meeting place was agreed upon, and it was agreed that the teacher, as well as the speaker, would come all the way to this place. Since such an arrangement between a superior and an inferior is against the common practice in the Japanese culture, even when it is true, one prefers to use (8b) to (8a) for expressing this fact.

When we have a physically immovable object, *to* becomes impossible. Observe the following sentences:

(9) a. Tom no atama ga Mary no atama *to*   butukatta.
        's head   's head   with collided
    'Tom's head collided with Mary's head.'
    Mary no atama ga Tom no atama *to*   butukatta.
        's head   's head   with collided
    [Tom no atama *to*   Mary no atama] ga butukatta.
        's head   and   's head   collided
    [Mary no atama *to*   Tom no atama] ga butukatta.
        's head   and   's head   collided

    b. Tom no atama ga Mary no atama *ni* butukatta.
        's head   's head   to collided
    'Tom's head collided (lit.) to Mary's head.'

(10) a. *Tom no atama ga kabe *to*   butukatta.
          's head   wall with collided
     'Tom's head collided with the wall.'
     *Kabe ga Tom no atama *to*   butukatta.
     wall   's head   with collided
     '*The wall collided with Tom's head.'
     *[Tom no atama *to*   kabe] ga butukatta.
          's head   and wall   collided
     '*Tom's head and the wall collided.'

*[Kabe *to*   Tom no atama] ga butukatta.
     and   's head   collided
'*The wall and Tom's head collided.'

b.   Tom no atama ga kabe *ni* butukatta.
        's head   wall to collided
'Tom's head hit the wall.'

Sentence (9a) indicates that Mary's head, as well as Tom's, was moving, and the two heads hit each other; (9b) indicates that Mary's head was still, and that Tom's head came all the way to bump into Mary's; (10a) is ungrammatical because *kabe* 'wall' is physically immovable and could not have participated in the reciprocal collision. Therefore, only *ni* is allowable, as shown in (10b). More examples of the same type follow:

(11) a. John no te   ga Mary no te $\begin{Bmatrix} to \\ ni \end{Bmatrix}$ hureta.
          's hand   's hand   touched
'John's hand touched Mary's hand.'

   b. John no te   ga kinko no kagi $\begin{Bmatrix} *to \\ ni \end{Bmatrix}$ hureta.
        's hand   safe 's lock   touched
'John's hand touched the lock of the safe.'

(12) a. Watakusi wa John $\begin{Bmatrix} to \\ ni \end{Bmatrix}$ atta.
          I   met
'I met John.'

   b. Watakusi wa sainan $\begin{Bmatrix} *to \\ ni \end{Bmatrix}$ atta.[3]
               calamities   met
'I encountered calamities.'

Example (12b) shows that, to the Japanese mentality, *sainan* 'calamity' is something that sits still and waits for poor victims to fall into its trap. Similarly,

(13) a. Watakusi wa suri $\begin{Bmatrix} to \\ ni \end{Bmatrix}$ atta.
          I   pickpocket   met
'I met a pickpocket.'

   b. Watakusi wa suri $\begin{Bmatrix} *to \\ ni \end{Bmatrix}$ atta.
          I   picking-of-pocket   met
'I had my pocket picked.'

---

[3] This example is due to David Perlmutter (personal communication).

Example (13b) shows that *suri* 'picking of the pocket' waits for victims. It is interesting to note that *ni au*, when it takes inanimate objects, allows only noun phrases denoting calamities, and not those denoting good luck.

(14) a. *arasi* ni au   'to encounter a tempest'
          tempest

          hubuki ni au   'to encounter a blizzard'
          blizzard

          zisin ni au   'to encounter an earthquake'
          earthquake

          hidoi me ni au   'to encounter a hardship'
          hard experience

          kanasii me ni au   'to encounter a sad event'
          sad experience

     b. *soyo-kaze ni au   'to encounter a cool breeze'
          breeze

        *otenki ni au   'to encounter fine weather'
          fine weather

        *uresii me ni au   'to encounter a happy experience'
          happy experience

          Compare: *uresii me* o   suru '(lit.) to do a happy ex-
                    happy experience do
          perience'

This may be due to the traditional Japanese psychology of resignation that disasters are there and luckless people fall into their hands unavoidably.

7†
Made, Made Ni, and Made De

Compare the following sentences:

(1) a. Ohiru *made* kore o site-kudasai.
       noon   this   do-please
       'Please do this until noon.'

   b. Ohiru *made ni* kore o site-kudasai.
       noon   this   do-please
       'Please do this by noon.'

   c. *Ohiru *made de* kore o site-kudasai.
       noon   this   do-please

   d. Ohiru *made de* kore o yamete-kudasai.
       noon   this   stop-please
       'Please stop this at noon.'

In such sentences X *made* means 'continuously until/to X' and requires verbs of durative states or actions. Thus (1a) would be literally translated as 'Please do this continuously until noon'. On the other hand, X *made ni* defines the limit of the domain in which discrete actions or states take place. It means 'in the domain delimited by X at the farthest end'. The difference between (1a) and (1b) should thus be obvious. The former is a request to keep doing something continuously until noon, while the latter is a request to finish doing something by noon. Since *made ni* gives a deadline, verbs that are paired with *made ni* very often acquire the perfective interpretation. Thus, in (1b) the phrase *site-kudasai* really means 'please finish', while in (1a) the same phrase means 'please (continue to) do'.

On the other hand, X *made de* means '(do something) continuously until/up to X, (and stop it at X)', where X is an intermediate limit tentatively set up. Sentence (1d) is literally translated as '(Please do this) continuously until noon, and then stop it.' It implies that the work could potentially be continued, if the speaker so wishes, in the afternoon, but he has set up an arbitrary deadline at noon. *Made de* is explicitly or implicitly followed by verbs implying 'to stop'. In the rest of this chapter,

†This chapter is mainly for students and teachers of Japanese.

I shall give examples that clarify the previously mentioned differences in meaning among *made, made ni,* and *made de.*

First, observe the following sentences:

(2) Tokyo kara Kyoto ⎰ a. *made   ⎱ Hikari ga tomaru eki   ga
         from   ⎱ b. *made ni* ⎰   stop   stations
                       c. *made de*

ikutu   aru ka?
how-many are
'How many stations are there between Tokyo and Kyoto where the superspecial express Hikari stops?'

Sentence (2a) is ungrammatical because no continuous action is implied by *ikutu aru ka* 'How many are there?' The difference between (2b) and (2c) is that, in the latter, the speaker implies that Kyoto is an arbitrary limit that he has set up. (The Hikari, in fact, goes to Okayama.) Sentence (2c) would be literally translated as 'From Tokyo to Kyoto (stop here although Hikari goes farther), how many stations ... ?' Since *made de* implies that an intermediate location (or time) has been arbitrarily chosen as a limit, if *X* of *X made de* is known to be the absolute limit, we get counterfactual sentences.

(3) *Tokyo kara Okayama *made de,* Hikari ga tomaru eki ga ikutu aru ka?
    'How many stations are there from Tokyo to Okayama (stop counting here) where the Hikari stops?

Similarly,

(4) Hikari wa, Tokyo kara Okayama ⎰ *made*   ⎱ yozikan,
                   from   ⎱ *made de ⎰ four hours
    Nagoya *made de* nizikan   no hayasa desu.
                     two hours 's   speed   is
    'Hikari has (lit., is) the speed of four hours from Tokyo to Okayama, and two hours up to Nagoya.'

Nagoya made de in (4) implies "stop counting at the intermediate location Nagoya." *Okayama made de* would result in a counterfactual sentence because Okayama is the terminal stop of the Hikari superspecial express. Incidentally, *Okayama made,* and not *Okayama made ni,* is used in (4) because the continuous-action verb *hasiru* 'to run' is implied here. The following sentences also illustrate the difference in the meanings of *made*, *made ni*, and *made de*:

(5) Yuka kara tenzyoo ⎧ a.   *made*   ⎫ nan-meetoru   arimasu ka?
     floor from ceiling ⎨ b. *made ni ⎬ how-many-meters are
                         ⎩ c.   *made de* ⎭
     'How many meters from the floor to the ceiling?'

In (5c) the speaker implies by the use of *made de* instead of *made* that the ceiling is not the absolute limit. Sentence (5c) would naturally follow questions such as:

(6) Yuka kara yane *made* nan-meetoru   arimasu ka?
     floor from roof   how-many-meters are
     'How many meters from the floor to the roof?'

Sentence (5b) is ungrammatical because the height is continuous, so to speak, from the floor to the ceiling, while *made ni* implies that some discrete actions or states take place. *Yuka kara tenzyoo made ni* 'from the floor to the ceiling' would be perfectly acceptable if the continuity is not implied, as in (7).

(7) Yuka kara tenzyoo *made ni* ita   no tugime ga ikutu
     floor from ceiling to   wood-panel 's joints   how-many
     arimasu ka.
     are
     'How many wood-panel joints are there from the floor to the ceiling?'

Made, made ni, and *made de* as conjunctions behave in exactly the same manner. Observe the following sentences:

(8) a. Ressya ga Osaka ni tuku   *made* syokuzi o sita.
         train   to arrive until meal   took
         'We kept eating the meal until the train arrived at Osaka.'

     b. Ressya ga Osaka ni tuku   *made ni*   syokuzi o sita.
         train   to arrive by-the-time meal   took
         'We finished eating the meal before the train arrived at Osaka.'

     c. *Ressya ga Osaka ni tuku   *made de* syokuzi o sita.
         train   to arrive   meal   took

Sentence (8c) is ungrammatical because *made de* is not followed by an explicit or implicit "stopping" verb.[1]

All three forms are possible in the following sentence:

(9) Ressya ga Nagoya ni tuku ⎰ a. *made* ⎱ zassi   o yomu no o

train   to arrive ⎨ b. *made ni* ⎬ magazine   read   ing

                               ⎩ c. *made de* ⎭

yameta.

stopped

  (a) *made*: 'I refrained from reading magazines until the train arrived at Nagoya.'

  (b) *made ni*: 'I stopped reading magazines before the train arrived at Nagoya.'

  (c) *made de*: '(I continued reading magazines) up until the train arrived at Nagoya, and I stopped it then (and thereafter, I did something else).'

Since *made* requires a durative verb, and 'to stop' (the first meaning of *yameru*) is not a durative verb, (9a) imposes the durative meaning 'to refrain from' on *yameru*.[2] Sentence (9a) says that the speaker did not read magazines at all until the train arrived at Nagoya. Sentence (9b) indicates that the speaker read magazines but stopped reading sometime before the train arrived at Nagoya. On the other hand, (9c) says that the speaker continued to read magazines up until the train arrived at Nagoya, that he stopped reading then, and that the arrival time at Nagoya is an arbitrarily set limit, and the speaker could have continued to read if he so wanted.

---

[1] Note that *syokuzi o sita* can mean 'continued to eat', as in (8a), or 'finished eating', as in (8b), but it cannot mean 'stopped eating'.

[2] For example,

Tabako o zutto   *yamete*-imasu.

cigarette   for-a-long-time refraining-am

'I have been refraining from smoking for a long time.'

8[†]

Coordinating Particles *To*, *Ni*, and *Ya*

Japanese is rich in what can be called coordinating particles. For example, corresponding to the English sentence (1), we have the three versions in Japanese shown in example (2).

(1) John *and* Mary *and* Tom came.

(2) a. John *to*   Mary *to*   Tom (*to*) ga kita.
          and   and   and

   b. John *ni* Mary *ni* Tom ga kita.

   c. John *ya* Mary *ya* Tom ga kita.

The objective of this chapter is to clarify the difference in meaning and usage of these particles and to contrast them with *and*.

First of all, *to*, *ni*, and *ya* are used almost exclusively to connect nouns. In connecting sentences, clauses, verbs, adjectives, and nominal adjectives, the gerundive form of the verbals is used. For example,

(3) a. *John ga Tokyo ni iku *to/ni/ya*, Mary ga Osaka ni iku.¹
                        to go and   to go

   b. John ga Tokyo ni *ik-i*,   Mary ga Osaka ni iku.
                          go-ing
       'John goes to Tokyo, and Mary goes to Osaka.'

(4) a. *Kono hon wa omosiroi   *to/ni/ya*, wakari-yasui.
          this   book   interesting-is and   understand-easy-is

   b. Kono hon wa omosiro-ku,   wakari-yasui.
                      interesting-be-ing
       'This book is interesting and easy to understand.'

---

†This chapter is for all readers.
¹ Sentence (3a) with *to* is grammatical, but it does not mean 'John goes to Tokyo, and Mary goes to Osaka.' It means 'Upon John's going to Tokyo, Mary will go to Osaka.' For the use of *to* as a temporal particle, see Chapter 16. It must be the case that the temporal particle *to* is historically related to the coordinating particle *to* 'and', but in present-day Japanese, they are felt to be two different particles.

(5) a. *Koko wa sizuka (da) *to/ni/ya*, suzusii.
         here   quiet   is   and   cool-is

    b. Koko wa sizuka *de*,   suzusii.
                      being

             'This place is quiet and cool.'

This feature stands in marked contrast to that of the English *and*, which can be used for connecting almost any constructions as long as they are of the same type.

In English, the following sentence is ambiguous:[2]

(6) John and Mary got married.

It can mean either that John and Mary became man and wife or that John married someone other than Mary and Mary married someone else. In the former interpretation *John and Mary* forms a tight unit in that it represents a group of people who jointly participate in a state or action that requires collaboration; in the second interpretation it forms a loose unit in that there is no joint action or state involved. In the second interpretation (6) can be paraphrased as

(7) John got married, *and* Mary got married.

Note that (7) does not have the first interpretation of (6), namely, that of 'John and Mary became man and wife'. The *NP and NP* pattern in general has two sources: one derived from the deep structure noun phrase conjunction *NP and NP*, the other derived from conjoined sentences as in (7). The former will be referred to as P-conjunction (for phrasal conjunction), and the latter as S-conjunction (for sentential conjunction).

It is not the case that all occurrences of *NP and NP* are ambiguous with respect to P-conjunction and S-conjunction. For example, sentence (8) cannot be paraphrased as (9).

(8) *John and Mary* are alike.

(9) *John is alike and Mary is alike.

Therefore, we can say that *John and Mary* in (8) has only one source, namely, that of P-conjunction. On the other hand, although (10) is

---

[2] The description of the English coordinating conjunction *and* that follows is based on the analysis proposed by Lakoff and Peters (1969). Detailed analysis of the Japanese particles *to*, *ni*, and *ya* can be found in Kuno (1967–1968).

amenable to the paraphrase in (11), it cannot mean that John and Mary are jointly or reciprocally tall.

(10) *John and Mary* are tall.

(11) John is tall and Mary is tall.

Therefore, (11) has only one source—that of S-conjunction.

There are verbs and adjectives that require P-conjunctions and those that cannot take P-conjunctions. To the former class belong such verbs and adjectives as *confer, meet, identical, similar*. To the latter belong *understand, hear, erudite, clever*, and many others.

The fact that *NP to NP* 'NP and NP' in Japanese has the same ambiguity as *NP and NP* in English can be seen from the following:

(12) *John to   Mary* ga kekkonsita.
      and   married
   (i) 'John and Mary became man and wife.'   (P-conjunction)
  (ii) 'John got married and Mary got married.'   (S-conjunction)

(13) *John to   Mary* wa baka da.
      and   fool   are
'John is a fool and Mary is a fool.'   (S-conjunction)

(14) *John to   Mary* ga nite   iru.
      and   resembling are
'John and Mary are alike.'   (P-conjunction)

On the other hand, *NP ni/ya NP* cannot receive the NP-conjunction interpretation. For example, (15) cannot mean that John and Mary became man and wife.

(15) a. John *ni*   Mary ga kekkonsita.
      and   married
   b. John *ya*   Mary ga kekkonsita.
      and

The examples can mean only that John got married and Mary got married. *Ni* is used for listing. Usually, it requires more than two items to be enumerated. Thus, (15a), with only two items, is slightly awkward. *Ya* is used for giving examples. Therefore, (15b) means that John and Mary (and others) got married, or that John and Mary among others got married.

It was mentioned in Chapter 2 that NP-*ga* as the subject of stative predicates receives the exhaustive-listing interpretation. For example,

(16) a. *John ga* gakusei desu.
                student is
        'John (and only John) is a student.'

     b. *Kono hon ga* omosiroi.
        this book   interesting-is
        'This book (and only this book) is interesting.'

The concept of giving examples is not compatible with the concept of exhaustive listing. Therefore, as predicted, *ya* cannot appear in the NP-*ga* construction when followed by a stative predicate. For example, although (17a) and (17b) are perfectly acceptable as an answer to 'Who is a student?' example (17c) is extremely awkward.

(17) a.   John *to* Mary *to* Bill ga gakusei desu.
                             student are
           'John, Mary, and Bill (and only they) are students.'

     b.   John *ni* Mary *ni* Bill ga gakusei desu.

     c.   ?*John *ya* Mary *ya* Bill ga gakusei desu.

In English, for a sentence with a P-conjunction subject, there is a paraphrase that does not involve the P-conjunction. For example,

(18) a. *John and Mary* conferred.

     b. *John* conferred *with Mary*.

(19) a. *John and Mary* are similar.

     b. *John* is similar *to Mary*.

(20) a. *A and B* are identical.

     b. *A* is identical *with B*.

In these paraphrases, one of the conjuncts in the P-conjunctions appears as a prepositional phrase preceded by *with* or *to*.[3] On the other hand,

---

[3] For some verbs and adjectives, prepositions are obligatorily deleted. For example,

(i) a.   John and Mary married.
     b.   *John married with Mary.
     c.   John married Mary.   *(Continued overleaf)*

sentences with the S-conjunction subject are not amenable to such para-phrases. For example,

(21) a. John and Mary are tall.

   b. *John is tall with/to Mary.

(22) a. John and Mary understood me.

   b. *John understood me with Mary.

   The same phenomena are observable in Japanese. Note, in particular, the ungrammaticality of (26b).

(23) a. [*John to   Mary*] ga kekkonsita.
          and   married
         'John and Mary married.'

   b. *Mary* ga *John* to   kekkonsita.
                    with married
         'Mary married John.'

(24) a. [*John to Mary*] ga soodansita.
                          conferred
         'John and Mary conferred.'

   b. *Mary* ga *John* to   soodansita.
                    with
         'Mary conferred with John.'

(25) a. [*John to   Mary*] ga nite   iru.
          and   resembling are
         'John and Mary are alike.'

   b. *Mary* ga *John* to nite iru.
         'Mary is like John.'

(26) a. [*John to   Mary*] ga baka da.
          and   fool are
         'John and Mary are stupid.'

   b. **Mary* ga *John* to baka da.
         '*Mary is stupid with John.'

(ii) a. John and Mary are alike.

   b. *John is alike to Mary.

   c. John is like Mary.

In the foregoing (a) sentences, it is intended that *John to Mary* is pronounced as constituting a single noun phrase. In the (b) sentences, *John to*
definitely serves an adverbial function, as indicated by the translation
'with John'. What is interesting is that *to* as 'and' and *to* as 'with' in
Japanese have the same form. This fact cannot be accidental and must be
due to the fact that they are semantically synonymous. Namely, it must
be the case that *John to* 'with John' in the preceding (b) sentences must be
transformationally related to *John to* 'John and' in the corresponding (a)
sentences. Incidentally, *John to* 'with John' of the (b) sentences can be
preposed for emphasis, as in

(27) *John to*,   Mary ga soodansita.
           with   conferred
      'With John, Mary conferred.'

John to and *Mary* in this sentence are pronounced, not as a single noun
phrase, but as two separate phrases. Thus, (28) is syntactically ambiguous
between (29a) and (29b).

(28) John to Mary ga soodansita.

(29) a. [John to Mary ga] soodansita.
          'John and Mary conferred.'
      b. John to [Mary ga] soodansita.
          'With John, Mary conferred.'

However, these two sentences are logically equivalent in meaning.
   Another peculiarity of the Japanese coordinating particle *to* is that it can
optionally appear after the last conjunct. For example,

(30) a.   John to Mary to Bill *to* ga kekkonsita.
                                           married
           'John, Mary, and Bill got married.'
      b. *John ni Mary ni Bill *ni* ga kekkonsita.
      c. *John ya Mary ya Bill *ya* ga kekkonsita.

Phrasal conjunctions can be embedded in another and larger phrasal
conjunction. For example,

(31) a. Stalin to Roosevelt ga kaidansita.
                                       conferred
          'Stalin and Roosevelt conferred.'

b. Stalin to [Roosevelt to Churchill] ga kaidansita.
'Stalin and [Roosevelt and Churchill] conferred.'

Together with (31b), the following two forms are also acceptable:

(31) c. Stalin to [Roosevelt to Churchill] *to* ga kaidansita.
     d. Stalin to [Roosevelt to Churchill *to*] *to* ga kaidansita.

The rightmost *to* in (31c) and (31d) is for the last member [*Roosevelt to Churchill*] of the larger phrasal conjunction, while the second-to-last *to* of (31d) is for the last member [*Churchill*] of the embedded phrasal conjunction. The repetition of *to* as seen in (31d) is possible only when *Roosevelt to Churchill to* is pronounced as a constituent, that is, only when the sentence receives the interpretation that two parties—namely, Stalin on one side, and Roosevelt and Churchill on the other side—were involved. If the sentence is intended for the conference among three parties—namely, among Stalin, Roosevelt, and Churchill—it would be ungrammatical. For example,

(32) *Stalin to Roosevelt to Churchill to to ga kaidansita.
     'Stalin, Roosevelt, and Churchill conferred.'

From the foregoing explanation, it might be expected that (33) would be grammatical, but it is not.

(33) *[Roosevelt to Churchill *to*] *to* Stalin (to) ga kaidansita.
     '[Roosevelt and Churchill] and Stalin conferred.'

The reason that (33) is ungrammatical seems to be that Japanese tries to avoid the repetition of the same particle. Therefore, *to to* of (33) is obligatorily changed to *to*. On the other hand, *to to ga* of (31d) is reinterpreted as *to toga*, and comes to be regarded as a sequence of two different particles.

This explanation seems to apply to other totally independent phenomena. First, observe the following:

(34) a. akai hana to   siroi *hana*
        red flower and white flower
        'a red flower and a white flower.'
     b. akai hana to siroi *no*
                           one
        'a red flower and a white one'

(35) a. John ga katta   hon   to   Mary ga katta   *hon*
              bought book and   bought book
         'the book that John bought and the book that Mary bought.'
     b. John ga katta hon to Mary ga katta *no*
                                            one
         'the book that John bought and the one that Mary bought.'

No is a formal noun that roughly corresponds to the pronominal *one* in English. Now, when this *no* is preceded by the genitive *no* or the copulative *no*, we get a single occurrence of *no*, and not *no no*.

(36) a.   John no hon   to   Mary no *hon*
               's book and   's book
          'John's book and Mary's book'
     b. *John no hon to Mary no *no*
                                's one
     c.   John no hon to Mary *no*

(37) a.   akai hana   to   tyairo no *hana*
          red flower and brown is flower
          'a red flower and a brown flower (lit., a flower that is red and a flower that is brown)'
     b. *akai hana to tyairo no *no*
     c.   akai hana to tyairo *no*

Since (36b) and (37b) are the expected forms, the ungrammaticality of these two must be due to an obligatory contraction of *no no* to a single *no*.

Second, there is a very peculiar phenomenon of particle duplications in Japanese. For example,

(38) a. John wa Tokyo *ni* itta.
                        to went
         'John went to Tokyo.'
     b. John wa Tokyo *ni wa* itta   ga, Osaka *ni wa* ikanakatta.
                       to   went but   did-not-go
         'John went to Tokyo, but did not go to Osaka.'

In (38b), *wa* is used to show contrast between 'to Tokyo' and 'to Osaka.' Now, along with (38b), we have

(38) c. John wa Tokyo *ni ni wa* itta ga, Osaka *ni ni wa* ikanakatta.

One of the two occurrences of *ni* in *ni ni wa* must be due to *ni* of (38a) and (38b), but the other must be due to reduplication conditional on the presence of *wa*.[4] What is interesting is that (38d) is ungrammatical.

(38) d. *John wa Tokyo *ni ni* itta ga, Osaka *ni ni* ikanakatta.

It seems that (38d) is ungrammatical for two reasons. First, because *wa* does not appear, there is no triggering element for reduplication. Thus, *ni* should not have been reduplicated in this sentence. Second, (38d) has a sequence of two occurrences of the same particle, which, it has been assumed, Japanese seems to avoid. On the other hand, (38c) is acceptable because *ni ni wa* is reinterpreted as *ni niwa*, namely, as a sequence of two different particles. This is exactly how this particle sequence is pronounced. The same phenomenon is observable in the use of many other particles, also.

(39) a. John wa Tokyo *de* Mary ni atta.
                  in   to met
     'John met Mary in Tokyo.'

    b. John wa Tokyo *de wa* Mary ni atta ga, Osaka *de wa* kanozyo ni
                                        but   she
       awanakatta.
       did-not-meet
       'John met Mary in Tokyo, but did not meet her in Osaka.'

    c. John wa Tokyo *de de wa* Mary ni atta ga, Osaka *de de wa*
       kanozyo ni awanakatta.

    d. *John wa Tokyo *de de* Mary ni atta ga, Osaka *de de* kanozyo ni
       awanakatta.

(40) a. Boku wa John ga baka da *to*   itta.
       I   fool is that said
     'I said that John is a fool.'

---

[4] The same reduplication is also triggered by particle *mo* 'also'. For example,

John wa Tokyo *ni ni mo*, Osaka *ni ni mo* itta.
                                           went
'John went to Tokyo and to Osaka, also.'

   b. Boku wa John ga baka da *to wa* itta ga, usotuki da *to wa*
                                                but liar

      iwanakatta.
      did-not-say
      'I said that John is a fool, but did not say that he is a liar.'

   c. Boku wa John ga baka da *to to wa* itta ga, usotuki da *to to wa*
      iwanakatta.

   d. *Boku wa John ga baka da *to to* itta ga, usotuki da *to to*
      iwanakatta.

In (39c) and (40c), the particle sequences are pronounced as *de dewa*, and *to towa*, respectively.

   In the preceding I have discussed uses of *to*, *ni*, and *ya*, with emphasis on the first particle. Besides these three particles, Japanese has *yara* and *toka* in the repertoire of coordinating particles.

(41) a. John *yara* Mary (*yara*) ga yattekita.
             and   and   came
          'John and Mary (among others) came.'

     b. John *toka* Mary (*toka*) ga yattekita.
         (same as a)

     c. John *da toka* Mary *da toka* ga yattekita.
         (same as a)

Yara and *toka* are similar to *ya* in that they are used for giving typical examples. *Yara* is highly colloquial. *Yara* and *toka* are different from *to*, *ni*, and *ya* in that they can be used for connecting verbals.

(42) a. John wa naku   *yara*, wameku   *yara* sita.
             cry (present)   scream (present)   did
          'John did such things as crying and screaming.'

     b. Syuumatu o, benkyoosuru *toka* hon o yomu *toka* site,
         weekend   study   book read   doing
         sugosita.
         spent
         'I spent the weekend doing things such as studying and reading
         books.'

For some reason or another, *yara* seems to be suitable only when the speaker is annoyed (or affected) by actions or states enumerated by the construction.

The presence of *da* 'is' to the left of *toka* in (41c) is not an isolated phenomenon. We have

(43) a. John ka Mary ga kuru desyoo.
             or   come I-suppose
      'I suppose that John or Mary will come.'

    b. John *da* ka Mary *da* ka ga kuru desyoo.
      '(Lit.) (Someone)—is it John, or is it Mary?—I suppose, will come./John or Mary will come.'

    c. John *datta* ka Mary *datta* ka ga kita.
          was   was
      '(Lit.) (Someone)—was it John, or was it Mary?—came.'

Thus, (41c) can be literally translated as 'People such as it was John and it was Mary came.'

With respect to *or* conjunctions, we have *ka* and *nari*.

(44) a. John *ka* Mary (*ka*) ga kuru desyoo.
          or   or   come I-suppose
      'John or Mary will come.'

    b. John *nari* Mary *nari* ni kikinasai.
          or   or   ask (imperative)
      'Ask John or Mary.'

It is interesting to note that the same form *ka* can also be used as a final particle in forming questions.

(45) John wa kuru *ka?*
             come
    'Will John come?'

This fact cannot be accidental but must be because *A or B* is semantically very closely related to the question "Is it A? Is it B?"

Nari 'or' implies that there might be a better alternative. Thus, (44b) means 'Ask John, or Mary, or someone else better than they, if there is any.' Therefore, the use of *nari* is limited to those cases in which such alternative choices are possible; namely, it can be used only in imperatives, requests, cohortatives (that is "let us . . ."), counterfactual conditionals, etc. It cannot be used in factual statements. In this respect, it resembles the use of "Be it . . ." in English. Consider the following examples:

(46) a. *John *nari* Mary *nari* ga kita.
         '(Lit.) *Someone, be it John or Mary, came.'

    b. *John *nari* Mary *nari* ga kuru.
         '(Lit.) *Someone, be it John, or be it Mary, is coming.'

(47) a. John *nari* Mary *nari* ni kikimasyoo.
         'Let's ask John, or Mary, or some better person.'

    b. John *nari* Mary *nari* ni kikeba, yokatta.
         'It would have been good if I had asked John, Mary, or some better person.'

III
Verbs

9 †

Giving and Receiving Verbs

In conventional grammars, typical explanations of giving and receiving verbs *kureru, kudasaru, yaru, ageru, sasiageru, morau, itadaku,* etc., proceed as follows:

(1) *yaru*: someone gives something to a person equal or inferior to him
   ageru: someone gives something to a person superior to him
   kureru: someone equal or inferior to the speaker gives something to him
   morau: someone receives something from a person equal to or inferior to him
   itadaku: someone receives something from a person superior to him, etc.

Such an explanation does not clarify the range of noun phrases that the subject and the indirect object of these giving and receiving verbs can take. I shall show that not only the concept of *the speaker* but also that of *someone who belongs to the speaker* plays a distinctive role in the use of some of these verbs.

Observe the following construction:

(2) a. *X* ga *Y* ni *Z* o kureru   '*X* gives *Z* to *Y*'
       X ga *Y* ni *Z* o kudasaru   '*X* gives *Z* to *Y*'

In these examples, *Y* can be not only *the speaker* but also *someone/something that belongs to the speaker.*

Consider the following sentences:

(3) a.   Mary ga *boku* ni kono hon o kureta.
                I   this book gave
         'Mary has given me this book.'

   b.   Mary ga *otooto*   ni kono hon o kureta.
                brother
         'Mary has given *my* brother this book.'

†This chapter is mainly for students of Japanese.

    c. *Mary ga *otooto* ni kono hon o kureta.
       'Mary has given *her* brother this book.'

    d. *Mary ga *John* ni kono hon o kureta.[1]
       'Mary has given this book to John.'

There is no problem with (3a) because the indirect object of *kureta* is the speaker (*boku*). Now, compare (3b) and (3c). The sentence is acceptable if *otooto* is meant for the speaker's brother, but not if it is meant for Mary's. This is due to the fact that *otooto* in (3b) is something that belongs to the speaker, so that Mary's having given a book to the brother is taken by the speaker as a favor to him (the speaker). What (3b) really means is 'Mary has given my brother this book *for me*.' On the other hand, *otooto* in (3c), if it is taken as someone else's brother, is not something that belongs to the speaker—hence, the ungrammaticality of (3c). Similarly, example (3d) is ungrammatical unless John is the speaker's brother, his protégé, etc. The same applies to *kudasaru*.

    Even the hearer can appear in the position of *Y* if he is regarded by the speaker as someone who belongs to him.

(4) a. Dare ga kono hon o anata ni kudasatta no?
      who   this book you   gave
      'Who has given this book to you?'

    b. Mary ga anata ni kono hon o kuremasita yo.
      'Mary has given this book to you.'

For this reason, (5) is ungrammatical except when *dare* is meant for 'which one of us' or 'which one of you.'

(5) *Sensei wa dare ni kono hon o kudasatta no?
     teacher   whom this book gave
     'Whom has the teacher given this book to?'[2]

    The presence of the speaker is not required for *yaru* and *ageru*.

(6) a. *X* ga *Y* ni *Z* o yaru.   '*X* gives *Z* to *Y*.'
    b. *X* ga *Y* ni *Z* o ageru.   '*X* gives *Z* to *Y*.'

[1] Grammatical expressions of the intended meaning of (3c) and (3d) are
(i) Mary ga otooto ni kono hon o yatta.
(ii) Mary ga John ni kono hon o yatta.
[2] A correct grammatical expression of this intended meaning is
Sensei wa dare ni kono hon o o-age-ni natta no?

In (6), X does not have to be the speaker. On the other hand, Y cannot be the speaker.

(7) a. Boku ga otooto   ni kono hon o yatta.
       I   brother   this book   gave
       'I gave this book to my brother.'

   b. John ga Mary ni kono hon o yatta.
      'John gave this book to Mary.'

Yaru can be used only between close friends, or when Y is really low in status, as is the case with a beggar, a dog, etc.

(8) a. Boku ga tomodati ni hana   o ageta.
        I   friend   flowers gave
        'I gave flowers to my friend.'

   b. Mary ga okaasan ni hana   o ageta.
                 mother   flowers gave
        'Mary gave flowers to her mother.'

(9) a. *Mary ga boku ni kono hon o yatta.
                me   this book   gave
       'Mary has given me this book.'

   b. *Mary ga boku ni kono hon o ageta.
      'Mary has given me this book.'

Sasiageru, on the other hand, requires that the subject be the speaker or someone who belongs to him.

(10) a. *Boku* (or *otooto*) ga sensei   ni kono hon o sasiageta.
         I   brother   teacher   this book   gave
         'I (or my brother) gave this book to the teacher.'

   b. ?**Mary* ga sensei ni kono hon o sasiageta.
      'Mary gave this book to the teacher.'

Although (10b) is unacceptable, it is less so than sentences such as those in (9). This seems to be due to the fact that there are no better ways of expressing the meaning of (10b). A use of *ageru* in the place of *sasiageru* in such a context would strike us as showing a lack of due respect for the teacher.

The subject of *morau* does not have to be the speaker, but that of *itadaku* does. Observe the following sentences:

(11) a.   *Boku* wa Mary ni kono hon o moratta.
        I   this book   received
        'I received from Mary this book.'

    b.   *John* wa Mary ni kono hon o moratta.

    c.   * *John* wa boku ni kono hon o moratta.
        'John received from me this book.'

(12) a.   *Boku* wa sensei   ni kono hon   o itadaita.
        I   teacher   this book   received
        'I received from the teacher this book.'

    b.   *Otooto*   wa sensei   ni kono hon o itadaita.
        brother   teacher   this book   received

    c. ?* *Mary no otooto* wa sensei ni kono hon o itadaita.
        'Mary's brother received this book from the teacher.'

    d. ?* *John* wa sensei ni kono hon o itadaita.
        'John received this book from the teacher.'

Strictly speaking, (12c) and (12d) are ungrammatical but are used often because there is no better way of expressing the intended meaning: a use of *morau* in the place of *itadaku* in (12c) and (12d) would result in sentences expressing a lack of proper respect for the teacher.

    The preceding observations can be summarized in diagram (13). Here, $X > Y$, $X < Y$, etc., indicate the relationship between X and Y in X-*ga*-Y-*ni*-V. For example, $X > Y$ shows that the V to which it is attached requires that X be higher in status than Y. The forms that are enclosed in boxes require the presence of the speaker or something that belongs to him, either in X or Y.

(13) 'X gives to Y'   'X gives to Y'   'X receives from Y'

    $X \neq$ speaker $Y \neq$ speaker $Y \neq$ speaker

	yaru $(X > Y)$	
kureru $(X \leq Y)$	*ageru* $(X \leq Y)$	*morau* $(X \geq Y)$
kudasaru $(X > Y)$	*sasiageru* $(X < Y)$	*itadaku* $(X < Y)$
$Y =$ speaker	$X =$ speaker	

That the *kureru/kudasaru/sasiageru/itadaku* series requires the presence of the speaker (or something that belongs to the speaker) may be accounted for by the nature of these honorific and condescending forms: the degree to which they are honorific or condescending is based on the *speaker's* status relative to that of the other people concerned and therefore presupposes the presence of the speaker either as the subject or as the indirect object of the verb.

The analysis represented in (13) applies to the use of these forms as auxiliary verbs, also. Consider the following sentences:

(14) a. Mary ga boku ni hon o yonde *kureta*.
                me   book   reading gave (the favor of)
          'Mary read the book to me (for me).'

   b. Mary ga otooto ni hon o yonde *kureta*.
               brother
         'Mary read the book to my brother (for me).'

   c. *Mary ga John ni hon o yonde *kureta*.
         'Mary read the book to John.'

Sentence (14b) would be unacceptable if *otooto* were meant for, say, Mary's brother. Example (14c) would be acceptable only when John is the speaker's brother or his protégé.

(15) a.   Sensei ga boku ni hon o yonde   *kudasatta*.
          teacher   me   book   reading gave (the favor of)

   b.   Sensei ga otooto ni hon o yonde *kudasatta*.
                   brother

   c.   *Sensei ga John ni hon o yonde *kudasatta*.

(16) a.   Boku ga Mary ni hon o yonde   *yatta/ageta*.
          I   book   reading gave (the favor of)

   b.   John ga Mary ni hon o yonde *yatta/ageta*.

(17) a.   Boku ga sensei   ni hon o yonde   *sasiageta*.
          I   teacher   book   reading gave (the favor of)

   b.   Otooto ga sensei ni hon o yonde *sasiageta*.
         brother

   c.   ?*John ga sensei ni hon o yonde *sasiageta*.

Sentence (17b) would be ungrammatical if *otooto* were meant for someone else's brother, and not the *speaker's*. Sentence (17c) is ungrammatical
unless John is the speaker's brother, protégé, etc.

(18) a. Boku ga Mary ni hon o yonde   *moratta.*
         I   book   reading received (the favor of)
         'I had Mary read the book to me (for me).'

     b. John ga Mary ni hon o yonde *moratta.*
        'John had Mary read the book to him.'

(19) a. Boku ga sensei ni hon o yonde   *itadaita.*
         I   teacher   book   reading received (the favor of)
         'I had the teacher read the book.'

     b. *John ga sensei ni hon o yonde *itadaita.*
        'John had the teacher read the book.'

When the subject or the indirect object of giving and receiving verbs is
missing, it is possible in many cases to determine what the missing noun
phrase must be. For example, (20) invariably means 'I (or my brother,
etc.) received this from the teacher', and not 'He/she/they/etc. received
this from the teacher.'

(20) Kore o sensei   ni itadakimasita.
      this   teacher   received (the favor of)

This is because *itadaku*, as shown in diagram (13), requires that its subject
be the speaker or someone who belongs to him. Similarly, when *yaru*, *ageru*,
and *morau* are used without a subject, it is most likely that the missing
subject is "I" (or my brother, etc.), although these three allow other
possibilities. The following examples should be read in reference to (13):

(21) a. Mary ga hon o yonde   kureta.
             book   reading gave (the favor of)
         'Mary read the book for me/my brother, etc.', and not 'Mary
         read the book for someone else.'

     b. Mary ga kutu o migaite   ageta.
             shoes   polishing gave (the favor of)
         'Mary shined the shoes for someone', and not 'Mary shined the
         shoes for me.'

   c. Sensei   no kutu o migaite   sasiageta.
      teacher 's shoes   polishing gave (the favor of)
      'I shined the teacher's shoes for him', and not 'Someone shined
      the teacher's shoes for him.'

   d. Hon o yonde   moratta.
      book   reading received (the favor of)
      'I (or someone) had the book read by someone else.'

Giving and receiving verbs as auxiliaries can be combined to represent
actions with complex status-favor relationships. For example,

(22) a. John wa Mary ni (tanonde) Jane ni hon o yonde
                asking   book   reading
     yatte   moratta.
     giving (the favor of) received (the favor of)
     'John had Mary read books to Jane'—(more literally) 'John
     (asked for and) received the favor of Mary's giving the favor of
     reading books to Jane.'

   b. Watakusi wa sensei   ni (tanonde) kodomo ni hon o yonde
     I   teacher   asking   child   book   reading
     yatte   itadaita.
     giving (the favor of) received (the favor of)
     'I received the favor of the teacher's giving me the favor of read-
     ing books to my child.'

(23) a. Mary wa otooto ni hon o yonde   yatte
             brother   book   reading giving (the favor of)
     kureta.
     gave (the favor of)
     'Mary gave me the favor of giving my brother the favor of reading
     books to him.'

   b. Sensei wa kodomo ni hon o yonde   yatte
     teacher   child   book   reading giving (the favor of)
     kudasatta.
     gave (the favor of)
     'The teacher gave me the favor of giving my child the favor of
     reading books to him.'

(24) a. Mary wa John no tame ni Jane ni tegami o kaite
                  's sake for   letter   writing
    moratte   yatta.
    receiving (the favor of) gave (the favor of)
    'Mary gave John the favor of asking for and receiving the favor
    of Jane's writing the letter.'

    b. Watakusi wa John no tame ni sensei   ni tegami o
       I   's sake   teacher   letter
      kaite   itadaite   yatta/ageta.
      writing receiving (the favor of) gave (the favor of)
      'I gave John the favor of asking for and receiving the favor of the
      teacher's writing the letter.'

(25) a. John wa Jane ni tegami o kaite   moratte
                    letter   writing receiving (the favor of)
    kureta.
    gave (the favor of)
    'John gave me the favor of asking for and receiving the favor of
    Jane's writing the letter.'

    b. Sensei wa Jane ni tegami o kaite   moratte
      teacher   letter   writing receiving (the favor of)
      kudasatta.
      gave (the favor of)
      'The teacher gave me the favor of asking Jane the favor of writing
      the letter.'

In these cases of double auxiliaries, also, it is often possible to supply the
missing subjects or indirect objects not so much on the basis of contexts as
on the basis of the scopes of these phrases as shown in (13).

(26) a. Koko ni sign   o site   moratte
      here   signing   doing receiving (the favor of)
    kudasai.
    please give (the favor of)
    'Please give *me* the favor of asking *him/her/*etc. to sign here.'

    b. Sign   o site   itadaite   agemasyoo.
      signing   doing receiving (the favor of) will give (the favor of)
      '*I* will give *you* the favor of asking *someone (superior to me)* for the
      favor of signing.'

  c. Sign o site yatte   kudasai.

       giving (the favor of) please give (the favor of)

    'Please give *me* the favor of giving *him/her*/etc. the favor of signing.'

  d. Sensei o tetudatte sasiagete   kudasai.

     teacher helping giving (the favor of) please give (the favor of)

    'Please give *me* the favor of giving the teacher the favor of helping him.'[3]

---

[3] An analysis of giving and receiving verbs very similar to the one proposed here has been presented in Sakai (1970). In the paper she sets up a feature [B is K than A] (the speaker thinks the referent of B to be closer or more familiar to him than that of A) and assigns this feature to *kureru, sasiageru, itadaku,* and *kudasaru.* In her analysis what counts is the relative closeness to the speaker of A and B, while in my analysis what is important is the absolute closeness of B to the speaker. I feel that there is some truth in both analyses. On the one hand, even if B is closer to the speaker than A is, if B is still not close enough to the speaker, *kureru/kudasaru,* for example, cannot be used.

(i) *Sooridaizin ga kootyoosensei ni kunsyoo o kudasatta.
  prime-minister principal-of-school to medal gave
  'The Prime Minister has given a medal to the principal of our school.'

Thus, (i) is a counterexample to Sakai's criterion. On the other hand, if both A and B are close to the speaker, whether A or B is closer to him plays a decisive role.

(ii) Obasan ga otooto ni okasi o kudasatta.
   aunt   brother candies gave
   'Aunt has given candies to my brother.'

(iii) *Otooto ga obasan ni okasi o kudasatta.
   'My brother has given candies to Aunt.'

The ungrammaticality of (iii) cannot be accounted for by the analysis I have presented in this chapter because *obasan* 'aunt' can certainly be someone who belongs to the speaker. It seems that Sakai's criterion forms a primary filter, and mine is superimposed on it as a secondary filter.

10†

Stative and Nonstative Verbals

Some verbals represent actions, and others states. For example, *kuru* 'to come', *yomu* 'to read', *hanasu* 'to speak', *sinu* 'to die', *otiru* 'to fall off', *deau* 'to encounter', all represent actions. On the other hand, *samui* 'to be cold', *akai* 'to be red', *hosii* 'to want', *urayamasii* 'to be jealous of', *sizuka (da)* 'to be quiet', *yukai (da)* 'to be merry', *suki (da)* 'to be fond of', all represent states. Note that whether a given verbal represents an action or a state is a semantic matter and has, by itself, nothing to do with syntax. Let us assume that verbals that represent states are marked in the lexicon as [+stative], and those that represent actions as [−stative]. All adjectives and nominal adjectives are inherently [+stative]. Most verbs are [−stative]. Semantically [+stative] verbs are *wakaru* 'to understand', *dekiru* 'to be able to', *kikoeru* 'to hear', *mieru* 'to see', *iru* 'to need', *aru* 'to exist', *aru* 'to have'.

When verbals are used in the present tense, the following generalization holds:

(1) a. The [+stative] verbals refer to present time.

    b. The [−stative] verbals usually refer to future time unless they represent habitual or generic actions, in which case they refer to present time, or they are used as "historical present," in which case they refer to past time.[1]

For example, all of the following represent present states:

(2) a. Koko wa samui.
      here   cold
      'It is cold here.'

---

†This chapter is mainly for students of Japanese.

[1] The same applies to English. For example, (i) refers to present time because *sick* is stative.

(i) John is sick.

On the other hand, (ii) refers to future time, as in (iii), or represents John's habitual actions.

(ii) John goes to school.

(iii) John goes to school at ten tomorrow.

b. Kono hana   wa akai.
   this   flower   red-is
   'This flower is red.'

c. Boku wa okane ga hosii.
   I   money   want
   'I want money.'

d. John wa Mary ga suki   da.
               fond-of is
   'John likes Mary.'

On the other hand, the following represent future actions:

(3) a. John ga kuru.
         come
     'John is coming. John will come.'

b. John ga kono hon o yomu.
         this book   read
    'John will read this book.'

c. John ga Mary ni tegami o kaku.
           to letter   write
    'John will write a letter to Mary.'

However, if these [−stative] verbs are used to represent habits or generic actions, they can refer to present time.

(4) a. John wa mainiti   koko ni kuru.
         everyday here to come
     'John comes here every day.'

b. John wa Mary ni mainiti   tegami o kaku.
            to everyday letter   write
    'John writes a letter to Mary every day.'

c. Ningen wa osokare-hayakare sinu.
   man   sooner-or-later   die
   'Man dies sooner or later.'

In the preceding, (4a,b) represent habitual actions, and (4c) a generic action.

Exceptional verbs that are semantically [+stative] behave just like adjectives and nominal adjectives in this respect. The present tense of these verbs refers to present time.

(5) a. John wa nihongo ga wakaru.
         Japanese   understand
    'John understands Japanese.'

   b. John wa nihongo ga dekiru.
          Japanese   can
     'John can (speak) Japanese.'

   c. Boku wa okane ga iru.
       I   money   need
     'I need money.'

   d. Boku wa okane ga aru.
       I   money   have
     'I have money.'

   e. Hen   na oto   ga kikoeru.
      strange is sound   hear
     'I hear a strange sound.'

   f. Tukue no ue ni hon ga aru.
      table 's top on book   exist
     'On the table are books.'

Note that semantically [+stative] verbals, if they are transitive, take *ga* for marking their object. This is why *ga* appears after the object in (2c,d) and (5a–e).[2]

Derived verbals ordinarily acquire the feature that is attributable to their derivational affix. Potential -(r)e, -(r)are and desiderative -ta are [+stative]; causative -(s)ase and passive -(r)are are [−stative]. Observe the following:

(6) a. John wa nihongo ⎰ o ⎱ hanas-(r)e-ru.
         Japanese   ⎱ ga ⎰ speak-can
    'John can speak Japanese.'

   b. Boku wa gohan ⎰ o ⎱ tabe-ta-i.
            meal   ⎱ ga ⎰ eat-want
     'I am anxious to eat a meal.'

---

[2] See Chapter 4, "*Ga* for Object Marking."

(7) a. John wa Mary ni hon   o yom-(s)ase-ru.
                      to book   read-cause
       'John will make Mary read a book.'
       'John habitually makes Mary read a book.'

   b. John wa Mary ni koros-(r)are-ru.
                     by kill-passive
      'John will be killed by Mary.'

Note that in (6) both *ga* and *o* can be used for marking the object of derived
[+stative] verbals. What seems to be happening here is that in (6a), for
example, *o* is used if *nihongo* 'Japanese' is felt to be the object of the lexically
[−stative] *hanas* 'to speak', and *ga* is used if *nihongo* is felt to be the object
of the derived [+stative] *hanas-(r)e* 'to be able to speak'. On the other
hand, if the rightmost derivational affix is [−stative], there is no way to
mark the object of the stem with *ga* even if the stem itself is [+stative]. For
example,

(8) John wa (itumo) gohan ⎰ o ⎱ tabe-ta-gar-ru.
                  always meal ⎱ *ga ⎰ eat-want-show a sign of
    'John (always) shows a sign of wanting to eat.'

(9) a. Mary wa kore ⎰ ga ⎱ wakaru.
                this ⎱ *o ⎰ understand
       'Mary understands this.'

   b. Boku wa Mary ni kore ⎰ o ⎱ wakar-(s)ase-ru.
      I   to this ⎱ *ga ⎰ understand-cause
      'I will make Mary understand this.'

Sentence (8) is formed by adding *-gar* 'to show a sign of' to *tabe-ta* 'to be
anxious to eat' of (6b). The verbal *-gar* is semantically and lexically
[−stative]. Therefore, the derived form *tabe-ta-gar* 'to show a sign of wanting to eat' is [−stative]. For this reason there is no way to retain in (8) the
object marker *ga* of (6b). Similarly, (9a) shows that *wakar* 'to understand'
is [+stative] and thus takes *ga* for marking its object. When it is followed
by the causative *-(s)ase*, however, the whole form *wakar-(s)ase* 'to make
(someone) understand' becomes [−stative] because of the [−stative]
feature of *-(s)ase*. Thus, *ga* cannot be used to mark the object of this
derived form.

Affixes seem to influence the case markings of the object of the derived forms only when they are bound forms. In (6) and (7) -$(r)e$, -ta, -$(s)ase$, and -$(r)are$ are all bound forms that cannot be used as independent verbs. On the other hand, *i-ru* 'to be in the state of',[3] *mi-ru* 'to try to', and *simaw-u* 'to end up -ing', which are used as elements of compound verb forms, can also be used as independent verbs. Thus, compound forms

[3] Many English verbals that are [+stative] have their counterparts in Japanese as [−stative]. For example, *know* is [+stative], but *siru* is [−stative], meaning 'to get to know.' Similarly, *live* and *love* are [+stative] in (i), but *sumu* 'to live' and *aisuru* 'to love' are [−stative].

(i) a. John lives here.

   b. John loves Mary.

Thus, the following sentences are ungrammatical in representing current states:

(ii) a. *John wa sore o siru.
             it   get-to-know
         'John knows it.'

   b. *John wa koko ni sumu.
             here in live
         'John lives here.'

   c. *John wa Mary o aisuru.
                       love
         'John loves Mary.'

Instead, the *i-ru* form 'to be in the state of' has to be used:

(iii) a. John wa sore o sit-te iru.
         'John knows it.'

    b. John wa koko ni sun-de iru.
         'John lives here.'

    c. John wa Mary o aisi-te iru.
         'John loves Mary.'

Similarly, observe the following:

(iv) a. *Sore wa minna ni sir-(r)are-ru.
             it   all   by know-passive
         'It is known to everyone.'

    b. Sore wa minna ni sir-(r)are-te iru.

(v) a. *Mary wa John ni ais-(r)are-ru.
                        by love-passive
         'Mary is loved by John.'

   b. Mary wa John ni ais-(r)are-te iru.

The ungrammaticality of (iv-a) and (v-a) for representing present states shows that the passive forms in Japanese are [−stative]. Note that in all the examples the present tense in the English translation refers to present time.

derived by adding *iru*, *miru*, and *simau* to the *-te* gerundive form of verbs, although they acquire the semantic feature of *iru* ([+stative]), *miru* ([−stative]), and *simau* ([−stative]), retain the object case marker of the stem verbs.

(10) a. John wa hon $\left\{\begin{array}{c} \text{o} \\ \text{*ga} \end{array}\right\}$ yon-*de iru*.
            book   read
     'John is reading a book.'

     b. John wa hon $\left\{\begin{array}{c} \text{o} \\ \text{*ga} \end{array}\right\}$ yon-*de miru*.

       'John will try to read the book.'

     c. John wa hon $\left\{\begin{array}{c} \text{o} \\ \text{*ga} \end{array}\right\}$ yon-*de simau*.

       'John will finish reading the book.'

Note again that *yonde iru* is [+stative], while *yonde miru* and *yonde simau* are [−stative].

Hazime-ru is an independent verb that means 'to begin'. It can follow the *-i* continuative form of verbs to make up compound verbs meaning 'to begin to'. Since *hazime-ru* in itself implies an action, the derived compound verbs are also [−stative]. However, it does not influence the case marking of the object of the verbs to which it is added.

(11) a. John wa hon *o* yomi hazime-ru.
             book   read begin
     'John will begin to read the book.'

     b. John wa nihongo *ga* wakar-i   hazime-ta.
              Japanese   understand begin
     'John began to understand Japanese.'

Note that *ga* of (11b) cannot be replaced by *o* although *wakar-i hazime* 'to begin to understand' as a whole is a [−stative] verb.

There is yet another type of compound verb formation. First observe the following sentences:

(12) a. John wa hutoru.
           get-fat
     'John will get fat.'

     b. John wa hutori-sugi-ru.
       'John will get excessively fat.'

(13) a. Koko wa samui.
       here   cold
       'It is cold here.'

   b. Koko wa samu-sugi-ru.
      'It is excessively cold here.'

Sugi-ru can be used as an independent verb meaning 'to go beyond a limit, to pass by'. It is also added to the *-i* continuative form of verbs and to the adjectival stems (and to the nominal adjectives) to form compound verbs meaning 'to excessively do something, to be excessively . . .'. Note in (12a) that *hutoru* 'to get fat' is not [+stative], but [−stative]. This is why, in referring to a present state, one must use the *-te iru* form for such a verb, as in

(14) a. John wa hutot-*te iru*.
        'John is fat.'

That *hutori-sugi-ru* 'to get excessively fat' is also [−stative] can be seen from the fact that (12b) cannot be used for representing a present state. Again, the *-te iru* form must be used:

(14) b. John wa hutori-sugi-*te iru*.
        'John is excessively fat.'

Samu-i 'to be cold' is [+stative], and thus (13a) refers to present time. The grammaticality of (13b) for referring to present time shows that *samu-sugi-ru* is [+stative], meaning 'to be excessively cold, to be too cold'. Note that (15) is totally ungrammatical.

(15) *Koko wa samu-sugi-*te iru*.
      here   cold
      'It is too cold here.'

Similarly, (16) shows that the same holds true when the stem to which *sugi-ru* is added is a [+stative] verb instead of an adjective as in (12).

(16) a. John wa sore ga wakaru.
                 it   understand
        'John understands it.'

   b. John wa sore ga wakari-sugi-ru.
      'John understands it too well.'

Thus, compound verbs with *sugi-ru* are [+stative] or [−stative] depending upon whether verbals to which it is added are [+stative] or [−stative], respectively. In other words, *sugi-ru* itself is neutral and does not determine the semantic nature, with respect to stativity, of the compound verbals. As far as I know, there are no other forms that share this characteristic of *sugi-ru*.

I have shown four types of [+stative] and [−stative] verbals:

Type 1: Some verbals are lexically [+stative], and the others lexically [−stative]. The [−stative] verbals mark their object with *o* (for example, *yom* 'to read'), while the [+stative] verbals mark their object with *ga* (for example, *deki* 'to be able to').

Type 2: Compound verbals derived by adding bound forms such as -(*r*)*e*, -(*r*)*are* (potential), -*ta* (desiderative), -(*s*)*ase* (causative), -(*r*)*are* (passive) are [+stative] or [−stative] depending upon whether the bound forms are [+stative] or [−stative], respectively. The [−stative] compound verbals of this type mark their object with *o*, and the [+stative] compound verbals mark their object with *ga/o*.

Type 3: Compound verbals derived by adding free forms such as *iru* 'to be in the state of', *miru* 'to try to' are [+stative] or [−stative] depending upon whether the free forms (compound verb formatives) are [+stative] or [−stative], respectively. However, the case marking of the object of such compound verbals is not influenced by the [±stative] features of these formatives.

Type 4: There is at least one compound verbal formative (namely, *sugi-ru*) that is neutral with respect to stativity. If the verbal to which it is added is [+stative], the derived compound verbal is also [+stative]. Similarly, if the verbal to which it is added is [−stative], the derived compound verbal is also [−stative].

The semantic feature [±stative] plays an important role in syntax. First, as has been mentioned, it determines whether the object of a transitive verbal (of Type 1 or 2) receives *ga* or *o* as a case marker. Second, as has also been mentioned, it determines the interpretation of the present tense. Namely, the present tense of a [−stative] verbal cannot refer to present time unless it represents a habitual or generic action. I shall list here several other constructions in which this distinction between [+stative] and [−stative] plays a crucial role.

Only [−stative] verbs can be used in neutral and adversity passives. For example,

(17) a. John wa, kodomo ni *byooki ni nar* -(r)are-te,   komatta.
                child   by sick   -ly become-passive was-troubled
                'John had a hard time because the child got sick (on him).'

    b. John wa, musuko ni *byoosis*   -(r)are-te, hikansi-te iru.
                son   by die-of-sickness -passive   in despair is
                'John is in despair because his son died of sickness (on him).'

    c. Mary wa, John ni *sissyokus*   -(r)are-te, yowatta.
                    by lose-employment -passive   was troubled
                'Mary was at a loss because John lost his job (on her).'

(18) a. *John wa, kodomo ni okane ga ir-(r)are-te,   komatta.
                child   by money   need-passive was troubled
                'John was troubled because his child needed money.'

    b. *John wa, seito   ni zibun yori umaku nihongo o
                students by self   than better Japanese
        hanas-(r)e-rare-te, yowatta.
        speak-can-passive was-troubled
        'John had a hard time because his students could speak Japanese better than he (himself).'

    c. *John wa, seito   ni zibun yori umaku nihongo ga
                students by self   than better Japanese
        deki-rare-te, yowatta.
        can-passive was-troubled
        'John had a hard time because his students could (speak) Japanese better than he (himself).'

The sentences in (17) are grammatical because *byooki ni nar-u* 'to become sick', *byoosisu-ru* 'to die of sickness', and *sissyokusu-ru* 'to lose a job' all represent actions, although the actions are such that the subject has no control over them. On the other hand, the sentences in (18) are ungrammatical because *ir-u* 'to need', *hanas-(r)e-ru* 'to be able to speak', and *deki-ru* 'to be able (to speak)' represent states, and not actions.[4]

---

[4] *Wakar* 'to understand' is [+stative], and therefore (i) is ungrammatical.

(i) *John wa, Mary ni sore o wakar-(r)are-te,   komatta.
             by it   understand-passive was-troubled
    'John was troubled because Mary understood it.'

It is well known that the present tense in relative clauses receives the past time interpretation if the main verbs are in the past tense. For example,

(19) a. John wa, densya no naka de, sinbun   o *yonde*   *iru*
                         tram   's inside in newspaper   reading-is
         hito   ni hanasikake*ta*.
         person to spoke
         'John spoke to a man who (lit.) is reading a newspaper in the streetcar.'

     b. John wa, densya no naka de, sinbun o *yonde-ita*   hito ni
                                        was
         hanasikake*ta*.

Sentences (19a) and (19b) are more or less synonymous.[5] In (19a) the present tense verb *yonde iru* 'is reading' receives the past time *yonde-ita* interpretation because of the past tense of the main verb *hanasikaketa* 'talked to'. This use of the present tense verbals in relative clauses for referring to past time is limited to [+stative] verbals. Note that *yonde iru* as a whole represents a state. Observe the following examples:

(20) a. *John wa, *kau* hon o yon*da*.
               buy book   read
                      (past)
         'John read the book that he bought.'

     b. John wa, *katta*   hon o yon*da*.
               bought

However, (i) is far better than

(ii) **John wa, Mary ni sore *ga* wakar-(r)are-te, komatta.

Note that (ii) has *ga* as the case marker of the object of *wakar* in the place of *o* of (i). Recall that *wakar*, in isolation, takes *ga* for object case marking:

(iii) a. *Mary wa sore *o* wakaru.
         'Mary understands it.'

     b. Mary wa sore *ga* wakaru.

It seems that (ii) is ungrammatical on two counts. First, the stative *wakar* appears before the passive -(r)*are*, which requires [−stative] verbs. Second, -(r)*are*, as a [−stative] affix, obligatorily marks the object of the compound verb form with *o*. Therefore, *sore ga* of (ii) should have been changed to *sore o*, as in (i).

5 See Chapter 22 ("Tense in Relative Clauses") for the subtle difference in meaning that exists between (19a) and (19b).

(21) a. John wa, *yomu*   hon   o katazuke*ta*.
              read   book   put aside
              (pres)   (past)
        'John put aside the book that he was about to read.'

    b. John wa, *yonda*   hon o katazuke*ta*.
              read
              (past)
        'John put aside the book that he had read.'

    c. John wa, *yonde*   *iru* hon o katazuke*ta*.
              reading is
        'John put aside the book that he was reading.'

    d. John wa, *yonde*   *ita* hon o katazuke*ta*.
              reading was
        'John put aside the book that he was reading.'

Kau is a [−stative] verb. Thus, (20b) is grammatical, but (20a) is not in the intended reading. Namely, *kau* 'buy' of (20a) cannot receive the *katta* 'bought' interpretation in spite of the fact that the main verb is in the past tense. Sentence (20a) would be grammatical if it meant 'John read the book that he was about to buy'. Note that the future time reference of the present tense [−stative] verbals is observable here, too. Similarly, (21a), with the present tense of the [−stative] verb *yomu* 'to read', does not mean 'John put aside the book that he read'. This shows again that *yomu* 'read (present)' cannot receive the *yonda* 'read (past)' interpretation in spite of the past tense of *katazuketa* 'put aside' of the main verb. *Yomu* in (21a) refers to future time with respect to the time referred to by *katazuketa* 'put aside (past)'. On the other hand, *yonde iru* 'is reading' of (21c) is a stative verb. Therefore, it can receive the *yonde ita* 'was reading' interpretation. Thus, (21c) is more or less synonymous with (21d).

    On the other hand, in (22) *wakaru* 'to understand' and *dekiru* 'to be able (to speak)' can refer to past time because they are [+stative].

(22) a. John wa, eigo   ga *wakaru*   hito   ni atta.
               English   understand person   met
        'John met a man who understood English.'

    b. John wa eigo   ga *dekiru* hito   o sagasita.
              English   can   person   looked-for
        'John looked for someone who could speak English.'

There is a formative *-sugi (da)*, which is attached to [−stative] verbals, lexical or derived, to form [+stative] nominal adjectives. Observe the following:

(23) a. John wa benkyoo o *si*-sugi da.
            study   do
            'John studies excessively.' '(Lit.) John is in the excessive state of studying.'

   b. John wa *hutori*-sugi da.
            get-fat
            'John is too fat.'

   c. John wa nandemo *siri*-sugi   da.
            everything get-to-know
            'John knows too much of everything.'

   d. John wa Mary ni hon   o *yom-(s)ase*-sugi da.
                    to book   read-cause
            'John makes Mary read books excessively.'

   e. John wa *izime-rare*-sugi da.[6]
            'John is bullied too much.'

(24) a. *John wa okane ga *iri*-sugi da.
                money   need
            'John needs money excessively.'

   b. *John wa nihongo ga *deki*-sugi da.
                Japanese   can
            'John is too good at Japanese.'

   c. *John wa nandemo *wakari*-sugi da.
                everything understand
            'John understands everything too much.'

   d. *John wa nihongo ga *hanas-(r)e*-sugi da.
                Japanese   speak-can
            'John can speak Japanese too well.'

The sentences in (23) are grammatical because verbals to which *sugi (da)* is attached are all [−stative]. On the other hand, the sentences in (24) are ungrammatical because verbals to the left of *sugi* are [+stative].

[6] Note that here again the passive form *izime-rare* 'to be bullied' behaves as [−stative] predicate.

Finally, stativity plays an important role in the interpretation of *ga* as the subject marker. It has been mentioned elsewhere that sentence (25) is ambiguous between neutral description ('Oh, John has come') and exhaustive listing ('Among those under discussion, it was John who came').

(25) John ga kita.
           came
  'John came.'

On the other hand, sentence (26) can receive only the exhaustive-listing interpretation ('Among those under discussion, it is only John who is a student').

(26) John ga gakusei desu.
    'John is a student.'

Roughly speaking, if the predicate is [−stative], as in (25), *ga* receives ambiguous interpretations between neutral description and exhaustive listing, whereas, if the predicate is [+stative], as in (26), only the exhaustive-listing interpretation is possible. Predicates that represent habitual or generic actions behave as [+stative]. For example,

(27) a. John ga mainiti   gakkoo ni iku.
               every-day school to go
      'It is John who goes to school every day.'
    b. Ningen ga osokare-hayakare sinu.
       man   sooner-or-later   die
       '(Among those under discussion), it is man who dies sooner or later.'

What determines the interpretation of subject particle *ga* between neutral description and exhaustive listing, however, is not identical with the stativity that we have been discussing thus far. For example, the -*te iru* form, which I have considered to be [+stative] because (28) can refer to present time, functions as if it were [−stative] in that (28) can receive the neutral-description interpretation as well as the exhaustive-listing one.

(28) John ga hon   o yon*de*   *iru*.
           book   reading is
    'John is reading a book.'

Similarly, I have considered all adjectives to be [+stative] because they can refer to present time when used in the present tense. For example, (29) represents the present state, and not the future one.

(29) Sora ga aoi.
     sky   blue
     'The sky is blue.'

On the other hand, some adjectives can act as if they were [−stative] with respect to the interpretation of subject particle *ga*. For example, (29) is ambiguous between neutral description ('Oh, look. The sky is blue') and exhaustive listing ('[Among the things that we have been discussing] it is only the sky that is blue'). The ambiguity of (29) is, no doubt, due to the fact that the sky can assume many colors and that the blueness of the sky at present represents only a temporary state.

There is another feature of verbs which is as important for syntax as stativity. That is self-controllability. Some verbs represent actions that their subject can take by self-control, and the others represent actions that their subject cannot take by self-control. For example, *kuru* 'to come', *yomu* 'to read', *hanasu* 'to speak', and *sinu* 'to die' are [+self-controllable], while *otiru* 'to fall off', *deau* 'to encounter', *kyuusisuru* 'to die suddenly' are [−self-controllable]. The [+stative] verbals are all [−self-controllable].

The causative affix -(s)ase can be added only to [+self-controllable] verbs. For example,

(30) a.   John wa Mary ni hon   o *yom*-(s)ase-ta.
                        to book   read-cause
          'John made Mary read the book.'

     b. *John wa Mary o gake kara, *oti*-sase-ta.
                        cliff from fall-off-cause
          'John made Mary fall off the cliff.'

Since passive forms *yom*-(r)are 'to be read', *tabe-rare* 'to be eaten', etc., are [−stative] but [−self-controllable], they can never be followed by the causative -(s)ase. Similarly, since potential forms *yom*-(r)e 'to be able to read', *tabe-rare* 'to be able to eat', etc., are [−self-controllable], they cannot be followed by the causative affix.

Mai is a form that is attached to the present tense of verbs to form a negative compound which means either 'I *will not*' (negative intentional) or 'I suppose . . . not . . .' (negative suppositional). When the subject is the first person, the negative intentional interpretation of *mai* results if the verbs are [+self-controllable], and the negative suppositional interpretation results if the verbs are [−self-controllable].

(31) a. Ore wa nanimo *suru* mai.
       I   anything do
                          [+self-controllable]
      'I *will not* do anything.'

     b. Ore wa nanimo *wakaru*   mai.
       I   anything understand
                        [−self-controllable]
      'I *suppose* I will *not* understand anything.'

Note here that *suru* 'to do' of (31a) is [+self-controllable], while *wakaru* 'to understand' of (31b) is [−self-controllable]. This difference is responsible for the difference in meaning of *mai* in the two sentences.

Imperatives are possible only with [+self-controllable] verbs. Purpose clauses ending with *yoo to* 'in order that', or *tame ni* 'for the purpose of' also require the [+self-controllable] predicates in the clauses. There are many other constructions that require [+self-controllable] predicates.

IV

Temporal and Conditional Clauses

11†

Before Clauses in *Uti Ni* and *Mae Ni*

The noun *uti* means 'interval, inside, one's home'. The expression *uti ni* is used as a subordinate conjunction meaning, literally, 'in the interval that something is happening; while something is happening' when it is preceded by verbs denoting states, durative actions, or habitual actions. Verbals are always in the nonpast form.

(1) a. Kodomo ga 〔 nete-iru 〕 *uti ni*, hon o yomimasyoo.
      children   sleeping-is   while book   let's read
                *neru
                fall asleep
    'While the children are asleep, let's read books.'

    b. Oni   ga inai   *uti ni*, asobimasyoo.
       demon   is-not while let's play
      'Let's play while the devil is away (lit., is not here).'

    c. Tegami o 〔 kaite-iru 〕 *uti ni* nemuku natta.
       letter   writing-is   while sleepy   became
                *kaku
                write
                *kaita
                wrote
                *kaite-ita
                writing-was
    'I got sleepy while writing a letter.'

    d. Kikoo   ga yoi   *uti ni* ryokoo ni ikimasyoo.
       weather   is-good while trip   to let's go
      'Let's go on a trip while the weather is favorable.'

When *uti ni* is preceded by the *negative* form of action verbs, it means, literally, 'in the interval that something doesn't happen; before something happens'. Thus, it acquires a meaning close to that of *mae ni*, literally, 'in advance, in front; before something happens', which is preceded by the affirmative form of verbs.

†This chapter is mainly for students of Japanese.

(2) a. Sensei ga *konai*   *uti ni* asobimasyoo.
       teacher   come-not before let's play
       'Let's play before the teacher gets here.'

   b. Sensei ga *kuru mae ni* asobimasyoo.
      teacher   come before let's play
      Let's play before the teacher gets here.'

The objective of this chapter is to elucidate the difference in meaning between *mae ni* and negative + *uti ni*.

When some future time is referred to, it appears that *uti ni* and *mae ni*
can be used interchangeably. Observe the following pairs of sentences:

(3) Kuraku ⎧ a. naranai   *uti ni* ⎫ kaerimasyoo.
    darkly ⎨   become-not before ⎬ let's go home
           ⎪ b. naru   *mae ni* ⎪
           ⎩   become before   ⎭

    'Let's go home before it gets dark.'

(4) Otera no kane ga ⎧ a. naranai *uti ni* ⎫ kaette   kuru no
    temple 's bell   ⎨   ring-not before ⎬ returning come that
                      ⎪ b. naru *mae ni*   ⎪
                      ⎩   ring before   ⎭

    desu yo.
    should
    'Remember to come back before the bell of the temple rings.'

However, there are some subtle differences of meaning between (a) and
(b) sentences of (3) and (4). First, when *mae ni* is used, *the speaker knows
when something is going to happen.* Therefore, (3b), for example, has the connotation that the speaker knows when it gets dark and that he proposes to
the hearer that they should go home before that time. *Uti ni*, on the other
hand, is used when *the speaker knows that something is about to happen but is
not certain when it is to happen.* Therefore, (2a) has the connotation that the
teacher is about to come, though the speaker does not know exactly when,
and he urges the hearer to play with him in the short interval before the
teacher arrives. Sentence (2b) is different from (2a) in that, in (2b), the
speaker knows when the teacher is coming, and he expresses no sense of
immediacy.

The foregoing distinctions will become clearer by observing the following pairs of sentences:

(5) Ame ga ⎰ a.   huranai *uti ni*   ⎱ kaerimasyoo.
      rain   ⎱   fall-not before ⎰ let's go home
             ⎱ b. ?huru *mae ni*   ⎰
             ⎱   fall   before   ⎰

'Let's go home before it rains.'

(6) ⎰ a.   Wasurenai *uti ni*   ⎱ henzi   o kakimasyoo.
     ⎱   forget-not before ⎰ answer   let's write
     ⎱ b. ?Wasureru *mae ni*   ⎰
     ⎱   forget   before ⎰

'I will write an answer before I forget it.'

(7) ⎰ a.   Sinanai *uti ni* ⎱ oisii   mono o takusan
     ⎱   die-not before ⎰ delicious things   a-lot
     ⎱ b. ?Sinu *mae ni*   ⎰
     ⎱   die   before   ⎰

tabete-okimasyoo.
let's eat (in advance)
'I will eat a lot of delicious things before I die.'

(8) ⎰ a.   Sikararenai   *uti ni* ⎱ yamemasyoo.
     ⎱   be-scolded-not before   ⎰ let's stop
     ⎱ b. ?Sikarareru *mae ni*   ⎰
     ⎱   be-scolded before   ⎰

'Let's stop this before we are scolded.'

(9) ⎰ a. Okane ga nakunaranai *uti ni*   ⎱ eiga   o mi ni ikimasyoo.
     ⎱   money   disappear-not before ⎰ movie   see to let's go
     ⎱ b. Okane ga nakunaru *mae ni*   ⎰
     ⎱   money   disappear before   ⎰

Sentence (5a) is perfectly grammatical if it is uttered when it looks as
though it is going to rain or if the weather forecaster has predicted rain,
say, in the afternoon. On the other hand, (5b) is very awkward because it
sounds as if the speaker knew what time it was going to rain. Example
(6a) is a natural sentence, which implies that the speaker feels that he is
going to forget to write an answer soon. On the other hand, (6b) is extremely awkward and probably ungrammatical because it sounds as if he
knows when he is going to forget, or as if he could willfully forget, to
write an answer. Sentence (7a) would be grammatical when uttered by
someone who feels that he is about to die. On the other hand, (7b) sounds
as if the speaker knows exactly when he is going to die, or as if the speaker

is about to commit suicide. Example (8a) is a perfectly natural sentence containing the speaker's sense of immediacy of their being scolded. He urges the hearers to join him in stopping whatever they are doing right now. On the other hand, there is no such sense of immediacy involved in (8b). Example (8b) sounds as if the speaker has made a calculation and knows exactly when they are going to be scolded. He may not be urging the hearers to stop right now. According to his calculation, there may still be some time left before they get scolded. Sentence (9a) with *nai uti ni* shows that the speaker is afraid of his money running out very soon and that the speaker plans to go to (see) the movies before this happens. On the other hand, (9b) with *mae ni* implies that the speaker has a definite idea of when he will run out of his money and probably has some plan to spend it all on a certain day.

When it is past rather than future time that is referred to, there is an additional complication: it seems that when some definite event, which is known to have occurred, is referred to, *mae ni* can be used, but not negative + *uti ni*. Observe the following sentences:

(10) a. John ga sinanai *uti ni*   okane o karite-okimasyoo.
               die-not before money   let's borrow (in advance)
      'I will borrow money from John before he dies.'

    b. *John ga sinanai *uti ni*   okane o karite-oita.
               die-not before money   borrowed (in advance)
      'I borrowed money from John before he died.'

Example (10a) is a perfectly natural sentence. Example (10b) would be ungrammatical if it were the case that John was already dead. It would be acceptable only if John were still alive when it was uttered: literally, 'I borrowed money from John before he dies.' In other words, if John's death refers to future time, (10b) is acceptable, and if it refers to past time, it is unacceptable.[1] Similarly,

---

[1] However, the following sentence is acceptable even though John's death occurred in the past:

John ga sinanai *uti ni*   okane o karite-oite   yokatta.
          die-not before money   having-borrowed (in advance) good-was
'I am glad that I borrowed money from John before he died.'

I don't know why the presence of *yokatta* 'I am glad, I am relieved, it was good, etc.,' makes this difference. This observation applies to (11b) and (12b) also.

(11) a.   Daisanzi sekaitaisen ga hazimaranai *uti ni*   bookuugoo o
          third   world-war   begin-not   before shelter
          tukutte   okoo/oita.
          making   do/did-in-advance
          'I will build/have built air-raid shelters before the third world
          war starts.'

     b.   *Dainizi sekaitaisen ga hazimaranai *uti ni*   bookuugoo o
          second world-war   begin-not   before shelter
          tukette oita.
          made (in advance)
          'I had built an air-raid shelter before the Second World War
          started.'

(12) a.   Jane-taihuu   ga konai   *uti ni* tabemono no kaidame   o
          typhoon-Jane   come-not before food   's stocking-up
          site-okoo.
          let's do (in advance)
          'I will stock up on foods before Typhoon Jane gets here.'

     b.   *Jane-taihuu   ga konai   *uti ni* tabemono no kaidame   o
          typhoon-Jane   come-not before food   's stocking-up
          site-oita.
          did (in advance)
          'I stocked up on foods before Typhoon Jane got here.'

(13)   *John wa kyonen   Tokyo ni ikimasita ga, Tokyo ni ikanai
                      last-year   to went   but   to go-not
          uti ni   byooki ni natta.
          before sick-   ly became
          'John went to Tokyo last year; before he went to Tokyo, he got
          sick.'

Example (11b) is ungrammatical because the Second World War is an
event in the past. Example (12b) would be ungrammatical if Typhoon
Jane had already arrived and would be acceptable if it had not come yet.
Example (13) is ungrammatical because the first half of the sentence
asserts that John's visit to Tokyo did take place, and therefore the *uti ni*
clause refers to a definite event that is known to have taken place in the
past. Incidentally, the use of *mae ni* or *nai uti kara* instead of *nai uti ni* in
(11b, 12b, 13) would result in grammatical sentences.

On the other hand, if a past event, which might not have taken place, is referred to, sentences with *uti ni* are grammatical. For example,

(14) a. John wa kyonen   Tokyo ni iku keikaku desita ga, Tokyo
             last-year   to go plan   was
          ni ika*nai uti ni*   byooki ni natte-simatta.
          to go-not before sick-   ly becoming-ended-up-with
          'John planned to go to Tokyo last year, but before going to Tokyo, he got sick.'

      b. John ga kaera*nai   uti ni*   Mary ga kita.
               return-not before   came
          'Mary came before John returned.'

Sentence (14a) does not specifically say whether John went to Tokyo, nor does (14b) say whether he came back. Hence, these sentences are grammatical since John's going to Tokyo and his coming back are not definite past events. A comparison of (13) and (14a) should clarify the proposed analysis, namely, S_1 of S_1 *nai uti ni* S_2 cannot refer to a definite past event whose occurrence is well established.

12†

After Clauses in *Te Kara Ato, De, Ato Ni,* and *Ato*

Japanese has two expressions corresponding to the English conjunction *after*. The first is *kara* 'from' preceded by the gerundive form of a verb; the second is *ato de*, literally, 'at later time', preceded by the perfect form of a verb.

(1) a. Gohan o tabe*te kara*, eiga   o mi ni ikimasita.
        meal   eating from movie   see to went
        'I went to see a movie after eating.'

    b. Gohan o tabe*ta ato de*, eiga   o mi ni ikimasita.
        meal   ate   after movie   see to went
        'I went to see a movie after I had eaten.'

Martin (1962, p. 156) observes that "The principal difference of use is that the *-te kara* construction refers to actions IN SEQUENCE (either time sequence or logical sequence), whereas *-ta ato de* is used for actions not necessarily in immediate sequence, just separated in time."[1] He states that (1a) implies that there is a direct sequence, with nothing else of importance happening between the time the speaker ate and the time he saw the movie: 'I saw the show right after dinner.' However, (1b) does not imply this sequence. According to Martin, perhaps the speaker did the dishes, studied for a while, and then went for a walk before taking in a late show.

---

†This chapter is mainly for students of Japanese.

[1] It seems that this distinction corresponds, to a certain extent, to that between *from* and *after*:

(i) a. *From* dinner, I went to a movie.

    b. *After* dinner, I went to a movie.

In the preceding, "from dinner" implies directly after eating dinner. Similarly,

(ii) a. *From* his arrival in Tokyo, John was engrossed in his research.

    b. *After* his arrival in Tokyo, John became engrossed in his research.

I am indebted to John Haig for this observation.

It seems that Martin's analysis just given is basically correct. For example, observe the following:

(2) 'I left home after (lit.) it became ten o'clock.'

    a.   Zyuuzi   ni nat*te*   *kara* ie   o deta.
        ten o'clock -ly becoming after home   left

    b. ?*Zyuuzi   ni nat*ta*   *ato de* ie   o deta.
        ten o'clock -ly became after home   left

Sentence (2a) means that I left home at or immediately after ten o'clock. Example (2b) is ungrammatical, but if one were to assign a reading to it, it would be 'I left home some time after ten o'clock'. The speaker might have left home at eleven or twelve. That (2b) is ungrammatical may be because the sentence is semantically unbalanced in the sense that its first component points to a very exact moment in time while the latter component is quite vague with respect to the time of its occurrence. In general, we get awkward sentences if either the first or the second component of *ato de* sentences points to some exact time.

(3) 'I went to see a movie (at seven o'clock) after having dinner (at six).'

    a.   Rokuzi   ni gohan o tabe*te kara*, sitizi   ni
        six o'clock at meal   eating after seven o'clock at
        eiga   o mi ni itta.
        movie   see to went

    b. ?Rokuzi   ni gohan o tabe*ta ato de*, eiga   o mi ni itta.
        six o'clock at meal   ate   after movie   see to went
        ?Gohan o tabe*ta ato de*, sitizi ni eiga o mi ni itta.
        ?Rokuzi ni gohan o tabe*ta ato de*, sitizi ni eiga o mi ni itta.

Sentence (3a) gives one the impression that the dinner took one hour or that dishwashing, etc., after the dinner extended until close to seven o'clock. Now, compare this with (4).

(4) ?*Rokuzi   no kane ga nat*te*   *kara*, sitizi   ni eiga o
    six o'clock 's bell   ringing after seven o'clock   movie
    mi ni itta.
    see to went
    'I went to see a movie at seven after the bell for six o'clock rang.'

Example (4) is ungrammatical because the ringing of the bell, in contrast to the dinner of (3a), does not take one hour, and therefore (4) contains a violation of the requirement that *te kara* connect two events or actions that are in immediate time sequence. Similarly, note the following:

(5) a.   Rokuzi   ni Bill to   at*te*   *kara*, sitizi   ni
          six o'clock at   with meeting after seven o'clock at
          eiga   o mi ni itta.
          movie   see to went
          'After seeing Bill at six o'clock, I went to see a movie at seven.'

  b. ?*Rokuzi   ni Bill to   wakare*te kara*, sitizi   ni
          six o'clock at   with departing after seven o'clock at
                      (from)
          eiga   o mi ni itta.
          movie   see to went
          'After saying good-bye to Bill at six, I went to see a movie at seven.'

Sentence (5a) is grammatical because the meeting with Bill might have taken an hour. On the other hand, (5b) is extremely awkward because saying good-bye to someone would not ordinarily take as much as an hour.

  Martin's analysis, although it is applicable to the preceding sentences, cannot account for the grammaticality and ungrammaticality/awkwardness of the following sentences:

(6) 'Mary came after John had eaten.'
  a. ?John ga gohan o tabe*te kara*, Mary ga yattekita.
              meal   eating after   came
  b. John ga gohan o tabe*ta ato de*, Mary ga yattekita.
              ate   after

(7) 'It started raining after it thundered.'
  a. ?Kaminari ga nat*te   kara*, ame ga huri   dasita.
          thunder   striking after rain   falling began
  b. Kaminari ga nat*ta   ato de*, ame ga huri dasita.
              struck after

(8) 'I had a call from Bill after I got home.'
  a. ?Ie   ni kaet*te   kara*, Bill kara denwa ga arimasita.
          home to returning after   from phone   there was
  b. Ie ni kaet*ta   ato de*, Bill kara denwa ga arimasita.
              returned after

(9) 'I had a call from Bill after Mary left.'

    a. ?Mary ga kae*tte   kara*, Bill kara denwa ga arimasita.[2]
            returning after   from phone   there was

    b. Mary ga kae*tta   ato de*, Bill kara denwa ga arimasita.
        returned after

(10) 'John died after the war ended.'

    a. ?John wa sensoo ga owa*tte kara* sinda.
              war   ending after died

    b. John wa sensoo ga owa*tta ato de* sinda.
                   ended after

What is characteristic of all the preceding examples is that the second event or action in each sentence could not have been planned so that it should occur after the first event or action. For example, in (6) John's finishing dinner is an independent action that cannot be controlled by Mary, who is presumed to have been somewhere else. Hence, (6a) is awkward, if not ungrammatical. Similarly, in (8), the speaker's returning home and the occurrence of a call from Bill are two independent events, and the subject of the second clause, namely, *denwa* (telephone, which is inanimate), could not have planned the time sequence as specified. Therefore, (8a) is extremely awkward. Note the grammaticality of the following:

(11) a. Ie   ni kaette   kara, Bill ni denwa o simasita.
       home to returning after   to phone   did
       'I called up Bill after I returned home.'

    b. Watakusi ga ie   ni kaette   kara, Bill ga denwa   o
       I   home to returning after   phone-call
       kuremasita.
       gave me
       'Bill called me up after I returned home.'

In (11a) the speaker could plan his telephone call to Bill so that it would take place after his (the speaker's) returning home. Similarly, in (11b)

---

[2] For some reason or other, the following example sounds perfectly grammatical:

Anata ga okaerininatte kara, Bill kara denwa ga arimasite ne . . .
you   returning   after   from phone   there-was-and
'After you left, there was a call from Bill, and . . .'

I do not understand why the use of the gerundive form would make this difference.

Bill could plan his call to the speaker so that it was timed after the speaker returned home. In both of these sentences, the requirement for the planned time sequence is fulfilled, and hence the sentences are grammatical.

The same explanation holds for the grammatical sentences of (1) through (4). For example, in (1a), the speaker could have planned his schedule in such a way that going to see a movie took place after eating. In other words, (1a) implies that he waited until he finished his own dinner and then went to see a movie. This accounts for the connotation that many speakers of Japanese derive from (1a) that the speaker finished his dinner in a hurry. The foregoing indicates that the S_1 *te kara* S_2 construction requires that S_2 be an action or event that can be intentionally controlled by the subject. The difference between (1a) and (1b), then, is not only the presence or absence of the sense of immediate time sequence but also the presence or absence of planning by the subject of S_2 for the second action or event. The two sentences could be literally translated as

(12) a. Gohan o tabe*te kara* eiga   o mi ni ikimasita.
          meal   eating after movie   see to went
          'I planned it in such a way that I went to see a movie shortly after I had dinner.'
      b. Gohan o tabe*ta ato de* eiga   o mi ni ikimasita
          meal   ate   after movie   see to went
          'I went to see a movie at some point of time after I had dinner.'

Similarly, note the following examples:

(13) a. John ga kaet*te   kara*, Mary ga kita.
              returning after   came
      b. John ga kaet*ta   ato de*, Mary ga kita.
              returned after

Sentence (13a) is different from (13b) in that it implies that Mary had timed her visit in such a way that she arrived shortly after John had left, while (13b) does not have such an implication. Likewise, consider the following:

(14) 'I left home after the bell rang.'
      a. Kane ga nat*te   kara* ie   o deta.
          bell   ringing after home   left
      b. Kane ga nat*ta ato de* ie o deta.
                      rang after

Sentence (14a) implies that the speaker waited until the bell rang before he left home, while there is no such implication in (14b). Sentence (14b) gives one the impression that the speaker is reconstructing a sequence of events or actions occurring sometime in the past, say, in the courtroom for establishing an alibi.

In the foregoing I have contrasted the meanings of *te kara* and *ato de*, and I have concluded that in S_1 *te kara* S_2, S_2 occurs immediately after S_1 and that this time sequence is potentially due to the intention or preplanning of the subject of S_2, while there is no such immediate sequence or pre-planning implied in S_1 *ato de* S_2. *Ato de* also contrasts with *ato ni* 'after', and *ato* 'after'. Observe the following examples:

(15) 'Mary came after John had left.'
   a. John ga kaetta   *ato de*, Mary ga yattekita.
             returned after   came
   b. John ga kaetta *ato ni*, Mary ga yattekita.
   c. John ga kaetta *ato*, Mary ga yattekita.

(16) 'Mary was born after John died.'
   a. John ga sinda *ato de*, Mary ga umareta.
             died after   was born
   b. John ga sinda *ato ni*, Mary ga umareta.
   c. John ga sinda *ato*, Mary ga umareta.

(17) 'I studied Japanese after I had dinner.'
   a. Syokuzi o sita *ato de*, nihongo no benkyoo o sita.
          meal   took after Japanese 's study   did
   b. *Syokuzi o sita *ato ni*, nihongo no benkyoo o sita.
   c. Syokuzi o sita *ato*, nihongo no benkyoo o sita.

(18) 'John died of cancer after the war ended.'
   a. John wa sensoo ga owatta *ato de*, gan   de sinda.
              war   ended after cancer of died
   b. *John wa sensoo ga owatta *ato ni*, gan de sinda.
   c. John wa sensoo ga owatta *ato*, gan de sinda.

(19) 'Ten years passed since the war ended.'
   a. *Sensoo ga owatta *ato de*, zyuunen tatta.
          war   ended after ten-years passed

  b. *Sensoo ga owatta *ato ni*, zyuunen tatta.

  c. Sensoo ga owatta *ato*, zyuunen tatta.

(20) 'I have been studying since I had dinner at six.'
  a. *Rokuzi ni syokuzi o sita *ato de*, zutto
    six o'clock at meal took after continuously
    benkyoosite-imasu.
    studying-am

  b. *Rokuzi ni syokuzi o sita *ato ni*, zutto benkyoosite-imasu.

  c. Rokuzi ni syokuzi o sita *ato*, zutto benkyoosite-imasu.

The S_1 *ato ni* S_2 construction seems to require that the semantic content of S_1 and S_2 be such that the vacuum left by S_1 is filled by S_2. Thus S_2 must end with verbs of coming and going or coming into existence and going out of existence. For example, (15b) literally means that Mary came to fill in the vacuum left by John when he departed. Similarly, (16b) means that Mary was born to fill in the vacuum left by John when he died. Since such an interpretation is impossible for (17b), (18b), (19b), and (20b), they are ungrammatical sentences. Similarly, in the following set of examples, (21b) is ungrammatical because Mary's leaving does not fill in the vacuum left by John's departure:

(21) a. John ga kaetta *ato ni*, Mary ga yattekita.
     returned after   came

  b. *John ga kaetta *ato ni*, Mary ga kaetta.
     returned after   returned
    'Mary left after John had left.'

  Likewise in the following set, (22a) is grammatical because Mary's birth filled in the vaccum left by John's death, while (22b) is ungrammatical because the vacuum left by John's death has not been filled yet by Mary's death:

(22) a. John ga sinda *ato ni*, Mary ga umareta.
     died after   was born
    'Mary was born after John had died.'

  b. *John ga sinda *ato ni*, Mary ga sinda.
     died after   died
    'Mary died after John had died.'

It seems that *ato* is the most neutral of all the forms under discussion. Note that it can be used in all the contexts given in (15) through (20). As a matter of fact, most grammatical sentences that have been used as examples in the present chapter thus far would still be grammatical using *ato* in the place of *te kara*, *ato de*, and so on. It can also be used in the same context as *te kara* 'ever since', which has not been discussed in this study.

(23) 'It is ten years since the war ended.'

    a. Sensoo ga owat*te kara*, *zyuunen*   *ni* narimasu.
        war   ending after ten-years to become

    b. *Sensoo ga owatta *ato de*, zyuunen ni narimasu.

    c. *Sensoo ga owatta *ato ni*, zyuunen ni narimasu.

    d. Sensoo ga owatta *ato*, zyuunen ni narimasu.

(24) 'It is that I have not been feeling well ever since I caught a cold the other day.'

    a. Kono mae kaze o hii*te*   *kara*, zutto
        last   time cold   catching after continuously
        kibun ga warui no   desu.
        feeling   is bad that (it is)

    b. *Kono mae kaze o hiita *ato de*, zutto kibun ga warui no desu.

    c. *Kono mae kaze o hiita *ato ni*, zutto kibun ga warui no desu.

    d. Kono mae kaze o hiita *ato*, zutto kibun ga warui no desu.

(25) 'I feel that my house is empty since my father died.'

    a. Titi ga sin*de kara*, uti   mo sabisiku narimasita.
        father dying after home also lonely   became

    b. *Titi ga sinda *ato de*, uti mo sabisiku narimasita.

    c. *Titi ga sinda *ato ni*, uti mo sabisiku narimasita.

    d. Titi ga sinda *ato*, uti mo sabisiku narimasita.

The fact that *te kara* can be used in the sense of 'since' gives additional support to the analysis that its basic meaning is 'immediately after'.[3] Sentence (23a) literally means that it amounts to ten years immediately after the war ended (up until now). Example (23b) is ungrammatical because

---

[3] Note that *te kara* in this sense does not have the 'preplanning' connotation that *te kara* of 'immediately after' has been shown to have. It requires that the S_2 represent continuous or repetitive actions or states, usually not self-controllable.

it means that ten years have passed at some point after the war ended, which is anomalous. Example (23c) is ungrammatical because the ten years that have passed do not fill the vacuum left by the termination of the war.[4] On the other hand, (23d) is grammatical because *ato*, being the most neutral form, does not have the peculiar connotation that *ato de* and *ato ni* have.

In summary, the following shows the distinction in usages among *te kara, ato de, ato ni,* and *ato*:

S_1 *te kara* S_2: The subject of S_2 plans in such a way that S_2 takes place immediately (either physically or psychologically) after S_1.

S_1 *ta ato de* S_2: S_2 occurs at a time after S_1 has taken place. (S_2 cannot be a continuous action or event right after the occurrence of S_1 up to the present time.)

S_1 *ta ato ni* S_2: S_2 takes place after S_1 does, and S_2 fills in the vacuum left by S_1.

S_1 *ta ato* S_2: S_2 takes place after S_1 does. (S_2 can be a continuous action or event right after the occurrence of S_1 up to the present time.)

---

[4] Again, the following would be perfectly grammatical because the vacuum left by the ending of the war was filled by the famine:

Sensoo ga owatta *ato ni*, kiga   ga yattekita.
war   ended after famine   came
'After the war ended, a famine came.'

13†

Assertive *Nara* Clauses

In this chapter, I shall examine the use of the S_1 *nara* S_2 pattern, as in

(1) John ga kuru *nara*, boku wa kaeru.
        come if   I   leave
    'If it is the case that John comes, I will leave.'

It is usually said that this pattern has a strong degree of assertion about the statement represented by S_1. Whose assertion is involved—the speaker's or the hearer's—will be clear from the following examples:

(2) a. Mary ga iku tumori   nara, John mo sono tumori
               go intention if   also same intention
      desyoo.
      I suppose
      'If Mary is intending to go, John will also be intending to go.'

    b. *Boku ga iku tumori   nara, John mo sono tumori desyoo.
       I   go intention if
       'If I am intending to go, John will also be intending to go.'

(3) a. Mary ga ikitagatte   iru nara, John mo ikitagatte
               go-wanting is   if   also go-wanting
      iru desyoo.
      is I suppose
      'If Mary wants to go, John will also want to go.'

    b. *Boku ga ikitai   nara, John mo ikitagatte iru desyoo.
       I   go-want if
       'If I want to go, John will also want to go.'

(4) a. Nihon ni iku keikaku nara, okane ga iru   desyoo.
      Japan to go plan   if   money   need I suppose
      'If *you* are planning to go to Japan, you must be in need of money.'

    b. *Nihon ni iku keikaku nara, okane ga iru desyoo.
       'If *I* am planning to go to Japan, I will need money.'

†This chapter is mainly for students and teachers of Japanese.

(5) a. Samui nara, motto kinasai.
         cold   if   more put-on (imperative)
         'If *you* are cold, put on more clothes.'

  b. *Samui nara, motto kimasu.
                                (I) put-on
         'If *I* am cold, I will put on more clothes.'

Note that the preceding (b) sentences, which are ungrammatical, have the speaker as the subject of the S_1. If we assume that the agent of the assertion contained in *nara* is the hearer (or someone else, people in general), and not the speaker, then we can account for the ungrammaticality of the (b) sentences because the speaker's intention, plan, or internal feeling represented in S_1 of these sentences is something that the hearer or the third party cannot assert. In this connection, note that (5b) would be perfectly grammatical if it were meant for 'If it is cold out (as you say it is), I will put on more clothes'. This is so because, although the hearer cannot make an assertion about the speaker's feeling cold, he can legitimately make an assertion about the coldness of the atmospheric temperature.

This observation does not mean that the first person cannot be the subject of the S_1 in the *nara* construction. If the action or state of S_1 is by design or judgment of the hearer (or a third party), and not of the speaker, it is possible to have the explicit or implicit *boku ga* in S_1.

(6) a. Boku ga matigatte iru nara, ayamarimasu.
         I   wrongly am if   apologize
         'If I am at fault (as you assert), I will apologize.'

  b. Boku ga baka nara, kimi mo baka desu.
         I   fool if   you also fool are
         'If I am stupid (as you say I am), so are you.'

  c. Boku ga siken ni pasusuru nara, Mary mo pasusuru
         I   exam in pass   if   also pass
         desyoo.
         I suppose
         'If I am to pass the examination (as you say I will), so will Mary.'

  d. Doose   sinu nara, hayaku sinda hoo   ga ii.
         by-any-means die if   soon   died choice   is-better
         'If I am going to die (as they say I am or as is asserted), I would rather die soon.'

Note that in (6a) and (6b), the speaker has not yet admitted that he is at fault or that he is stupid. From the preceding examples, it must be clear that the S_1 *nara* S_2 sentence is ungrammatical unless S_1 represents a state or an action that the hearer can assert.

When S_1 is an event that is certain to happen, *nara* cannot be used. A possible explanation might be that such an event need not be asserted strongly since it is a matter-of-fact event. Observe the following:

(7) a. *Natu   ni naru   nara, New York ni ikimasu.
     summer   become if   to go
     'If summer is to come, I will go to New York.'

  b. Ima sugu   natu   ni naru   nara, New York ni
      now immediately summer   become if
      ikimasu.
      'If summer is to come right now, I will go to New York.'

Example (7a) is ungrammatical because *natu ni naru* 'summer comes' is presented here as if there could be some possibility that the summer would not come. Sentence (7b) is grammatical because *ima sugu natu ni naru* 'summer comes right now' is not a matter-of-fact event.

Let us now examine the tenses of S_1 and S_2 in the S_1 *nara* S_2 construction. First consider these sentences:

(8) a. John ga ku*ru*   *nara*, kaeri*masu*.
          come if   return
      'If John comes, I will leave.'

  b. *John ga ku*ru*   *nara*, Mary ga kaeri*masita*.
          come if   returned
      'When John came, Mary left.'

  c. John ga ki*ta*   *nara*, kaeri*masu*.
          came if   return
      'If John has come, I will leave.'

  d. *John ga ki*ta*   *nara*, Mary ga kaeri*masita*.
          came if   returned
      'When John came, Mary left.'

Although both the present tense and the past tense can appear in front of *nara*, S_2 cannot represent a past event. This is due to the constraint that S_2 of S_1 *nara* S_2 must represent the speaker's evaluation, will, resolution, request, or order. For example,

(9) a.   John ga kuru nara (watakusi wa) kaerimasu. (resolution)
             come if   I   return
        'If John comes, I will leave.'

    b. *John ga kuru nara, Mary ga kaerimasu. (pure future)
             come if   return
        'If John comes, Mary will leave.'

(10) a. Samuku naru   nara, danboo o iremasu. (will)
            coldly   become if   heating put-on
        'If it becomes cold, I *will* turn on the heat.'

    b. *Samuku naru   nara, danboo ga hairimasu.
            coldly   become if   heating be-put-on
        (pure statement of fact)
        'If it becomes cold, the heat will be turned on.'

(11) a. John ga kita   nara, Mary ga kaetta   ni tigai nai.
            came if   returned   must
        (evaluation of past event)
        'If John has come, Mary must have returned.'

    b. *John ga kita   nara, Mary wa kaetta.   (pure past)
            came if   returned
        'If/when John came, Mary left.'

(12) a. Samuku natta   nara, danboo o irete-okeba yokatta.
            coldly   became if   heating   turn-on   should have
        (evaluation)
        'If (as you have asserted) it became cold, I should have turned
        on the heat.'

    b. *Samuku natta   nara, danboo o ireta.   (pure past)
            coldly   became if   heating turned-on
        'If/when it became cold, I turned on the heat.'

In the foregoing, (9b) would be acceptable if one imposes upon *Mary ga kaerimasu* 'Mary will leave' the causative interpretation 'I will make Mary leave'. The sentence would also become grammatical if *Mary ga kaerimasu* is replaced by *Mary ga kaeru hazu desu* 'Mary is expected to leave' or *Mary ga kaeru desyoo* 'I suppose that Mary will leave', both of which represent the speaker's judgment.

This generalization still does not account for all the peculiarities of the *nara* construction. Observe the following sentences:

(13) a. Nihon ni iku nara, okane ga iru   desyoo.
      Japan to go if   money   need I suppose
      'If you are going to Japan (as you assert), you must be in need
      of money.'

    b. *Nihon ni iku nara, Amerika ga natukasiku naru   desyoo.
                                 missing-ly   become I suppose
      'If you are going to Japan (as you assert), you will miss America.'

(14) a. Tabako o nomu nara, seiramu ga ii.
      cigarette   smoke if   Salem   is good
      'If you are going to smoke (as you say you are), Salem is the
      best.'

    b. *Tabako o nomu nara, yamerarenaku naru   desyoo.
                         addicted   become
      'If you are going to smoke (as you say you are), you will be
      addicted to it.'

(15) a. Eigo   o hanasu nara, tadasii eigo   o tukaimasyoo.
      English   speak if   correct English   let's use
      'If we are going to speak English (as you say we are), let's use
      correct English.'

    b. *Eigo   o hanasu nara, Tanaka-san ni wakaranai   desyoo.
      English   speak if   Mr. to unintelligible
      'If we are going to speak English (as you say we are), Mr.
      Tanaka won't understand it.'

(16) a. Kono hon o yomu nara, zibiki   ga irimasu.
      this   book   read if   dictionary   need
      'If you read this book (as you say you will), you will need a
      dictionary.'

    b. *Kono hon o yomu nara, hakusiki   ni naru   desyoo.
                       knowledgeable -ly become
      'If you read this book (as you say you will), you will become
      knowledgeable.'

Note that the (b) sentences are such that the action or state represented
by S_2 relies upon the *realization* or *completion* of the action or state repre-

sented by S_1. For example, in (13b), that the hearer will miss America can happen only after his visit to Japan. Similarly, in (14b), that the hearer will become unable to stop smoking can take place only after he has started smoking. The generalization here seems to be that the S_1 *nara* S_2 construction, with the present tense action verb in S_1, cannot have an action or event in S_2 whose realization depends upon that of a future action or event represented by S_1. When the verb of S_1 is not a present tense action verb, the preceding rule does not apply.

(17) a. Ame ga hutte iru nara, taxi de kaerimasu.
         rain   falling is if   by return
         'If it is raining now (as you assert), I will go home by taxi.'

   b. John ga Boston ni kite   iru   nara, boku ni ai ni
                     come have if   I   to see to
      kuru desyoo.
      come
      'If John is here in Boston (as you say he is), he will come to see me.'

The S_1 in (17), because a stative verb is being used, represents an already realized present state.[1] Since S_2 represents a present or future time action or event, there are no contradictions in the time sequence. Similarly, if the S_1 refers to a past action or event, the rule does not hold. For example,

(18) a. John ga sinda (no) nara, Mary ni isan   ga hairu
                 died   that if   to inheritance   enter
      hazu   desu.
      expectation is
      'If John died (as you say he did), it is expected that Mary will inherit some of his fortune.'

   b. Boku ga siken ni pasusita (no) nara, kimi mo pasu dekimasu.
      I   exam in passed   that if   you also pass can
      'If I have passed the examination (as is asserted), then you can pass it, too.'

It seems that the sequence of time for S_1 *nara* S_2 holds the relationships

[1] This is according to the very general rule in Japanese that the present form of stative verbals refers to present time, while the present form of action verbals refers to future time (or to present habits). See Chapter 10 for details.

shown in the accompanying diagram, depending upon what types of
verbs are used in what tenses in S_1 and S_2.

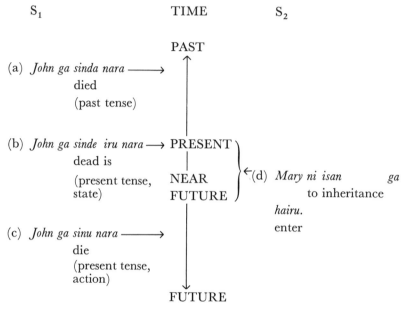

In the diagram, (a) can be combined with (d) because the time for the
former, which is past, precedes the time for the latter, which is either
present or near future. Similarly, (b) can be combined with (d) because
the time for (b) either precedes or is synchronic with the time for (d). On
the other hand, (c) cannot be combined with (d) because the time for (c),
which is future, follows the time for (d), while the event represented by
(d) should follow the event represented by (c).[2]

   This generalization seems to account for many peculiarities of the *nara*
construction which would otherwise be unexplained. For example,

(19) a. *John ga sinu nara, Mary ni isan   ga hairu hazu   desu.
             die   if   to inheritance   enter should
          'If John dies (as you assert), it is expected that Mary will inherit
          his fortune.'

---

[2] If (d) represents an action or state that holds prior to the realization of (c), we get grammatical sentences as is expected:

John ga sinu nara, kan-oke o yooisite   okimasu.
             die   if   coffin   have-ready in-advance
'If John is to die (as you assert), I will have a coffin ready in advance.'

b. *Ame ga huru nara, kimoti ga ii   (desyoo).
   rain fall if   feeling is-good
   'If it is to rain (as you assert), I will feel refreshed.'

c. *Kimi ga Nihon ni iku nara, sabisiku naru   desyoo.
   you   Japan to go if   lonely become
   'If you are to go to Japan (as you assert), I will miss you.'

d. *Nihon ni iku nara, nihongo ga zyoozu ni naru   desyoo.
   Japan to go if   Japanese good-at -ly become
   'If you are to go to Japan (as you assert), you will become fluent
   in Japanese.'

e. *Gohan o tabenai nara, onaka   ga sukimasu   yo.
   meal   eat-not if   stomach   get-hungry
   'If you are not going to eat (as you say you are not), you will get
   hungry.'

This constraint on the time sequencing between S_1 and S_2 does not
seem to apply when S_2 represents requests, commands, volition, and determination. Observe the following sentences:

(20) a. Nihon ni iku nara, kamera o katte   kite   kudasai.
        Japan to go if   camera buying come please
        'If you are going to Japan (as you assert), please buy a camera
        for me.'

     b. John ni au nara, nooto   o karite   kite kudasai.
             to see if   notebook borrowing come please
        'If you are going to see John (as you assert), please borrow his
        course notebook for me.'

     c. John ga kuru nara, issyo ni syokuzi ga sitai.
             come if   together meal   want-to-have
        'If John is coming (as you say he is), I want to have dinner with
        him.'

     d. John ga kuru nara, ie   ni tomatte moraimasu.
             come if   home at stay   here
        'If John is coming (as you assert), I will have him stay with me.'

These examples are not really counterexamples to the proposed generalization. What S_1 *nara* is paired with is not the action verbs in S_2, but the implicit abstract verbs "I REQUEST, I WANT, I AM DETERMINED,"

which are superficially realized as *kudasai*, *tai*, and *moraimasu*. For example, (20a) really means 'If you are going to Japan (as you assert), I REQUEST THAT you buy a camera for me there.' That is, the action of S_2 (namely, the request) takes place at present, and it does not depend upon the realization of the hearer's visit to Japan.

In summary, the S_1 *nara* S_2 pattern is subject to the following constraints:

(i) The speaker presents S_1 as the assertion by the hearer (or people in general) without completely agreeing with it.

(ii) It is ungrammatical unless S_1 represents a state or an action that the hearer (or people in general) can assert.

(iii) This pattern cannot be used when S_1 is an event that is certain to happen (for example, "summer comes").

(iv) S_2 must represent the speaker's evaluation, supposition, will, resolution, request, or order.

(v) It is ungrammatical if S_2 represents a state or action whose realization depends upon the future realization or completion of the action represented by S_1.

(vi) If S_2 represents requests, commands, volition, or determination, then (v) does not apply.

14†

Perfective *Tara* Clauses[1]

In this chapter, I shall examine the uses of the S_1 *tara* S_2 pattern, as in (1), and contrast them with those of the S_1 *nara* S_2 pattern.

(1) a. John ga ki*tara*,　　boku wa kaeru.
　　　　　 come-if　 I　　　　 leave
　　　'If John has come, I will leave.'
　　 b. John ga ki*tara*,　　　Mary ga kaetta.
　　　　　 come-when　　　　 left
　　　'When John came, Mary left.'

Formally, the *tara* form results from adding *ra* to the past form of verbs, adjectives, and nominal adjectives (such as *ittara* 'if you go', *samukattara* 'if it is cold', *sizuka dattara* 'if it is quiet'). In other words, *ta* of *tara* is the perfect tense suffix *ta,* and this fact is the key to understanding various uses of *tara* forms.

　Semantically, *tara* in S_1 *tara* S_2 always presupposes that the action or state represented by the verb it is attached to *is completed* or *finished before* S_2 takes place, while *nara* in S_1 *nara* S_2 does not have such a presupposition.[2] This implies that if S_2 pertains to an action or an event to take place before S_1 is completed, *tara* cannot be used. That this is indeed the case can be seen in the following examples:

(2) a. Asu　　　Tokyo ni　⎧ *iku nara* ⎫ , issyo ni　turete itte kudasai.
　　　 tomorrow　　　　 to ⎨ 　go if 　⎬ 　 together taking go　please
　　　　　　　　　　　　 ⎪ **ittara* ⎪
　　　　　　　　　　　　 ⎩ went-if ⎭
　　　'Please take me with you if you are going to go to Tokyo tomorrow.'
　　 b. Benkyoo　⎧ *suru nara* ⎫ , hayaku site　　simainasai.
　　　　 study　　 ⎨ 　do　if 　⎬ 　 quickly doing finish
　　　　　　　　　 ⎪ **sitara* ⎪
　　　　　　　　　 ⎩ did-if ⎭
　　　'If you are going to study, finish it quickly.'

---

†This chapter is mainly for students and teachers of Japanese.
[1] The use of these forms for the counterfactual conditional will not be touched on in this chapter.
[2] This analysis is due to Alfonso (1966, pp. 691–693). Examples (2) through (7), which are to follow, are essentially his.

c. Ensoku   ni   ┌ *iku nara* ┐ , Nikko ni irassyai.
   excursion on   │   go if   │   to come/go
                  │ **ittara* │
                  └ went if ┘

'If you are going to go on a school excursion, come to Nikko.'

Note that in the preceding, the action represented by S_2 takes place *before* (or at the same time as) the action represented by S_1. The *nara* sentences are grammatical because the S_1 *nara* S_2 pattern can be used if S_2 takes place before S_1, while the *tara* sentences are ungrammatical because the pattern can be used only when S_2 takes place after S_1.

Note, however, that the following are possible:

(3) a. Asu   Tokyo ni iku no   dattara, issyo ni turete itte
       tomorrow   to go that was-if   together taking going
       kudasai.
       please

   b. Benkyoo suru no   dattara, hayaku site   simainasai.
      study   do   that was-if quickly doing finish

   c. Ensoku   ni iku no   dattara, Nikko ni irassyai.
      excursion on go that was-if   to come/go

In these examples, what is completed before S_2 is not the action *iku* 'to go', *suru* 'to do', and *iku* 'to go', but the assertion . . . *no da* 'it is the case that . . .': that is, the action is nominalized by *no*, and the assertion copula *da* is used in the past conditional form *dattara* in each of the preceding examples. These sentences could be literally translated as follows:

(3) a. If it has been the case (or you have asserted) that you are going to go to Tokyo tomorrow, would you take me with you?

   b. If it has been the case (or you have asserted) that you are going to study, finish it quickly.

   c. If it has been the case (or you have asserted) that you are going to go on a school excursion, come to Nikko.

In some sentences a choice between *nara* and *tara* results in a subtle but crucial difference in meaning. For example, observe the following:

(4) a. John ni osieru *nara*, boku ni mo osiete kudasai.
            to teach if   I   to also teach please
       'If you are to tell it to John, please tell it to me also.'

    b. John ni osie*tara*, boku ni mo osiete kudasai.
         to taught-if I   to also teach please
        'If you (will) have told it to John, please tell it to me also.'

In (4a) the speaker is asking the hearer to tell him something, but he does not specify as to whether this should be done before or after the hearer tells it to John. In (4b) the speaker is asking the hearer to tell him something only after having told it to John, which the hearer may or may not have done.

(5) a. John ga kuru *nara*, boku wa kaeru.
           come if   I   go-home.
      'If John is to come, I will leave.'

    b. John ga *kitara*, boku wa kaeru.
          came-if I   go-home
      'If John has come, I will leave.'

In (5a) the speaker is saying that he will leave if John is expected to come —even before John arrives there. On the other hand, in (5b) the speaker is saying that he will leave only after John has arrived.

(6) a. Kono hon o yomu *nara*, ano hon mo yomu to ii   desu.
        this   book   read if   that book also read if good is
      'If you are to read this book, it is good for you to read that book also.'

    b. Kono hon o yon*dara*, ano hon mo yomu to ii   desu.
        this   book   read-if that book also read if good is
      'If you (will) have read this book, it is good for you to read that book also.'

In (6a) the speaker is advising the hearer to read that book probably prior to (but possibly subsequent to) the hearer's reading of this book. In (6b), on the other hand, the speaker is advising the hearer to read that book only after reading this book. Finally,

(7) a. Kono hon o yomu *nara* kasite   agemasu yo.
        this   book   read if   lending give-you-the-favor-of
      'If you are to read this book, I will lend it to you.'

    b. Kono hon o yon*dara*, kasite   agemasu yo.
        this   book   read-if lending give-you-the-favor-of
      'If I (will) have read this book, I will lend it to you.'

The subject of *yomu* in (7a) is unambiguously *anata* 'you' because 'If *I* am to read this book, I will lend it to you' would make no sense. On the other hand, the subject of *yondara* in (7b) is unambiguously *watakusi* 'I' because 'If *you* have read this book, I will lend it to you' would be nonsensical.

The S_1 *tara* S_2 pattern can be used also when S_2 refers to past time. For example,

(8) John ga ki*tara*,   Mary ga *kaetta*.
          came-when   left
    'When John came, Mary left.'

In (8), S_1 is not conditional, but refers to a real past action. In this case, also, S_2 represents an event that took place after S_1 did. In addition, there is a peculiar constraint on the use of this pattern for the past reference. Observe, first, the following sentences:

(9) a. *John wa, uwagi o nuidara,   hangaa ni kaketa.
              jacket   took-off-when hanger on hung
         'When John took off his jacket, he hung it on a hanger.'
     b. John ga uwagi o nuidara,   Mary ga hangaa ni kaketa.
              jacket   took-off-when   hanger on hung
         'When John took off his jacket, Mary hung it on a hanger.'

(10) a. *Gakkoo ni ittara,   benkyoosita.
          school   to went-when studied
         'When I went to school, I studied.'
     b. Gakkoo ni ittara,   benkyoosaserareta.
          school   to went-when was-made-to-study
         'When I went to school, I was made to study.'
     c. Gakkoo ni ittara,   mada dare mo kite   inakatta.
          school   to went-when yet   anyone come had not
         'When I went to school, no one had come yet.'

(11) a. *Ie   ni kaettara,   gohan o tukutta.
          home to returned-when meal   prepared
         'When I returned home, I cooked dinner.'
     b. Mary no ie   ni ittara,   gohan o gotisoosite
              's home to went-when meal   treating
          kureta.
          gave-me-the-favor-of
         'When I went to Mary's house, she treated me to dinner.'

   c. Ie   ni kaettara,   tegami ga kite   ita.
       home to returned-when letter   arrived had
       'When I returned home, the letter had arrived.'

(12) a. *John wa, ie   ni kaettara,   gohan o tukutta.
             home to returned-when meal   prepared
         'John, returning home, cooked dinner.'

   b. John ga ie   ni kaettara,   Mary ga naite ita.
         home to returned-when   crying was
       'When John returned home, Mary was crying.'

   c. John ga ie   ni kaettara,   Mary kara tegami ga kite   ita.
         home to returned-when   from letter   come had
       'When John returned home, a letter had arrived from Mary.'

The foregoing examples show that there cannot be self-controllable timing between the action or event represented by S_1 and that represented by S_2 when the *tara* construction is used for referring to past time.[3] For example, in (9a) the agent of S_1 and that of S_2 are identical (namely, John), and since the action of taking off one's jacket and that of hanging it on a hanger are both self-controllable, it is considered that there was a self-controllable time sequence between S_1 and S_2. Hence, the sentence is ungrammatical. On the other hand, in (9b) the agent of S_1 and the agent of S_2 are not identical, and although each action must have been self-controllable on the part of each agent, the time sequence between the two events might have been accidental. Namely, this sentence does not imply that Mary hung John's jacket after waiting for him to take it off. It simply means that Mary's hanging John's jacket on a hanger followed John's taking it off.

Compare next the sentences of (12). Example (12a) is ungrammatical because John's returning home and his cooking dinner represent a self-controllable time sequence. On the other hand, in (12b) that Mary was crying was an event over which John had no control. Therefore, John could not have planned the time sequencing of the two events. Hence, the sentence is grammatical.

It seems that the requirement that S_1 and S_2 in S_1 *tara* S_2 have no self-controllable time sequence is responsible for the peculiar overtone at-

---

[3] I am indebted to Mineko Masamune (personal communication) for her valuable suggestions, from which this analysis has emerged.

tached to the pattern: namely, S_2 normally represents an unexpected or surprising event. Incidentally, this requirement is the opposite of what we have observed to be the case between S_1 and S_2 of S_1 *te kara* S_2. In the latter there must be a time sequence planned by the subject of S_2 for S_2 to follow S_1 immediately.

The ungrammaticality of (10a) and the grammaticality of (10b) are also illustrative of the proposed generalization. Although the speaker of both these sentences is the subject for S_1 and S_2, *benkyoosita* 'I studied' is an action controllable by the speaker, while *benkyoosaserareta* 'I was made to study' is an event over which the speaker did not have control. In this light, observe the following sentences:

(13) a. John ga inaku nattara,   (watakusi wa) benkyoo
           absent became-when I   study
      dekiru yoo ni natta.
      can   became
      'When John had left, I came to be able to study.'

   b. *John ga inaku nattara,   (watakusi wa) benkyoosita.
           absent became-when I   studied
      'When John had left, I studied.'

(14) a. New York ni ittara,   John ni aimasu.
            to went-when   to meet
      'I will see John if I go to New York.'

   b. New York ni ittara,   John ni aimasita.
            to went-when   to met
      'I met John when I went to New York.'

Note that (13a) is grammatical because *yoo ni naru* 'come to' does not represent a self-controllable action, but results from a natural course of events. In (14) both (a) and (b) are grammatical. However, the meanings of the verb *au* 'to meet' are different. In (14a), *aimasu* is a self-controllable verb meaning 'to meet with, interview'. Note that the constraint of the non-self-controllable time sequence applies only to the past time reference of *tara*, and not to the future time reference. Therefore, (14a) is perfectly grammatical with this self-controllable verb *au*. On the other hand, the *tara* construction in (14b) represents a past event, and so there cannot be a self-controllable time sequence between S_1 and S_2. Therefore, *au* is interpreted, not as 'to meet with, interview', but as 'to encounter, accidentally meet'. Meeting John in this sense was an accidental event that the speaker did not and could not plan. Hence, the sentence is grammatical. It is interesting to note that it is not possible to assign this 'encounter' interpretation to *au* of (14a) since *John ni aimasu* designates the speaker's intention, and one cannot intend to do what he cannot control.

Past habits, viewed retrospectively, also constitute a natural course of events, and not a self-controllable action. Therefore, the following sentences are grammatical:

(15) a. Natu   ni nattara, yoku New York ni ikimasita.
      summer   became often   to went
      'I often went to New York when the summer had arrived.'

     b. Natu   ni nattara, yoku New York ni itta mono   desu.
      summer   became   custom was
      'I used to go to New York when the summer had arrived.'

To summarize, the *tara* pattern (S_1 *tara* S_2) has the following characteristics:

(i) S_2 happens after S_1 is completed.

(ii)   When this pattern is used to refer to past events, there cannot be self-controllable timing between the action or event represented by S_1 and that represented by S_2.

(iii) Therefore, S_2 often represents an unexpected or surprising event.

15[†]

To as a Temporal Particle

In this chapter, I shall examine two uses of *to* as a temporal particle:

(1) a. With the present tense verb in the second clause:
   Kono ie   wa natu   ni naru   *to* totemo atui.
   this   house   summer -ly become   very   hot
   '(Lit.) This house is very hot when it becomes summer.'
   b. With the past tense verb in the second clause:
   Gakkoo ni iku *to* Mary ga kite   ita.
   school   to go   coming was
   'When I got to school, Mary had already been there.'

Alfonso (1966, pp. 652–655) states that this construction represents two facts related as *antecedent* and natural, habitual, inevitable, or immediate *consequent*. He also adds, correctly, that the S_2 can be neither a command nor a request nor some form showing determination. In this chapter I shall show that Alfonso's observation is correct for (1a), where a habitual general statement is given, but that it does not apply to (1b), where specific events are referred to.

First, I shall contrast S_1 *to* S_2 in the generic use with the S_1 *tara* S_2 and S_1 *nara* S_2 constructions and show that Alfonso's analysis, so far as this usage is concerned, is correct and accounts for the subtle differences in meanings among them and for the ungrammaticality of certain *to* sentences.

Observe the following triplets:

(2) 'When the summer comes, I go to New York.'
   a. Natu   ni naru   *to* New York ni ikimasu.
   summer -ly become   to go
   b. Natu ni nat*tara*, New York ni ikimasu.
   c. *Natu ni naru *nara*, New York ni ikimasu.

(3) 'When next summer comes, I go to New York.'
   a. ??Rainen   no natu   ni naru   *to*, New York ni ikimasu.
   next-year 's summer -ly become   to go
   b. Rainen no natu ni nat*tara*, New York ni ikimasu.
   c. *Rainen no natu ni naru *nara*, New York ni ikimasu.

[†]This chapter is mainly for students and teachers of Japanese.

(4) 'If I don't eat, I (will) feel hungry.'

    a.   Gohan o tabenai *to* onaka   ga sukimasu.

          meal   eat-not   stomach   get-hungry

    b.   Gohan o tabenaka*ttara* onaka ga sukimasu.

    c.   *Gohan o tabenai *nara*, onaka ga sukimasu.

(5) 'It is pleasant when/if it rains.'

    a.   Ame ga huru *to* kimoti ga ii.

          rain   fall   feeling   is-good

    b.   *Ame ga hut*tara* kimoti ga ii.

    c.   *Ame ga huru *nara* kimoti ga ii.

Sentence (2a) means that the speaker goes to New York every summer, while (2b) says that he intends to go to New York the coming summer. In other words, (2a), with *to*, represents habitual actions, while (2b), with *tara*, represents a single future action. Therefore, if the context forces a "single future action" interpretation to the *to* construction, as in (3a), we get an unnatural sentence. Examples (2c) and (3c) are ungrammatical because *natu ni naru* 'the summer will come' is presented here as if there could be some doubt of its coming. Similarly, (4a) represents a habitual or inevitable antecedent-consequent relationship ('Whenever one skips a meal, one gets hungry', 'If one doesn't eat, one naturally gets hungry'), while (4b) says that the speaker (or the hearer) will feel hungry if he misses the next meal. Example (4c) is ungrammatical because *onaka ga suku* 'I get hungry' is a future state that is expected to occur if *gohan o tabenai* 'I will not eat' takes place, while syntactically, as was discussed in the previous chapter, *tabenai* refers to (remote) future time, and *onaka ga suku* to immediate future time, yielding a contradictory time sequence. Sentence (5a) represents a habitual antecedent-consequent relationship 'I feel refreshed whenever it rains.' Example (5b) is ungrammatical because the time referred to by *kimoti ga ii* 'it is pleasant' syntactically precedes that referred to by *ame ga huttara* 'if it rains', while in reality it will become pleasant *after* it has rained. Example (5c) is ungrammatical for the same reason. Similarly, note the following group of examples:

(6) 'When John got angry, he became red.'

    a.   John wa okoru   *to* akaku natta.

                   get-angry   red-ly became

    b. ?John wa oko*tara* akaku natta.

    c. *John wa okoru *nara*, akaku natta.

Sentence (6a) represents a habitual antecedent-consequent relationship, meaning 'John, whenever he got angry, became red.' It is not clear to me why (6b) is awkward in the intended interpretation.[1] This sentence would be perfectly grammatical if it meant 'John, when *I* got angry (at that time), became red'. Example (6c) is ungrammatical because *akaku natta* 'he became red' does not satisfy the requirement that S_2 of the S_1 *nara* S_2 must represent the speaker's evaluation, will, resolution, request, or order. Example (6c) would be literally translated as 'If you assert that John got angry, he became red', which does not make much sense.

    The following *to* sentences are ungrammatical because S_2 represents either a command, request, or determination, which the S_1 *to* S_2 construction cannot take:

(7) 'If you are cold, put on more clothes.'
    a. *Samui *to*, motto kinasai.
       be-cold   more put-on

    b. Samuka*tara*, motto kinasai.

    c. Samui *nara*, motto kinasai.

(8) 'When the summer comes, please go to New York for me.'
    a. *Natu ni naru   *to* New York ni itte kudasai.
       summer -ly become   to go please

    b. Natu ni nat*tara*, New York ni itte kudasai.

    c. *Natu ni naru *nara*, New York ni itte kudasai.

(9) 'I will leave if John comes.'
    a. *John ga kuru *to*, kaerimasu.
           come   return

    b. John ga ki*tara*, kaerimasu.

    c. John ga kuru *nara*, kaerimasu.

---

[1] This must have something to do with the meaning of *okoru* 'get angry', because the following is a perfectly natural sentence:

John wa sake o non*dara*   akaku natta.
            drank-when red-ly became
'John became red when he drank sake (at that time).'

(10) 'If John comes, I intend (want) to have dinner with him.'

a. *John ga kuru *to*, issyo   ni syokuzi ⎧o suru tumori desu.
       when   together -ly meal ⎪   have intention be
                                   ⎨ga sitai
                                   ⎩   want-to-have

b. John ga ki*tara*, issyo ni syokuzi ⎧o suru tumori desu.
                                      ⎩ga sitai.

c. John ga kuru *nara*, issyo ni syokuzi ⎧o suru tumori desu.
                                         ⎩ga sitai.

Similarly,

(11) a. Sonna ni takai   *to*, dare mo kaimasen yo.
        such   -ly expensive   anyone buy-not
        'If it is that expensive, no one will buy it.'

b. *Sonna ni takai *to*, watakusi wa kaimasen yo.
                         I   buy-not
        'If it is that expensive, I am not going to buy it.'

Sentence (11a) is grammatical because, being a statement about every-one, it does not represent the speaker's determination. On the other hand, (11b) is ungrammatical because it represents the speaker's determination.

As is true for the *tara* construction, the S_1 *to* S_2 construction requires that the action or state represented by S_2 take place *after* that represented by S_1 is completed. This is so because this construction represents the antecedent-consequent relationship. Observe the following sentences:

(12) a. *Nihon ni iku *to*, otooto o turete ikimasu.
        Japan to go   brother taking go
        'Whenever I go to Japan, I take my brother with me.'

b. Nihon ni iku to, Tanaka-san no ie   ni tomaru.
                              's house in stay
        'Whenever I go to Japan, I stay at Mr. Tanaka's house.'

(13) a. *Sukii ni iku *to*, yooi   ga taihen   desu.[2]
        ski   to go   preparation painstaking is
        'Whenever I go skiing, the preparation for it is a problem.'

[2] This sentence would be grammatical if it meant 'Whenever I go skiing, the preparation at the skiing site is a problem.'

b.   Sukii ni iku to, kega   o suru.
                  injury do
          'Whenever I go skiing, I get injured.'

(14) a. ??Ame ga huru to, dosyaburi da.
              rain   fall   squall   is
          'Whenever it rains, it pours.'

    b.   Ame ga huru to, nukarumi da.
                          muddy   is
          'Whenever it rains, it becomes muddy.'

In (14a), *dosyaburi da* 'it is a squall' represents an attribute of the rain, and
not a result of it. Therefore, the sentence is awkward, if not ungrammatical. On the other hand, *nukarumi da* 'it is muddy' represents the logical
or habitual consequence of the rain in the place that is under discussion
(for example, *kono toori wa* 'This street gets muddy when it rains'). Hence,
(14b) is grammatical.

    Thus far, I have examined the S_1 *to* S_2 construction only as representing
the habitual antecedent-consequent relationship. That is, all the examples
given in (2) through (14) represent general statements, and they do not
refer to any specific events. The second usage of the S_1 *to* S_2 construction,
as exemplified by (1b), is to present two specific events, S_1 and S_2, either
in past or in future time, as occurring concurrently or successively. There
is no "logical antecedent-consequent" relationship implied in this usage.
For example, in (15) there is no logical connection between the speaker's
leaving home and its raining, or between the speaker's lying in bed at
home and Bill's coming to visit him.

(15) a. Ie   o deru *to*, ame ga hutte-ita.
              house leave rain   falling-was
          'On my leaving home, it was raining.'

    b. Ie   de nete-iru *to*, Bill ga tazunete kita.
        house at lying-be   visiting came
        'While I was lying in bed at home, Bill came to call on me.'

At the same time, S_1 and S_2 cannot be two independent events: S_1 *to* S_2
is acceptable only when the events represented by S_1 and S_2 are such that

they are amenable to the paraphrase "Upon S_1's happening (or while S_1 was happening), *what do you think happened?* S_2 did." Observe the following:

(16) a. ?*Ie   de nete-iru to, Bill ga Mary o tazuneta.
         house at lying-be   visited
         'While I was lying in bed at home, what do you think happened? Bill called on Mary.'

     b.   Ie de nete-iru to, Bill ga Mary o tazunete-simatta.
                                        visiting-finished (on me)
         'While I was lying in bed at home, what do you think happened? Bill visited Mary ahead of me.'

Compare (15b) and (16a). In the former, S_2 is closely related to S_1 in the sense that Bill came to visit the speaker, who is the subject of S_1. Thus, S_1 and S_2 are amenable to the "What do you think happened next?" paraphrase. On the other hand, in (16a), S_2 (namely Bill's visiting Mary) has little to do with S_1. Hence, S_1 and S_2 are not amenable to the "What do you think happened next?" paraphrase. This accounts for the extreme awkwardness, bordering on ungrammaticality, of (16a) devoid of appropriate contexts. In contrast, (16b) would be a natural sentence if the speaker had planned to visit Mary, but if Bill visited her ahead of him while he was idling at home. *Simatta* 'ended up with, did such and such to me' at the end of S_2 implies that the speaker was affected by Bill's having visited Mary. Thus, S_1 and S_2 of (16b) are in some close relationship that would allow the "What do you think happened next?" paraphrase. Hence, the sentence is grammatical.

Because of the "What do you think happened next?" connotation, the S_1 *to* S_2 construction brings the flavor of suspense or surprise. It stands in marked contrast with S_1 *toki* S_2 'When S_1, S_2', which does not carry with it any such connotation.

(17) Ie   de nete-iru toki, Bill ga tazunete kita.
        house at lying-be when   visiting came
        'When I was lying in bed at home, Bill came to call on me.'

Compare (15b) with (17). Sentence (17) is a neutral, colorless statement of two successive events, while (15b) presents the two events suspensefully. Likewise, observe the following pairs of sentences:

(18) a. John ga Mary o naguru *to*, Tom mo Jane o nagutta.
             hit   hit
'On John's hitting Mary, what do you think happened? I observed that Tom, too, hit Jane.'

b. John ga Mary o nagutta *toki*, Tom mo Jane o nagutta.
'At the time when John hit Mary, Tom, too, hit Jane.'

(19) a. Soto   ni deru   *to*, ame ga hutte-ita.
       outside go-out   rain   falling-was
'On going out, what do you think happened? I discovered that it was raining.'

b. Soto ni deta *toki*, ame ga hutte-ita.
'At the time when I went out, it was raining.'

(20) a. Bar ni   hairu *to*, Bill ga sake o nonde-ita.
           into enter   drinking-was
'On entering the bar, what do you think happened? I discovered that Bill was drinking.'

b. Bar ni haitta *toki*, Bill ga sake o nonde-ita.
'At the time when I entered the bar, Bill was drinking.'

The (a) sentences just cited have the connotation of 'What did I see but Tom's hitting Jane', etc., which is lacking in the (b) sentences. The two events represented in (18b), for example, can be totally independent. It might be that John and Mary were in Tokyo, that Tom and Jane were in Osaka, and that the speaker knew that John's hitting Mary and Tom's hitting Jane occurred at the same time. In (18a), because of the connotation of "What do you think happened next? I observed that . . ." carried by the S_1 *to* S_2 construction, such an interpretation is not plausible. Tom's hitting Jane must have occurred in the same place immediately after John's hitting Mary took place.

What seems to be responsible for the "What do you think happened next?" connotation of the S_1 *to* S_2 construction is that the two events, S_1 and S_2, are presented in this construction through the speaker's view. In other words, this construction really means "After/while S_1 happened, what do you think happened next? *I* (=the speaker) *observed/discovered* S_2

happened." It would not make sense to report on the speaker's own voluntary action as an objective event observed by the speaker himself. Thus, many sentences of this construction with the first person subject in S_2 are ungrammatical.

(21) a. Mary ga kuru to John ga kaetta.
             come   left
      'Upon Mary's coming, what do you think happened? I observed that John left.'

b. Boku ga tuku to John ga kaetta.
       I   arrive   left
      'Upon my arriving, what do you think happened? I observed that John left.'

c. *Mary ga kuru to boku ga kaetta.
          come   I   left
      'Upon Mary's coming, what do you think happened? *I observed that I left.'

On the other hand, if S_2 represents an involuntary action or state on the part of the speaker, the sentence may have the first person subject.

(22) a. Sono hon ga syuppansareru to, boku wa minna   no
       the book   published-is   I   everyone 's
      tyuumoku no mato to natta.
      attention 's target as became
      'When the book was published, what do you think happened? I observed that I became the focus of attention of everyone.'

b. Hikoozyoo ni tuku to, boku wa atama ga itaku   natta.
      airport   to arrive I   head   painfully became
      'When I arrived at the airport, what do you think happened? I observed that I came to have a headache.'

Note that in (22a) and (22b) the events represented by S_2 are such that they can be observed objectively by the speaker.

In narratives the narrator (namely, the speaker) is allowed to talk about the first person as if it refers to a third party. Thus, although (23) is ungrammatical in colloquial speech, it is acceptable as a sentence in narratives.

(23) *Boku wa, uwagi o nugu   to hangaa ni kaketa.
      I   jacket take-off   hanger on hung
      'When I took off my jacket, what do you think happened? I ob-
      served that I hung it on a hanger.'

When S_1 refers to a state, it must be of a reasonably short duration. For example,

(24) a. Aru hi, aru kaisya   de hataraite iru to, Bill ni atta.
         one day one company in working   am   met
         'One day, when I was working in a company, I met Bill.'

     b. *Tokyo de aru kaisya   ni tutomete iru to, Bill ni atta.
                 in one company in employed am   met
         'While I worked for a company in Tokyo, I met Bill.'

(25) a. Aru hi, Tokyo de asonde iru to, Bill ni atta.
         one day   in idling am   met
         'One day, when I was idling in Tokyo, I met Bill.'

     b. *1960-nen, Tokyo ni sunde iru to, Bill ni atta.
          year   in living am   met
         'In 1960, when I was living in Tokyo, I met Bill.'

It will not be amiss here to compare the S_1 *to* S_2 pattern with the S_1 *tara* S_2 pattern discussed earlier. Observe the following sentences:

(26) a. Mary ga ki*tara*,   John ga kaetta.
                 came-when   left
         'When Mary came, John left.'

     b. *Mary ga ki*tara*,   boku ga kaetta.
                 came-when I   left
         'When Mary came, I left.'

(27) a. Mary ga kuru *to*, John ga kaetta.
                 come   left
         'When Mary came, what do you think happened? I observed
         that John left.'

     b. *Mary ga kuru *to*, boku ga kaetta.
                 come I   left
         'When Mary came, what do you think happened? I observed
         that I left.'

Example (27b) is ungrammatical because the speaker cannot talk about his own voluntary action as if it were an event, while the S_1 *to* S_2 pattern requires that S_2 be an event (this constraint is implicit in the test that I have been using: "What do you think happened? I observed that . . ."). On the other hand, (26b) is ungrammatical for the same reason, but only indirectly so. The speaker cannot talk about his own voluntary action (namely, leaving) as if it were an event. Therefore, S_2 in (26b) must represent a self-controllable action. Since it represents a self-controllable action, it must be that the time sequencing between S_1 and S_2 was by the speaker's design, which is not allowable in the S_1 *tara* S_2 pattern. Hence, (26b) is ungrammatical.

To repeat, two different constraints are applicable to S_1 *tara* S_2 and S_1 *to* S_2. For the former, there must not be a self-controllable time sequence between S_1 and S_2. For the latter, S_2 must be an event that the speaker could observe objectively. This difference manifests itself in the following:

(28) a. *John wa, uwagi o nui*dara*,   hangaa ni kaketa.
                   jacket   took-off-when hanger to hung
        'John, when he took off his jacket, hung it on a hanger.'

    b. John wa, uwagi o nugu *to*, hangaa ni kaketa.
        'After John took off his jacket, what do you think happened? I observed that he hung it on a hanger.'

Taking off one's jacket and hanging it on a hanger are both self-controllable actions. When both actions are taken by the same agent, it is considered that there was a planned time sequencing between the two actions. This is not compatible with the constraint of the *tara* pattern; hence, (28a) is ungrammatical. On the other hand, since John's hanging his jacket on a hanger is something that the speaker can observe objectively, (28b) does not violate the constraint of the S_1 *to* S_2 pattern. Hence, the sentence is grammatical.

In summary, the following are some of the characteristics of the S_1 *to* S_2 construction:

A. When it represents a general statement:
(i) It represents a habitual or logical antecedent-consequent relationship.
(ii) S_2 cannot represent a command, a request, or some form showing determination.

(iii) It requires that the action or state represented by S_2 take place after that represented by S_1 is completed.

B. When it refers to two specific events:

(i) The construction lacks any "logical antecedent-consequent" implication.

(ii) The sentence must be amenable to the paraphrase "After/while S_1 happened, what do you think happened? I observed/discovered that S_2 happened." In other words, S_2 must represent an event that the speaker could observe objectively. Consequently, the construction carries with it the connotation of suspense and surprise.

(iii) Therefore, S_2 cannot represent the speaker's voluntary action.

(iv) However, (iii) does not apply in narratives, where the narrator can talk about the first person as if the latter were a third party.

(v) If S_1 refers to a state, it must be of a short duration.

16†

The -*Te* Gerundive Form
and the -*I* Continuative Form

The -*te* gerundive form and the -*i* continuative form of verbs can be used for representing time sequence. For example,

(1) John wa uwagi o nui-*de*[1] hangaa ni kaketa.
           jacket   take off hanger on hung
    'John took off his jacket and put it on a hanger.'

(2) John wa uwagi o nug-*i*   hangaa ni kaketa.
                  take off
    'John took off his jacket and put it on a hanger.'

In this chapter, I shall examine the difference in meaning between these two forms and contrast them with the *to* temporal clause.

Sentences (1) and (2) are very similar in meaning except that the -*te* form (namely, *nui-de*) has the connotation of "V and then" or "having V-ed." This connotation is lacking in the -*i* form in (2). This is, no doubt, due to the fact that -*te* of the gerundive form originates from the perfect tense auxiliary *tari* of classical Japanese, from which the perfect tense suffix -*ta* of the present-day Japanese is also derived. The V_1 -*te* V_2 pattern cannot be used when two simultaneous actions or states are involved. For example,

(3) a. John wa yoku asob-*i* yoku benkyoosuru.
               well play well study
      'John plays a lot and studies a lot.'
    b. *John wa yoku ason-*de* yoku benkyoosuru.

Example (3b) is ungrammatical in the intended sense 'John both plays and studies a lot'. It would be grammatical only if it meant 'John studies a lot after he plays a lot'. Similarly,

(4) a. John wa Mary o nikum-*i* Jane o aisi-te iru.
                  hate   loving is
      'John hates Mary and loves Jane.'

---

†This chapter is mainly for students and teachers of Japanese.
[1] -*Te* is realized as -*de* after stems that end with a voiced consonant. For example, *yom*: *yon-de* 'read', *sin*: *sin-de* 'die', *nug*: *nui-de* 'take off'.

b. *John wa Mary o nikun-*de* Jane o aisi-te iru.

(5) a.   John wa zibun o nikum-*i*, hito   o nikunda.
              self   hate   people   hated
    'John hated himself and hated others.'

  b.   *John wa zibun o nikun-*de*, hito o nikunda.

Another difference between the -*te* form and the -*i* form is that, for the former, the two actions involved must be either both self-controllable or both non-self-controllable, while such a constraint does not seem to hold for the -*i* form. Observe the following example:

(6) a.   John wa asa   oki-*te*, kao o aratta.
              morning get-up face   washed
    'John got up in the morning and washed his face.'

  b.   *John wa asa   me o samas-i-*te*, kao o aratta.
              morning   wake   face   washed
    'John woke up in the morning and washed his face.'

Oki 'to get up' can be a self-controllable action, and *araw* 'to wash' is definitely a self-controllable action. Therefore, both actions in (6a) are self-controllable. Thus, the sentence is grammatical. On the other hand, *me o samasu* 'to wake up' is a non-self-controllable action; hence, (6b) is ungrammatical. Similarly,

(7) a.   John wa hikoozyoo ni tui-*te*, nimotu no kensa   o uketa.
              airport   to arrive luggage 's inspection   underwent
    'John arrived at the airport and underwent the inspection of his luggage.'

  b.   *John wa hikoozyoo ni tui-*te*, ie   ni denwasita.
              airport   to arrive home to telephoned
    'John arrived at the airport and called home.'

(8) a.   John wa hikoozyoo ni it-*te*, nimotu no kensa   o uketa.
              airport   to go   luggage 's inspection   underwent
    'John went to the airport and underwent luggage inspection.'

  b.   John wa hikoozyoo ni it-*te*, ie   ni denwa   o sita.
              airport   to go   home to telephone   made
    'John went to the airport and called home.'

(9) a.   John wa Mary ni at-*te*, sono hanasi o sita.
                         to meet the   talk   did
         'John saw Mary and talked about it.'
    b. *John wa Mary ni guuzen   de at-*te*, sono hanasi o sita.
                         to accidentally   meet the   talk   did
         'John met Mary accidentally and talked about it.'

Sentence (7a) is grammatical because both arriving at the airport and
undergoing luggage inspection are non-self-controllable. On the other
hand, (7b) is ungrammatical because, while arriving at the airport is a
non-self-controllable action, calling home is a self-controllable action.
Compare (7a) and (8a). In the latter, the self-controllability of going to
the airport forces *nimotu no kensa o uketa* 'underwent luggage inspection' to
be interpreted as a self-controllable (voluntary) action. This is why (8a)
has, in one of its readings, the connotation that the speaker went to the
airport in order to undergo the luggage inspection. Similarly, compare
(7b) with (8b). While *tuku* 'to arrive' is non-self-controllable, *iku* 'to go' is
a self-controllable action. Hence, the two actions in (8b) are both self-
controllable. This is why (8b) is grammatical, while (7b) is not. Likewise,
in (9a), *au* 'to meet' is taken as a planned meeting because of the self-
controllable nature of *sono hanasi o sita* 'talked about it'. Example (9b) is
ungrammatical because the self-controllable interpretation cannot be
forced upon *guuzen deau* 'to meet accidentally'.

This constraint does not seem to be mandatory, though applicable to
some extent, in the -*i* form. The following sentences, although slightly
awkward, are not as unacceptable as the corresponding -*te* form sentences.

(10) a.   John wa, hikoozyoo ni tuk-*i*, ie   ni denwa   o sita.
                   airport   to arrive home to telephone   did
          'John arrived at the airport and called home.'
     b.   John wa Mary ni guuzen   a-*i*, sono hanasi o sita.
                   to accidentally meet the   talk   did
          'John met Mary accidentally, and talked about it.'

Now, we are ready to compare three forms: the -*te* form, the -*i* form,
and the *to* clause. First, observe the following triplet:

(11) 'John went to school and studied.'
     a.   John wa gakkoo ni it-*te* benkyoosita.
                   school to go   studied

b. John wa gakkoo ni ik-*i* benkyoosita.

                  go

c. John wa gakkoo ni iku *to* benkyoosita.

Sentences (11a) and (11b) are different from (11c) in that they do not have the connotation of suspense and surprise represented in "What do you think happened? I observed that. . . ." Sentence (11a) is different from (11b) in that the former contains the connotation of the perfection of V_1, while the latter does not. Next, observe the following:

(12) a. John ga Mary o nagut-*te*, boku ga Jane o nagutta.

                  hit   I   hit

       'John hit Mary, and then I hit Jane.'

b. John ga Mary o nagur-*i*, boku ga Jane o nagutta.

c. *John ga Mary o naguru *to*, boku ga Jane o nagutta.

Example (12c) is ungrammatical in colloquial speech because 'I observed that I hit Jane' would not make very much sense.

(13) a. *John wa me o samas-i-*te* kao o aratta.

                         wake-up face   washed

       'John woke up and washed his face.'

b. John wa me o samas-*i* kao o aratta.

c. John wa me o samasu *to* kao o aratta.

Example (13a) is ungrammatical because the -*te* form requires that actions involved be either both self-controllable or both non-self-controllable, while in (13a) waking up is non-self-controllable, and washing the face is self-controllable. Since such a constraint does not apply to the -*i* form and the *to* clause, (13b) and (13c) are both grammatical.

(14) a. John wa hitokoto   mo   iwanai-*de* gohan o tabeta.

                  single-word even say-not   meal   ate

       'John ate without saying a word.'

b. John wa hitokoto mo iwa*zu*, gohan o tabeta.

c. *John wa hitokoto mo iwanai *to*, gohan o tabeta.

In the preceding, *iwanai-de* is the -*te* form, and *iwazu* the -*i* form, of the negative of *iu* 'to say'. Example (14c) is ungrammatical because it would not make sense to say that event S_2 occurred *after* something did not happen. On the other hand, (14a) and (14b) are grammatical because the -*te* and -*i* forms can represent attendant circumstances, namely, what the situation was when S_2 took place.

To summarize,

(i)   The S_1 -*te* S_2 construction implies that S_1 has taken place before S_2 does.

(ii) In the S_1 -*te* S_2 construction, S_1 and S_2 must be both self-controllable or both non-self-controllable.

(iii) S_1 of the two constructions can represent an attendant circumstance when S_2 took place.

17†

Degrees of Subordination

In the preceding chapters, I examined various types of temporal and conditional clauses: *before* clauses in *uti ni* and *mae ni*; *after* clauses in *te kara, ato de, ato ni,* and *ato*; assertive *nara* clauses; perfective *tara* clauses; temporal *to* clauses; and the *-te* gerundive form and the *-i* continuative form. These clauses are felt to have different degrees of subordination to the main clauses. For example, observe the following sentences:

(1) a. John wa uwagi o nui-   *de,* hangaa ni ⎧ kaketa.
           jacket   take-off ing hanger on ⎨ hung

                                   kake-mas-ita.
                                   hang-polite-past

     'John, taking off his jacket, hung it on a hanger.'

     b. John wa uwagi o nug-*i,*   hangaa ni ⎰ kaketa.
                      and   ⎱ kakemasita.

     'John took off his jacket and hung it on a hanger.'

     c. John wa uwagi o nugu *to,* hangaa ni ⎰ kaketa.
                                         ⎱ kakemasita.

     'John, upon taking off his jacket, hung it on a hanger.'

In (1a) and (1b) the *-te* gerundive and the *-i* continuative forms appear, while in (1c) the temporal particle *to* is used. It is intuitively felt that *uwagi o nui-de/nug-i* 'taking off his jacket' forms a tighter unit with *hangaa ni kaketa* 'hung it on a hanger' than does *uwagi o nugu to* 'upon taking off his jacket'. In other words, V_1 *-te*/V_1 *-i* is felt to be more subordinate to V_2 than V_1 *to* is to V_2.[1] I shall show in this chapter that this intuitive feeling

---

†This chapter is for all readers.

[1] Mikami (1970, pp. 11–15) observes that (1a) and (1c) can be distinguished as

(i)   John wa ——— nui-de kaketa.

(ii) John wa ———⎰ nugu to,
                ⎱ kaketa.

What he means is that in (1a) it is felt that the understood subject *John ga* appears only once, namely, as the subject of *nui-de kaketa.* On the other hand, in (1c) it is felt that *John ga* appears twice: once as the subject of *nugu to* and the second time as the subject of

has some syntactic basis. In many patterns, V_1 *-te* V_2 and V_1 *-i* V_2 behave as if they were single constituents, while V_1 *to* V_2 behaves as if it formed two independent constituents.[2] In the following the same three examples (1a), (1b), and (1c) will be tested in various syntactic patterns. Other patterns, such as S_1 *toki* S_2 (which means 'when S_1, S_2') and S_1 *node* S_2 ('because of S_1, S_2'), will also be examined.

1. Questions

In the following pair of sentences, (2a) is ambiguous, but (2b) is not.

(2) a. John wa uwagi o nui-*de*/nug-*i*, hangaa ni kakemasita *ka?*

   b. John wa uwagi o nugu *to*, hangaa ni kakemasita *ka?*

In (2a), the question particle *ka* has in its domain either V_1 *-te*/*-i* V_2 or only V_2.

(3) a. John wa [uwagi o $\begin{Bmatrix} \text{nui-de} \\ \text{nug-i} \end{Bmatrix}$, hangaa ni kakemasita]-ka?

   'Did John take off his jacket and hang it on a hanger?'

   b. John wa uwagi o $\begin{Bmatrix} \text{nui-de} \\ \text{nug-i} \end{Bmatrix}$, [hangaa ni kakemasita]-ka?

   'Taking off his jacket, did John hang it on a hanger?'

The square brackets indicate the domain of the interrogative particle *ka*. In (3a) whether it was true that John took off his jacket and hung it on a hanger is being questioned. In (3b) the speaker takes for granted that John took off his jacket and then questions whether he hung it on a hanger or not. On the other hand, (2b) has only one interpretation, namely, the one that corresponds to (3b). The speaker takes for granted that it is true that John took off his jacket. The preceding examples show that the command power of *ka* can be easily extended to the left of *-te*, but not to the left of *to*.

---

kaketa. In other words, in (1a) [*nui-de kaketa*] behaves as a single verb phrase requiring only one subject, while in (1b) [*nugu to*] [*kaketa*] behaves as two verb phrases, each requiring its own subject.

[2] In this chapter, expressions such as "the *-te* gerundive form" and "V_1 *-te* V_2" will be used exclusively, unless otherwise noted, to refer to the use of *-te* for representing time sequences, as in (1a). When the same pattern is used for designating cause or means, it does not always follow the same rules. Similarly, the expression "V_1 *to* V_2" will be used to refer to the use of this construction for representing two specific past events occurring one after another, and not to the use of the construction for representing the habitual antecedent-consequent relationships.

Let us examine here other types of subordinate clauses. Observe the following sentences:

(4) a. Mary wa John ga butta *toki*   nakimasita.
                              hit   when cried
          'Mary cried when John hit (her).'

    b. Mary wa John ga butta *toki* nakimasita *ka?*
          'Did Mary cry...'

(5) a.   Mary wa John ga butta *node*   nakimasita.
                                    because
          'Mary cried because John hit (her).'

    b. *Mary wa John ga butta *node* nakimasita *ka?*[3]
          'Did Mary cry...'

    c.   Mary wa John ga butta *node* naita *no desu ka?*
                                          cried
          'Is it the case that...'

(6) a.   John wa e   o kaku *si*   haiku o tukuru.
                      picture   paint and poem   compose
          'John paints pictures and composes poems.'

    b. *John wa e o kaku *si* haiku o tukuru *ka?*
          'Does John paint...'

    c. ?John wa e o kaku *si* haiku o tukuru *no desu ka?*
          'Is it the case that...'

Sentence (4b) is ambiguous: it can be a question as to whether it was when John hit her that Mary cried or as to whether Mary cried or not. In the former interpretation, *ka*'s command extends to the left of *toki*.

Sentence (5a) presupposes that it is true that Mary cried, and it gives the reason for Mary's crying. In (5b) the intended meaning is 'Is it because John hit her that Mary cried?' However, the sentence is ungrammatical in this interpretation. Thus, it seems that *node* prevents *ka* from extending its influence to the left of it. Therefore, *ka* in (5b) can have as its domain only *nakimasita* 'cried'. However, this is the part of the sentence whose truth-value is presupposed and which cannot be questioned. Hence

---

[3] The ungrammaticality of (5b) was first pointed out to me by Sige-Yuki Kuroda (personal communication, 1967).

(5b) is ungrammatical. On the other hand, the nominalizing particle *no* has a stronger command power than *ka*, and its influence can go to the left of *node*. Thus, in (5c) we have

(7) Mary wa [John ga butta node, naita]-no desu ka?

Namely, in order to make (5a) an interrogative sentence, it is necessary first to make *John ga butta node, naita* 'Mary cried because John hit (her)' a noun clause by adding the nominalizing particle *no* and then to let *ka* command "[Noun Clause]-*no desu.*"[4]

Sentence (6a) is an example of pure coordination by *si* 'and', which is used to juxtapose two events without saying which took place first. It seems that the command power of *ka* cannot be extended to the left of *si*. Example (6b) is ungrammatical because the intended function of *ka* is to make the whole sentence a question, while *si* prevents the command power of *ka* from being extended to the left of it. Thus, (6b) ends up with the juxtaposition of a declarative clause and an interrogative clause, which is an ungrammatical combination in Japanese, as well as in English and many other languages.

2. Negation

Observe the following sentences:

(8) a.   John wa [uwagi o {nui-de / nug-i} , hangaa ni kake]-nakatta.
                                                       did not

      'John did not take off his jacket and hang it on a hanger.'

   b.   ??John wa uwagi o {nui-de / nug-i} , [hangaa ni kake]-nakatta.

      'John, taking off his jacket, did not hang it on a hanger.'

(9) a.   *John wa [uwagi o nugu to, hangaa ni kake]-nakatta.
      'It was not the case that John took off his jacket and hung it on a hanger.'

   b.   ??John wa, uwagi o nugu to, [hangaa ni kake]-nakatta.
      'John, upon taking off his jacket, did not hang it on a hanger.'

---

[4] Sentence (5c) cannot have the reading corresponding to the following example for the same reason that (5b) is ungrammatical:

(i) *Mary wa John ga butta node,   [naita]-no desu ka?
                   hit   because cried
   'Because John hit Mary, is it that she cried?'

The grammaticality of (8a) shows that the command power of the negative morpheme *na* can be extended to the left of the gerundive *-te* and the continuative *-i*. The ungrammaticality of (9a) indicates that the command power of *na* cannot be extended to the left of *to*. Sentence (9b) is not totally acceptable because the V_1 *to* V_2 construction requires that V_2 represent observable events, while *hangaa ni kake-nakatta* 'did not hang it on a hanger' in this sentence represents, not an event, but the lack of an event.

Example (8b) is ungrammatical for a similar reason. The V_1 *-te* V_2 construction requires that if V_1 represents an action, V_2 should also represent an action and that if V_1 represents a state, V_2 should also represent a state. Again, *nui-de* of (8b) represents an action, but *hangaa ni kake-nakatta* 'did not hang it on a hanger' represents, not an action, but a lack of action. Hence, (8b) is ungrammatical.[5]

The following examples show that the command power of *na* cannot be extended to the left of *toki* 'at the time when' or to the left of *node* 'because':

(10) a.   Mary wa, John ga butta toki [nak]-anakatta.
                          hit   time cry   did not
          'Mary did not cry when John hit her.'

     b. *Mary wa [John ga butta toki nak]-anakatta.
          'It wasn't that Mary cried when John hit her.'

     c.   Mary wa [John ga butta toki naita]-*no* de wa nai.
                                        cried   is   not

(11) a.   Mary wa, John ga nagusameta node,   [nak]-anakatta.
                          comforted   because cry   did not
          'Mary, because John consoled her, did not cry.'

     b. *Mary wa, [John ga nagusameta node, nak]-anakatta.
          'It wasn't that Mary cried because John consoled her.'

     c.   Mary wa, [John ga nagusameta node, naita]-*no* de wa nai.
                                                      is   not

Note that in order to negate *John ga butta toki/node naita*, it is necessary first to nominalize the clause by adding *no* and then negate the [*Noun Clause*]-*no da*.

---

[5] This sentence, with *nug-i*, is almost grammatical. See Chapter 16.

3. Modal
Consider the following:

(12) a.   John wa [uwagi o $\{$ nui-de $\}$, hangaa ni kake]-*yoo to   sita.
          $\qquad\qquad\qquad\quad\{$ nug-i $\}$ was about to
          'John was about to take off his jacket and hang it on a hanger.'

   b.   John wa uwagi o $\{$ nui-de $\}$, [hangaa ni kake]-*yoo to sita.*
        $\qquad\qquad\qquad\{$ nug-i $\}$
        'John took off his jacket and was about to hang it on a hanger.'

(13) a.   *John wa [uwagi o nugu to, hangaa ni kake]-*yoo to sita.*
          'John was about to take off his jacket and hang it on a hanger.'

   b.   John wa uwagi o nugu to, [hangaa ni kake]-*yoo to sita.*
        'John, upon taking off his jacket, was about to hang it on a
        hanger.'

Yoo to suru is a modal that means 'be about to do something', in which *yoo*
'appearance' is a formal noun that is modified by a preceding verb phrase.
Literally translated, (12a) means 'John did [that is, made] an appearance
of taking off his jacket and hanging it on a hanger'. The ungrammaticality
of (13a) shows that the modal *yoo to suru* cannot extend its command to the
left of *to*.

4. Scrambling
Observe the following sentences:

(14) a.   John wa boosi o $\{$ nui-de $\}$, Mary ni aisatusita.
          $\qquad\quad$ hat $\quad\{$ nug-i $\}$ $\qquad\quad$ to greeted
          $\qquad\qquad\qquad$ take-off
        'John took off his hat and greeted Mary.'

   b.   John wa, Mary ni, boosi o $\{$ nui-de $\}$ aisatusita.
        $\qquad\qquad\qquad\qquad\qquad\{$ nug-i $\}$

(15) a.   John wa, boosi o nugu to, Mary ni aisatusita.
          'John, upon taking off his hat, greeted Mary.'

   b.   ?John wa, Mary ni, boosi o nugu to, aisatusita.

In both (14b) and (15b), *Mary ni*, an element of V_2, has been preposed to
the left of V_1. Sentence (14b) is perfectly normal, while (15b) is awkward
even though the sentence is still felt to be grammatical. This must be due
to the fact that V_1 *to* is not as closely subordinated to the V_2 as V_1-*te*/-*i* is.

On the other hand, the grammaticality (in spite of its awkwardness) of (15b) indicates that V_1 *to* is still subordinate to V_2. If V_1 and V_2 formed a coordinate structure "V_1 and V_2," no element of V_2 could be preposed to the left of V_1. For example, observe the following:

(16) a. John wa, e   o kaku *si*, haiku o tukuru.
                 picture   paint and poem   compose
         'John paints pictures and composes poems.'

     b. John wa, e o kaita   si,   haiku o tukutta.
                     painted and poem   composed
         'John painted pictures and composed poems.'

     c. *John wa, haiku o, e o kaita si, tukutta.[6]

The awkwardness of (15b) indicates that V_1 *to* V_2 has a status somewhere between the "subordinate phrase–main phrase" construction and the co-ordinating construction (probably closer to the former than to the latter).

Toki 'time when' and *node* 'because' behave in the following manner with respect to the pattern under consideration:

(17) a. John wa, Mary ga Tokyo ni kita   *toki*, kanozyo ni   atta.
                                  to came time she   with met
        'John met Mary when she came to Tokyo.'

     b. John wa, Mary ni, kanozyo ga Tokyo ni kita *toki*, atta.

(18) a. John wa, yoozi   ga atta *node*,   Mary ni   atta.
                 business   had because   with met
        'John met Mary because he had some business (to discuss with her).'

     b. John wa, Mary ni, yoozi ga atta *node*, atta.

The grammaticality of (17b) and (18b) shows that the *toki* clause and the *node* clause have a full status as subordinate clauses as far as the preposing of an element of V_2 to the left of V_1 is concerned.

[6] The same holds when V_1-*i* V_2 represents, not two successive actions, but two independent actions. Although (14a) is grammatical, (ii) is ungrammatical:

(i)   John wa e   o kak-*i*, haiku o tukuru.
              picture   paint poem   compose
      'John paints pictures and composes poems.'

(ii) *John wa haiku o, e   o kak-i, tukuru.
              poem   picture   paint compose

5. Subjects

Consider the following sentences (ϕ marks the position of the underlying subject for the latter half of each sentence):

(19) a. John *ga* uwagi o (nui-*de*) , ϕ hangaa ni kaketa.
　　　　　　　　　　 (nug-*i*)

　　　　'John took off his jacket and ϕ hung it on a hanger.'
　　　　(ϕ must be John)

　　 b. John *ga* uwagi o nugu *to*, ϕ hangaa ni kaketa.
　　　　'John took off his jacket and ϕ hung it on a hanger.'
　　　　(ϕ can be someone else)

Sentences (19a,b) are different from (1a,b,c) in that the subject particle *ga* appears instead of the thematic particle *wa*. The subject of V_2 in (19a) is invariably *John*. On the other hand, the subject of V_2 in (19b) can be either *John* or someone else under discussion.[7] This difference, it seems, is due to the fact that V_1 -*te*/-*i* V_2 forms a single verb phrase constituent such that the command power of NP-*ga* is obligatorily extended to VP_2, while VP_1 *to* VP_2 consists of two separate verb phrases $[VP_1$ *to*] $[VP_2]$ so that the command power of NP-*ga* may optionally be terminated at the first constituent without being extended to VP_2.

When V_1 -*te*/-*i* V_2 appears with two different subjects, V_1 ceases to be subordinate to V_2.

(20) John ga uwagi o (nui-de) , Mary ga hangaa ni kaketa.
　　　　　　　　　 (nug-i)

　　　'John took off his jacket, and Mary hung it on a hanger.'

That (20) represents two juxtaposed (coordinated) events can be witnessed by the fact that *Mary*, an element of the second clause, cannot become the topic of the sentence.

(21) **Mary wa*, John ga uwagi o (nui-de) , hangaa ni kaketa.
　　　　　　　　　　　　　　 (nug-i)

　　　'Speaking of Mary, John took off his jacket, and (she) hung it on a hanger.'

---

[7] This observation is due to Mikami (1970).

Note that the same applies to the coordinating structures connected by *si*.

(22) a. *John ga* e   o kaita   *si,*   *Mary ga haiku* o tukutta.
                  picture   painted and   poem   composed
          'John painted a picture, and Mary composed a poem.'

   b. **Mary wa,* John ga e o kaita *si,* haiku o tukutta.
          'Speaking of Mary, John painted a picture, and (she) composed
          a poem.'

On the other hand, S_1 *to* of S_1 *to* S_2, even when two different subjects are involved, still retains its subordinate nature. *Mary* of (23a) can become the topic of the sentence.

(23) a. John ga uwagi o nugu to, Mary ga hangaa ni kaketa.
          'Upon John's taking off his jacket, Mary hung it on a hanger.'

   b. Mary wa, John ga uwagi o nugu *to,* hangaa ni kaketa.
          'Speaking of Mary, upon John's taking off his jacket, (she) hung
          it on a hanger.'

We have seen in (19) that in *NP-ga* V_1 *-te/-i* V_2 the subject of V_2 must be NP-*ga* but that in *NP-ga* V_1 *to* V_2 it can be someone else. Moreover, V_1 *si* V_2 ('V_1 and V_2') behaves like V_1 *-te/-i* V_2, while V_1 *toki* V_2 ('when V_1, V_2') and V_1 *node* V_2 ('since V_1, V_2') behave like V_1 *to* V_2. Observe the following examples:

(24) a. John ga e   o kaku *si,* ϕ haiku o tukuru.
                  picture   paint and   poem   compose
          'John paints pictures and composes poems.' (ϕ must be John)

   b. John ga kita *toki,* ϕ atta.
                came when   met
          'When John came, *I/he/she* met him.' (ϕ is someone else)

   c. John ga kita *node,* ϕ atta.
                came because   met
          'Since John came, *I/he/she* met him.' (ϕ is someone else)

There is an instance in which the command of *NP-ga* V_1 *-te* V_2 may end at V_1: that is when the construction represents the cause-effect relationship.[8] For example,

[8] This observation is due to Kazue Campbell (personal communication).

(25) a. John ga ki-*te*, hotto sita.
                    come was-relieved
      'I was relieved by John's coming.'

   b. *John ga* ki-*te*, nigiyaka-ni natta.
               come lively   became
      'It became lively due to John's coming.'

6. Summary

Diagram (26) summarizes the observations given in this section.

(26)

		Subordination			Coordination	
	tight ————————————→loose					
	-*te*/-*i*	*toki*	*node*	*to*	-*te*/-*i*	*si*
	'-ing then'	'when'	'because'	'upon -ing'	'and'	'and'
a. Can *ka?* command V_1?	yes	yes	no	no	no	no
b. Can sentence-final negative negate V_1?	yes	yes	no	no	no	no
c. Can sentence-final modal command V_1?	yes	yes	no	no	no	no
d. Can an element of V_2 be preposed to the left of V_1?	yes	yes	yes	yes?	no	no
e. Can the command of NP-*ga* end at V_1?	no	yes	yes	yes	no	no

The diagram is simply a typological categorization of various subordinating and coordinating constructions in Japanese. Why these differences exist in the degree of subordination and how they can be represented in sentence structures are the questions that I have not attempted to answer. These questions deserve careful and exhaustive examination.

V
Nominal and Adjectival Clauses

18†

Koto, No, and *To*

Some verbs take noun clauses ending with *koto* as their object, certain others take those ending with *no*, and still others take those ending with *to*. Observe the following:

(1) a. Watakusi wa John ga Mary o butu *no* o (**koto* o/**to*) mita.
    I   hits   saw
    'I saw John hitting Mary.'

    b. Watakusi wa nihongo ga muzukasii *koto* o (**no* o/**to*) mananda.
    I   Japanese   difficult-is   learned
    'I learned that Japanese is difficult.'

    c. John wa nihongo ga muzukasii *to* (**koto* o/**no* o) itta.
               Japanese   difficult-is   said
    'John said that Japanese is difficult.'

The question is whether, given a verb and its meaning, one can predict which of the three forms, *koto o, no o,* or *to,* to use for this verb or whether one has to learn, for each verb, whether it takes *koto o, no o,* or *to.* The answer to this question is that one can predict, to a certain degree, although there are a great many idiosyncratic factors still involved.

    There is a fairly clear-cut distinction between *koto* and *no,* on the one hand, and *to,* on the other. The *koto* and *no* clauses represent an action, state, or event that the speaker presupposes to be true, while the *to* clause represents an action, state, or event that does not have such a presupposition. The term "presupposition" requires some explanation. Compare the following sentences in English:

(2) a. John thought that Mary had left.

    b. John heard that Mary had left.

    c. John believed that Mary had left.

(3) a. John regretted that Mary had left.

    b. John remembered that Mary had left.

    c. John was glad that Mary had left.

†This chapter should be interesting both to linguists and to students of Japanese.

In (2) the speaker (or the writer) does not presuppose that *Mary had left* is a true proposition.[1] Compare this with (3). In (3) that Mary had left is presupposed to be true by the speaker. That the presupposition in (3) is made by the speaker, and not by the subject of the sentences, is clear from the following examples:

(4) a. John knew that Mary had left.

    b. John did not know that Mary had left.

In (4b) John did not know that Mary had left, and therefore he could not have formed that presupposition. Sentence (4b) could be paraphrased as

(4) c. Mary had left, but John did not know it.

The absence and the presence of presuppositions in (2) and (3), respectively, become clearer in (5), where a context is given in which it is denied that Mary had left.

(5) a.   John thought that Mary had left, but in fact she had not left yet.

    b. *John regretted that Mary had left, but in fact she had not left.

Also observe that the presupposition of (3) remains intact even when the entire sentences are negated.

(6) a. John did not regret that Mary had left.

    b. John did not remember that Mary had left.

    c. John was not glad that Mary had left.

    d. John did not think that Mary had left.

In (6a,b,c) the presupposition that Mary had left is still present.[2]

    It should be pointed out that presupposition is a concept distinct from that of assertion. Compare the following two sentences:

(7) a. I was aware that Mary had left.

    b. I asserted that Mary had left.

In both sentences the speaker asserts that Mary had left. However, there

---

[1] Hereafter, the term "presupposition" will be used as an abbreviation for "the speaker's presupposition that the proposition of the action, state, or event represented by the noun clause has the truth-value true."

[2] The significance of the concept of presupposition for syntactic description was first pointed out by Paul Kiparsky and Carol Kiparsky (1971).

is no presupposition in (7b) that the proposition is true, while there is in (7a). Therefore, when the two sentences are negated, the presupposition that Mary had left is still present in the negative form of (7a), but not in that of (7b). Sentence (7d) neither presupposes nor asserts that Mary had left.

(7) c. I was not aware that Mary had left.

    d. I did not assert that Mary had left.

Similarly, a proposition occurring with a presupposition of its own truth can be preceded by *the fact that*, while a proposition with only an assertion cannot be.

(8) a.   I was aware of the fact that Mary had left.

    b. *I asserted the fact that Mary had left.

With regard to our Japanese examples, it is natural that *to*, which was originally a particle for reporting someone else's statement, be used for representing an action, state, or event about which the speaker has not made a presupposition. Observe the following sentences:

(9) a.   John wa Mary ga baka   da *to* omotta.
                      stupid is   thought
    'John thought that Mary was stupid.'
    *John wa Mary ga baka na *koto* o omotta.

    b. John wa Mary ga tunbo de aru ⎧ *koto* ⎫ o wasurete ita.
                      deaf   is   ⎩ *no* ⎭ forgot
    'John forgot that Mary was deaf.'
    *John wa Mary ga tunbo de aru *to* wasurete-ita.

Omou 'to think' does not contain a presupposition, and therefore *to*, and not *koto o*, is used in (9a). On the other hand, *wasureru* 'to forget' presupposes the truth-value of what precedes it, and therefore *koto o*, *no o*, and not *to*, is used in (9b).

There are some verbs that can take both *to* and *koto/no*. Consider the subtle difference in meaning depending upon which of the two classes is used.

(10) a. John wa Mary ga baka   da *to* nageita.
                   stupid is   deplored

'(Lit.) John deplored that Mary was stupid (she might or might not have been stupid).'

b. John wa Mary ga baka na *koto* o negeita.
'John deplored the fact that Mary was stupid (she was stupid).'

(11) a. John wa Mary ga sinda *to* sinzinakatta.
                    died   not-believed
'John did not believe that Mary was dead (Mary might or might not have been dead).'

b. John wa Mary ga sinda *koto* o sinzinakatta.
'John did not believe that Mary was dead (she was dead).'

(12) a. John wa Mary ga sinda *to* utagawanakatta.
                    died   not-doubted
'John did not doubt, (believing) that Mary was dead (Mary might or might not have been dead).'

b. John wa Mary ga sinda *koto* o utagawanakatta.
'John did not doubt that Mary was dead (she was dead).'

(13) a. John wa Mary ga hannin da *to* suiteisita.
                    culprit is   inferred
'John inferred that Mary was the culprit (Mary might or might not have been the culprit).'

b. John wa Mary ga hannin de aru *koto* o suiteisita.
                              is
'John inferred, correctly, that Mary was the culprit.'

(14) a. John wa Mary o korosite simatta   *to* zihakusita.
                    killing ended-up-with   confessed
'John confessed that he had killed Mary (he might have given a false confession).'

b. John wa Mary o korosite simatta *koto* o zihakusita.
'John confessed the fact that he had killed Mary.'

(15) a. John wa Mary ga sinde simatta   *to* kiita.
                    dying ended-up-with   heard.
'John heard that Mary had died.'

   b. John wa Mary ga sinde simatta *koto* o kiita.
      'John heard about the fact that Mary had died.'

The following are examples of verbs that can take only *to* clauses:

(16) a. John wa Mary ga sinda *to* (*koto o/*no o)
                 died

      haya-gattensita.
      formed-the-hasty-conclusion
      'John formed the hasty conclusion that Mary had died.'

   b. John wa Mary ga sinda *to* (*koto o/*no o) itta.
                 died   said
      'John said that Mary had died.'

   c. John wa Mary ga sinda *to* (*koto o/*no o) kantigaisita.
                 died   made-the-wrong-guess
      'John made the wrong guess that Mary had died.'

   d. John wa Mary sa sinda *to* (*koto o/*no o) gokaisita.
      'John formed the wrong notion that Mary had died.'

The following are examples of verbs that can take only *koto/no* clauses:

(17) a. John wa Mary ga tunbo de aru *koto* o/*no* o (*to) omoidasita.
                      deaf   is   recalled
      'John recalled that Mary was deaf.'

   b. John wa Mary ga tunbo de aru *koto* o/*no* o (*to) wasurete-ita.
                      deaf   is   had-forgotten
      'John had forgotten that Mary was deaf.'

For some mysterious reason, *siru* 'to get to know' can be used with *to* in certain contexts.

(18) a. *Anata wa Mary ga tunbo da *to* sitte-imasu ka?
      you   deaf is   know
      'Do you know that Mary is deaf?'

   b. Watakusi wa Mary ga tunbo da *to* sono toki sitta.
      I   deaf is   that time got-to-know
      'I got to know then that Mary was deaf.'

   c. Watakusi ga Mary ga tunbo da *to* sitta   no wa sono
      I   deaf is   got-to-know that   that
      toki datta.
      time was
      'It was then that I got to know that Mary was deaf.'

(19) a. *Mary ga konna baka da *to* sitte-imasita ka?
                such fool is   knew
         'Did you know that Mary was such a fool?'

     b. *Mary ga konna baka da *to* wa sitte-imasita ka?
                such fool is   know
         'Did you know that Mary was such a fool?'

     c. Mary ga konna baka da *to* sirimasen desita.
               such fool is   did-not-know
        'I didn't know that Mary was such a fool.'

     d. Mary ga konna baka da *to* wa sirimasen desita.
               such fool is   did-not-know
        'I did not know that Mary was such a fool.'

It is unclear why (18b,c) and (19c,d) are acceptable. The fact that it is difficult to find acceptable contexts, such as those of (18b,c) and (19c,d), and that it is easy to find unacceptable sentences, such as (18a) and (19a,b), indicates that the acceptability of (18b,c) and (19c,d) is what requires special explanation. Both sentences have some peculiar story-telling flavor and are suspect of being the remnants of old expressions.

So far, we have discussed all those cases in which noun clauses are the objects of transitive verbs. When noun clauses are used as subjects, complications arise because *to* cannot form subject noun clauses. Two compound forms *to yuu koto* and *to yuu no*, both literally meaning 'the thing that says that', are used instead. When the predicate of a subject noun clause contains the presupposition of the truth of the clause, all the four forms—namely, *koto*, *no*, *to yuu koto*, and *to yuu no*—can potentially be used as complementizers. For example,

(20) a. John ga kekkon tyokugo   sinde simatta ⎰ *koto/no* ⎱
            marriage right-after died   ⎱ *to yuu koto/no* ⎰
      wa higeki   da.
          tragedy
      'It is a tragedy that John died right after he got married.'

b. John ga sono yuuwaku o kippari sirizoketa (*koto/no*)
      the temptation resolutely rejected (*to yuu koto/no*)
wa migoto   da.
admirable is
'It is admirable that John rejected the temptation resolutely.'

On the other hand, when the predicate does not contain a presupposition, *koto* and *no* cannot be used.

(21) a. John ga Mary o nagutta (**koto/*no*) wa ariuru koto da.
               hit   (*to yuu koto/no*) possible thing is
    'It is probable that John hit Mary.'

    b. John ga Mary o nagutta (**koto/*no*) wa uso da.[3]
                hit   (*to yuu koto/no*) lie is
    'It is false that John hit Mary.'

With regard to the uses of *koto, no*, and *to* for sentential object marking, there are several classes that can take *koto/no* for which there doesn't seem to be any presupposition involved. For example,

(22) a. Watakusi wa oyogu *koto* ga dekiru.
      I   swim to   am-able
    'I can swim.'

    b. Eigo   o hanasu *no* wa muzukasii.
      English speak to   is-difficult
    'To speak English is difficult.'

Neither (22a) nor (22b) contains any presupposition about the truth-value of someone's swimming or speaking English. What is common to all these classes is the fact that only the present tense is allowable for the verbs of their object clauses. It is quite likely that the *koto* and *no* of this usage are of a different origin from those which I have been discussing until now. What follows is an examination of the uses of *koto* and *no* that do not involve presuppositions.

    Verbs of perception can take only *no* clauses. Observe the following:

(23) a. Watakusi wa John ga Mary o butu (*no*) o mita.
      I   hit (**koto*) saw
    'I saw John hitting Mary.'

[3] This paragraph is based on the observation presented by Masako Inoue (1971).

    b. Watakusi wa John ga piano o hiku (*no*) o kiita.
      I   play (**koto*) heard
      'I heard John playing the piano.'

    c. Watakusi wa sesuzi ga samuku naru (*no*) o kanzita.
      I   spine   cold   get (**koto*) felt
      'I felt a cold shiver running down my spine.'

Sentence (23b) with *koto* would be acceptable, but it would no longer be a statement of perception by any of the five senses: it would mean 'I heard that John plays the piano'. Similarly, *kanziru* 'to feel' can take a *koto* clause, but then it would mean no longer 'to feel by five senses', but 'to think'.

    Verbs of ordering can take *koto* clauses, but not *no* clauses.

(24) a. Watakusi wa John ni hatarake   *to* meizita.
      I   to work (imperative)   ordered
      '(Lit.) I ordered John "Work!"'

    b. Watakusi wa John ni hataraku *koto* (**no*) o meizita.
      I   work   ordered
      'I ordered John to work.'

(25) Watakusi wa John ni hataraku *koto* (**no*) o yookyuusita/
    I   work   demanded
    tanonda/kyooseisita.
    asked   forced
    'I demanded/asked/forced John to work.'

That *no* cannot be used for ordering verbs might be due to the fact that actions ordered cannot yet be perceived by any of the five senses.

    With verbs of expecting it is preferable to use *koto*, but *no* and *to* are also acceptable.

(26) a. Mary wa John ga kuru *koto* o kitaisite-ita.
                    come   was-expecting
        'Mary was expecting that John would come.'

    b. Mary wa John ga kuru *no* o kitaisite-ita.

    c. Mary wa John ga kuru *to* kitaisite-ita.

There seems to be some subtle difference in meaning among these three sentences. Sentence (26c) most likely means that the expectation did not come true. This seems to be related to the nonpresuppositional nature of *to*. Between (26a) and (26b), it seems to be the case that the latter represents a stronger conviction on the part of the subject that John would come. This might be due, again, to the fact that *no* represents a concrete action, state, or event directly perceived by any of five (or six) senses, while *koto* represents a more abstract concept.

Verbs of waiting ordinarily take *no*, but they can take *koto* when the clause represents a general and abstract concept.

(27) a. Watakusi wa John ga kuru   *no* (**koto*) o matta.
      I   coming   waited
      'I waited for John to come.'

    b. Watakusi wa sekai ni heiwa ga otozureru ⎰ *no* ⎱ o matte-imasu.
       I   world to peace   visits   ⎱ *koto* ⎰ am-waiting
       'I am waiting for peace to descend on the world.'

As has been mentioned before, *koto* is used for nominalizing a proposition and forming an abstract concept out of the proposition, while *no* is used for representing a concrete event. From this point of view, it is natural that only *no* can be used for marking the object of perceptive verbs, as in (23). One can see or hear a concrete event, but not an abstract concept. There are verbs that can take only a concrete event as their object, such as those of perception, and there are verbs that can take only an abstract concept, such as *kangaeru* 'to think', *omou* 'to think'. There are also some verbs that can take both an abstract concept and a concrete event as their object: *wasureru* 'to forget', *omoidasu* 'to recall', *nageku* 'to deplore', *sinziru* 'to believe', etc. In this connection, it should be pointed out that there are propositions that cannot be events. For example,

(28) a. Columbus ga Amerika o hakkensita.
               America   discovered
      'Columbus discovered America.'

    b. Kuzira wa honyuu-doobutu de aru.
       whale   mammal   is
       'A whale is a mammal.'

Sentence (28a) can be an abstract concept or a concrete event, but (28b) cannot be a concrete event. Therefore, it is expected that nominalizing

(28b) with *no* would result in an awkward clause. That this is so can be seen from the following examples:

(29) a. Watakusi wa Columbus ga Amerika o hakkensita
      I   discovered

$\begin{Bmatrix} koto \\ no \end{Bmatrix}$ o siranakatta.
        knew-not

'I did not know (the fact) that Columbus discovered America.'

  b. Watakusi wa kuzira ga honyuu-doobutu de aru
       I   whale   mammal   is

$\begin{Bmatrix} koto \\ *no \end{Bmatrix}$ o siranakatta.
        knew-not

'I did not know the fact that a whale is a mammal.'

The ungrammaticality/awkwardness of some of the following sentences can be accounted for by the same argument:

(30) a. Columbus ga Amerika o hakkensita $\begin{Bmatrix} koto \\ no \end{Bmatrix}$ wa syuuti
                              discovered   well-known
     no zizitu desu.
        fact   is

'That Columbus discovered America is a well-known fact.'

  b. Kuzira ga honyuu-doobutu de aru $\begin{Bmatrix} koto \\ *?no \end{Bmatrix}$ wa syuuti
     whale   mammal   is   well-known
     no zizitu desu.
        fact   is

'That a whale is a mammal is a well-known fact.'

(31) a. John ga sinda $\begin{Bmatrix} no \\ koto \end{Bmatrix}$ wa tasika desu.
           died   certain is

'It is certain that John has died.'

  b. John ga zyussai   de aru $\begin{Bmatrix} koto \\ *?no \end{Bmatrix}$ wa tasika desu.
         ten-years-old   is   certain is

'It is certain that John is ten years old.'

What is interesting about these examples is that the relation between *koto* and *no* is controlled not only by verbs, adjectives, and nominal adjectives of the main sentences but also secondarily by the semantic content of the subordinate clause.

19†

No Desu 'It Is That'

In Japanese, the peculiar patterns *no da* (informal), *no desu* (polite), and *no de aru* (formal writing), which can be roughly translated as 'it is that', are extensively used in connected discourses. In formal speech even *no de aru no de aru* 'it is that it is that' appears. In this chapter I shall clarify the meaning of this pattern by giving contexts in which sentences either with or without *no desu*, but not both, are acceptable, contrast it with *kara desu* 'it is because', and discuss the syntactic role of subjects in *no desu* sentences.

Observe the following pairs of sentences:

(1) a. Kaze o hiita.
     cold   drew
     'I've caught a cold.'

   b. Kaze o hiita *no desu.*
     'It is that I've caught a cold.'

(2) a. Watakusi wa baka da.
     I   fool am
     'I am a fool.'

   b. Watakusi wa baka na[1] no desu.
     'It is that I am a fool.'

From a purely formal point of view, *no desu* consists of the nominalizing particle *no* and the copulative *desu*. Therefore, for example, (1b) is literally translated as '(It) is that (I) have caught a cold'. The meaning of this

---

†This chapter should be of interest both to linguists and to students of Japanese.
[1] Copulative *da* is realized as *na* (or *no*) in an adjectival clause. For example,

(i)   Kimi wa baka da.
     you   fool are
     'You are a fool.'

(ii) Kimi wa baka *na* otoko da.
                   is   man
     'You are a stupid man.'

(iii) Kimi ga baka na koto wa minna   ga sitte-iru.
      you   fool are fact-that everyone   knowing-is
     'Everyone knows the fact that you are a fool.'

construction is lucidly described in Alfonso (1966, p. 405), as quoted here:

Basically, the meaning of a sentence does not change by the addition of NO DESU to it. However, the presence of NO DESU adds certain overtones to the statement, for it indicates some EXPLANATION, either of what was said or done, or will be said or done, and as such always suggests some context or situation. Contrast sentences without and with NO DESU:

(a) Hanashi ga arimasu.
　　　talk　　　　have
　　　'I have something to tell you.'
　　　Chotto matte kudasai. Hanashi ga aru　n(o) desu.
　　　a little wait　please　　talk　　　　have
　　　'Just a moment please. I have something to tell you.'
　　　('Hanashi ga aru n desu' explains why the other is requested to wait.)

(b) Tsutomeru tokoro ga nai desu.
　　　work　　　place　　exist-not
　　　'There are no jobs available anywhere.'
　　　Oota san wa tsutomete imasen ne.
　　　　　　　　　　working　is-not
　　　'Mr. Oota, you are not employed, are you.'
　　　Tsutomeru tokoro ga nai n desu.
　　　work　　　place　　exist-not
　　　(Oota san explains why he is not employed.)

(c) Omoshiroi desu ka, sono hon　wa?
　　　interesting is　　　　that book
　　　'That book, is it interesting?' (You ask of someone who is reading one.)
　　　Omoshiroi n desu ka?
　　　(You ask of someone whose attention is visibly absorbed, or who has broken into a smile or a laugh.)

(d) Are wa doo shimashita ka?
　　　that　how did
　　　'What happened to that business (you told me about)?'
　　　Doo shita n desu ka?
　　　'What's the matter?'
　　　(In the first case you merely asked your friend a question for information. In the second case you are asking for an explanation of his worried look or his sickly appearance or his unusual haste or the like. If he were not looking well his answer might be:
　　　Atama ga itai　　n desu. 'It is that I have a headache.')
　　　head　　painful

The following are some more examples of the *no desu* construction:

(3) a. Kaze o hikimasita. Ame ni hurarete　　nureta *no desu*.
　　　　cold　drew　　　rain by fallen-being got-wet
　　　　'I have caught a cold. (Lit.) The explanation for my having caught a cold is that I was rained on and drenched.'

b. Kinoo   yasunde simaimasita.   Kibun ga warukatta *no desu*.
   yesterday resting ended-up-with feeling   bad-was
   'I absented myself yesterday. (Lit.) The explanation for my
   absence is that I didn't feel well.'

c. Taizyuu ga zyuppondo herimasita. Byooki na *no desu*.
   weight   ten-pounds lessened   sick
   'I have lost ten pounds. (Lit.) The explanation for my loss of
   weight is that I am sick.'

The interrogative *no desu ka* asks for the hearer's explanation of what
the speaker has heard or observed.

(4) a. Kaoiro   ga warui desu ne. Byooki na *no desu* ka?
      complexion bad   sick
      'You don't look well. Is the explanation for your not looking well
      that you are sick?'

   b. Kibun ga warui *no desu* ka?
      feeling   bad-is
      '(I have observed that you don't look well.) Is the explanation for
      this that you don't feel well?'

   c. Dokoka   e iku *no desu* ka?
      somewhere go
      '(I see that you are preparing to go out.) Is the explanation for
      this that you are going somewhere?'

   d. Doko e iku *no desu* ka?
      where to go
      '(I see that you are ready to go out.) Where is it that you are
      going?'

   e. Nani o site-imasu ka?
      what doing-are
      'What are you doing?'

      Nani o site-iru *no desu* ka?
      '(You seem to be involved in something.) What is it that you are
      doing?'

   f. Naze naite-imasu ka?
      why crying-are
      'Why are you crying?' (a neutral question and hence very un-
      natural when used in addressing someone who is crying now)

Naze naite-iru *no desu* ka?
'(You are crying.) Why is it that you are crying?'

g. Ame ga hutte-imasu ka?
    rain   falling-is
    'Is it raining?'

Ame ga hutte-iru *no desu* ka?
'(You have an umbrella, you look drenched, etc.) Is it the case that it is raining?'

h. Benkyoosite-imasu ka?
    studying-are
    'Are you studying?' (ordinarily a question, not about the present moment, but about habitual actions, namely, 'Are you studying these days?')

Benkyoosite-iru *no desu* ka?
'(You look absorbed in something.) Is it that you are studying now?'

In the examples given in (3), the explanation given for what has been said happens to be the cause of the stated fact, also. Therefore, we get grammatical sentences with *no desu* replaced by *kara desu* 'it is because'. For example, parallel to (3a), we can have

(5) Kaze o hikimasita. Ame ni hurarete   nureta *kara desu*.
    cold   drew   rain by fallen-being got-wet
    'I have caught a cold. It is because I was rained on and drenched.'

However, not all explanations give causes. The following sentences would become extremely awkward or ungrammatical if *no desu* were to be replaced by *kara desu*.

(6) a. Byooki desu. Taizyuu ga zyuppondo hetta   *no desu*.
       sick   weight   ten-pounds lessened
       'I am sick. The explanation (or evidence) for my being sick is that I have lost ten pounds.'

b. Boku wa baka desu. Ikura   benkyoosite mo   dame na *no desu*.
    I   fool   how-hard if-I-study   even no-good
    'I am a fool. The explanation (or evidence) for my being a fool is that I am no good however hard I may study.'

   c. John wa kitigai desu. Dare   ni demo kenka o hukikakete
           insane   everyone to   quarrel provoking
   kuru *no desu.*
   come
   'John is insane. The explanation (or evidence) for John's insanity
   is that he provokes a quarrel with everyone.'

Compare (6a) with (3c). The speaker's being sick is the reason for his having lost ten pounds. In (3c) his being sick is used as an explanation for his having lost ten pounds. On the other hand, in (6a) his having lost ten pounds is presented as an explanation (or as evidence) of his being sick. Sentence (6a) with *kara desu* would mean that the speaker has become sick because he lost ten pounds and would be grammatical only in that peculiar interpretation. The *kara desu* construction is grammatical only when what has been said can become the subject of this construction with *no wa*. For example,

  (7) a. Taizyuu ga zyuppondo herimasita. Byooki da *kara desu.*
          weight   ten-pounds lessened   sick
      b. Taizyuu ga zyuppondo hetta *no wa* byooki da *kara desu.*
          'It is because I am sick that I have lost ten pounds.'

  (8) a.   Byooki desu. *Taizyuu ga zyuppondo hetta *kara desu.*
      b. *Byooki na *no wa* taizyuu ga zyuppondo hetta *kara desu.*
          'It is because I have lost ten pounds that I am sick.'

In (7) the *no wa . . . kara desu* construction is acceptable, and hence (7a) is grammatical. In (8), on the other hand, the *no wa . . . kara desu* construction is unacceptable in its ordinary interpretation, and therefore (8a) is ungrammatical. The main differences between *no desu* and *kara desu* are that (i) the former gives an explanation, and the latter a reason, for what has been said; and (ii) while the former accepts as its understood subject some vague circumstances such as the hearer's appearing to be ready to go out or not looking well, the latter requires that what has been said be syntactically qualified as its subject. The point will become clearer by observing the following examples:

  (9) a. Okane o kudasai.   Hon ga kaitai   *no desu.*
        money give-please book   want-to-buy
        'Please give me money. The explanation for this request is that I
        want to buy books.'

b. Okane o kudasai. *Hon ga kaitai *kara desu.*
'Please give me money. *That please give me money is because I want to buy books.'

c. Okane o kudasaru yoo   onegaisimasu. Hon ga kaitai *kara desu.*
                 so-that request
'I request that you give me money. That I request that you give me money is because I want to buy books.'

Sentence (9a) is grammatical because *no desu* in this example has as its implicit subject something like 'the explanation for this request'. Sentence (9b) is ungrammatical because the imperative *Okane o kudasai* 'Give me money' cannot become the subject of the *kara desu* construction. On the other hand, (9c) is grammatical because now we have a declarative sentence, and not an imperative one, preceding the *kara desu* sentence, and because the following construction is grammatical:

(9) d. Okane o kudasaru yoo onegaisuru *no wa* hon ga kaitai *kara desu.*
'It is because I want to buy books that I request that you give me money.'

Similarly,

(10) a. Kibun ga warui *no desu* ka?
         feeling   bad-is
         'Is it that you don't feel well?'
     b. *Kibun ga warui *kara desu* ka?

Sentence (10a) is grammatical, with the understood subject of the *no desu* construction being approximately 'the explanation for your not looking well', while such a vague and syntactically unspecified concept cannot become the subject of *kara desu*; hence, (10b) is ungrammatical.

More examples of the *no desu* construction follow:

(11) a. Okane ga amari arimasen kara,   mudazukai o sinaide
        money   much exist-not because waste   do-not
        kudasai.
        please
        'Since there isn't too much money, please don't use it wastefully.'
     b. Okane ga amari nai   *no desu* kara, mudazukai o sinaide
                        exist-not
        kudasai.

Example (11a) is a simple neutral request. On the other hand, (11b) implies that the speaker has some basis for suspecting that the hearer has been wasting money. It would be literally translated as 'The explanation for my worry is that there isn't too much money; therefore, please don't waste money'. Example (11b), if uttered to someone who has not shown signs of wasting money, would be a very impolite request.

(12) a. Hatizi   ni ie   o denakereba ikemasen. Sitizi
        eight o'clock   home   must-leave   seven o'clock
        made ni gohan ni site-kudasai.
        by   meal   serve please
        'I must leave home at eight. Please serve dinner by seven.'

     b. Hatizi ni ie o denakereba naranai *no desu*. Sitizi made ni gohan
        ni site-kudasai.
        'The explanation for my worry is that I must leave home at eight.
        Please serve dinner by seven.'

Sentence (12b) is appropriate only when there is a sign that the dinner may not be served in time. Even under such a circumstance, it has an overtone of reproach and should not be used unless the speaker is on friendly terms with the hearer (for example, the hearer is the wife of the speaker).

(13) a. ?*Nando   onazi koto o ittara,   wakarimasu ka?
           how-often same thing   if-I-said understand

     b.   Nando onazi koto o ittara, wakaru *no desu* ka?
          '(You seem not to have understood me.) How many times is it
          that I have to repeat the same thing to make you understand?'

The first part of the sentence, *nando onazi koto o ittara* '(lit.) how many times if I have said the same thing', is emphatic and shows the speaker's irritation at the hearer's not having understood him. Therefore, the neutral question *wakarimasu ka* 'do you understand?' is out of place and does not follow the first part naturally. Only the *no desu* construction is acceptable.

(14) a. Okane ga nakute   komatte-imasu. Sukosi kasite kudasai.
        money   have-not troubled-am   a little lend   please
        'I am in trouble because I don't have any money. Please lend me
        some.'

     b. Okane ga nakute komatte-iru *no desu*. Sukosi kasite kudasai.

Sentence (14a) is a neutral request. On the other hand, (14b) may imply that the hearer is supposed to have lent the speaker some money, and it has a reproachful tone: 'The explanation for my irritation with you is that I am in trouble since I don't have any money. Please lend me some'. Sentence (14b) may also mean 'The explanation of my looking worried is that I am in trouble because . . .'. In this interpretation, it does not have a reproachful tone.

(15) Kore kara kaimono ni iku *no desu* ga, nani ka   o-iriyoo no
      now from shopping on go   but anything in need be
      mono wa arimasen ka?
      things   exist-not
      'My explanation for being prepared to go out (for being dressed up, for calling you up, etc.) is that I am going shopping now. Is there anything that you need?'

I mentioned at the beginning of this chapter that, syntactically speaking, *no desu* consists of the nominalizing particle *no* and the copulative *desu*. Does *no* nominalize the entire string that precedes it? Recall that the thematic particle *wa* does not appear in a subordinate clause and that NP-*ga* with a stative predicate generally has the exhaustive-listing interpretation:[2]

(16) a.   [John *ga* baka na] koto wa minna   ga sitte-iru.
                  fool is that   everyone   knowing-is
      b. *[John *wa* baka na] koto wa minna ga sitte-iru.
          'That John is a fool is known to everyone.'

(17) John *ga* baka desu.
      'It is John who is a fool; John and only John is a fool.'

Now, observe the following sentence:

(18) John wa hon o yomu koto ga dekimasen. Kare *wa* mekura na
               book read to   cannot   he   blind is
      no desu.
      'John cannot read books. It is that he is blind.'

If *kare* were in a subordinate clause, forming a constituent with *mekura na* 'is blind', *ga* would appear after it just as *ga* appears in (16). The fact that

---

[2] See Chapter 3, "*Wa* and *Ga* (Part II)—Subjectivization."

wa is the form that appears here shows that the sentence has the *NP-wa S-no desu* pattern instead of [*NP-wa VP*]*-no desu*.

(19) Kare wa [baka na] no desu.

The preceding sentence would be literally translated as 'Talking about him, it is that (he) is stupid'. Similarly,

(20) John wa keisatu ni taihosaremasita. Kare *ga* hannin datta *no desu*.
           police by arrested-was   he   culprit was
     'John was arrested by the police. It was he who was the culprit.'

Kare in this example distinctly has the exhaustive-listing interpretation, thus indicating that it is not in a subordinate clause.

(21) Kare ga [hannin datta] no desu.

Likewise, replacing *kare wa* of (18) by *kare ga* would force a peculiar in-terpretation to the sentence: 'John cannot read books. (Therefore,) it must be he who is blind'. This is in accordance with the exhaustive-listing in-terpretation of *kare ga* with the stative predicate *mekura na no desu*. The foregoing two examples show that NP-*wa* and the NP-*ga* at the beginning of the *no desu* construction can be outside a subordinate clause that the particle *no* nominalizes.

It is not the case, however, that the NP-*ga* initiating the *no desu* con-struction must always be outside the *no* clause. Observe the following examples:

(22) Okane ga kakatte sikata   ga arimasen. Kodomo *ga*
     money   costing no-way-out   exist-not   child
     daigakusei   na *no desu*.
     college-student
     'It's costing me a hopeless amount of money. It is that my child is a college student.'

(23) Dare ka ii   onna no hito   wa imasen ka? John *ga* mada
     someone good girl is person   exist-not   still
     dokusin   na *no desu*.
     bachelor
     'Don't you know some nice girl? It is that John is still single.'

(24) Watakusi wa baka de wa arimasen. Anata *ga* rikoosugiru *no desu.*
      I   fool   am-not   you   too-bright-are
      'I am not a fool. It is that you are too bright.'

The italicized *ga*'s in the preceding examples do not have the exhaustive-listing reading in spite of the fact that the predicates in the *no* clauses are all stative. Therefore, we must conclude that these NP-*ga*'s are part of the subordinate clauses nominalized by *no*. For example, the second sentence of (22) has the following constituent structure:

(25) [Kodomo ga daigakusei na] *no desu.*

This conclusion is not at all contradictory with the previous one—that is, that the NP-*ga*, as in (20), is outside the *no* clause. In fact, it is possible to have two NP-*ga*'s in a *no desu* sentence: one outside the *no* clause, the other inside.

(26) Watakusi *ga* [kodomo *ga* sinda] *no desu.*
      I   child   died
      '(Lit.) It is I who it is the case that (my) child has died.'

(27) John *ga* [seiseki *ga* warui] *no desu.*
               grades   bad-is
      '(Lit.) It is John who it is that (his) grades are bad.'[3]

In summary, the following are some of the characteristics of the *no desu* construction:

(i) *No desu* gives some explanation for what the speaker has said or done or the state he is in.

(ii) *No desu ka* asks for the hearer's explanation for what the speaker has heard or observed.

[3] Sentences (26) and (27), respectively, are derived from the following by application of the Subjectivization transformation (see Chapter 3).

[Watakusi no kodomo ga sinda] no desu.
'It is that my child has died.'

[John no seiseki ga warui] no desu.
'It is that John's grades are bad.'

In parallel with the bracketing of (26) and (27) we also get

[Watakusi ga kodomo ga sinda] no desu.
'(Lit.) It is that I—my child has died.'

[John ga seiseki ga warui] no desu.
'(Lit.) It is that John—his grades are bad.'

(iii) When the *no desu* construction is paired with a request, it often acquires a reproachful tone. For example, see (11b).

(iv) In the immediate environment in which the speaker has made some observation, questions about the observation without using the *no desu* construction are often out of place. For example, in talking to a girl who is crying, the (a) sentences that follow are out of place:

    a.   *Naite-imasu ka?
        'Are you crying?'
      *Naze naite-imasu ka?
        'Why are you crying?'

    b.   Naite-iru *no desu* ka?
        'Is it that you are crying?'
      Naze naite-iru *no desu* ka?
        'Why is it that you are crying?'

See also (13).

(v) The NP-*ga* initiating the *no desu* construction can be either inside the *no* clause or outside it. For example,

Kare ga [hannin datta] no desu.
'It was he who was the culprit.'

[*Kodomo ga* daigakusei na] no desu.
'It is that my child is a college student.'

20[†]
Relative Clauses

Japanese relative clauses have several peculiarities in contrast to the corresponding construction in English.

1. Prenominal Position of Relative Clauses

They precede their "antecedents," while English relative clauses follow their antecedents. For example,

(1) a. Kore wa [*watakusi ga kaita*] *hon*   desu.
      this   I   wrote book is

    b. This is a *book* [*that I have written*].

In (1a) the relative clause *watakusi ga kaita* 'that I have written' precedes its antecedent *hon* 'book', while in (1b) the relative clause *that I have written* follows its antecedent *a book*.

2. Absence of Relative Words

Except in formal writings of direct-translation flavor,[1] Japanese lacks relative words corresponding to English *who, whom, whose, which, that, where,* etc. In (1b) the relative clause is initiated by the relative pronoun *that,* while in (1a) *watakusi ga kaita* is neither preceded nor followed by any form that might be called a relative pronoun.[2]

---

†This chapter should be of interest both to linguists and to students of Japanese.

[1] The phrase *tokoro no,* literally translated as 'of the place', is used as a relative pronoun in direct translation. For example,

(i) Kore wa John ga kaita *tokoro no* hon de aru.
    this   wrote   book is
    'This is the book that John has written.'

[2] The verb form that appears at the end of a relative clause is identical with that of a sentence-final verb. For example, the same form *kaita* 'wrote' is used for (1a) and

(i) Watakusi ga kono hon o *kaita.*
    'I wrote this.'

Unaccented adjectives appear without an accent in relative clauses, but with an accent sentence-finally.

(ii) Kore wa *atui*   hon desu.
     this   is-thick book is
    'This is a thick book.'

3. Restrictive and Nonrestrictive Clauses

Japanese has no phonological, morphological, or syntactic distinctions between restrictive and nonrestrictive relative clauses. Proper names and personal pronouns can be freely preceded by relative clauses. Observe the following:

(2) a. watakusi ni eigo   o osiete-iru   Mary (nonrestrictive)
       I   to English teaching-is
       'Mary, who is teaching me English'

   b. watakusi ga sitte-iru   Mary (restrictive)
       I   knowing-is
       'the Mary that I know'

(3) a. honyuu-doobutu de aru kuzira (nonrestrictive)
       mammal   is   whale
       'the whale, which is a mammal'

   b. nihon-kai ni sunde iru kuzira (restrictive)
       Japan sea in living is   whale
       'whales that live in the Japan Sea'

(4) a. anata no koto o itumo kangaete-iru watakusi (nonrestrictive)
       you 's thing always thinking-am I
       'I, who am thinking about you all the time'

   b. watakusi o nikunde-iru anata (nonrestrictive)
       I   hating-are you
       'you, who hate me'

4. Pronomial Trace after Relativization

In certain constructions in Japanese, a noun phrase in the relative clause that has been relativized can leave its trace as a pronoun. This is not possible in standard English. Before I explain the meaning of this statement,

---

(iii) Kono hon wa *atúi*.
      this book is-thick
      'This book is thick.'

The copula *da* appears as *na/no* in relative clauses. For example,

(iv) baka *na* hito
     stupid is person
     'a person who is stupid'

(v) Kono hito wa baka *da*.
    this man   stupid is
    'This man is stupid.'

I shall describe how English relative clauses are produced according to the hypothesis. Let us assume that (1b) is produced from an underlying abstract structure informally represented as follows:

(5) This is [[a book]$_{NP}$ [I have written the book]$_S$]$_{NP}$

Example (5) shows that *a book* is an NP (noun phrase), that *I have written the book* is an S (sentence), and that *a book* [*I have written the book*], in its entirety, is also an NP. The last string has the structure graphically representable as follows:

(6)

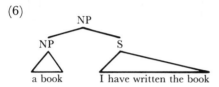

Now, a syntactic process called Relativization applies to (5). This process (or transformation) replaces *the book* (dominated by the S) with the relative pronoun *that* and moves the latter to the head of the relative clause, thus yielding (1b). The process of Relativization is very similar to what one might have been asked to do in a grade-school grammar course when given the following problem:

(7) Compose a single sentence using the following two sentences:
    This is a book. I have written the book.

In Japanese, let us tentatively assume[3] that Relativization is a process of simply deleting a noun phrase that is identical with the relative clause's antecedent. Therefore, (1a) is assumed to be derived from

(8) Kore wa [watakusi ga *sono hon*   o kaita] *hon*   desu.
    this   I   the book   wrote book is

Now, in English, *the book* of the relative clause in (5) is completely replaced by *that*, and after Relativization has been applied, there is no trace of its original presence in its original location (that is, after *written*). The following is not a grammatical sentence:

(9) *This is a book that I have written ⎰ *the book*.[4]
                                       ⎱ *it*.

---

[3] This assumption will be discussed in detail in the next chapter.
[4] In colloquial English, when certain conditions are met, it is possible to leave pronouns. For example,
(i) This is the man that, when I went to see *him*, I took Mary with me.

In Japanese, on the other hand, if certain conditions, which I shall not elaborate on here,[5] are met, a trace of the noun phrase to be relativized can be left in the form of a pronoun. The following is awkward, but not ungrammatical:

(10) a. [watakusi ga *sono okyaku-san* no namae o wasurete-simatta]
　　　 I　　　　　　　that guest　　　's　name　　have-forgotten
　　　okyaku-san
　　　guest

　　 b. [watakusi ga ⎰ *sono hito* ⎱ no namae o wasurete-simatta]
　　　　　　　　　　 that person
　　　　　　　　　　 kare
　　　　　　　　　　 he
　　　　　　　　　　 so
　　　　　　　　　　 that
　　　okyaku-san
　　　'a guest whose name I have forgotten'

In (10a) we have the abstract structure to which Relativization is presumed to apply. Observe that (10b) retains the trace of the original presence of *sono okyaku-san* 'the guest' in its original position in the form of quasi-pronominal *sono hito* 'that person' or pronominal *kare* 'he' or *so* 'that'. This phrase would be literally translated as 'a guest that I have forgotten *that person's* (or *his, that*) name', which, of course, is unacceptable in English.

5. Relativization from Adverbial Clauses

Another characteristic of Japanese relative clauses is that an element of an adverbial clause can be relativized. This again is not usually possible in English.[6] Observe the following phrases:

(11) a. sinda no de　 minna　 ga kanasinda　　 hito
　　　　died　because everyone　　was-distressed person

---

[5] The conditions will be discussed in some detail in the next chapter.
[6] It is, however, possible to relativize an element in *if* clauses in colloquial English:
(i) He is the man that I would be pleased if I could see.
Note that the following is ungrammatical:
(ii) *He is the man that if I could see, I would be pleased.
It seems that the *if* clause, for some reason or another, plays a noun-clause-like function in the embedded clause of (i).

b. '*a person who, because (he) died, everyone was saddened'

(12) a. hara-ippai tabetara, geri   o site   simatta   okasi[7]
     belly-full   when-ate diarrhea   doing ended-up-with cookies

    b. '*cookies which, when we had glutted ourselves with (them), we ended up with diarrhea'

In (11a) and (12a) the subject of *sinu* 'to die' and the object of *taberu* 'to eat', both of which are in adverbial clauses, have been relativized. The direct translation of these sentences results in ungrammatical English sentences, as shown in (11b) and (12b).

6. Relativization from Complex Noun Phrases

Let us define a *complex noun phrase* as a noun phrase followed by a relative clause or an appositional clause. There is a general constraint in English that no element in a relative clause or an appositional clause may be moved out of the complex NP of which the relative or appositional clause is a part.[8] For example, consider the following sentences:

(13) a. I believed the claim that Otto was wearing *this hat*.

    b. I believed that Otto was wearing *this hat*.

Since *Otto was wearing this hat* in (13a) is an appositional clause, that is, a clause appositional to *the claim*, we have a complex NP here. On the other hand, the same clause in (13b) plays the role of a sentential object of *believed*, and therefore (13b) does not contain a complex NP. The constraint stated earlier says that *this hat* of (13a) cannot be moved out of the complex NP *the claim that . . . this hat* by any transformation. Now, observe the following pairs of sentences:

(14) *Topicalization*

    a. *This hat, I believed the claim that Otto was wearing.

    b. This hat, I believed that Otto was wearing.

---

[7] For example, as in the following:
Kore wa kono-aida, *anata ga hara-ippai tabetara geri o site-simatta okasi desu kara, kyoo wa amari takusan tabete wa ikemasen yo*. 'These are cookies which, (lit.) when you glutted yourself the other day with (them), you ended up having diarrhea, so, don't eat too much today.'

[8] This constraint has been hypothesized by Ross (1967) as a constraint that is more or less a language universal and is applicable not simply to English but to many other languages that he has examined.

(15) *Cleft Sentence*
   a. *It is this hat that I believed the claim that Otto was wearing.
   b. It is this hat that I believed that Otto was wearing.

(16) *Wh-Question*
   a. *What did you believe the claim that Otto was wearing?
   b. What did you believe that Otto was wearing?

(17) *Relativization*
   a. *The hat which I believed the claim that Otto was wearing is red.
   b. The hat which I believed that Otto was wearing is red.

Example (17a) shows that Relativization, as well as Topicalization, Cleft Sentence Formation, and *Wh*-Question Formation, is subject to this constraint. Compare the preceding with this example:

(18) [[kawaigatte-ita]$_S$ inu ga sinde simatta]$_S$ kodomo
        was-fond-of   dog   dying ended-up-with child
    'the child who the dog (he) was fond of died'

In (18) what has been relativized (and deleted consequently) is *sono kodomo* (*ga*) 'the child', the subject of *kawaigatte-ita* 'was fond of'. However, *sono kodomo ga kawaigatte-ita* is a relative clause whose head noun is *inu* 'dog'. Therefore, we have here a complex NP *sono kodomo ga kawaigatte-ita inu* 'the dog that the child was fond of', to which Relativization has presumably been applied. Example (18) should be an ungrammatical noun phrase if the constraint that was shown to be applicable to English were also applicable to Japanese. However, (18) is a grammatical phrase.

More examples of the same type follow. Direct translation is given to each Japanese expression.

(20) [kite-iru   yoohuku ga yogorete-iru] sinsi
        wearing-is suit   dirty-is   gentleman
    'a gentleman who the suit that (he) is wearing is dirty'

(21) [osiete-ita   seito   ga rakudaisita] sensei
        teaching-was student   flunked   teacher
    'the teacher who the students that (he) was teaching flunked'

(22) [ooensite-ita   team ga maketa] hitotati
        backing-were   lost   people
    'people who the team (they) were backing has lost'

(23) [dasita tegami ga todokanakatta] hito
    mailed letter   did-not-reach   person
    'persons who the letters that (they) mailed have not reached (the
    addresses)'

   The preceding observation does not mean that a noun phrase in a complex NP is freely relativizable. Besides, the native speakers' intuition varies
a great deal with respect to the grammaticality or ungrammaticality of
these complex sentences. Native speakers agree that (20) through (23) are
all grammatical expressions. Some native speakers accept the following
phrases, while some others do not:

(24) a. ?[Bill ga korosita to yuu zihaku   o keisatu ga mada
         he   killed   that   confession police   yet
         urazukesite-inai]   onna
         substantiating-is-not woman
         'the woman who the police have not substantiated yet Bill's
         confession that he has killed (her)'
    b. ?[John o korosita zizitu o watakusi ga tukitometa] onna
         killed   fact   I   ascertained woman
         'the woman who I have ascertained the fact that (she) killed
         John'
    c. ?[John o korosita zizitu o watakusi ga nagai
         killed   fact   I   long
         aida siranakatta] onna
         while knew-not   woman
         'the woman who I did not know for a long while the fact
         that (she) killed John'
    d. ?[syuppansita kaisya   ga kazi de yakete-simatta]   hon[9]
         published   company   fire by was-burned-down book
         'a book which the company that published (it) was burned
         down by a fire'

7. Relativization from Sentential Subjects

There is another constraint that applies to English but does not seem to
apply to Japanese. This constraint, called the Sentential Subject Con-

---

[9] The fact that some of these expressions are of dubious acceptability seems to be because
they involve a very peculiar characterization of the head nouns. For example, one would
rarely characterize a book as one such that the publisher that published it was burned
down.

straint,[10] states that no element may be moved out of a sentential subject. Compare the following two sentences:

(25) a. [That the principal would fire *the teacher*] was expected.

   b. The reporters expected [that the principal would fire *the teacher*].

The teacher in (25a) is an element in the sentential subject *that the principal would fire the teacher*, while *the teacher* in (25b) is an element in a sentential object, and not in a sentential subject. Now, observe the following pairs of sentences:

(26) a. *This teacher, that the principal would fire was expected.

   b. This teacher, the reporters expected that the principal would fire.

(27) a. *It was this teacher that that the principal would fire was expected.

   b. It was this teacher that the reporters expected that the principal would fire.

(28) a. *This is the teacher that that the principal would fire was expected.

   b. This is the teacher that the reporters expected that the principal would fire.

Sentence (28a) shows that the Sentential Subject Constraint applies to English Relativization. In Japanese, on the other hand, we have the following:

(29) a. [watakusi ga au   koto/no] ga muzukasii hito
        I   meet that   difficult   person
        '(lit.) the person whom that I see (him) is difficult'

   b. [kimi ga au   koto/no] ga atarimae   no hito
        you   meet that   matter-of-fact   person
        '(lit.) the person whom that you see (him) is matter-of-fact'

   c. [kare ga kaita koto] ga yoku sirarete-iru bun
        he   wrote that   well known-is   article
        '(lit.) the article which that he has written (it) is well known'

<hr>

[10] Also proposed by Ross (1967).

I have shown here some of the peculiarities of Japanese relative clauses in contrast to those of English relative clauses. In addition, I have shown that some of the constraints that are applicable to English relative clauses do not seem to apply to the Japanese. In the next chapter I shall show the similarities between the conditions for Japanese Relativization and Japanese Thematization (that is, NP-*wa*) and shall suggest that what is relativized in Japanese is not an ordinary noun phrase, but the theme NP-*wa* in the relative clause.

21[†]

Themes and Relative Clauses

In this chapter I shall point out the similarity of several constraints that apply both to relative clauses and to themes of sentences. I shall suggest in conclusion that what is relativized in a relative clause is not an ordinary noun phrase, but a noun phrase followed by the thematic particle *wa*.[1]

1. Deletion of Particles

Observe the following sentences:

(1) a. Oozei no hito   ga sono mura *ni kita.*
      many   people   the village to came
      'Many people came to the village.'

    b. Sono mura *ni wa* oozei no hito ga kita.
      'To that village, many people came.'

    c. Sono mura ϕ *wa*, oozei no hito ga kita.
      'As for that village, many people came (there).'

    d. Oozei no hito   ga kita   mura
      many   people   came village
      'the village that many people came to'

Example (1a) is a sentence with no theme. Sentence (1b) contains what I shall informally call a theme: *sono mura ni wa* 'as for (lit.) to that village'. Example (1c) shows that *ni* of (1b) can be deleted. The corresponding relative clause construction (1d) is grammatical. Now, consider the following:

(2) a. John ga sono mura *kara* kita.
                the village from came
      'John came from the village.'

    b. Sono mura *kara wa* John ga kita.
      'John came from the village.'

[†]This chapter should be of interest both to linguists and to students of Japanese.
[1] The distinction that I made in Chapter 2 between the thematic *wa* and the contrastive *wa* seems irrelevant here. I shall use the cover term "theme" for both in this chapter.

    c. *Sono mura φ wa, John ga kita.
       'As for that village, John came.'
    d. *John ga kita   mura
              came village
       'the village that John came from'[2]

Example (2c) shows that *kara*, in the context of (2b), cannot be deleted. Example (2d) shows that, in such a case, we obtain an ungrammatical relative clause construction.

    This observation is not meant to imply that *kara* can never be deleted. Observe the following sentences:

  (3) a. Sono tomodati *kara* tegami ga takusan kita.
           friend   from letters   many-ly came
        'Many letters came from the friend.'
      b. Sono tomodati *kara wa* tegami ga takusan kita.
      c. Sono tomodati φ *wa* tegami ga takusan kita.
      d. Tegami ga takusan kita tomodati ga oozei ita.
          letters   many-ly came friend   many were
        'There were many friends from whom many letters came (to me).'

Sentence (3c), without *kara*, seems to be perfectly grammatical in the intended reading, and so does the relativized version in (3d).[3] Similarly, examine the following:

  (4) a. Tokyo ya Osaka *kara* oozei no daihyoo   ga kita.
              and   from many   representative   came
        Hiroshima to   Fukuoka *kara wa* daihyoo   ga
                 and   from   representative
        hitori   mo konakatta.
        single-person   came-not
        'Many representatives came from Tokyo and Osaka. No representatives came from Hiroshima and Fukuoka.'
      b. Tokyo ya Osaka *kara* oozei no daihyoo ga kita. Hiroshima *to* Fukuoka φ *wa* hitori mo daihyoo ga konakatta.

---

[2] Example (2d) is grammatical if interpreted as 'the village that John came to'.
[3] Sentences (3c) and (3d) are ambiguous. They mean 'Speaking of those friends, many letters came *to/from* them' and 'There were many friends *to/from* whom many letters came'. The first reading that native speakers obtain for these sentences is that of *to* rather than *from*.

c. Tokyo ya Osaka kara oozei no daihyoo   ga kita.
      and   from many   representative   came
Daihyoo   ga hitori   mo konakatta tosi wa Hiroshima
representative   one-person   came-not city
to Fukuoka dake da.
and   only is
'Many representatives came from Tokyo and Osaka. Cities (from
which) no representatives came are (limited to) only Hiroshima
and Fukuoka.'

In both (4b) and (4c) the first sentence specifies that what is under discussion is *from* where representatives came. Thus, the missing particle in (4b) and (4c) is unambiguously recoverable. Hence, these sentences are grammatical.[4]

Parallelisms between the deletability of particles before *wa* and relativizability can be seen from the following examples, also:

(5) a. Mary ga John *to*   benkyoosita.
               with studied
      'Mary studied with John.'

    b. John *to wa* Mary ga benkyoosita.

    c. *John ϕ *wa* Mary ga benkyoosita.

    d. *Mary ga benkyoosita John
      'John, with whom Mary studied'

Example (5c) shows that *to* 'with' in the context of (5b) is not deletable. The corresponding relative clause construction is unacceptable, as shown in (5d). On the other hand, (6c) shows that *to* 'with' is deletable if *issyo-ni* 'together' is in the sentence. Predictably, we obtain a grammatical relative clause corresponding to it.[5]

(6) a. Mary ga John *to*   *issyo-ni*   benkyoosita.
                with together studied
      'Mary studied together with John.'

    b. John *to wa* Mary ga *issyo-ni* benkyoosita.

    c. John ϕ *wa* Mary ga *issyo-ni* benkyoosita.

---

[4] I am indebted to Kunihiko Ogawa (personal communication) for this example.
[5] I am indebted to Lewis Josephs (personal communication, 1969) for this observation.

d. Mary ga *issyo-ni* benkyoosita John
   'John, (with whom) Mary studied together'[6]

2. Reflexive Pronouns

Both themes and relative clauses can, under certain conditions, retain (reflexive) pronouns in the position formerly occupied by the original noun phrase that has been thematized or relativized. Observe the following:

(7) a. [Sono kodomo ga kawaigatte-ita] inu ga sinde-simatta.
       the child   fond-of-was   dog   died
       'The dog that the child was fond of died.'

---

[6] The foregoing phenomenon does not immediately show that what is relativized is the theme of the relative clause. This is because the same phenomenon is observed in two other classes of constructions. First, particles *mo* 'also', *sika* 'only', *sae* 'even', etc., behave just like *wa*. For example, parallel to (1) and (5), we have (i) and (ii), respectively.

(i) a. Sono mura *ni mo*, oozei no hito   ga kita.
        the village to also many   people came
        'Many people came to the village, also.'
     b. Sono mura *ɸ mo*, oozei no hito ga kita.

(ii) a. John *to   mo*, Mary ga benkyoosita.
        with also   studied
        'Mary studied with John, also.'
     b. *John *ɸ mo*, Mary ga benkyoosita.

Second, particle deletion before the copula follows the same principle.

(iii) a. John ga kita   no wa, Osaka *ni da*.
         came that   to is
         'It is *to* Osaka that John came.'
      b. John ga kita no wa, Osaka *ɸ da*.

(iv) a. John ga kita   no wa, Osaka *kara da*.
         came that   from is
         'It is *from* Osaka that John came.'
     b. *John ga kita no wa Osaka *ɸ da*.

(v) a. Mary ga benkyoosita no wa John *to   da*.
         studied   that   with is
         'It is *with* John that Mary studied.'
     b. *Mary ga benkyoosita no wa John *ɸ da*.

Since Relativization involves deletion of the particle that follows the relativized noun phrase, what determines relativizability or unrelativizability may simply be the deletability or undeletability of particles, and it may not have anything specifically to do with Thematization. I am indebted to James McCawley (personal communication) for this observation.

b. Sono kodomo wa [*zibun* ga kawaigatte-ita] inu ga sinde-simatta.
            self
    'Speaking of the child, the dog that (he) himself was fond of died.'

c. [[*zibun* ga kawaigatte-ita] inu ga sinde-simatta] kodomo
    'the child who the dog that (he) himself was fond of died'

In (7b) the reflexive pronoun *zibun* appears as the trace of the original full-fledged noun phrase *sono kodomo* 'the child' as the subject of *kawaigatte-ita* 'was fond of'. The same reflexive pronoun appears in (7c) in the corresponding relative clause. Example (7d), with *zibun* missing, is also a grammatical expression.

(7) d. [[kawaigatte-ita] inu ga sinde-simatta] kodomo
            fond-of-was   dog died   child
        'the child who the dog that (he) was fond of died'

It is not the case that the original noun phrase can freely remain as a (reflexive) pronoun. Examples (8b) and (8c) are ungrammatical.

(8) a. Sono kodomo ga Mary o butta.
            the   child   struck
        'The child struck Mary.'

b. *Sono kodomo wa $\left\{\begin{array}{l} \textit{zibun} \\ \text{self} \\ \textit{kare} \\ \text{he} \end{array}\right\}$ ga Mary o butta.

    'Speaking of the child, himself/he hit Mary.'

c. *$\left\{\begin{array}{l} \textit{zibun} \\ \textit{kare} \end{array}\right\}$ ga Mary o butta kodomo
                                    struck child
    'the child who himself/he struck Mary'

It is not completely clear under what conditions original noun phrases can remain in the form of (reflexive) pronouns after thematization. One thing that is clear is that such noun phrases must be left-branching noun phrases. Note that when the thematized form is ungrammatical as in (8b), the corresponding relative clause is also ungrammatical, as in (8c). More examples follow:

(9) a. Sono kodomo no gakkoo no sensei ga kootuuziko   de sinda.
            the   child   's school 's teacher   traffic-accident in died
        '(Lit.) The child's school's teacher died in a traffic accident.'

b. Sono kodomo wa *zibun* no gakkoo no sensei ga kootuuziko de sinda.
'Speaking of the child, the teacher of his own school died in a traffic accident.'

c. *Zibun* no gakkoo no sensei ga kootuuziko de sinda kodomo
'the child whose (his own) school's teacher died in a traffic accident'

(10) a. Zoo no hana ga nagai.
'An elephant's trunk is long.'

b. Zoo   wa (*sono*   ) hana ga nagai.
elephant   { *sore no* } trunk   long-is
             (*zibun no*)
'Speaking of an elephant, its trunk is long.'

c. (*sono*   ) hana ga nagai zoo
   { *sore no* } trunk   long-is elephant
   (*zibun no*)
'an elephant whose (its) trunk is long'

(11) a. Cyrano de Bergerac no hana wa kiwamete ookikatta.
                          's nose   extremely big-was
'Cyrano de Bergerac's nose was extremely big.'

b. Cyrano de Bergerac wa ((*sono*   )) hana ga kiwamete
                        (({ *kare no* }))
                        ((*zibun no*))
ookikatta.

c. ((*sono*   )) hana ga kiwamete ookikatta Cyrano de Bergerac
   (({ *kare no* }))
   ((*zibun no*))
'Cyrano de Bergerac, whose (its) nose was extremely big'

Examples (10b,c) and (11b,c) are in the written style and would not be used in colloquial speech. Note that we have *so* 'that' in the place of the original noun phrase both for nonhuman *zoo* 'elephant' and human *Cyrano de Bergerac*.[7]

3. Thematization and Relativization

Both the themes and the relative clauses can involve elements in adverbial clauses, complex noun phrases, and sentential subjects. Recall that these

---

[7] The use of *sono* in the place of *kare no* or *kanozyo no* 'his or her' as in *Alibaba to sono yonzyuu-nin-no toozoku* 'Ali Baba and His (lit., its) 40 Thieves' has a formal archaic and literary tone.

features were discussed in the preceding chapter as characteristics of Japanese relative clauses that are not shared by English relative clauses.

(12) a. sinda node   minna ga kanasinda   hito
    died because all   saddened-were person
    '(lit.) the person, who, because (he) died, everyone was saddened'

    b. Sono hito   wa, sinda node,   minna ga kanasinda.
        the   person   died because all   saddened-were
        'Speaking of that person, everyone was saddened because he died.'

(13) a. sinda noni   dare mo kanasimanakatta hito
    died although anyone saddened-not-was person
    '(lit.) the person who, although (he) died, no one was saddened'

    b. Sono hito   wa, sinda noni   dare mo kanasimanakatta.
        the   person   died although anyone saddened-not-was
        'Speaking of that person, no one was saddened although (he) died.'

(14) a. kite-iru   yoohuku ga yogorete iru sinsi
    wearing-is suit   dirty   is gentleman
    '(lit.) a gentleman who the suit that (he) is wearing is dirty'

    b. Sono sinsi   wa, kite   iru yoohuku ga yogorete iru.
        the gentleman   wearing is suit   dirty   is
        'Speaking of that gentleman, the suit he is wearing is dirty.'

(15) a. watakusi ga au   koto ga muzukasii hito
    I   meet that   difficult-is person
    '(lit.) the person whom for me to see (him) is difficult'

    b. Sono hito   wa, watakusi ga au   koto ga muzukasii.
        the   person   I   meet that   difficult-is
        'Speaking of that person, for me to see (him) is difficult.'

In the preceding, (12) and (13) are instances of Thematization and Relativization involving an element in adverbial clauses, while (14) and (15) concern a complex noun phrase and a sentential subject, respectively. These examples show that when Relativization is possible, Thematization is also possible.

    It is not the case, however, that Relativization is freely applicable to elements in adverbial clauses, complex noun phrases, and sentential subjects. Although it is not clear under what conditions it is possible, or under what conditions it is not, it is clear that when Thematization is possible, then Relativization is also possible. Observe the following sentences:

(16) a. Sono hito   ga dekinakereba, watakusi ga yaru.
         the   person if-cannot-do I   do
         'If that man cannot do it, I will do it.'

     b. *Sono hito wa, [dekinakereba, watakusi ga yaru].
         'Speaking of that man, if he cannot do it, I will do it.'

     c. *[dekinakereba, watakusi ga yaru] hito
         'the person who, if (he) cannot do it, I will do it'

(17) a. Sono hito   ga tokenai   mondai o, watakusi ga toita.
         the   person cannot-solve problem I   solved
         'I solved the problem that the man could not solve.'

     b. *Sono hito wa, [tokenai mondai o, watakusi ga toita].[8]
         'Speaking of that man, I solved the problem that (he) could not
         solve.'

     c. *[tokenai mondai o watakusi ga toita] hito
         'the man who I solved the problem that (he) could not solve'

It seems that (16b) and (17b) are unacceptable because what follows the theme is not a statement about the theme. For example, *dekinakereba, watakusi ga yaru* 'if (he) cannot do it, I will do it' of (16b) is not a statement about *sono hito* 'that man', but a statement about something that the speaker says he will do if *sono hito* cannot do it. Hence, a non sequitur results. It seems that (16c) is unacceptable for the same reason.

4. Source of Thematic Sentences

There are thematic sentences for which there are no corresponding theme-less sentences. For some of these sentences, it is possible to construct corresponding relative clause expressions. Observe the following sentences:

(18) a. *Sakana wa* tai   ga ii.
         fish   red-snapper good-is
         'Speaking of fish, red snapper is the best.'

[8] Example (17b) is ungrammatical if *sono hito wa* is to be taken as the theme of the whole sentence, as it should be taken in this example. However, it would be grammatical if it were pronounced as [*sono hito wa tokenai mondai o*] *watakusi ga toita*. Then *sono hito wa* would not be the theme of the entire sentence, but would be the contrastive subject of the relative clause. The sentence would mean 'I solved the problem that that man could not solve'.

b. *Hana*   *wa* sakura   ga ii.
   blossoms   cherry-blossoms
   'Speaking of flowers, cherry blossoms are the best.'

There are no corresponding themeless sentences for (18) which are grammatical.

(19) a. Sakana $\left\{ \begin{array}{l} *no \text{ 'of'} \\ *de \text{ 'among'} \\ *ni \text{ 'in'} \\ \text{etc.} \end{array} \right\}$ tai ga ii.[9]

b. Hana $\left\{ \begin{array}{l} *no \\ *de \\ *ni \\ \text{etc.} \end{array} \right\}$ sakura ga ii.

No uti de and *no naka de*, both meaning '(lit.) in the class of, in the middle of, among', are "compound particles" that come closest to the meaning of (18).

(20) a. ?Sakana *no uti/naka de* tai ga ii.
        'Among fish, red snapper is the best.'

   b. ?Hana *no uti/naka de* sakura ga ii.
        'Among blossoms, cherry blossoms are the best.'

One might be tempted to hypothesize that (18a) and (18b) are derived from the pair of sentences in (21) via deletion of *no uti/naka de*.

---

[9] Minoru Nakau (1971) has proposed that (18a) is derived from the following, where *no* is not a particle, but the attributive form of the copulative *da*:

(i) Sakana *no* tai   ga ii.
    fish   is red-snapper   good-is
    'Red snapper, which is a fish, is the best.'

Thus, *sakana no* is regarded as an appositional modifier of *tai* 'red snapper'.

   The preceding analysis does not seem to be tenable because, in general, appositive noun phrases cannot be thematized. For example,

(ii) a. Soori-daizin   *no* Ikeda-si   ga sinda.
        prime-minister is   Mr.   died
        'Mr. Sato, Prime Minister, has died.'

    b. *Soori-daizin *wa* Ikeda-si ga sinda.

Furthermore, there are no known transformations that move or delete noun phrases before copulas.

(21) a. Sakana *no uti/naka de wa* tai ga ii.

    b. Hana *no uti/naka de wa* sakura ga ii.[10]

However, there are several things wrong with this hypothesis. First, (21a) and (21b) are not synonymous with (18a) and (18b), respectively. For example, (18a) is a statement about fish, and it says that among fish, red snapper is the best. On the other hand, (21a) is not a statement about fish alone. It has a highly contrastive connotation: it means that if one restricts one's scope of discussion to fish, red snapper is the best (but if one talks about sea products, then something else might be the best). Furthermore, there is no justification for transformationally deleting *no uti/naka de*, which contain nouns *uti* and *naka* (both meaning 'inside'), while there are monosyllabic particles that cannot be deleted.[11]

Moreover, *no uti/naka de* is a "compound particle" that is not ordinarily deletable. Observe the following examples:

(22) a.   John to   Bill to   Mary *no uti/naka de,* Mary ga itiban yoku

               and   and   among   most well

        dekiru.

        does-well

        'Among John, Bill, and Mary, Mary does the best.'

    b. ??John to Bill to Mary ϕ *wa,* Mary ga itiban yoku dekiru.

(23) a.   Sono densya *no naka de* John ni atta.

        the   train   in   met

        'I met John on the train.'

    b. ??Sono densya ϕ *wa* John ni atta.

Finally, there are sentences of the same pattern as that of (18) that cannot be paraphrased using *no uti/naka de*. For example,

(24) a.   Kagaku   wa, 1970-nen X ga gooseisareta.

        chemistry   -year   was-synthesized

        'Speaking of chemistry, X was synthesized in 1970.'

    b. *Kagaku *no uti/naka de* wa, X ga gooseisareta.

[10] Masatake Muraki (1970, Chapter 4) has proposed deriving (18a) from (21a) with *no naka de*.

[11] This is particularly so because, as is shown later, the *de* of *no uti/naka de* happens to be a particle that cannot be deleted.

(25) a. Buturigaku *wa*, syuusyoku   ga taihen   da.
         physics   employment   difficult is
         'Speaking of physics, finding jobs is very difficult.'

    b. *Buturigaku *no uti/naka de* wa, syuusyoku ga taihen da.

Thus, we are forced to assume that themes exist as themes in the deep structure of thematic sentences. For this reason it is hypothesized that (18a) is derived from the deep structure informally represented in diagram (26).[12]

---

[12] Muraki argues that if *Sakana wa tai ga ii* 'Speaking of fish, red snapper is the best' is not derived from the deep structure corresponding to the following, but is derived from a deep structure with *sakana* already as the theme of the sentence, then NP-*wa* would have to be generated by the base rules independently of the predication.

(i) Sakana no naka de tai ga ii.

He seems to have in mind sentences such as

(ii) *Sakana wa Mary ga byooki da.
      fish   sick   is
      'Speaking of fish, Mary is sick.'

According to my analysis, (ii) is anomalous because the predication *Mary ga byooki da* has nothing to do with the theme. In other words, (ii) is anomalous for the same reason that the examples in (iii) are anomalous out of context.

(iii) a. *Speaking of fish, Mary is sick.
      b. *If I am to speak of fish, Mary is sick.

It would be next to impossible to give syntactic constraints for marking (iii) as ungrammatical because the following sentences are grammatical:

(iv) a. Speaking of chemistry, John's book is very interesting.
      b. Speaking of fish, Mary got sick after last night's banquet. I suspect that the red snapper served there was not fresh.

The following examples, all due to Mikami (1960), also show clearly that it is not possible to derive all themes from nonthematic sentences:

(v) a. *Are wa*, zettai   ni Amerika ga warui.
         that   absolutely   wrong-is
         'Speaking of that matter, absolutely, America is to blame.'

    b. *Sinbun   o yomitai   hito   wa*, koko ni arimasu.
         newspaper   read-want   people   here   exist
         'Speaking of those who want to read newspapers, they (=newspapers) are here.'

    c. *Basyo wa*, okunai-setu   ga attooteki   datta.
         place   indoor-theory   predominant was
         'Speaking of the place (of the murder), the "indoor" theory was predominant.'

(*Continued overleaf*)

(26)

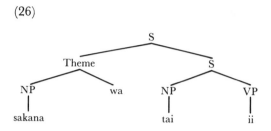

5. Relativization as Theme Deletion

Now, I propose that what is relativized is not an ordinary noun phrase, but the theme (NP-*wa*) of the relative clause. According to this hypothesis, (27a) will be derived from the deep structure containing (27b) as follows:

(27) a. Kore wa John ga kaita hon da.
　　　　 this　　　　　　　 wrote book is
　　　　 'This is the book that John wrote.'

　　 b. [*sono hon wa* [John ga *sono hon* o kaita]ₛ]ₛ hon

The second *sono hon* 'the book' in the most deeply embedded clause is obligatorily deleted under identity with the theme of the embedded clause, yielding

(27) c. [*sono hon wa* John ga kaita]ₛ hon

Since the theme of the embedded clause is identical with the head noun, it is deleted because of Relativization, yielding [*John ga kaita*] *hon*.

In none of the preceding sentences is it possible to replace *wa* with nonthematic particles.

On the other hand, we do not always obtain grammatical sentences if the comment part has something to do with the theme. Observe the following sentence, which is due to James McCawley (personal communication):

(vi) *U.S. Steel wa boku no apaato　　no mado　ga kitanai.
　　　　　　　　　　 I　 's apartment's　window　 dirty
　　 'Speaking of U.S. Steel, the windows of my apartment are dirty.'

This sentence is ungrammatical, even if it is the case that the U.S. Steel is responsible for the speaker's windows being dirty.

At present it is not clear what kind of relationship the theme and the comment must hold for the sentence to be grammatical. What is clear is that it cannot be a simple syntactic constraint, as has been suggested by Muraki and others to the effect that the theme must be present in nonthematic form in the comment part.

Now, observe the following sentence:

(28) *Syuusyoku   ga taihen   na buturigaku, sotugyoo   ga taihen*
employment   difficult is physics   graduation   difficult
na gengogaku—dono gakumon mo yooi de wa nai.
is linguistics every discipline   easy is-not
'Physics, where finding a job is difficult, and linguistics, where graduation is difficult—no discipline is easy.'

If we assumed that what is relativized was an ordinary noun phrase, there would be no plausible way to derive the italicized noun phrases of (28).

(29) a. [buturigaku *no/*de/*ni/*no-naka-de syuusyoku ga taihen da]
buturigaku

b. [gengogaku *no/*de/*ni/*no-naka-de sotugyoo ga taihen da]
gengogaku

On the other hand, if we assume that what is relativized is an NP-*wa*, then these noun phrases can be readily accounted for. They are derived from

(30) a. [[*buturigaku wa*]$_{theme}$ syuusyoku   ga taihen   da]$_S$ buturigaku
physics   employment   difficult is   physics

b. [[*gengogaku wa*]$_{theme}$ sotugyoo   ga taihen   da]$_S$ gengogaku
linguistics   graduation   difficult is   linguistics

6. Counterexamples to Hypothesis

I have presented the hypothesis that Relativization in Japanese applies, not to an ordinary noun phrase, but to the theme NP-*wa* of the relative clause. This hypothesis is still very speculative and requires further investigation. There are some counterexamples—some easily explainable, but some very challenging—to this hypothesis. For example, consider the following:

(31) a.   Sakana wa tai ga ii.
'Speaking of fish, red snapper is the best.'

b.   *tai ga ii sakana[13]
'fish, as for which red snapper is the best'

[13] This phrase should be read as [*tai ga ii*] *sakana*, where [*tai ga ii*] is a modifier of *sakana*. The phrase has another reading, namely, *Tai ga* [*ii*] *sakana* (*da*) 'Red snapper (and only red snapper) (is) a good fish'. In this reading, it is grammatical.

(32) a.   America wa California ni itta.
          'Speaking of America, I went to California.'

   b. *California ni itta America
          'America, as for which I went to California'

(33) a.   Nekutai wa aoi   no o katta.
          tie   blue one bought
          'Speaking of ties, I bought a blue one.'

   b. *aoi no o katta nekutai
          'ties, as for which I bought a blue one'

(34) a.   Hana wa zoo   ga nagai.
          trunk   elephant   long-is
          'Speaking of trunks, an elephant (lit.) is long.'

   b. *zoo ga nagai hana[14]
          'trunks, as for which an elephant('s) is long'

The (b) phrases given are indeed unacceptable in isolation, as has been
pointed out by Muraki (1970). However, the unacceptability of these
phrases seems to be due, not to any syntactic reason, but to a semantic
reason. First of all, observe that the relative clauses involved in the (b)
phrases are all nonrestrictive and that their antecedents are either generic
noun phrases or proper nouns. One rarely characterizes something
generic by some specific event or state; to be more concrete, one does not
characterize fish in general as something such that the red snapper is the
most delicious, America as a country such that I went to California,
neckties in general as something such that I bought a blue one, and
trunks in general as something such that an elephant has a long one.
However, in certain limited contexts, this pattern becomes perfectly
plausible. Observe the following examples:

(35) a. *California ni itta   America, Eiffel Tower ni nobotta   France,*
                  to went   climbed
        zoo   ni notta Indo   no koto ga wasurerarenai.
        elephant   rode India 's   matters cannot-forget
        'I cannot forget about America, as for which I went to California,
        France, as for which I climbed the Eiffel Tower, and India, as for
        which I rode on an elephant.'

[14] Examples (32) through (34) are due to Muraki (1970).

b. *California-syuu ga Nihon yori   ooki America* wa hontooni
          state   Japan than big   really
ooki kuni   desu.
big country is
'America, as for which the state of California is larger than Japan,
is really a big country.'

c. *Zoo*   *ga nagai hana* wa, eigo   de wa, 'trunk' to yuu.
   elephant   long nose   English   in   as call
'The nose, as for which the elephant's is long, is called a trunk in
English.'

d. *Boko ga itumo   onazi no o simete   iru nekutai* wa muyoo
   I   always same one wearing am tie   useless
no soosyokuhin desu.
   accessory   is
'Ties, as for which I always wear the same one, are useless
accessories.'

In the preceding the noun phrases in italics have the same pattern as those labeled as unacceptable in (31) through (34). This shows that (31) through (33) do not really constitute counterexamples to the proposed generalization.[15]

[15] Observe the following:

(i)   Asa wa itumo usugurai uti ni okita.
     morning always semidark while got-up
     'In the morning, I always got up while it was still semidark.'

(ii) *itumo usugurai uti ni okita asa
     'the morning such that I always got up while it was still semidark'

It seems to be impossible to come up with a situation in which (ii) would become acceptable. Again, this is simply because one does not characterize the morning in general as something such that he got up while it was still dark. In this connection, compare the preceding with these examples:

(iii) (Sono) asa   wa usugurai uti ni okita.
     the   morning   semidark while got-up
     'In the morning (in those mornings), I got up while it was still semidark.'

(iv) usugurai uti ni okita asa
     'those mornings when I woke up while it was still semidark'

Sentence (iii) is different from (i) in that it does not have *itumo* 'always', and that, therefore, *asa* can be specific, and not generic as is the case with (i). Example (iv) is now perfectly acceptable because it characterizes specific morning(s) as one(s) such that the speaker woke up while it was still dark.

Next, observe the following examples:

(36) a.   Okane wa John ga aru.
      money   have
      'As for money, John has (a lot).'

     b.   *John ga aru okane
        'money, as for which John has (a lot)'

Here again, (36b) is the characterization of money in general as something that John has; hence, the phrase is unacceptable. It is not possible
to assign the reading 'the money that John has' to (36b) because the
corresponding interpretation of (36a) is ruled out. Example (36a) cannot
mean 'As for that money, John has it.' This is because the object of *aru*
'to have' must be indefinite.

(37) a.   John ga okane ga aru.
               money   have
      'John has money.'

     b.   *John ga *sono* okane ga aru.
        'John has the money.'

     c.   *Sono* okane wa John ga aru.
        'Speaking of that money, John has it.'

The following examples seem to indicate what is relativized is not
an ordinary noun phrase, and not an *NP + particle + wa*, but a noun
phrase *immediately* followed by *wa*:

(5) a.   Mary ga John to   benkyoosita.
               with studied
     'Mary studied with John.'

    b.   John to wa Mary ga benkyoosita.

    c.   *John wa Mary ga benkyoosita.

    d.   *Mary ga benkyoosita John
              studied
      'John, with whom Mary studied'

(6) a. Mary ga John to   issyo-ni benkyoosita.
               with together studied
     'Mary studied together with John.'

    b. John to wa Mary ga issyo-ni benkyoosita.

    c. John wa Mary ga issyo-ni benkyoosita.

    d. Mary ga issyo-ni   benkyoosita John
            together studied
     'John, with whom Mary studied together'

Example (5d) is ungrammatical because its source, (5c), is ungrammatical, and (6d) is grammatical because (6c) is grammatical.

    The claim that what is relativized is the theme, *immediately followed by wa*, of the embedded clause might be too strong. There are relative clause constructions for which corresponding NP-*wa* sentences do not exist. These counterexamples, due to Muraki, all involve the particle *de* in its various usages and the dative *ni*. Observe the following examples:

(38) *De* for Instrument

    a.   Mary ga sono naihu *de*   John o sasita.
               the knife with   stabbed
        'Mary stabbed John with that knife.'

    b.   Sono naihu *de wa* Mary ga John o sasita.

    c.   *Sono naihu *wa* Mary ga John o sasita.

    d.   Mary ga John o sasita   naihu
                           stabbed knife
        'the knife with which Mary stabbed John'

(39) *De* for Degree

    a.   Kono cake o sono ondo   *de* yaita.
               this   the temperature   baked
        'I baked this cake at that temperature.'

    b.   ?Sono ondo *de wa* kono cake o yaita.

    c.   *Sono ondo *wa* kono cake o yaita.

    d.   kono cake o yaita   ondo
               this   baked temperature
        'the temperature at which I baked this cake'

(40) *De* for Reason, Manner

    a.   John ga sono riyuu   *de* kessekisita.
                     the   reason   absented-oneself
        'John absented himself for that reason.'

    b.   ?Sono riyuu *de wa* John ga kessekisita.

   c. *Sono riyuu *wa* John ga kessekisita.

   d. John ga kessekisita   riyuu
                absented-oneself reason
          'the reason for which John absented himself'

(41) *De* for Locative

   a. John ga Tokyo *de* Mary ni atta.
                        met
          'John met Mary in Tokyo.'

   b. Tokyo *de wa* John ga Mary ni atta.

   c. *Tokyo *wa* John ga Mary ni atta.

   d. John ga Mary ni atta Tokyo
          'Tokyo, where John met Mary'

(42) Dative *Ni*[16]

   a. John ga Mary o sono isya   *ni* syookaisita.
                   the   doctor to introduced
          'John introduced Mary to that doctor.'

   b. Sono isya *ni wa* John ga Mary o syookaisita.

   c. *Sono isya *wa* John ga Mary o syookaisita.

   d. John ga Mary o syookaisita isya
                  introduced doctor
          'the doctor John introduced Mary to'

I do not know at present how to reconcile these two contradictory phenomena. On the one hand, examples (38) through (42) suggest that one should make the weaker claim that what is relativized in a relative clause is a noun phrase followed by *wa* with or without intervening particles. On the other hand, an explanation for the phenomenon observed in examples (1) through (6) would be greatly simplified if it could be claimed that what is relativized is a noun phrase immediately followed by *wa*. Since the counterexamples at present are limited to those involving the particles *de* and *ni* (dative), the latter generalization, which is stronger, seems to be more promising. At present, I do not have any explanation as to why *de* and dative *ni* resist the NP-*wa* pattern and yet are amenable to relativization at the same time.

---

[16] Note that, as was shown in example (1), directional *ni* can be deleted before *wa*.

22†

Tense in Relative Clauses

In English, there is a general rule for agreement of tense. For example, (1a) is realized in the reported speech as (1b), and not as (1c).

(1) a. When I met him ten years ago, John said, "I *am* writing a book."
   b. When I met him ten years ago, John said that he *was* writing a book.
   c. *When I met him ten years ago, John said that he *is* writing a book.

Similarly, in relative clauses the action or state simultaneous with that of the main clause must be represented in the past tense if the main verb is in the past tense:

(2) a. *John took away the book that Mary *is* reading.
   b. John took away the book that Mary *was* reading.

In Japanese, there is basically no agreement of tense. Observe the following sentences:

(3) a. John wa hon o kaite *iru* to itta.
            book writing is that said
      'John said that he was (lit., is) writing a book.'
   b. John wa hon o kaite *ita* to itta.
            book writing was   said
      'John said that he *had been* writing a book.'

(4) a. John wa zibun ga baka *da* to   itta.
            self   fool is that said
      'John said that he was (lit., is) stupid.'
   b. John wa zibun ga baka *datta* to itta.
                            was
      'John said that he *had been* a fool.'

(5) a. John wa Mary ga kare o aisite *iru* koto o sitta.
                      he   loving is that   knew
      'John found out that Mary was (lit., is) in love with him.'

†This chapter is for all readers.

b. John wa Mary ga kare o aisite *ita*   koto o sitta.

                                   was

'John found out that Mary *had been* in love with him.'

Note that (3b), (4b), and (5b) are ungrammatical if they are to mean 'John said that he was writing a book', 'John said that he was stupid', and 'John found out that Mary was in love with him', respectively. These examples show that in complement clauses in Japanese, the present tense must be used if an action or state represented by the verb of the complement clause is meant to be simultaneous with that of the main clause.

In certain relative clauses both the present tense and the past tense can be used without obvious difference of meaning:

(6) a. John wa Mary ga yonde   *iru* hon   o toriageta.

                      reading is   book   took-away

'John took away the book that Mary was (lit., *is*) reading.'

b. John wa Mary ga yonde *ita*   hon o toriageta.

                      was

'John took away the book that Mary *was* reading.'

This phenomenon has led to an erroneous belief that there is a more or less free variation in the tense of Japanese relative clauses when the main verb is in the past tense: if the action or state represented by the verb of the relative clause is simultaneous with that represented by the verb of the main clause, which is in the past tense, the former can be either in the present tense or in the past tense. In this chapter I shall examine those cases in which this generalization will not hold.

First of all, when a relative clause ends with a copula or an adjective, the past tense cannot be used unless the clause represents a state prior to that of the main clause. For example,

(7) a.   John wa *ooki*   apaato   ni sunde ita.

                 big-is apartment in living was

'John lived in an apartment which was (lit., is) big.'

b. *John wa *ookikatta* apaato ni sunde ita.

              big-was

(8) a.   John wa baka *na* onna   to   kekkonsita.

               stupid is woman with married

'John married a woman who was (lit., is) stupid.'

b. *John wa baka *datta* onna   to   kekkonsita.
stupid was woman with married

Examples (7b) and (8b) would be grammatical only if they were to mean 'John lived in an apartment which had been big', and 'John married a woman who had been stupid', respectively.[1]

Second, Josephs (1971) has observed that when relative clauses have adverbs that refer to past time, the present tense cannot be used.

(9) a.   John wa Mary ga yonde   *iru* hon o toriageta.
                          reading is book   took away
'John took away the book that Mary was (lit., is) reading.'

b. *John wa Mary ga *sono toki*   yonde *iru* hon o toriageta.
                    that time
'John took away the book that Mary was (lit., is) reading that time.'

c.   John wa Mary ga *sono toki* yonde *ita*   hon o toriageta.
                                        was
'John took away the book that Mary was reading that time.'

(10) a.   John wa eigo   ga dekinai gaikokuzin to   kekkonsita.
               English   cannot foreigner with married
'John married a foreigner who (lit.) cannot speak English.'

b. *John wa eigo ga *dekinakatta* gaikokuzin to kekkonsita.
                    could not

c. *John wa *sono toki*   mada eigo ga *dekinai* gaikokuzin to
             that time yet   cannot
kekkonsita.
'John married a foreigner who (lit.) cannot yet at that time speak English.'

d.   John wa *sono toki* mada eigo ga *dekinakatta* gaikokuzin to
                                        could not
kekkonsita.
'John married a foreigner who could not yet at that time speak English.'

[1] This phenomenon in Japanese stands in marked contrast with the corresponding feature of Korean. In Korean, attributive adjectives *must* be in the past tense.

Third, as Josephs (1971) has observed, if the relative clause modifies
the subject of an adjectival or copulative predicate, the past tense must
be used in the relative clause if it refers to past time.[2] For example,

(11) a. John ga yonde   { *iru } hon   wa Shakespeare datta.
              reading   { ita } book   was
       'The book that John was reading was Shakespeare.'
     b. John ga sanposasete { *iru } inu wa tiisakatta.
              walking   { ita } dog   small-was
       'The dog that John was walking was small.'

This phenomenon is undoubtedly related to the fact that the predicate
of these sentences can be in the present tense without substantial difference
in meaning.

(12) a. John ga yonde   ita   hon   wa Shakespeare da.
              reading was book   is
       'The book that John was reading is Shakespeare.'
     b. John ga sanposasete ita   inu wa tiisai.
              walking   was dog   small-is
       'The dog that John was walking is small.'

Josephs observes that sentence (13) is acceptable, in spite of the fact that
(11a) with iru is ungrammatical.

(13) Watakusi ga tuku   to Taroo ga yonde   iru hon   wa Shakespeare
                 arrive   reading is book
     datta.
     was
     'When I arrived, the book Taroo (lit.) is reading was Shakespeare.'

This seems to be related to the fact that datta of (13) cannot be changed to
the present tense.

(14) *Watakusi ga tuku   to Taroo ga yonde   ita hon   wa Shakespeare
      I   arrive   reading is book
     da.
     is
     'When I arrived, the book Taroo was reading (lit.) is Shakespeare.'

[2] This applies only when the relative clause represents a nonhabitual nonfuture state
represented by the -te iru form. Predicates that represent future or habitual actions will
be discussed later in the chapter.

From the foregoing it can be assumed that in (11) and (12) the verb in the relative clause is, semantically speaking, the principal verb of the sentence and thus determines the time referred to by the sentence, and that the copula or adjective in the main clause can optionally take the past tense form in tense agreement. On the other hand, in (13) the copula of the main clause must be in the past tense, thus determining the time reference and giving the verb of the relative clause the option of being in the present tense.

Fourth, in relative clauses whose predicate represents an action, the use of past and present tenses would result in significant differences in meaning.[3] For example, observe the following:

(15) a. John wa *kau* hon   o yonda.
              buy book   read
         'John read the book that he *was to buy*.'

     b. John wa *katta*   hon   o yonda.
              bought book   read
         'John read the book that he *(had) bought*.'

(16) a. John wa miti   de deau hito   ni hanasikaketa.
              street   meet person to talked
         'John talked to whomever he met on the street.'

     b. John wa miti   de deatta hito   ni hanasikaketa.
              street on met   person to talked
         'John talked to a person whom he met on the street.'

The relative clause of (15a) has the future (with respect to the time referred to by the main clause) connotation, while the relative clause of (16a) has the habitual connotation. This phenomenon is consistent with the fact that the present tense of action verbs in Japanese refers either to future time or to present habit. Consider the following sentences:

(17) a. John wa kono hon o *kau*.
              this book buy
         'John will buy this book. John is to buy this book.'

     b. John wa mainiti   gakkoo ni *iku*.
              every-day school to go
         'John goes to school every day.'

---

[3] Compare (15) and (16) with (6). In the latter, the predicate of the relative clause is in the *-te iru/ita* form and represents a state, not an action.

The same difference in meaning that holds between (15a) and (15b) and between (16a) and (16b) seems to hold between the following sentences, which are due to Josephs:

(18) a. John wa basu o *oriru*   toki ni wa itumo tyuuisita.
              bus   get-off when   always careful-was

    b. John wa basu o *orita*   toki ni wa itumo tyuuisita.
                   got-off

Both are roughly translatable as 'John was always careful when he got off the bus'. The presence of *itumo* 'always' imposes the habitual interpretation both to *oriru* 'get off' and to *orita* 'got off'. However, since the present tense action verb basically refers to future time, (18a) means that John was always careful when he *was about to get off* the bus. On the other hand, since the past tense action verb basically represents an action perfected, (18b) means that John was always careful when *he had gotten off* the bus.

The same explanation seems to account for the subtle difference in meaning that exists between the following two sentences, also due to Josephs:

(19) a. Maisyuu   *kuru* hito   wa John to Mary desita.
        every-week come person   were

    b. Maisyuu *kita*   hito wa John to Mary desita.
             came

Both mean roughly 'The ones who came every week were John and Mary'. However, the former implies that John's and Mary's weekly visits were part of a fixed habit that might be, for example, the result of a mutual agreement between the speaker and John and Mary. On the other hand, (19b) lacks such habitual connotation and implies that their weekly visits were accidental as far as the speaker was concerned; that is, they just turned out that way.

At the beginning of this chapter, I noted that (6b) was synonymous with (6a).

(6) a. John wa Mary ga yonde   *iru* hon o toriageta.
                    reading is   book   took-away
    'John took away the book that Mary was (lit., is) reading.'

    b. John wa Mary ga yonde *ita*   hon o toriageta.

                            was

    'John took away the book that Mary was reading.'

There seems to be a subtle difference in meaning, however, between the two sentences. The use of *-te ita* in (6b) seems to imply that the speaker "had for some time directed particular attention to, or had special awareness of" Mary's reading the book.[4] This is undoubtedly due to the perfective sense of the *-te ita* form. Thus, (6b) can be literally translated as 'John took away the book that Mary had been and was reading; John took away the book that I had noticed Mary was reading'. Alternatively, if (6b) is taken to be a sentence in a third person narrative, it would literally mean 'John took away the book that he (=John) had noticed Mary was reading'.[5] Similarly, compare the following pairs of sentences:

(20) a. John wa densya no naka de kasa o   motte *ita* hito   ni

                train   in   umbrella having was person to

    hanasikaketa.

    talked

    'In the train, John struck up a conversation with a man who (I/he had observed) had an umbrella.'

    b. John wa densya no naka de kasa o motte *iru* hito ni hanasikaketa.

    'In the train, John struck up a conversation with a man who had an umbrella.'

(21) a. John wa densya no naka de kirei   na kimono o kite

                train   in   pretty is dress   wearing

    ita onna   no hito   ni hanasikaketa.

    was woman   person to talk

    'In the train, John struck up a conversation with a lady who (I/he had noticed) wore a beautiful dress.'

    b. John wa densya no naka de kirei na kimono o kite *iru* onna no hito ni hanasikaketa.

    'In the train, John struck up a conversation with a lady who wore a beautiful dress.'

---

[4] This observation is also due to Josephs (1971).

[5] For the identity of the speaker and a third person (such as *John* in this sentence) in a third person narrative, see Chapter 26 of this book.

The following sentences have low acceptability because the context rules out the connotation of previous awareness:

(22) a. ??Densya ni tobinoru to, kasa   o motte *ita* hito   ga
            train   to jump   into umbrella   having was person
            hanasikakete kita.
            talking   came
            'When I hurriedly got on the train, a man who had an umbrella started talking to me.'

    b. ??Miti de kirei   na kimono o kite *ita* onna   no hito   ni
           street   pretty is dress   wore   woman   person to
           deatta.
           encountered
           'On the street, I met a lady who wore a beautiful dress.'

These sentences are awkward or ungrammatical because they are not, in ordinary contexts, amenable to the interpretation "who I (or *he*) *had noticed* had an umbrella/wore a beautiful dress." Replacement of *ita* with *iru* in these sentences results in perfect grammaticality.

   In summary, the following generalizations hold with respect to the tense of relative clauses that refer to past time:

(i)   Basically, there is no agreement of tense. Therefore, if both the main clause and the relative clause represent past states, the present tense is used in the former.

(ii)   However, if the relative clause has an adverb that refers to past time, the present tense cannot be used.

(iii) If the relative clause that refers to past time modifies the subject of a past tense adjectival or copulative predicate,
     (a) only the past tense can be used if the past tense predicate can be changed to the present tense predicate without significantly changing the meaning of the sentence,
     (b) either the past or present tense can be used if the main clause predicate is in the past tense.

(iv) If the predicate of the relative clause represents an action, the use of the past and present tenses would result in significant differences in meaning, namely,
     (a) if the past tense is used, the relative clause represents a past

action simultaneous with, or prior to, the action represented by the main clause predicate;

(b) if the present tense is used, the relative clause represents a habitual action or action in the future (future with respect to the time referred to by the main clause predicate).

(v) The -*te ita* form in the relative clause implies that the speaker, or the subject of the main clause, had for some time directed particular attention to, or had some special awareness of, the state represented by the relative clause.

VI

Deictics—Yes, No, and Pronouns

23†
Yes and No

According to conventional grammars, Japanese *hai* 'yes' and *iie* 'no', as answers to negative questions, correspond to English *no* and *yes*, respectively. For example, Martin (1962, pp. 364–365) states the following:

The words *hai* (or *ē*) and *iie* are used to mean 'what you've said is correct' and 'what you've said is incorrect'. So if you state a question in a negative way, the standard Japanese answer turns out to be the opposite of standard English 'yes' and 'no', which affirm or deny the FACTS rather than the STATEMENT of the facts.

Kumamoto e ikimasen deshita ka?	Didn't you go to Kumamoto?
Hai, ikimasen deshita.	*No*, I didn't.
Iie, ikimashita yo.	*Yes*, I did indeed.

Martin correctly adds that if the negative question is really just an oblique request, then one indicates assent with *hai* and one's refusal with *iie*, as one would in English:

Kaban o motte kite kudasaimasen ka?	Won't you please bring the suitcase over here?
Hai, kashikomarimashita.	*Yes*, gladly.
Mō sukoshi meshiagarimasen ka?	Won't you have a little more (to eat)?
Iie, mō kekkō de gozaimasu.	*No* (thanks), I've had enough.

The fact of the matter is not as simple as is implied by Martin's explanation. For example, observe the following sentences by Speakers A and B:

(1) A. Kinoo   gakkoo ni ikimasen desita ka?
yesterday school to go-not   did
'Did you not go to school yesterday?'

B. *Hai*, ikimasen desita.
yes go-not   did
'No, I did not go.'

Iie, ikimasita.
no went
'*Yes*, I did.'

†This chapter is for all readers.

(2) A. Kinoo   gakkoo ni itta   n zya arimasen ka?
       yesterday school to went that is-not
       'Isn't it the case that you went to school yesterday?'

   B. *Hai*, ikimasita yo.
      '*Yes*, I did.'

      Iie, ikimasen desita yo.
      '*No*, I didn't.'

Both (1A) and (2A) are negative questions. In (1B) *hai* and *iie* are used for 'no' and 'yes' respectively, while in (2B) they are used just like English 'yes' and 'no'. What is at issue here is not the presence or absence of the syntactic negative (as manifested by *masen*) but the presence or absence of the semantic negative in questions. In other words, the deciding factor here is whether the questioner (A) is expecting a negative answer or not from the hearer. Example (1A) is a neutral (negative) question, and the speaker does not have any presupposition as to whether the hearer's answer will be in the affirmative or not. In such a case, *hai* corresponds to the English 'no', and *iie* to 'yes'. On the other hand, (2A) is a question in which the speaker presupposes that the hearer must have gone to school yesterday. Therefore, (2A) is not, semantically speaking, a negative question, but an affirmative sentence with a tag question at the end. Therefore, (2A) would best be translated as 'You went to school yesterday, didn't you?' In such a case, *hai* is used for the affirmative answer, and *iie* for the negative answer. Questions of the second type, that is, those which presuppose affirmative answers, are not peculiar to Japanese. Most negative questions in English are of this type:

(3) a. Didn't you go to school yesterday?   (You must have.)

   b. Isn't it the case that you gave it up?   (It must be the case.)

   c. Doesn't he look like a hippie?   (He looks like a hippie.)

   d. Isn't it too bad?   (It is too bad.)

   e. Aren't you sick?   (You must be sick.)

The use of *iie* 'no' for the affirmative answer to a negative question in Japanese is often likened to that of *si* in French. In French, the affirmative answer to a positive question is given with the use of *oui* 'yes', while the affirmative answer to a negative question starts with *si*.

(4) A. Est-il arrivé?   'Has he arrived?'

    B. *Oui*, il est arrivé.   'Yes, he has arrived.'

(5) A. N'est-il pas encore arrivé?   'Hasn't he arrived yet?'

    B. *Si*, il est déjà arrivé.   'Yes, he has already arrived.'

However, contrary to that of *iie*, the use of *si* in French is strictly conditioned syntactically: the questioner's presupposition does not play a role in the *oui-si* switch at all. Observe the following sentences:

(6) A. Ne voudriez-vous pas voyager?   'Wouldn't you like to travel?'

    B. *Si*.   'Yes, I would.'

(7) A. Jean, n'est-il pas intéressant?   'John, isn't he (=John) interesting?'

    B. *Si*.[1]   'Yes, he is.'

To recapitulate, the Japanese *hai* is used for introducing a negative-statement answer, and *iie* for introducing a positive-statement answer, to a negative question when it is a neutral question. On the other hand, if a negative question includes the questioner's expectation of the positive-statement answer, *hai* is used for introducing a positive-statement answer, and *iie* a negative-statement answer, just like 'yes' and 'no' in English. The issue, then, is whether, given a negative question, there are any syntactic clues to distinguish a semantically neutral question from one that contains the questioner's expectation of a positive answer. I cannot formulate a precise solution to this issue at present but shall try to give rules of thumb for its determination.

Observe the following sentences by Speakers A and B:

(8) a. A. *Nani mo* kaimasen desita ka?

      anything buy-not did

      'Didn't you buy anything?'

---

[1] *Si* is used in French for contradicting a negative statement. Its use is not restricted to answers to questions. Observe the following sentences:

Connaissez-vous Louise Bedel?	'Do you know Louise Bedel?'
Non, je ne la connais pas.	'No I don't know her.'
Mais *si*.	'Yes, you do.'

Similarly,

Qu'est-ce que vous avez, Marie?	'What is the matter with you, Marie?'
Je n'ai rien de tout, je vous assure.	'Nothing is the matter, really.'
Mais *si*, vous avez quelque chose.	'Yes, there is something wrong. You look
Vous avez l'air triste.	very sad.'

  B. *Hai*, nani mo kaimasen desita.
    yes, anything buy-not   did
    'No, I didn't buy anything.'

  Iie, hon o kaimasita.
    no book   bought
    'Yes, I bought a book.'

b. A. *Nani ka*   kaimasen desita ka?
    something buy-not   did
    'Didn't you buy something?'

  B. *Hai*, hon o kaimasita.
    yes book   bought
    'Yes, I bought a book.'

  Iie, nani mo kaimasen desita.
    no anything buy-not   did
    'No, I didn't buy anything.'

(9) a. A. *Dare mo* rusu   tyuu   ni kimasen   desita ka?
    anyone absence interval in come-not did
    'Didn't anyone come while I was out?'

  B. *Hai*, dare mo kimasen   desita.
    yes anyone come-not did
    'No, no one came.'

  Iie, Yamada-san ga kimasita.
    no   came
    'Yes, Mr. Yamada came.'

b. A. *Dare ka*   rusu   tyuu   ni kimasen   desita ka?
    someone absence interval in come-out did
    'Didn't someone come while I was out?'

  B. *Hai*, Yamada-san ga kimasita.
    yes   came
    'Yes, Mr. Yamada came.'

  Iie, dare mo kimasen   desita.
    no anyone   come-not did
    'No, no one came.'

(10) a. A. Mary wa *doko ni mo* ikimasen desita ka?
                      anywhere go-not   did
          'Didn't Mary go anywhere?'

      B. *Hai*, doko ni mo ikanakatta yoo   desu.
         yes   anywhere go-not-did semblance is
         'No, it seems that she didn't go anywhere.'

         Iie, doko ka   ni itta yoo   desu.
         no   somewhere to went semblance is
         'Yes, it seems that she went somewhere.'

   b. A. Mary wa *doko ka*   ni ikimasen desita ka?
                      somewhere to go-not   did
          'Didn't Mary go somewhere?'

      B. *Hai*, doko ka   ni itta yoo   desu.
         yes somewhere to went semblance is
         'Yes, it seems that she went somewhere.'

         Iie, doko ni mo ikanakatta yoo   desu.
         no   anywhere   go-not-did semblance is
         'No, it seems that she didn't go anywhere.'

As these examples show, negative questions with indefinite pronouns ending with *mo* (8a, 9a, 10a) constitute neutral questions, while those with indefinite pronouns ending with *ka* (8b, 9b, 10b) involve the questioner's presupposition for the positive answer. As the English translation suggests, this distinction between *nani mo, dare mo, doko ni mo* and *nani ka, dare ka, doko ka ni* parallels that between 'any' and 'some' in questions and conditional clauses in English.[2]

(11) a. Do you have *any* money with you now? (Neutral question—the speaker has an open mind as to the hearer having money.)

   b. Do you have *some* money for me? (The speaker thinks that the hearer has the money, but only asks if he is willing to lend him some.)

(12) a. If you have *any* money, please lend me some. (The speaker does not know whether the hearer has some money or not.)

   b. If you have *some* money, please lend me some. (The speaker thinks the hearer has some money.)

[2] See Kruisinga and Erades (1911, pp. 577–578).

When a question involves the ... *no/n desu* 'it is that ...' pattern, it appears to be a neutral question if the negative is in the clause preceding *no/n*, but a question with the expectation of a positive answer if the *desu* is negated. Compare the following sentences:

(13) a. A. Ika*na*katta no   desu ka?
             go-not-did that (it) is
             'Is it the case that you didn't go?'

       B. *Hai*, ikanakatta no   desu.
           yes go-not-did that (it) is
           'Yes, it is the case that I didn't go.'

           Iie, ikimasita yo.
           no went
           'No, I did go.'

     b. A. Itta no de wa ari*masen*   ka?
             went that   (it) is-not
             'Isn't it the case that you went?'

       B. *Hai*, ikimasita yo.
           yes went
           'Yes, I did go.'

           Iie, ikanakatta no/n desu.
           no go-not-did went (it) is
           'No, I didn't go.'

Questions with the negative forms of *omou* 'to think' contain the questioner's expectation of an affirmative answer.

(14) Kore, omosiroi to omoimasen ka? Un. Iya.[3]
      'Don't you think this is interesting? Yes (I think it is interesting).
      No (I don't think it is interesting).'

Negative statements ending with *ne* 'isn't it' with the interrogative intonation always contain the presupposition for the positive answer.

(15) A. Benkyoosite kimasen   desita ne?
          studying   come-not did
          'You didn't do the homework, did you?'

---

[3] *Un* and *iya* are informal forms of *hai* and *iie*, respectively.

B. *Hai.*
   yes
   'No, I didn't do the homework.'

Iie, site   kimasita yo.
no doing came
'Yes, I did do the homework.'

Hai in (15B) means 'yes, your guess is correct. I didn't do the homework'. Similarly, *iie* means 'No, your guess is not correct. I did do the
homework'.

Negative rhetorical questions presuppose the expectation of the
affirmative answer.

(16) John wa baka de wa nakaroo   ka? Sikari,[4] John wa baka de aru.
          fool   not-be-will   yes   fool   is
     'Isn't John stupid? Yes, he is.'

Finally, as was correctly observed by Martin, negative cohortative
questions with *masen* are answered with *hai* if the hearer agrees. If the
hearer does not agree, he would give an excuse instead of answering with
iie.

(17) A.   Sanpo ni ikimasen ka?
           stroll for go-out
           'How about going out for a walk?

     B.   Hai, ikimasyoo.
           yes let's go
           'Yes, let's go.'
           Ima isogasii desu kara, tyotto   matte
           now busy   am   since a minute waiting
           kudasai.
           give (me the favor of)
           'Since I am busy now, please wait for a minute.'
           Compare:
         *Iie, ikimasen.
           no go-not
           'No, I won't go.'

---

[4] *Sikari* and *ina* are archaic forms of *hai* and *iie*, respectively.

In the foregoing, I have given some examples of negative questions for which it can be syntactically determined whether they are neutral questions (or questions in anticipation of negative answers) or whether they are questions that anticipate positive answers. For these questions, the choice between *hai* and *iie* can be made automatically depending upon whether the answer is affirmative or negative.

(18)

	If answer is:	
	Affirmative	Negative
Negative question with no anticipation of positive or negative answer	iie	hai
Negative question with anticipation of negative answer		
Negative question with anticipation of positive answer	hai	iie

Unfortunately, in addition to those clear-cut cases in which *hai* or *iie* can be uniquely chosen, there are many negative questions that can be answered either by *hai* or *iie* regardless of whether the answer is positive or negative. It seems that in these cases, the choice depends upon whether the hearer assumes that the questioner expects a positive answer or a negative answer. Cues lie in intonations or in nonlinguistic environments and seem to be difficult to define syntactically.

(19) A. John ni aimasen desita?
          to meet-not   did
       (with a neutral interrogative intonation on *ta*)
       'Did you not see John?'[5]

    B. *Hai*, aimasen desita.
        yes   meet-not did
        'No, I didn't see him.'

        Iie, aimasen desita.
        no   met
        'No, I didn't see him.'

---

[5] This English translation is misleading because it usually involves the speaker's expectation of a positive answer. The Japanese original, with the specified intonation, is a neutral question not involving such an expectation.

(20) A. Jo⌐hn ni a⌐imase⌐n /desita?
              to meet-not   did
      (with the terminal rising intonation earlier than in (19))
      'Didn't you see John?'

    B. *Hai*, aimasita yo.
       yes met
       'Yes, I did see him.'

      *Iie, aimasita.
       no met
       'Yes, I saw him.'

24[†]

The Anaphoric Use of *Kore*, *Sore*, and *Are*

Table (1) presents a list of demonstratives in Japanese:

(1)

ko-series	*so*-series	*a*-series
kore 'this one'	sore 'that one'	are 'that one there'
koitu 'this guy'	soitu 'that guy'	aitu 'that guy there'
kono '(of) this'	sono '(of) that'	ano '(of) that over there'
konna 'like this'	sonna 'like that'	anna 'like that over there'
koko 'here'	soko 'there'	asoko 'over there'
kotira 'this way'	sotira 'that way'	atira 'that way over there'
koo 'in this way'	soo 'in that way'	aa 'in that way there'

Conventional grammars give adequate explanations of these demonstratives when they are used for referring to something *visible* to the speaker
and the hearer. The *ko*-series is used for referring to something near the
speaker, and the *so*-series for indicating something closer to the hearer
than to the speaker. On the other hand, the *a*-series is used for referring to
something at a distance from both the speaker and the hearer.[1]

However, these demonstratives are used not only for actually pointing
to objects but also for referring to something that the speaker or the hearer
has just mentioned but that is not visible to either the speaker or the hearer
at the time of the speech. Let us call this an *anaphoric* use of demonstratives. For example,

(2) Speaker A: Kinoo   Boston de Yamada-san ni aimasita.
          yesterday   in   met
          'Yesterday I met Mr. Yamada in Boston.'
    Speaker B: *Ano* hito   wa saikin   doosite imasu ka?
                 person   recently how   is
              'How is he (that man) doing these days?'

Ano in (2) does not refer to something visible that is at a distance from
both the speaker and the hearer. It is anaphoric to *Yamada-san* in A's

---

[†]This chapter is for all readers.
[1] There are dialectal differences in areas, relative to the speaker and the hearer, that are
referred to as *kore*, *sore*, and *are*. See Hattori (1968).

speech. Observe that the English demonstrative *this* and *that* also have the anaphoric usage as well as the deictic (that is, finger pointing) one:

(3) a. Nonanaphoric:
   This is a book. *That* is a notebook.
   b. Anaphoric:
   Speaker A: Yesterday, I met a Japanese girl called Hanako.
   Speaker B: Oh, I know *that* girl quite well.

There is an interesting distinction between the *so*-series and the *a*-series in the anaphoric usage. The *a*-series is used only when the speaker knows that the hearer, as well as the speaker himself, knows the referent of the anaphoric demonstrative. The *so*-series, on the other hand, is used either when the speaker knows the referent but thinks that the hearer does not or when the speaker does not know the referent. What I mean by "to know the referent" will become clearer later. First, observe the following conversation between Speakers A and B:

(4) A. Kinoo   Yamada-san ni aimasita. *Ano* (*sono) hito itumo
       yesterday   met   man always
       genki   desu ne.
       healthy is
       'Yesterday, I met Mr. Yamada. That man is always in high spirits.'
    B. Hontoo ni soo desu ne.
       truly   so is
       'Indeed so.'

The use of *ne* 'isn't it' at the end of A's speech shows that the speaker knows that B knows Yamada. Therefore, he can refer to Yamada as *ano hito*. The use of *sono hito* would result in a contradiction because it would show that the speaker knows that B does not know Yamada and yet he is soliciting B's concurrence about Yamada's being in high spirits. Now, observe the following:

(5) A. Kinoo   Yamada-san ni hazimete   aimasita. *Ano* (*sono)
       yesterday   for-the-first-time met
       hito,   zuibun kawatta hito   desu ne.
       person very   strange person is   isn't it
       'I met Mr. Yamada for the first time yesterday. That man is a very strange person, isn't he?'

    B. Ee, *ano* (*sono) hito wa henzin   desu yo.
       yes   man   eccentric is
       'Yes, that man is an eccentric.'

In (5A), Speaker A uses *ano* in referring to Yamada since he knows that
B knows him. Speaker B also refers to Yamada as *ano hito* because he
knows now that A knows Yamada as well. On the other hand, if A does
not know whether B knows Yamada or not, he would use *sono* for referring
to him.

    (6) A-1. Kinoo   Yamada to yuu   hito   ni aimasita. *Sono* (*ano)
             yesterday   as named person   met
             hito,   miti ni mayotte komatte-ita   node,   tasukete
             person way in lose   was-in-trouble because helping
             agemasita.
             gave (the favor of)
             'Yesterday, I met a man by the name of Yamada. Since he
             lost his way and was having difficulties, I helped him.'

       B-1. *Sono* (*ano) hito,   hige   o hayasita tyuunen   no
                           person beard   grew   middle-aged
             hito   desyoo?
             person is
             'Isn't that person a middle-aged man with a beard?'

       A-2. Hai, soo desu.
             yes so is
             'Yes, that's right.'

       B-2. { *Sono* } hito   nara, watasi mo sitte-imasu yo. Watasi mo
             { *Ano* } person if   I   too know   I   too
             { *sono* } hito   o tasukete ageta
             { *ano* } person   helping giving (the favor of)
             koto ga arimasu.
             have-an-experience-of
             'I know him, too. I have helped that man, too.'

In (6B-1), B answers with *sono* because he is not sure yet whether the
person that A has mentioned is the person that he knows well. Reply B-1
with *sono* would be literally translated as 'That person that you have
mentioned whom you have assumed that I don't know—isn't he a middle-

aged man with a beard?' On the other hand, B-1 with *ano* would be translated as 'That man that both you and I know well—isn't he a middle-aged man with a beard?' and thus is semantically anomalous. In (B-2), since B now knows that the person that A has been talking about is the person that he also knows, he can refer to him as *ano hito*, thus indicating that he knows the person very well. He could use *sono hito*, indicating that he had only a casual encounter and really does not know him well enough.

If B does not know Yamada, the person who is being dicussed, at all, he would continue to use *sono* throughout the conversation although he now knows of him because A has talked about him. Thus (6A-1) might be followed by (6B-3).

(6) B-3. *Sono* (*ano) hito,   doko ni iku tokoro datta no   desu ka?
             person where to go about was   that is
        'Where was it that he was going?'

This shows that an indirect acquaintance with someone through hearsay does not constitute "formally knowing him." On the other hand, in referring to public figures, for example, who are known to both the speaker and the hearer, *sono* is never used. The use of the *a*-series is acceptable but implies that the speaker knows the figures more or less personally or that he feels as if he knew them personally.

So far, I have discussed only the use of *sono* and *ano* in referring to humans. The use of these demonstratives in reference to things, events, places, time, and manner also shows the same characteristics. Observe the following conversation between A and B:

(7) A.   Sensyuu Harvard Square no soba   de kazi ga arimasita.
          last week   's proximity in fire   was
          Sono kazi de, gakusei ga hutari   sinda soo   desu.
                 fire by students   two-persons died hearsay is
          'Last week there was a fire near Harvard Square. I hear that two students were killed by that fire.'

    B-1. *Sono* kazi no koto wa sinbun   de yomimasita.
               fire 's story   newspaper in read
          'I have read about that fire in the newspaper.'

In (7) the use of *sono kazi* by B implies that B did not see the fire. But if B had been there at the place of the fire, he might have answered A in the following manner:

(7) B-2. Watakusi mo tyoodo Harvard Square no soba   ni ite
       I   too just   's proximity in being
      sono (*ano*) kazi o mimasita. *Are* (*sore) wa hidoi   kazi
               fire   saw   terrible fire
      desita ne.
      was
      'I also happened to be in the Harvard Square area and saw that fire. That was a devastating fire, wasn't it?'

The use of *are* by Speaker B implies that he thinks that Speaker A also witnessed the fire. More examples follow:

(8) A. Mary ni wa ninen   mae Tokyo de aimasita.
               two-years ago   in met
      Anata mo goissyo desita ne?
      you   too together were
      'I saw Mary two years ago in Tokyo. You were with me then, weren't you?'

    B. *Ano* (*sono) toki wa Mary mo mada genki   desita ga ...
                time   too still   healthy was   but
      'At that time, Mary was still healthy, but ...'

(9) A. Mary ni   wa ninen   mae Tokyo de aimasita.
             with   two-years ago   in met
      'I met Mary two years ago in Tokyo.'

    B. *Sono* (*ano) toki Mary wa hitori desita ka?
               time   alone was
      'Was Mary alone at that time?'

In (8), B uses *ano toki* 'that time' because he shared with A the knowledge of the specific time that A is alluding to: he knows 'that time' because he was with A. On the other hand, in (9) he uses *sono toki* because he does not share with A the knowledge of the time that A saw Mary. That B took part in the act of seeing Mary in (8), but not in (9), is the deciding factor here. Next, observe the following conversation:

(10) A. Watakusi ga Mary to   wakareta no wa moo   zyuunen
        I   from departed that   already ten-years
        mae desu yo.
        ago is
        'It is already ten years since I got separated from Mary.'

     B. *Ano* koro wa mina wakakatta   ne.
            times   all were-young
        'We were all young in those days, weren't we?'

In (10), B of course did not take part in A's separation from Mary. But he must have had some involvement in this matter, to the extent that 'that time' rings a bell with B. Thus, he shares with A the knowledge of the time that A got a separation from Mary. If he has not shared the knowledge of the time with A, he would not have used *ano*. In such a case, (10A) might have been followed by (11B).

(11) B. *Sono* (**ano*) koro wa, Mary wa mada genki   desita ka?
               times   still   healthy was
        'Was Mary still healthy around then?'

More examples follow:

(12) A. Kinoo   Nikkoo ni itte   kimasita.
        yesterday   to going came
        'I went to Nikko (and came back) yesterday.'

     B. *Asoko* wa itu   itte   mo ii   tokoro desu ne.
            there   whenever going   good place is
        'That place there is a nice place whenever you go.'

     A. Aa, anata mo Nikkoo ni irassyatta koto ga aru n desu ne?
        yes you too   went   have-an-experience-of
        'Ah, you have been to Nikko yourself, haven't you?'

     B. Hai, nando mo   ikimasita.
        yes many times went
        'Yes, I have been there many times.'

(13) A. John wa baka de   komarimasu.
                   stupid being I-am-annoyed
                   'I am annoyed that John is stupid.'

     B. Hontoo ni *sonna* (*anna) ni baka   na no desu ka?
        truly   that much   stupid is that is
        'Is it that he is really that stupid?'

(14) A. John wa baka de komarimasu.

     B. Hontoo ni *anna* (*sonna*) ni baka   de wa komarimasu ne.
        truly   that much   stupid is
        'I am annoyed that he is that stupid.'

In (13) the use of *sonna ni* by B indicates that B does not know to what degree John is stupid. On the other hand, in (14) the use of *anna ni* by B indicates that B knows from his own observation how stupid John is, and that he is concurring with A that he observed in John the same degree of stupidity that he believes A has observed.

    I have shown that when they are used anaphorically, the *so*-series and the *a*-series lose their original meaning of "closer to the hearer than to the speaker" and "at a distance both from the speaker and the hearer." The anaphoric *a*-series is used for referring to something (at a distance either in time or space) that the speaker knows both he and the hearer know personally or have shared experiences in, while the anaphoric *so*-series is used for referring to something that is not known personally to either the speaker or the hearer or has not been a shared experience between them. The *ko*-series can be used for indicating something as if it were visible to both the speaker and the hearer at the time of the conversation, and thus it imparts vividness to the conversation.

(15) Boku no tomodati ni   Yamada to yuu hito   ga iru n da ga,
     I   's friend   among   named person   exists   but
     kono otoko wa nakanaka   no rironka   de, . . .
     this man   considerable   theoretician is
     'I have a friend by the name of Yamada. This man is a theoretician of some caliber, and . . .'

Assume that Speaker B followed Speaker A's utterance given in (15) with

(16) Aa, *sono* (*ano,* *kono) hito   nara, boku mo yoku sitte imasu yo.
     ah   person if   I   also well know
     'Ah, I know that man well.'
     Ano (**sono,* *kono) hito   wa zuibun giron-zuki   desu ne.
                            person   very   argument-fond-of is
     'That man likes very much to argue, doesn't he?'

The first use of *sono* in (16) is probably nonanaphoric but demonstrative. It seems that Speaker B, in response to Speaker A's reference to Yamada as if he were present at his side, now refers to him as a person who is present at A's side (is closer to A than to B). What is interesting here is that the use of *kono* in (16) would result in ungrammaticality. In ordinary demonstrative uses Speaker B can refer with the *ko*-series to what Speaker A has already indicated by using the *ko*-series. For example, assume that A points to a ring on B's finger as if touching it. Then the following conversation is possible:

(17) A. *Kore,* nan   desu ka?
             what is
         'What is this?'

     B. *Kore,* engeizi   ringu yo.
             engagement ring
         'This is an engagement ring.'

Likewise, in (18) the reader would imagine the scene in which B is holding A's watch in his hand and examining it closely.

(18) A. *Kono* tokei kinoo   kaimasita.
             watch yesterday bought
         'I bought this watch yesterday.'

     B. *Kore,* doko-sei?
         this   where-make
         'What country's product is it?'

In this way, an object that is visible and referred to with the use of the *ko*-series can be tossed around, so to speak, between the speaker and the hearer, with each of them referring to it as something that is closer to himself than to the other. On the other hand, as has been seen in (15) and (16), an object that is not visible but is referred to by the *ko*-series semidemonstratively cannot be tossed around between the speaker and the hearer. Once the speaker has referred to Yamada as *kono hito* 'this person', the hearer can no longer refer to him as *kono hito*.

What is also interesting about (16) is that once the understanding is established, through B's first sentence, that both A and B know Yamada well, B can no longer use the *so*-series and A can no longer use the *ko*-series in referring to him. Hence, the second statement in (16) is ungrammatical if *sono* has been used. In subsequent conversations, both A and B must use the *a*-series in referring to Yamada. Thus, the *ko*-series, in this semianaphoric semidemonstrative usage, can be used only when only the speaker knows the object well.

In summary, anaphoric uses of the *ko*-, *so*-, and *a*-series have the following characteristics:

(i)   The *a*-series is used for referring to something (at a distance either in time or space) that the speaker knows both he and the hearer know personally or have shared experience in.

(ii) The *so*-series is used for referring to something that is not known personally to either the speaker or the hearer or has not been a shared experience between them.

(iii) The *ko*-series is used semianaphorically as if the object being talked about were visible and were at the speaker's side. The hearer cannot refer to the same object by using the *ko*-series in spite of the fact that in the ordinary demonstrative use of the *ko*-series the same object can occasionally be referred to with *ko* by both the speaker and the hearer. Once the understanding is established between the two that both know the object well, the *a*-series takes precedence, and the use of the *ko*-series results in unacceptability.

25†

The Reflexive Pronoun and the Passive and Causative Constructions

1. English and Japanese Reflexive Pronouns

There are four important differences between the English reflexive pronoun and the Japanese reflexive pronoun. First, in English, the form of reflexive pronouns varies according to the person, gender, and number of their antecedents. For example,

(1) a. *I* despise *myself*.

    b. *John* despises *himself*.

    c. *Mary* despises *herself*.

    d. *John and Mary* despise *themselves*.

In Japanese, the same form, *zibun*, is used for all persons, genders, and numbers.

(2) a. Boku ('I')

    b. John

    c. Mary

    d. John to Mary ('John and Mary')

    wa *zibun* o keibetusite-iru.

    self   despising-is

Second, in English, the antecedent of a reflexive pronoun can be inanimate. For example,

(3) a. *History* repeats *itself*.

    b. *The newspaper* unfolded *itself* in the wind.

On the other hand, the antecedent of *zibun* 'self' in Japanese must be something that is animate and has will power.[1] Thus, examples (4a) and (4b), as translations of (3a) and (3b), respectively, are ungrammatical.

(4) a. *Rekisi wa *zibun* o kurikaesu.

    history   self   repeat

†This chapter is linguistically oriented but should also be of interest to students of Japanese.
[1] This seems to be related to the fact that transitive constructions with inanimate subjects are ungrammatical in Japanese except in the direct translation style.

b. *Sono sinbun   wa kaze ni zibun o hirogeta.
   the newspaper   wind in self   unfolded
   '(Lit.) The newspaper unfolded itself in the wind.'

Third, in English, the antecedent of a reflexive pronoun can be either the subject of the sentence or some other element (for example, the object of the sentence). Observe the following examples:

(5) a. *John* talked to Mary about *himself*.

    b. Mary talked to *John* about *himself*.

    c. *John* talked to *Bill* about *himself*.

    d. *John* showed *Bill* a picture of *himself*.

In (5a), *John*, the antecedent of *himself*, is the subject of the sentence. In (5b), on the other hand, *John*, the antecedent of *himself*, is the indirect object of the verb of the sentence. Thus, ambiguous sentences such as (5c) and (5d) result. In these sentences, the antecedent of *himself* can be either the subject or the indirect object of the sentence.

In Japanese, on the other hand, in the ordinary style, the antecedent of a reflexive pronoun must be the subject of the sentence. For example, the following are not ambiguous:

(6) a. John ga Bill ni *zibun* no koto   o hanasita.
                  to self 's matter   talked
        'John talked to Bill about (lit.) self's matter.'

    b. John ga Bill ni *zibun* no syasin o miseta.
                  to self 's picture   showed
        'John showed Bill a picture of (lit.) self.'

In these sentences *zibun* refers to *John* and cannot refer to *Bill*, which is a nonsubject element in the sentences.

Fourth, in English, a reflexive pronoun and its antecedent must be in the same sentence. For example, (7) is grammatical because *John* and *himself* are in the same sentence.

(7) *John* will take good care of *himself*.

However, (8) is ungrammatical because *himself* is in a subordinate clause that does not contain *John*.

(8) **John* expects [that Mary will take good care of *himself*].

On the other hand, in Japanese, reflexive pronouns do not have to be in the same sentence as their antecedents. For example, (9) is ambiguous: *zibun* can refer to either *Mary* or *John*.

(9) John wa [Mary ga *zibun* o daizi-ni-suru   koto]o kitaisite-iru.
                    self   take-good-care-of that   expecting-is
    'John expects that Mary will take good care of (lit.) self.'

It is not the case that *zibun* in any subordinate clause can refer to the subject of the main sentence. For example,

(10) *John wa Mary ga *zibun* o korosita toki Jane to   nete   ita.
                    self   killed   when   with in-bed was
    'John was in bed with Jane when Mary killed (lit.) self.'

Example (10) is not grammatical with *zibun* coreferential with *John*.

It is not the purpose of this chapter to specify exactly under what conditions *zibun* in a subordinate sentence can be coreferential with the main sentence subject and under what conditions it cannot be.[2] The purpose of this chapter is to discuss, on the basis of the use of *zibun* in simple sentences, how causative and passive sentences are derived in Japanese.

2. Cases of Ambiguous Reference of *Zibun*

First, observe the following sentences:[3]

(11) a. *John ga Mary$_i$ o zibun$_i$ no uti   de korosita.
                        self   's house in killed
        'John killed Mary in her own house.

    b. *John ga Mary$_i$ o zibun$_i$ no uti   de mita.
                        self   's house in saw
        'John saw Mary in her own house.'

    c. *John ga Mary$_i$ o zibun$_i$ no imooto to   kurabeta.
                        self   's sister with compared
        'John compared Mary with her own sister.'

[2] This matter will be discussed in detail in the next chapter.
[3] Examples (11a) and (12), which are crucial for proving that Reflexivization must apply before embedded predicates lose their overt subjects, are due to Akatsuka (1970). Masayoshi Shibatani has also independently arrived at the same observation. See Shibatani (1971).

These sentences are grammatical if *zibun* is meant to be coreferential with *John*, the subject of the sentences. However, if *zibun* is to refer to *Mary*, as indicated in the translation, they are ungrammatical. These examples confirm the point presented earlier, namely, that the antecedent of the Japanese reflexive pronoun must be the subject of the sentence.

Now, consider the following sentence:

(12) John ga Mary ni zibun no uti   de hon o yom-(s)ase-ta.
                       self   's house in book   read-causative-ed
     'John made Mary read books in (lit) self's house.'

This sentence is ambiguous: *zibun no uti* can refer either to John's house or to Mary's. The first interpretation is no problem because the antecedent of *zibun* in this interpretation is the subject of the sentence. The second interpretation poses a problem because *zibun*'s antecedent would be *Mary*, which is not the subject of the sentence. Why is it that *zibun* of (12) can be coreferential with *Mary*, while *zibun* of (11) cannot be?

The major difference between (12) and (11) seems to be that the former, although it appears to be a simple sentence, is composed of two sentences:

(13) a. John ga Mary ni nanika   o saseta.
                       something   made-do
     'John made Mary do something.'

   b. Mary ga hon o yomu.
            books   read
     'Mary reads books.'

Sentence (13b) represents what that something is that John made Mary do. What is important to note here is that *Mary* is the semantic subject of (13b), which is contained in (12). Therefore, since (14) is perfectly grammatical with *zibun* referring to *Mary*, (12) is also grammatical in the interpretation in which *zibun* is coreferential with *Mary*.

(14) Mary ga zibun no uti   de hon o yomu.
               self   's house in book   read
     'Mary reads books in her own house.'

On the other hand, such an explanation is not possible for (11). It is not possible to claim that, for example, (11a) contains a subordinate clause whose subject is *Mary*.

This explanation shows that in order to preserve the simplest generalization that the antecedent of the reflexive *zibun* must be the subject of the sentence, example (12), in its interpretation with *zibun* coreferential with *Mary*, must be derived from the structure that has *Mary* as the subject of *hon o yomu* 'to read books', and that such an analysis is also semantically motivated. The theory of transformational grammar gives us tools for formally representing this fact in the following manner.

Example (12), with *zibun* coreferential with *Mary*, is derived from this deep structure:

(15) John ga Mary ni [Mary ga *Mary* no uti   de hon o yom]$_S$ sase-ta.[4]
                  to   's house   book   read cause-ed

'(Lit.) John caused Mary [Mary read books in Mary's house].'

Note that the causative *sase* is taken here to be a main verb that takes two objects: indirect object [*Mary ni*] and the sentential direct object, which is in square brackets in (15). *Mary* (*ga*), the subject of the embedded sentence, is deleted under identity with the indirect object of the main sentence. However, this deletion occurs after the embedded sentence has been transformed into that of (14) by a transformation that I shall henceforth refer to as Reflexivization. Namely, first, *Mary* of *Mary no uti de* 'in Mary's house' is reflexivized and becomes *zibun* because it is coreferential with the subject of the embedded sentence. Then, *Mary* (*ga*), which is the subject of the embedded sentence, is deleted because it is identical with the indirect object of the main sentence. Note that it would not do to delete the subject of the embedded sentence before reflexivizing *Mary*. By first deleting *Mary* (*ga*), the following structure would result:

(16) John ga Mary ni [Mary no uti   de hon o yom] sase-ta.
                            's house   book   read cause-ed

Now there is only one antecedent for *Mary* of the embedded sentence, namely, *Mary* (*ni*). Since the latter is not the subject of the main sentence, the former should not become *zibun*, and thus the interpretation of (12) with *zibun* coreferential with *Mary* would remain unaccounted for.

[4] More accurately, (12) is derived from the following less redundant structure, and particles *ga*, *ni*, and *o* are inserted at some points in the derivation of the sentence:
John Mary [Mary Mary no uti de hon yom]$_S$ sase-ta.
How these particles can be predicted is not the concern of this chapter, and therefore I shall use the representation of (15), with particles already inserted, as if it were the deep structure of (12).

This explanation is based on an assumption basic to the theory of transformational grammar that some transformations apply cyclically—namely, given transformations $T_1, T_2 \ldots, T_n$, they apply first to the most deeply embedded sentence, next to the second most deeply embedded sentence, and so on, and finally to the topmost (main) sentence. Such transformations are called cyclical transformations. Reflexivization is a cyclical transformation.

The derivation of (12) from (15), already given, can be more technically represented as the following:

(a) In the first cycle, Reflexivization applies to the embedded sentence, turning the second occurrence of *Mary* into *zibun*.

(b) In the second cycle, *Mary* (*ga*), the subject of the embedded sentence, is deleted under identity with *Mary* (*ni*), the indirect object of the main sentence.

Example (12) can also be taken as meaning that John made Mary read books in *his own* house. In this interpretation, (12) is derived from the following deep structure:

(17) John ga Mary ni [Mary ga *John* no uti   de hon o yom]$_S$
                          to   's house in book   read
     sase-ta.
     cause-ed
     '(Lit.) John caused Mary [Mary read books in John's house].'

The derivation of (12) from (17) proceeds in the following manner:

(a) In the first cycle, Reflexivization does not apply because there are no coreferential noun phrases in the embedded sentence.

(b) *Mary* (*ga*), the subject of the embedded sentence, is deleted under identity with *Mary* (*ni*), the indirect object of the main sentence. Then Reflexivization applies and turns the second occurrence of *John* to *zibun* because it is coreferential with the subject of the main sentence.

3. Deep Structure of Causative Sentences

In the foregoing it has been shown that one can give a very natural explanation for the fact that *zibun* in causative sentences such as (12) can be coreferential with the indirect object—an apparent violation of the principle that the antecedent of *zibun* must be the subject of the sentence. The explanation is that there used to be a coreferential noun phrase as the subject of the embedded clause, which is responsible for the reflexivization, but which in turn has been deleted because it is coreferential with the indirect object of the sentence.

There are independent justifications for hypothesizing the deep structure of the form of (15) for causative sentences. First of all, (15) represents naturally the meaning of the corresponding surface sentence of (12). Second, the transformation for deleting the subject of the embedded sentence under identity with the indirect object of the main sentence is needed independently for other constructions. For example, the same transformation will turn the (a) structures into (b) in the following:

(18) a. John ga Mary ni [Mary ga tegami o kak]$_S$ morat-ta.
                              letter   write receive-the-favor-of

   b. John ga Mary ni tegami o kaite moratta.
      'John asked for, and received, from Mary the favor of writing a letter.'

(19) a. John ga Mary ni [Mary ga tegami o kaku]$_S$ koto o meizita.
                              letter   write that   ordered

   b. John ga Mary ni tegami o kaku koto o meizita.
      'John ordered Mary to write a letter.'

Note here that (18) contains causative form *moraw* 'to politely ask for and receive the favor of'.

Third, *sase* is a highly productive morpheme and can be added to almost any active verb to produce causative forms. It also has a specific semantic content, namely, that of 'to cause'. It can be followed by the passive morpheme, *rare*, like other verbs, or by a tense marker. Thus, it has some of the characteristics of a verb.[5]

---

[5] The only thing that is peculiar to *sase* is that it is a bound form and cannot appear without being preceded by the stem form of some other verb and that it changes its form in certain contexts. Namely, if it is preceded by a verb whose stem ends in a consonant, the initial consonant of *sase* drops. For example,

tabe 'to eat' + sase = tabesase
yom 'to read' + sase = yomase

However, the latter feature is a part of a very general rule in Japanese that drops the initial consonant of a bound form if it is preceded by a morpheme that ends in a consonant:

tabe + ru 'present' = taberu
yom + ru   = yomu
tabe + rare 'passive' + ru 'present' = taberareru
yom + rare   + ru   = yomareru

Fourth, note that for sentences such as (18b) and (19b), for which there are independent syntactic justifications for hypothesizing the presence of embedded sentences in the deep structure, the same type of ambiguity results with respect to the reference of *zibun*. Observe the following sentences:

(20) a. John ga Mary ni *zibun* no uti   de benkyoosite-moratta.
                            self   's house in study-caused
'John asked for, and received, from Mary, the favor of (her) studying in *his/her* own house.'

b. John wa Mary ni *zibun* no uti   de tegami o kaku
                        self   's house in letter   write
$\left\{\begin{matrix} \text{koto o} \\ \text{yoo ni} \end{matrix}\right\}$ $\begin{matrix} \text{meizita.} \\ \text{ordered} \end{matrix}$
      to
'John ordered Mary to write a letter in *his/her* own house.'

c. John wa Mary ni *zibun* no uti   de benkyoosuru koto o
                        self   's house in study   that
kitaisuru.
expect
'John expects Mary to study in *his/her* own house.'

d. John wa Mary ni *zibun* no uti   de benkyoosuru yoo
                        self   's house in study   so-that
yookyunsita.
demanded
'John demanded that Mary study in *his/her* own house.'

These sentences give indisputable evidence for the hypothesis presented here that the antecedent of *zibun* must be the subject of a sentence (main or embedded) and that when there is an apparent counterexample, it is the case that what used to be the subject, with which *zibun* is coreferential, has been either deleted or moved out of the subject position by some transformation.[6]

---

[6] Some transformational grammarians claim that the verb *die* in English is derived from the deep structure representation corresponding to 'to COME to be dead', and that the verb *kill* is derived from the representation corresponding to 'to CAUSE (someone) to COME to be dead'. See, for example, Lakoff (1970, pp. 98–100).

4. Passive Sentences

Let us now turn to the passive sentences. Observe the following sentences:

(21) a. Mary wa John ni zibun no uti   de koros-(r)are-ta.
                        by self   's house in kill-passive-ed
         'Mary was killed by John in (lit.) self's house.'

      b. Mary wa John ni zibun no uti   de mi-rare-ta.
                        by self   's house in see-passive-ed
         'Mary was seen by John in (lit.) self's house.'

      c. Mary wa John ni zibun no imooto to   kurabe-rare-ta.
                        by self   's sister with compare-passive-ed
         'Mary was compared by John with (lit.) self's sister.'

These are the passive versions of (11). What is interesting here is that they are not ambiguous; *zibun* of these sentences is coreferential only with

---

With respect to this analysis, note that (i) is not ambiguous.

(i) John ga Mary o zibun no uti   de korosita.
                        self   's house in killed
    'John killed Mary in his own house.'

Zibun can refer only to *John*. Assume that *koros* 'to kill' is actually a causative verb and is derived from *sin* 'to die' + *SASE* where *SASE* is an abstract verb meaning 'to cause'. According to this proposal, (i) would be derived from a deep structure like

(ii) John [Mary ga John/Mary no uti de sin] SASE-ta.
                                      die cause

This deep structure would seem to represent the meaning of (i) accurately. However, the transformation for deriving *koros* 'to kill' from *sin-SASE* 'to cause to die' would be ad hoc in that it would have only one domain of application, that is, the domain for which it has been designed, namely, to turn *sin-SASE* into *koros*. There can be no morphological and phonological justification as to why *sin-SASE* changes into *koros*. It is interesting to note here that if (ii) were the deep structure for (i), then (i) should be ambiguous. That is, if (ii) had *John no uti de* 'in John's house', this *John* would be reflexivized under identity with the main sentence subject in the second cycle. If (i), on the other hand, had *Mary no uti de* 'in Mary's house', this *Mary* would be reflexivized in the first cycle under identity with the subject of the embedded sentence. Thus both cases would lead to (i). However, we have already noted that (i) is not ambiguous and cannot mean that John killed Mary in Mary's house. This shows that the deep structure of (ii), which is ad hoc in that it requires a very peculiar transformation that would change *sin-SASE* to *koros*, can be rejected as implausible on the basis of the phenomenon of reflexivization. As far as this process is concerned, (i) shows every characteristic of having been derived from a simple deep structure with no embedded sentence with *Mary* as its subject.

Shibatani (1971) has independently given the same explanation (and some others) for not deriving *koros* 'kill' from *sin* 'die' + *SASE*.

Mary and not with *John*. What this fact implies is that these passive sentences are derived from the corresponding active sentences and that *Reflexivization applies after Passivization has been applied.*[7] For example, (21a) is derived in the following manner:

(22) a. Deep structure:

      John wa Mary o *Mary* no uti   de korosita.

                          's house in killed

      'John killed Mary in Mary's house.'

    b. Passivization:

      Mary wa John ni Mary no uti de koros-(r)are-ta.

                by   passive

    c. Reflexivization:

      Mary wa John ni zibun no uti de koros-(r)are-ta.

This derivation explains why (21a) has the interpretation in which *zibun* is coreferential with *Mary*. On the other hand, the following derivation, whose deep structure has *John no uti* 'John's house' instead of *Mary no uti*, explains why (21a) does not mean that Mary was killed in John's house:

(23) a. Deep structure:

      John wa Mary o *John* no uti   de korosita.

                         's house in killed

    b. Passivization:

      Mary wa John ni John no uti de koros-(r)are-ta.

    c. Reflexivization:

      (does not apply because the first occurrence of *John* is not the subject of the sentence)

Therefore, Pronominalization instead of Reflexivization would apply, yielding

(24) Mary wa John ni *kare* no uti de korosareta.

                    he

      'Mary was killed by John in his house.'

Thus, the deep structure of (23a), which represents the meaning of (11a), cannot lead to the surface sentence (21a).

---

[7] Note that if Reflexivization were to apply before Passivization, (11a) and (21a) should be synonymous, and both should mean what (11a) means.

The preceding analysis suggests that passive sentences of the type given in (21) are not derived from complex deep structures such as

(25) Mary ga [John ga Mary o John/Mary no uti   de koros]
                                                's   house in kill

     rare-ta.
     passive-ed
     '(Lit.) Mary underwent [John kill Mary in John's/Mary's house].'

If this were the deep structure of (21a), the sentence should be ambiguous, but it is not.

5. Adversity Passives

If the simplex deep structure as represented in (22a) is the deep structure for (21a), then what is the deep structure for sentences such as (26), for which it is not possible to hypothesize simplex active sentences, as shown in (27)?

(26) a. John wa ame ni hur-(r)are-ta.
              rain by fall-passive-ed
          'John was rained on.'

    b. John wa tuma ni sin-(r)are-ta.
              wife by die-passive-ed
        '(Lit.) John was died by his wife. To John's chagrin, his wife died.'

(27) a. *Ame ga John ni hutta.
        rain   to fell
        'Rain fell on John.'

    b. *Tuma ga John ni sinda.
        wife   died
        'His wife died on John.'

For these passive sentences, one is forced to hypothesize complex deep structures such as

(28) a. John ga [ame ga hur]$_s$ rare-ta.
              rain   fall suffered
        'John suffered from rain's falling.'

b. John ga [tuma ga sin]$_S$ rare-ta.
            wife   die suffered
    'John suffered from his wife's dying.'

How, then, can one reconcile these two facts: some passive sentences must be derived from simplex deep structures, and some others from complex deep structures?

Note that the passive sentences of (21) and those of (26) are quite different semantically. The former are pure passive sentences, while the latter are what is usually called adversity passives. That is, the latter sentences imply that the subject of the main sentence has been inadvertently affected by the action represented in the rest of the sentence. This connotation of suffering or inadvertent effect on the part of the main subject is completely lacking in pure passive sentences of the former type. To make this point clearer, observe the following pairs of sentences:

(29) a. Kono ie   wa 1960-nen ni tate-rare-ta.
       this   house   year in build-passive-ed
       'This house was built in 1960.'

     b. John wa niwa no sugu mae ni ie   o tate-rare-ta.
               yard 's right front in house   build-passive-ed
       'John had a house built on him right in front of (his) yard.'

(30) a. Sono yubiwa wa doroboo ni nusum-(r)are-ta.
       the   ring   thief   by steal-passive-ed
       'The ring was stolen by the thief.'

     b. Mary wa sono yubiwa o doroboo ni nusum-(r)are-ta.
             the   ring   thief   by steal-passive-ed
       'Mary had the ring stolen on her by the thief.'

Again, (29a) and (30a) are pure passive sentences, and there is no connotation of adversity involved here. (How can a house be inadvertently affected by being built?) On the other hand, (29b) and (30b) definitely show that John and Mary were affected by a house being built, and the ring being stolen, respectively. Note that this connotation of adversity passive arises only when there is an extra noun phrase (*John* and *Mary* in the preceding examples) that cannot be accounted for by simplex deep structure of the active version—namely, only when the complex deep structure of the type of (28) is needed.

The conclusion that I have been led to in the foregoing is that pure passive sentences are derived from the simplex deep structure of the corresponding active sentences, while adversity passives are derived from complex deep structures.[8] This hypothesis[9] predicts that *zibun* in adversity passives can be ambiguous. This prediction is borne out by the following examples:

(31) a. John wa Mary ni zibun no kazoku no hanasi bakari
                by self   's family 's talk   only

    s-(r)are-ta.
    do-passive-ed
    'John was affected by Mary's talking only about (lit.) self's family.'

[8] Irwin Howard (1969) proposed that there are two types of passive sentences in Japanese —pure passives and adversity passives—and that the former type is derived from the simplex deep structure, the latter from the complex deep structure, as shown earlier. The difference between Howard's analysis and the one presented here is that, while I regard (i) as a pure passive sentence derivable only from the simplex deep structure of (ii), Howard thinks that (i) is ambiguous between pure passive and adversity passive and that it is derived from both (ii) and (iii).

(i)   Mary wa John ni koros-(r)are-ta
             by kill-passive-ed
   'Mary was killed by John.'
(ii) John wa Mary o koros-ita.
   'John killed Mary.'
(iii) Mary wa [John ga Mary o koros] (r)are-ta.
               kill   passive-ed

I do not get any adversity-passive interpretation for (i). Similarly, none of the following sentences have the adversity-passive interpretation, namely, the one that says that John was adversely affected by being elected as representative of the students, etc.:

(iv) a. John wa gakusei no daihyoo   ni erab-(r)are-ta.
            student 's representative as elect-passive-ed
     'John was elected as representative of the students.'
   b. John wa minna ni tensai to iw-(r)are-te   iru.
           all   by genius as say-passive-ing is
     'John is said by all to be a genius.'
   c. John wa hoobi   o atae-rare-ta.
           reward   give-passive-ed
     'John was given a reward.'

[9] The same hypothesis has been arrived at independently by Akatsuka (personal communication, 1971).

b. John wa Mary ni zibun no koto o zimans-(r)are-ta.
            by self   's matter boast-passive-ed
   'John suffered from Mary's bragging about (lit.) self's matter.'

c. John wa Mary ni zibun no uti   de nekom-(r)are-ta.
            by self   's house in become-sick-passive
   'John was affected by Mary's becoming bedridden in (lit.) self's house.'

d. John wa Mary ni zibun no zikka ni kaer-(r)are-ta.
            by self   's home to return
   'John had Mary (his wife) return to (lit.) self's family house.'

All of these sentences are ambiguous: *zibun* can be coreferential either with *John*, the subject of the sentences, or with *Mary*, a nonsubject element. This ambiguity can be explained easily in the following manner. For example, (31a) has two deep structures:

(32) a. John ga [Mary ga *John* no kazoku no hanasi bakari su]$_s$ rare-ta.
                      's family 's talk   only do
    '(Lit.) John suffered from Mary's talking only about John's family.'

b. John ga [Mary ga *Mary* no kazoku no hanasi bakari su]$_s$ rare-ta.
                     's family 's talk   only do
    '(Lit.) John suffered from Mary's talking only about Mary's family.'

For (32a) nothing of any significance here happens in the first cycle of the derivation. In the second cycle *Mary* (*ga*) is raised out of the embedded sentence, and becomes *Mary ni* 'by Mary'. Next, Reflexivization applies, turning *John* of the embedded sentence into *zibun* under identity with the main subject. This results in (31a). On the other hand, for (32b), Reflexivization applies in the first cycle, turning *Mary* to *zibun* under identity with the first *Mary*, the subject of the embedded sentence. In the second cycle *Mary ga* is raised out of the embedded clause and becomes *Mary ni* 'by Mary'. This derivation also produces (31a).

6. Additional Examples

Observe the following sentence:

(33) Mary wa John ni zibun no uti   de hon o
                        by self   's house in book
      yom-(s)ase-rare-ta.
      read-causative-passive-ed
      'Mary was made by John to read books in (lit.) self's house.'

This sentence is not ambiguous: *zibun* can refer only to *Mary*. This fact
is easily explainable by hypothesizing the following two deep structures
and respective derivations from them:

(34) a. Deep structure:
          John ga Mary ni [Mary ga *Mary* no uti   de hon o yom]
                                        's house in book   read
          (s)ase-ta.
          cause-ed

      b. First cycle:
          Reflexivization
          John ga Mary ni [Mary ga *zibun* no uti de hon o yom] (s)ase-ta.

      c. Second cycle:
          (i) Deletion of the embedded subject
          John ga Mary ni zibun no uti de hon o yom-(s)ase-ta.
          'John made Mary read a book in her own house.'
          (ii) Pure Passivization
          Mary ga John ni zibun no uti de hon o yom-(s)ase-rare-ta.
          'Mary was made by John to read a book in her own house.'

(35) a. Deep structure:
          John ga Mary ni [Mary ga *John* no uti   de hon o yom]
                                        's house in book   read
          (s)ase-ta.
          caused

      b. First cycle:
          Nothing happens.

      c. Second cycle:
          (i) Deletion of the embedded subject
          John ga Mary ni John no uti de hon o yom-(s)ase-ta.

(ii) Pure Passivization
Mary ga John ni John no uti de hon o yom-(s)ase-rare-ta.
'Mary was made by John to read a book in John's house.'
(iii) Reflexivization does not apply because the first occurrence
of *John* is not a subject.

Thus, the deep structure of (35) does not lead to (33). This explains why
(33) does not have the interpretation in which *zibun* refers to *John*. Note
that (33) is a pure passive sentence and therefore is derived from the active
version directly. For this reason the deep structure of (33) contains only
one embedded sentence. The following sentence contains two embedded
sentences:

(36) John wa Mary ni, kodomo ni zibun no heya de hon o
                          child   self   's room in book
     yom-(s)asete-moratta.
     read-cause-caused
     'John asked for, and received, from Mary, the favor of making the
     child read the book in (lit.) self's room.'

This sentence, more literally, means 'John (politely) caused Mary to make
the child read the book in self's room'. This double-causative construction
is triply ambiguous: *zibun* can refer to *John*, *Mary*, or *kodomo* 'the child'.
This fact can be explained automatically if we hypothesize the deep
structure like (37) for the sentence.

(37) John ga Mary ni [Mary ga kodomo ni [kodomo ga hon o yom]$_S$
                          child   child   book read
     sase]$_S$ moratta.
     cause cause
     'John caused Mary [Mary caused the child [the child read the
     book]].'

If *kodomo no heya de* 'in the child's room' is in the most deeply embedded
sentence (that is, *kodomo ga hon o yom*), Reflexivization applies in the first
cycle, turning it to *zibun no heya de* 'in self's room'. If *Mary no heya de* 'in
Mary's room' is in the most deeply embedded sentence, Reflexivization
would not apply in the first cycle but would apply in the second cycle,
turning it to *zibun no heya de*. On the other hand, if *John no heya de* is in the
most deeply embedded sentence, Reflexivization would apply neither in

the first cycle nor in the second cycle. It would apply in the third cycle, yielding *zibun no heya de*. Thus, regardless of whether one has *kodomo no heya de*, *Mary no heya de*, or *John no heya de*, the same form *zibun no heya de* 'in self's room' would be derived. This explains why (36) is triply ambiguous.

7. Summary

In this chapter I have given a systematic and natural explanation for the following problems relating to the interpretation of the reflexive pronoun *zibun*. Crucial examples are

(11) a. John ga Mary o *zibun* no uti   de korosita.
                      self 's house in killed
     'John killed Mary in *his* own house.'

(12) John ga Mary ni *zibun* no uti   de hon   o yom-(s)ase-ta.
                      self 's house in book   read-cause-ed
     'John made Mary read the book in *his/her* own house.'

(21) a. Mary wa John ni *zibun* no uti   de koros-(r)are-ta.
                      by self 's house in kill-passive-ed
     'Mary was killed by John in *her* own house.'

(31) a. John wa Mary ni *zibun* no kazoku no hanasi bakari
                      by self 's family 's talk   only
     s-(r)are-ta.
     do-passive-ed
     'John was affected by Mary's talking only about *his/her* own family.'

(33) Mary wa John ni *zibun* no uti   de hon   o
                   by self 's house in book
     yom-(s)ase-rare-ta.
     read-causative-passive-ed
     'Mary was made by John to read the book in *her* own house.'

(36) John wa Mary ni, kodomo ni *zibun* no heya de hon   o
                               self 's room in book
     yom-(s)asete-moratta.
     read-cause-caused
     'John (politely) caused Mary to make the child read the book in *John's/Mary's/the child's* room.'

I have explained why in (12) *zibun* can refer to either *John* or *Mary*, in spite of the fact that *zibun* of (11a) can refer only to *John*, why in (21a) *zibun* cannot refer to *John*, why in (31a) *zibun* can refer to either *John* or *Mary*, why in (33a) *zibun* cannot refer to *John*, and finally why *zibun* in (36) can refer to *John*, *Mary*, or *kodomo* 'the child'. In so doing, I have relied heavily upon the mechanisms of the transformational theory of grammar—in particular, the mechanism that allows us to hypothesize the presence in the deep structure of what is not present in the actual sentences, the mechanism for applying transformations cyclically, and the mechanism for applying transformations in a fixed order in each cycle. Without these mechanisms explanations for the phenomena under discussion would be inordinately difficult to formulate.

26†

The Reflexive Pronoun and Internal Feeling

1. *Kare* 'He' versus *Zibun* 'Self'

In the preceding chapter, I discussed the use of the reflexive pronoun *zibun* 'self' in simplex sentences. In this chapter I shall examine its use in complex sentences. First, observe the following sentences:

(1) a. John wa, [*kare* o nikunde iru] onna   to   kekkonsita.
               he   hating   is   woman with married
      'John married a woman who hated him.'

    b. John wa, [*zibun* o nikunde iru] onna   to   kekkonsita.
               self   hating   is   woman with married
      'John married a woman who hated him.'

Sentences (1a) and (1b) are different in that in the former the pronoun *kare* 'he' is used in the relative clause (in the square brackets) to refer to *John*, while in the latter the reflexive pronoun *zibun* is used.[1] The two sentences are almost synonymous, and few native speakers would be able to pinpoint the subtle difference in meaning that there is between them.

Is it the case, then, that in subordinate clauses in Japanese, the reflexive pronoun and the personal pronoun can be used in free variation in referring to noun phrases in matrix sentences? The answer is in the negative, as can be seen in the following examples:

(2) a. John wa, Mary ga ⎰ *kare* ⎱ o korosoo to sita toki,
                    ⎱ *zibun* ⎰   kill-try   did when

    Jane to   nete   ita.
      with sleeping was
    'John was in bed with Jane when Mary tried to kill him/self.'

†This chapter is for all readers. It is a greatly abbreviated version of my paper, which is entitled "Pronominalization, Reflexivization and Direct Discourse," *Linguistic Inquiry*, Vol. 3, No. 2 (1972). Refer to this paper for more thorough justifications of the proposed analysis and for various implications they entail.

[1] Sentence (1b) has another reading, namely, that in which *zibun* is coreferential with *onna* 'woman'. In this interpretation, it means 'John married a woman who hated herself'. Since this is a case of *zibun* in a simplex sentence, I shall not be concerned here with this interpretation. Some of the examples that I use in the rest of the chapter also have a second interpretation of the same type, which I shall ignore completely in the discussions.

b. John wa, Mary ga $\begin{Bmatrix} kare \\ *zibun \end{Bmatrix}$ o korosita toki,

                               killed   when

Jane to   nete   ita.

with   sleeping was

'John was in bed with Jane when Mary killed him/*self.'

(3) a. John wa $\begin{Bmatrix} kare \\ zibun \end{Bmatrix}$ o korosoo to sita sono otoko to

                        kill-try   did the   man with

mae ni atta koto ga atta.

before   had met

'John had met before the man who tried to kill him/self.'

b. John wa $\begin{Bmatrix} kare \\ *zibun \end{Bmatrix}$ o korosita sono otoko to

                      killed   the   man with

mae ni atta koto ga atta.

before   had met

'John had met before the man who killed him/*self.'

(4) a. John wa, kazoku ya   sinseki-tati ni, $\begin{Bmatrix} kare \\ zibun \end{Bmatrix}$

           family and relatives   to

ga sinu mae ni, denwa o kaketa.

   die before   phone   called

'John called up his family and relatives before he/self died.'

b. John wa, $\begin{Bmatrix} kare \\ *zibun \end{Bmatrix}$ ga sinda toki, issen mo motte inakatta.

                    died when penny even having was-not

'John, when he/*self died, didn't have a penny.'

In all the preceding sentences and those that follow, it is intended that *kare* and *zibun* are coreferential with *John*. What is it that makes the use of *zibun* acceptable in the (a) sentences but unacceptable in the (b) sentences? Note that, in the former, John could have been aware that Mary tried to kill him or that he was to die. In fact, in (4a), if *zibun* is used in the place of *kare*, the implication is that John committed suicide, or that he knew when he was going to die. If *kare* is used instead, the sentence lacks such an implication. On the other hand, note in the (b) sentences that John could not have been aware of the action or state represented by the embedded clauses. Namely, John could not have been aware that Mary killed him, or that he died, because he was dead. This difference seems to be responsible for the grammaticality of *zibun* in the (a) sentences, and the ungrammaticality of *zibun* in the (b) sentences. In other words, *zibun* is acceptable if it can be replaced by the first person pronoun in the direct representation of the internal feeling:

(5) a.   Mary ga *boku* o korosooto sita.
                      I   kill-try   did
         'Mary tried to kill me.'

    b. *Mary ga *boku* o korosita.
                      I   killed
         'Mary killed me.'

(6) a.   *Boku* wa sinu.
           I   die
         'I am going to die.'

    b. *Boku* wa sinda.
           I   died
         'I died.'

Sentences (2a) and (3a) with *zibun* are grammatical because (5a) is grammatical. Similarly, (4a) is grammatical because (6a) is grammatical. On the other hand, (2b) and (3b) are ungrammatical because (5b) is ungrammatical, and (4b) is ungrammatical because (6b) is ungrammatical.

The following phenomenon will make this point even clearer. First, observe (7a) and (7b):

(7) a.   Sono hito   ga *boku* o tasukete *kureta*.
           the   person   I   helping gave-me-the-favor-of
         'The person saved me.'

    b. *Sono hito   ga *boku* o tasukete *yatta*.
           the   person   I   helping gave-nonspeaker-the-favor-of

Kureru 'give' and *yaru* 'give' are used in conjunction with action verbs to specify who has received the favor from whom. The former indicates that the speaker (or someone who belongs to him) has received the favor, while the latter indicates that someone who is not the speaker has received the favor.[2] Example (7b) is ungrammatical because the sentence says that the speaker has received the favor, while the use of *yatta* indicates that someone other than the speaker has received the favor. Now, observe the following:

(8) a. John wa, $\begin{Bmatrix} kare \\ zibun \end{Bmatrix}$ o tasukete *kureta* hito   o korosita.
　　　　　　　　　　　helping gave person   killed
　　　'John killed the person who helped him/self.'

　　b. John wa, $\begin{Bmatrix} kare \\ *zibun \end{Bmatrix}$ o tasukete *yatta* hito o korosita.
　　　'John killed the person who helped him/*self.'

Example (8b) with *zibun* is totally ungrammatical. If *zibun* in a subordinate clause, as I have proposed, corresponds to the first person pronoun in the direct representation of the content of the clause, (8a) and (8b) with *zibun*, in their underlying structures, contain (7a) and (7b), respectively. Then, the ungrammaticality of (8b) with *zibun* is an automatic consequence of the fact that (7b) is ungrammatical.[3]

2. Awareness
The awareness, on the part of the referent of *zibun*, of the past action represented by the subordinate clause can be either at the time the action took place or at some later time. For example, sentence (9) is ambiguous between 'John was in the next room (overhearing it) when Mary was criticizing him' and 'John was in the next room when (as he later found out) Mary was criticizing him'.

(9) John wa, Mary ga *zibun* o hinansite iru toki,   tonari no
　　　　　　　　　　　　self   criticizing is   when next
　　heya ni ita.
　　room in was
　　'John was in the next room when Mary was criticizing him/self.'

Now we are ready to discuss the difference of meaning between (1a)

---

[2] See Chapter 9 ("Giving and Receiving Verbs") for details.
[3] I am indebted to James McCawley (personal communication) for suggesting to me the use of *kureru/yaru* patterns for supporting the proposed hypothesis.

and (1b). Sentence (1a) is a neutral statement to the effect that John married a woman who hated him. It does not say whether or not John was aware that the woman hated him. On the other hand, (1b) states either that John married a woman who (he knew) hated him or that John married a woman who (as he later found out) hated him. Similarly, consider the following:

(10) a. John wa Mary ga *kare* ni ai-tai toki ni wa itumo
with meet-want when always

ryokoo-tyuu datta.
traveling was

b. John wa Mary ga *zibun* ni ai-tai toki ni wa itumo ryokoo-tyuu datta.

Sentence (10b) means that John was always out of town when he knew Mary wanted to see him or that he was always out of town when (as he later found out) Mary wanted to see him. On the other hand, (10a) is a neutral, objective statement that does not involve John's internal feeling or awareness.

In the preceding chapter, it was mentioned that the antecedent of *zibun* in simplex sentences must be the subject of the sentence. For example, (11a) and (11b) are not ambiguous with respect to the reference of *zibun*.

(11) a. John ga Mary o *zibun* no uti de korosita.
's house in killed
'John killed Mary in (lit.) self's house.'

b. Mary ga John ni *zibun* no uti de koros-(r)are-ta.
by 's house in kill-passive-ed
'Mary was killed by John in (lit.) self's house.'

In (11a) it refers only to *John*, and in (11b) only to *Mary*. Note that *zibun* in simplex sentences does not have anything to do with the awareness on the part of its referent of the action represented by the sentences. Sentence (11b) does not mean that Mary was aware that she was killed by John in her own house.

Zibun in subordinate clauses, on the other hand, does not require that its antecedent be the subject of the matrix sentence. Observe the following sentences:

(12) a. *Zibun* ga baka na koto ga John o kanasimaseta.
              fool is that   saddened
        'The fact that he was a fool saddened John.'

   b. Mary ga *zibun* o aisite inai koto ga John o gakkarisaseta.[4]
                     loving is-not that   distressed
        'The fact that Mary did not love him distressed John.'

   c. *Zibun* ga Mary ni karakawareta   koto ga John o
                        by was-made-fun-of that
      zetuboo   e to oiyatta.[5]
      desperation to   drove
      'That he was made fun of by Mary drove John to desperation.'

In these examples, *zibun* is coreferential with *John*, which is not the subject, but the object of the matrix sentence. The use of *zibun* in these sentences is consistent with the hypothesis that it is derived from the first person pronoun in the direct representation of the internal feeling. The underlying structures of (12) contain the following direct representations:

(13) a. *Boku* wa baka da.
         I   fool am
         'I am a fool.'

   b. Mary wa *boku* o aisite inai.
                    I   loving is-not
        'Mary doesn't love me.'

   c. *Boku* wa Mary ni karakawareta.
         I   by was-made-fun-of
        'I was made fun of by Mary.'

   The following phenomena show that there is a strange mix of syntax and semantics in the use of *zibun*. First, consider the following examples:

(14) a. John wa Mary ga *zibun* o aisite iru koto o sitte   ita.
                              loving is that   knowing was
          'John knew that Mary loved him.'

[4] I am indebted to Noriko Akatsuka (personal communication) for (12a) and (12b).
[5] I am indebted to Sige-Yuki Kuroda (personal communication) for (12c).

   b. John wa Mary ga *zibun* o aisite iru koto o siranakatta.
                              loving is that   knew-not
      'John didn't know that Mary loved him.'

(15) a. John wa Mary ga *zibun* o matte   iru koto o wasurete inakatta.
                                 waiting is that   forgetting was-not
         'John hadn't forgotten that Mary was waiting for him.'

   b. John wa Mary ga *zibun* o matte   iru koto o wasurete
                            waiting is that   forgetting
      simatte ita.
      ended-up
      'John had forgotten that Mary was waiting for him.'

In (14a) and (15a), respectively, John was aware that Mary loved him and that Mary was waiting for him—hence the acceptability of *zibun*. In (14b) and (15b), on the other hand, John was not aware of these facts. It seems that once it is established that *zibun* can be used in the subordinate clause of the positive (or negative) form of a matrix verb, then it can also be used with the negative (or positive) form of the same verb.

3. Comparison with English

In the preceding, I have shown that the reflexive pronoun *zibun* shows up in subordinate clauses only when its antecedent, which is in the matrix sentence, is aware of the actions or states represented by the subordinate clauses.[6] I shall show next that this concept of awareness or internal feeling plays an important role in English, also, in the use of personal pronouns. First, observe the following sentences:

(16) a. John expects that he will be elected.

   b. That he will be elected is expected by John.

   c. *That John will be elected is expected by him.

---

[6] This constraint is violated when *zibun* is used contrastively. For example, in the Japanese version of "Although John received $20,000 as inheritance when his father died, he did not leave a penny to his children when *he himself* died" or "Although John always took care of funerals for other people, when *he himself* died, there was no one who would take care of the funeral for him," *zibun* can appear as the subject of *died*. This is because *he himself* (=John) is contrasted with *his father* and *other people*. It is a well-known fact that some grammatical constraints are relaxed when contrast is involved. For example,

(i) a. *John was killed by *himself*.

   b. John was killed, not by Mary, but by *himself*.

(17) a.   John claimed that he was the best boxer in the world.

   b.   That he was the best boxer in the world was claimed by John.

   c.   *That John was the best boxer in the world was claimed by him.

(18) a.   John denied that he was the best boxer in the world.

   b.   That he was the best boxer in the world was denied by John.

   c.   ?That John was the best boxer in the world was denied by him.

(19) a.   John forgot that he had an appointment at two.

   b.   That he had an appointment at two was forgotten by John.

   c.   ?That John had an appointment at two was forgotten by him.

In all these sentences and in all that follow, it is intended that *he* is co-referential with *John*. Examples (16c) and (17c) are ungrammatical, but (18c) and (19c) are not. This difference, I claim, is due to the fact that the complement clause of verbs such as *expect* and *claim* represents the internal feeling of the matrix subject, while it is not the case with verbs such as *deny* and *forget*. In (16a), for example, John's feeling is "*I* will be elected." On the other hand, in (18a), what John is denying is not his own internal feeling, but someone else's statement to the effect that John is the best boxer in the world.

   Let us hypothesize that the foregoing sentences are derived from under-lying structures that can be informally represented as

(20) a. John expects, "*I* will be elected."

   b. John claimed, "*I* am the best boxer in the world."

   c. John denied (someone else's statement) that John is the best boxer in the world.

   d. John forgot (the fact) that John had an appointment at two.

Namely, *expect* and *claim* have as their complements the direct discourse representation of John's internal feeling, while *deny* and *forget* have as their complement an abstract fact or someone else's statement. The first person pronoun *I* in (20a) and (20b) becomes *he* because of Indirect Discourse Formation, which is obligatory for verbs such as *expect*, *claim*, and *remember* but is optional for verbs such as *say*, *think*, and *ask*. Since the subject of the embedded clauses in (20a) and (20b) is a pronoun from the beginning, there is no possibility of its being realized as *John*. Hence, (16c) and (17c) are ungrammatical. On the other hand, in (20c) and (20d), the subject of the complement clauses is a full-fledged noun phrase, namely, *John*, and therefore it may appear in surface sentences unpronominalized, as is the case with (18c) and (19c).

3.1 Passive Sentences with Sentential Subjects

The hypothesis presented in the preceding section accounts for many otherwise unexplained phenomena in pronominalization in English. First, compare (21) and (22):

(21) a.   John expected that he would be elected.

   b.   *That John would be elected was expected by him.

(22) a.   Mary expected of John that he would do it.

   b.   That John would do it was expected of him by Mary.

Note that (21b) is ungrammatical, as has been observed before, but that (22b) is perfectly grammatical. According to the proposed hypothesis, (21a) and (22b) are derived from the following underlying structure:

(23) a.   John expected, "*I* will be elected."

   b.   Mary expected of John, "*John* will do it."

Since the subject of the complement clause in (23a) is the first person pronoun, it can never be realized as *John*, to which it is coreferential, regardless of where it appears in the surface sentence. Hence, (21b) is ungrammatical. On the other hand, in (23b) the subject of the complement clause is not *I*, but *John*, because the complement clause represents not John's feeling, as is the case with (23a), but Mary's feeling. Hence, it can remain unpronominalized if it appears in the context that does not force its pronominalization. Thus, (22b) is grammatical.

3.2 Rumor

Compare (24) and (25):

(24) a.   The rumor that he would become the president of the Corporation was spread by John.

   b.   *The rumor that John would become the president of the Corporation was spread by him.

(25) a. The rumor that he would become the president of the Corporation was denied by John.

   b. The rumor that John would become the president of the Corporation was denied by him.

Note that forward pronominalization is unacceptable in (24b), while it is acceptable in (25b). The difference between these two sentences lies in the fact that in (24) John himself was the author of the rumor, while in (25) someone other than John was the source of the rumor. Namely, examples (24) and (25) correspond to:

(26) a. The rumor, "*I* will become the president of the Corporation," was spread by John.

   b. The rumor that *John* will become the president of the Corporation was denied by John.

That is, the subject of the embedded clause in (24) is a pronoun in the underlying structure and therefore should never be realized as *John*. Hence, (24b) is ungrammatical. On the other hand, the subject of the embedded clause in (25) is *John*, and therefore it can remain unpronominalized, as in (25b).

3.3 Direct Internal Feeling
It has been observed that both (27a) and (27b) are grammatical:

(27) a. That he was sick worried John.

   b. That John was sick worried him.

To some speakers, however, the following (b) sentences have low acceptability:

(28) a. That he was secretly in love with Mary worried John.

   b. ?That John was secretly in love with Mary worried him.

(29) a. That he felt hungry all the time worried John.

   b. ?That John felt hungry all the time worried him.

(30) a. That he was always unhappy worried John.

   b. ?That John was always unhappy worried him.

The low acceptability of the (b) sentences seems to be related to the fact that ordinarily John knows, without being told by someone else, that he is secretly in love with Mary, that he feels hungry all the time, and that he was always unhappy. In other words, the content of the sentential subject of each of these sentences is such that it naturally describes John's own direct internal feeling: "I am secretly in love with Mary," "I feel hungry all the time," and "I am always unhappy"; and it is not amenable to the interpretation in which someone else said that John was secretly in love with Mary, that John felt hungry all the time, or that John was always unhappy. It seems that *worry* can take as its sentential subject either a direct internal feeling representation or an abstract fact, as in the following, where (31a) corresponds to (27a), and (31b) to (27b):

(31) a. "I am sick," worried John.

   b. The fact that John is sick worried John.

However, if the content of the sentential subject is such that it cannot readily assume the status of an abstract fact, as is the case with (28), (29), and (30) for some speakers, then the deep structure of the type of (31b) is ruled out.

3.4 Yiddish Movement
Observe the following sentences:

(32) a.   John thinks that Mary doesn't like the girl that he is living with.

   b. *He thinks that Mary doesn't like the girl that John is living with.

   c.   The girl that he is living with, John thinks that Mary doesn't like.

   d.   The girl that John is living with, he thinks that Mary doesn't like.

To some speakers of English, (32c) and (32d) are both grammatical. Since (32b), in the interpretation in which *he* is coreferential with *John*, is ungrammatical, it must be assumed that Pronominalization applies after the object of *like* has been preposed by a transformation called Yiddish Movement.[7] Now, compare (33) and (34).

[7] Backward Pronominalization in English (and in many other languages) is acceptable when the first of the two coreferential noun phrases is in a subordinate clause that does not contain the second. Thus, in the following, (i-b) is ungrammatical because Backward

(Continued overleaf)

(33) a. John's brother visited him.

    b. His brother visited John.

    c. John, his brother visited.

(34) a. John thinks that Mary likes him.

    b. *He thinks that Mary likes John.

    c. *John, he thinks Mary likes.

Now, what needs to be accounted for is why (34c) is ungrammatical in spite of the fact that (33c) is grammatical. According to the proposed hypothesis, the ungrammaticality of (34c) is an automatic consequence of the fact that in the underlying structure the object of *likes* is the first person pronoun:

(35) John thinks, "Mary likes *me*."

On the other hand, the underlying structure of (33) is presumably that shown in (36).

(36) John's brother visited *John*.

Therefore, the object of *visited* can remain in surface sentences unpronominalized if it appears, as it does in (33c), in the context that does not force its pronominalization.[8]

3.5 Quasi-Direct Discourse
The proposed hypothesis automatically accounts for the ungrammaticality of the (b) sentences in the quasi-direct discourse representation as follows:

Pronominalization has applied in spite of the fact that the first of the two coreferential noun phrases involved is not in a subordinate clause:

(i) a. John will do it if he can.

    b. *He will do it if John can.

    c. If John can, he will do it.

    d. If he can, John will do it.

On the other hand, (i-d) is grammatical because the first occurrence of *John* is in a subordinate clause that does not contain the second. See Ross (1969) for details.

[8] One might argue that (34c) is ungrammatical because its source, (34b), is ungrammatical and that (33c) is grammatical because its source, (33b), is grammatical. This argument is based on the assumption that Pronominalization applies before Yiddish Movement. It faces difficulty in accounting for the grammaticality of (32d) because its source, (32b), is ungrammatical.

(37) a. Was *he* going to lose, John wondered.

    b. *Was *John* going to lose, he wondered.

(38) a. Would *he* be allowed to come, John asked Mary.

    b. *Would *John*, be allowed to come, he asked Mary.

(39) a. Who should *he* see, John inquired of the secretary.

    b. *Who should *John* see, he inquired of the secretary.

3.6 As-for-Self Construction

Observe the following examples:

(40) a. As for myself, I won't be invited.

    b. ?As for yourself, you won't be invited.

    c. *As for himself, he won't be invited.

(41) a. John told Mary that, as for himself, he wouldn't be invited.

    b. ?Mary told John that, as for himself, he wouldn't be invited.

    c. *Mary told Betty that, as for himself, he wouldn't be invited.

The *as-for-self* construction requires that its reflexive pronoun be in the first person. When the second person reflexive appears, as in (40b), we get a marginal sentence, and when the third person reflexive appears, as in (40c), we get an ungrammatical sentence. Now, the awkwardness of (41b) and the ungrammaticality of (41c) would be an automatic consequence of this constraint if these sentences were derived from underlying structures that contained (40):

(42) a. John told Mary, "As for myself, I won't be invited."

    b. Mary told John, "?As for yourself, you won't be invited."

    c. Mary told Betty, "*As for himself, he won't be invited."

Similarly, in (43), sentence (43a) is acceptable because its underlying structure has (40a) as the complement of *expect*.

(43) a. John expects that, as for himself, he won't be invited.

    b. ?*John denies that, as for himself, he will be invited.

However, (43b) is unacceptable because its underlying structure has

(44) *As for himself, John will be invited.

3.7 *Seem*
Observe the following pair of sentences:

(45) a. *Realizing that *John* had cancer seemed to him to have bothered
          Mary.

     b. Realizing that he had cancer seemed to *John* to have bothered
          Mary.

No adequate explanations have been offered previously for the ungrammaticality of (45a). According to the proposed hypothesis, (45) has as
its underlying structure:

(46) "(Mary's) realizing that *I* have cancer has bothered Mary," (it)
      seemed to John.

Since the subject of *have cancer* is the first person pronoun from the beginning, it can never be realized as a full-fledged noun phrase regardless of
whether it appears to the left or to the right of its antecedent *John*. Hence,
(45a) is ungrammatical.

4. Summary
To summarize, in this chapter I have made the following observations
with respect to Reflexivization and Pronominalization in Japanese and
English:

(i)   The reflexive pronoun *zibun* 'self' in a simple sentence must be
      coreferential with the subject of the sentence.

(ii) *Zibun* in a constituent clause (A) is coreferential with a noun phrase
      (B) of the matrix sentence only if A represents an action or state
      that the referent of B is *aware of* at the time it takes place or has
      come to be aware of at some later time. In other words, *zibun* appears
      in subordinate clauses only when the clauses represent the internal
      feeling of the referent of *zibun* and the first person pronoun appears
      in its place in the direct representation of the internal feeling.

(iii) Verbs such as *expect, claim, remember, know,* and *ask* in English take
      as their complements the direct discourse representation of the
      internal feeling of the subject of these verbs.

(iv) The first person pronoun *I* becomes *he* or *she* if Indirect Discourse Formation is obligatory and if its antecedent is in the third person. It is not possible to replace *I* with a full-fledged noun phrase co-referential with it. Hence, ungrammatical sentences result if un-pronominalized noun phrases appear in the place of *I* in surface sentences.

It is interesting, although by no means surprising, that the same concept of "awareness" or "internal feeling" controls two apparently unrelated phenomena—a subset of reflexivization in Japanese, and a subset of pronominalization in English.

VII
Case Marking and Word Order

27†

Case Marking in Japanese

1. Uses of *Ga*, *O*, and *Ni*

In this chapter I shall examine occurrences of case-marking particles *ga*, *o*, and *ni* and propose a set of rules for predicting their appearance. Observe first the following sentences:

(1) a. John *ga* nihongo {*o* / **ga*} hanas-(r)u.
Japanese speak
'John speaks Japanese.'

b. John *ga* nihongo {*ga* / *o*} hanas-(r)e-ru.
Japanese speak-can
'John can speak Japanese.'

c. John *ni* nihongo *ga* hanas-(r)e-ru.
to
'John can speak Japanese.'

d. *John *ni* nihongo *o* hanas-(r)e-ru.

(2) a. John *ga* aruk-(r)u.
walk
'John walks.'

b. John *ga* aruk-(r)e-ru.
can
'John can walk.'

c. *John *ni* aruk-(r)e-ru.

In (1a), *o*, and not *ga*, is used in marking the object of *hanas-(r)u* 'speak'. In (1b), both *ga* and *o* can be used. In (1c), *ni* appears for marking the original subject, while in (1d) and (2c) *ni* cannot be used. Similarly, consider the following:

(3) a. Mary *ga* (iki-tai tokoro ni) ik-(r)u.
go-want place to go
'Mary goes (to places where she wants to go).'

†This chapter is linguistically oriented but should also be of interest to students of Japanese.

    b. John wa Mary *ni* (iki-tai   tokoro ni) ik-(s)ase-ru.
                    to go-want place to go-cause
      'John lets Mary go (to places that she wants to go).'

    c. John wa Mary *o* (ik-(s)ase-tai   tokoro ni) ik-(s)ase-ru.
                         go-cause-want place to go-cause
      'John makes Mary go (to places that he wants to make her go to).'

(4) a.   Mary *ga* hon o yom-(r)u.
              book   read
        'Mary reads books.'

    b.   John wa Mary *ni* hon o yom-(s)ase-ru.
                    to book   read-cause
        'John lets Mary read books.'

    c.   *John wa Mary *o* hon o yom-(s)ase-ru.
        'John makes Mary read books.'

The difference in meaning between (3b) and (3c) is as represented in the translation—(3b) with *ni* is a *let* causative and (3c) with *o* is a *make* causative. In the former it is assumed that the referent of the NP-*ni* is willing to perform the action represented by the stem of the causative verb, while in the latter the referent is forced to do it by the referent of the matrix sentence subject.[1] When the predicate involves a transitive construction, as in (4), the *make* causative with *o* is ungrammatical. Why is it that the same *ni/o* alternation that is possible in (3) is not acceptable in (4)? This chapter is an attempt to account for these peculiar conditions on particle alternations.

2. Deep Structure of Particles

I assume that some particles are in the deep structure and some are inserted by transformations. The subject case marker *ga*, the object case markers *o* and *ga*, and the indirect object case marker *ni* belong to the latter class. These are the particles that get changed depending upon what kind of derived structures the sentences take. Examples (1) through (4) show how these particles are interchanged. The following is another example:

---

[1] This difference was first observed by Kuroda (1965b).

(5) a. John *ga* Mary *o* korosi-ta.
                          killed
    'John killed Mary.'

   b. Mary *ga* John *ni*   koros-(s)are-ta.
                      by kill-passive-ed
    'Mary was killed by John.'

John, which is marked by the subject case marker in the active sentence, is marked by *ni* 'by' in the passive sentence, and *Mary*, which is marked by the object case marker in (5a), is marked in the passive by the subject marker *ga*. I assume that (5a) and (5b) have as their deep structure

(6) [John]$_{NP}$ [Mary]$_{NP}$ [koros-ta]$_V$.

Similarly, it is assumed that sentence (7) is derived from the deep structure shown in (8).

(7) John ga Mary ni okane o yatta.
                    to money   gave
    'John gave money to Mary.'

(8) [John]$_{NP}$ [Mary]$_{NP}$ [okane]$_{NP}$ [yatta]$_V$.

On the other hand, it is assumed that sentences such as those in (9) are derived from deep structures with the second particles specified as in (10).

(9) a. John *ga* Tokyo *ni* itta.
                          to went
    'John went to Tokyo.'

   b. John *ga* Tokyo *kara*   kita.
                      from came
    'John came from Tokyo.'

   c. John *ga* kawa *de* oyoida.
                  river in swam
    'John swam in the river.'

(10) a. [John]$_{NP}$ [Tokyo]$_{NP}$-*ni* [itta]$_V$.

    b. [John]$_{NP}$ [Tokyo]$_{NP}$-*kara* [kita]$_V$.

    c. [John]$_{NP}$ [kawa]$_{NP}$-*de* [oyoida]$_V$.

3. Basic Case-Marking Transformation

The most basic transformations are those that insert the subject marker *ga*, the indirect object marker *ni*, and the object marker *o* or *ga*. They can be stated as follows:

(11) a. Indirect Object Marking: Attach *ni* to the second of three unmarked NP's (noun phrases), that is, the NP's that do not yet have a particle.

    b. Subject Marking: Attach *ga* to the subject NP.

    c. Object Marking: Attach *o* to the first nonsubject unmarked NP to the left of the main verb if it is [−stative], and *ga* if it is [+stative].[2]

I shall show here the derivation of two sentences:

(12) a. Deep structure: $[John]_{NP}$ $[Mary]_{NP}$ $[okane]_{NP}$ $[yatta]_V$.
                      [−stative]
            'John gave money to Mary.'

    b. Indirect Object $[John]_{NP}$ $[Mary]_{NP}$ *ni* $[okane]_{NP}$
       Marking: $[yatta]_V$.

    c. Subject Marking: $[John]_{NP}$ *ga* $[Mary]_{NP}$ ni $[okane]_{NP}$
                        $[yatta]_V$.
                        [−stative]

    d. Object Marking: $[John]_{NP}$ ga $[Mary]_{NP}$ ni $[okane]_{NP}$ *o*
                      $[yatta]_V$.

(13) a. Deep structure: $[John]_{NP}$ $[Mary]_{NP}$ $[suki\ da]_V$.
                      [+stative]
            'John likes Mary.'

    b. Subject Marking: $[John]_{NP}$ *ga* $[Mary]_{NP}$ $[suki\ da]_V$.
                      [+stative]

    c. Object Marking: $[John]_{NP}$ ga $[Mary]_{NP}$ *ga* $[suki\ da]_V$.

In (12) *yatta* 'gave' is a [−stative] verb. Therefore, *o* is attached to *okane* by Object Marking. On the other hand, in (13) *suki (da)* '(be) fond of' is [+stative]. Therefore, *ga* is attached to *Mary* by Object Marking.

[2] See Chapter 4, "*Ga* for Object Marking" for (11c). Why Indirect Object Marking precedes Subject Marking will be discussed later in this chapter.

The preceding case-marking transformations apply cyclically, that is, first to the most deeply embedded sentence, next to the second most deeply embedded sentence, and so on. Observe the derivation shown in (14).

(14)

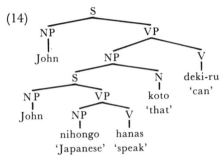

'John can speak Japanese.'[3]

[3] It is not clear whether Japanese has a constituent that can be called a VP. The question is whether (i) has the underlying structure represented in (ii-a) or (ii-b).

(i)   John ga hon o yonda.
                book   read
        'John read books.'

(ii) a.

b.

On the surface level, it seems to be very difficult to argue that *hon o yomu* 'reads books' forms a constituent. Intuitively, one does not feel that the sentence consists of two constituents: [John ga] [hon o yonda]. One feels that it consists of three components: [John ga] [hon o] [yonda]. On the other hand, for assigning semantic interpretations to the underlying structure, the presence of the VP node seems to be required. In Japanese, as in English, whether or not the predicate as a whole represents a self-controllable action or state plays an important role in determining the grammaticality or ungrammaticality of given sentences. It is sometimes the case that this determination cannot be based solely on the nature of the verb but has to be based on the amalgamation of the nature of the verb and its complements. I shall use English examples for ease of explanation. Verbs, adjectives, and nouns have to be marked in the lexicon with respect to whether or not they represent self-controllable states or actions.

(iii) a. Look at this picture.
            [+self-controllable]

      b. Be good.
            [+self-controllable]   *(Continued overleaf)*

a. Deep structure: [John]$_{NP}$ [[John nihongo hanas-ru]$_S$ koto]$_{NP}$ dekiru

b. First cycle
   (i) Subject Marking: [John]$_{NP}$ [[John *ga* nihongo hanas-ru]$_S$ koto]$_{NP}$ dekiru
   (ii) Object Marking: [John]$_{NP}$ [[John ga nihongo *o* hanas-ru]$_S$ koto]$_{NP}$ dekiru

c. Second cycle
   (i) Equi-NP Deletion: [John] [[ϕ nihongo o hanas-ru]$_S$ koto]$_{NP}$ dekiru
   (ii) Subject Marking: John *ga* [[nihongo o hanas-ru]$_S$ koto]$_{NP}$ dekiru
   (iii) Object Marking: John ga [[nihongo o hanas-ru]$_S$ koto]$_{NP}$ *ga* dekiru

Equi-NP Deletion is the transformation that deletes the subject of the constituent sentence under identity with the subject (or object) of the matrix sentence. Note that in (14c-iii), [*nihongo o hanas-ru koto*] is the first

---

c. Don't be a hypocrite.
   [+self-controllable]

(iv) a. *See this picture.
   [−self-controllable]
   b. *Be tall.
   [−self-controllable]
   c. *Be a girl.
   [−self-controllable]

Now this lexical information is not enough to mark the following sentences either as grammatical or as ungrammatical:

(v) a. Be a good girl.
   b. *Be a tall girl.
   c. Granted that you are a tall girl, be a good tall girl.
   d. *Granted that you are a tall girl, be a good and tall girl.

Note that (v-a) and (v-c) are grammatical in spite of the fact that (iv-c) is ungrammatical. Note also that although (v-c) is grammatical, (v-d) is not. In order to handle this phenomenon systematically, it is necessary to have semantic rules that assign semantic features to the predicate node on the basis of the lexical features of its constituent nodes. The same argument applies for the Japanese case. Imperative sentences are well-formed if the feature [+self-controllable] gets assigned to the entire predicate. Otherwise, they are ungrammatical. This necessitates the presence of the VP node in the deep structure.

unmarked NP to the left of *dekiru*. Since the verb is [+stative], this noun phrase is marked with *ga*.

Sentence (1b) is derived from the deep structure similar to (14a) except that the constituent sentence is not dominated by the NP node,[4] as shown in (15).

(15)

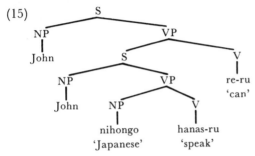

The derivation of (1b) from the deep structure of (15) follows the steps given in (16).

(16) a. Deep structure: [John]$_{NP}$ [John nihongo hanas-ru]$_S$ re-ru.

  b. First cycle
    (i) Subject Marking: [John] [John *ga* nihongo hanas-ru]$_S$ re-ru
    (ii) Object Marking: [John] [John ga nihongo *o* hanas-ru]$_S$ re-ru.

  c. Second cycle
    (i)   Equi-NP Deletion: [John] [ϕ nihongo o hanas-ru]$_S$ re-ru.
    (ii) Aux Deletion: [John] [nihongo o hanas-ϕ]$_S$ re-ru.
    (iii) Verb Raising: [John] [nihongo o] hanas-re-ru.
    (iv) Subject Marking: John *ga* nihongo o hanas-re-ru.
    (v)   Object Marking: John ga nihongo o *ga* hanas-re-ru.
    (vi) *Ga/O* Deletion: John ga nihongo ϕ ga hanas-re-ru.

The derivation given in (16) requires some explanations. Aux Deletion is a transformation that deletes the tense auxiliary of the constituent sentence when the constituent sentence is not followed by nominalizers such

---

[4] Kuroda (1965a) was the first person who proposed that bound forms such as *re* 'can', *ta(i)* 'want', and *sase* 'cause' appear as matrix verbs in the deep structure.

as *koto* 'that, the fact that' and *no* 'that, the fact that'. Constituent sentences of verbs such as *re* 'can', *sase* 'cause', *rare* 'be adversely affected', *ta(i)* 'want' undergo this transformation obligatorily. Verb Raising is a transformation that takes the tenseless verb out of the embedded clause and attaches it to the left of the matrix sentence verb. When this transformation applies, the constituent clause loses its status as a sentence because of its loss of the main verb, and therefore the node S that dominates it is automatically deleted.[5] The change in the phrase-marker configurations between (16c-i) and (16c-iii) is shown in (17).

(17) a. Before Aux   b. After Aux
        Deletion and   Deletion and
        Verb Raising   Verb Raising

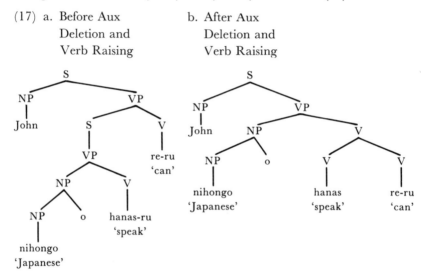

Now, *nihongo o* has come to occupy a position in the phrase marker that is in the same simplex sentence as the verb *re* 'can'. Let us assume that NP's that are followed by *ga* or *o* are *unmarked*. Since *nihongo o* is unmarked by definition, and since it is the first unmarked NP to the left of *re* [+stative], *ga* is attached to it by Object Marking,[6] as shown in (16c-v).

[5] Such a convention for deleting an intermediate node in the phrase marker when a transformation deletes its lower node(s) is called a tree-pruning convention. See Ross (1967). When Verb Raising applies, the VP node that used to dominate the verb of the embedded clause is also pruned because it has lost its verb.

[6] This idea for considering NP-*o* or NP-*ga* as unmarked is due to Kuroda (1965c). Incidentally, note that although (i) is grammatical, (ii) is ungrammatical.

(i) John ga nihongo *ga* hanas-(r)e-ru.
         Japanese   speak-can
    'John can speak Japanese.'

Ga/O Deletion that follows is a very general transformation[7] that deletes *ga* and *o* when they are followed by some other particle. The same transformation is responsible for deriving (b) from (a) in the following:

(18) a. John ga sono hon   *o* yonda.
             the   book   read
     'John read the book.'

    b. John ga sono hon *mo*   yonda.
                      also
     'John read the book also.'

(19) a. John ga eigo   *ga* dekiru.
             English   can
     'John can speak English.'

    b. John ga eigo *mo* dekiru.
     'John can speak English also.'

(20) a. John *ga* eigo   ga dekiru.
             English   can
     'John can speak English.'

    b. John *mo* eigo ga dekiru.
     'John, too, can speak English.'

Object Marking by *ga* is optional when the object is already followed by *o*. Thus, in (16c-iv), since *nihongo* is already followed by *o*, the transformation does not have to apply. For example, observe the following:

(21) John ga nihongo   *o* hanas-(r)e-ru.
          Japanese   speak-can
   'John can speak Japanese.'

(ii) *John ga nihongo *ga* hanas-(r)u koto ga deki-ru.
      Japanese   speak   that   can
  'John can speak Japanese.'

This is due to the fact that, at the time of application of Object Marking, (ii) looks like

(iii) John ga [[nihongo o hanas-ru]$_S$ koto]$_{NP}$ deki-ru.

The constituent [*nihongo o*] is an unmarked NP, but it is inside the embedded clause, and case-marking rules never apply to a noun phrase not in the topmost sentence of the current cycle. This is why neither Indirect Object Marking nor Object Marking applies to [*nihongo o*] of (iii). On the other hand, in (16c-iv), because of the deletion of the S node after Verb Raising, [*nihongo o*] has come to be a constituent of the topmost S. Thus, Object Marking applies to it, attaching *ga*.

[7] This transformation is also due to Kuroda (1965c).

Sentence (21) is derived by not applying Object Marking to (16c-iv).

The derivation of sentences involving the desiderative *ta(i)* follows the same steps:

(22) a. Deep structure: Boku [boku hon   yom-ru]$_S$ ta-i.

                                   I   I   book read   want

                                   'I want to read the book.'

      b. First cycle

           (i) Subject Marking: Boku [boku *ga* hon yom-ru]$_S$ ta-i.

           (ii) Object Marking: Boku [boku ga hon *o* yom-ru]$_S$ ta-i.

      c. Second cycle:

           (i)   Equi-NP Deletion: Boku [ϕ hon o yom-ru] ta-i.

           (ii) Aux Deletion: Boku [hon o yom-ϕ]$_S$ ta-i.

           (iii) Verb Raising: Boku hon o yom-ta-i.

           (iv) Subject Marking: Boku *ga* hon o yom-ta-i.

           (v)   Object Marking: Boku ga hon o *ga* yom-ta-i.

           (vi) *Ga/O* Deletion: Boku ga hon ϕ ga yom-ta-i.

Later, *-i-* is inserted between *yom* and *ta-i* as an affix, yielding

(22) c. (vii) Boku ga hon ga yom-*i*-ta-i.   'I want to read the book.'

If Object Marking is not applied to (22c-iv), sentence (22c-viii) is derived.

(22) c. (viii) Boku ga hon o yom-*i*-ta-i.   'I want to read the book.'

The *ta-i* derivatives require that their subject be the first person pronoun.[8] When the subject is a third person, the *ta-gar-(r)u* derivatives must be used.

(23) John ga hon o yom-i-ta-gar-(r)u.

                book   read

'John shows a sign of wanting to read books.'

---

[8] This is only approximately true. It applies only when *ta-i* appears in the matrix declarative sentences. In questions, the subject of *ta-i* must be the second person.

(i) Kono hon ga yom-i-ta-i?

     this book   read-want

     'Do you want to read this book?'

In subordinate clauses, this constraint can be violated:

(ii) Benkyoosi-ta-i mono wa benkyoosi, asob-i-ta-i mono wa asonda.

     study-want   people   study-and play-want people   played

     'Those who wanted to study studied, and those who wanted to play played.'

There are many other contexts in which it can appear with a non-first-person subject.

Gar is a bound form that has the meaning of 'to show a visible sign of'. Sentence (23) is assumed to be derived from the deep structure shown in (24).

(24)

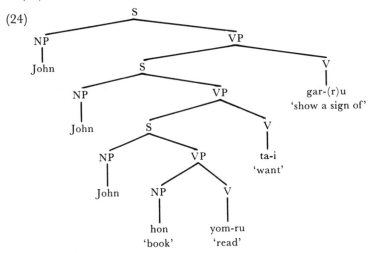

In the first and the second cycles of applications of transformations, exactly the same steps are taken as in (22). The third cycle, namely the cycle for the topmost sentence, is entered with the following phrase-structure configuration:

(25) a. Third cycle: John [John ga hon ga/o yom-i-ta-i]_S gar-ru.

   b. Equi-NP Deletion: John [φ hon ga/o yom-i-ta-i]_S gar-ru.

   c. Aux Deletion: John [hon ga/o yom-i-ta-φ]_S gar-(r)u.

   d. Verb Raising: John hon ga/o yom-i-ta-gar-(r)u.

   e. Subject Marking: John *ga* hon ga/o yom-i-ta-gar-(r)u.

   f. Object Marking: John ga hon ga/o *o* yom-i-ta-gar-(r)u.

   g. *Ga/O* Deletion: John ga hon φ o yom-i-ta-gar-(r)u.

Object Marking with *o* is obligatory. Thus, the following is ungrammatical:

(26) *John ga hon *ga* yom-i-ta-gar-(r)u.
              book   read
      'John shows a sign of wanting to read books.'

4. *Ga/Ni* Conversion

Many of the verbals that can enter into the *NP-ga NP-ga Verbal* construction, in which the first NP-*ga* is the subject and the second NP-*ga* the object, can undergo the transformation that changes the first NP-*ga* to NP-*ni*. I shall call this transformation *Ga/Ni* Conversion. Observe the following pairs of sentences:

(27) a. John *ga* nihongo *ga* nigate da.
             Japanese   bad-at is
       'John is bad at Japanese.'
   b. John *ni* nihongo *ga* nigate da.

(28) a. John *ga* nihongo *ga* dekiru.
             Japanese   can
       'John can speak Japanese.'
   b. John *ni* nihongo *ga* dekiru.

(29) a. John *ga* nihongo o hanasu koto *ga* dekiru.
             Japanese   speak   to   can
       'John can speak Japanese.'
   b. John *ni* nihongo o hanasu koto *ga* dekiru.

(30) a. John *ga* nihongo *ga* hanas-(r)e-ru.
             Japanese   speak-can
       'John can speak Japanese.'
   b. John *ni* nihongo *ga* hanas-(r)e-ru.

Since *Ga/Ni* Conversion applies only when there is an *NP-ga NP-ga V* pattern, it does not apply when the object of (30a) is marked with *o* or when the intransitive construction appears to the left of *re*. Consider the following examples:

(31) a. John *ga* nihongo *o* hanas-(r)e-ru.
             Japanese speak-can
       'John can speak Japanese.'
   b. *John *ni* nihongo *o* hanas-(r)e-ru.

(32) a. John *ga* aruk-(r)e-ru.
             walk-can
       'John can walk.'
   b. *John *ni* aruk-(r)e-ru.

(iv) Subject Marking: John *ga* Mary ga ni okane o nusum-rare-ta.

(v) Object Marking: John ga Mary ga ni okane o *o* nusum-rare-ta.

(vi) *Ga/O* Deletion: John ga Mary ϕ ni okane ϕ o nusum-rare-ta.

At the time of application of Object Marking in (39c-iv), *okane o* is the first unmarked NP (note that noun phrases followed by *o* are unmarked by definition) to the left of the verb *rare*. Since *rare* is [−stative],[11] Object Marking with *o* applies obligatorily, producing *okane o o*. The first of the two *o*'s is deleted by *Ga/O* Deletion.

6. *Ni* and *O* Causatives

The *let* causative (or *ni* causative) and the *make* causative (or *o* causative) are assumed to be derived from two different deep structures. For example, (3b) and (3c) have (40a) and (40b), respectively, as their deep structure.

(3) b. John ga Mary *ni* ik-(s)ase-ru.
                to go-cause
     'John lets Mary go.'

     c. John ga Mary *o* ik-(s)ase-ru.
                go-cause
     'John makes Mary go.'

(40) a. *Ni* causative   b. *O* causative

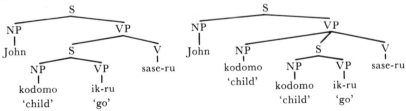

The difference between (40a) and (40b) is that in the former *sase* takes a single sentential object, while in the latter it takes an indirect object and a sentential object. The indirect object of (40b) specifies the person or the thing toward which John's causative action is directed. The sentential object of *ni* causative must be such that it represents an action that can be

---

[11] See Chapter 10, "Stative and Nonstative Verbals," for the [−stative] nature of *rare*.

controlled by the subject of the clause, while there is no such constraint on the sentential object of the *o* causative.[12] For example,

(41) a. *John ga bakudan *ni* bakuhatus-(s)ase-ta.
                    bomb   explode
           'John let the bomb explode.'

      b. John ga bakudan *o* bakuhatus-(s)ase-ta.
          'John made the bomb explode.'

(42) a. *John wa ame *ni* hur-(s)ase-ru koto ga dekiru.
                   rain   fall   that   can
          'John can let it rain.'

      b. John wa ame *o* hur-(s)ase-ru koto ga dekiru.
          'John can make it rain.'

The following gives the step-by-step derivation of (3b) from (40a):

(43) *Ni* causative (intransitive construction)
      a. Deep structure: John [Mary ik-ru]$_S$ sase-ru.
      b. First cycle
          (i) Subject Marking: John [Mary *ga* ik-ru]$_S$ sase-ru.
      c. Second cycle
          (i) Agentive-*Ni*
               Attachment: John [Mary ga *ni* ik-ru]$_S$ sase-ru.
          (ii) Aux Deletion: John [Mary ga ni ik-ϕ]$_S$ sase-ru.
          (iii) Verb Raising: John Mary ga ni ik-sase-ru.
          (iv) Subject Marking: John *ga* Mary ga ni ik-sase-ru.
          (v)   *Ga*/*O* Deletion: John ga Mary ϕ ni ik-sase-ru.

On the other hand, (3c) is derived from (40b) in the following manner:

(44) *O* causative (intransitive construction)
      a. Deep structure: John Mary [Mary ik-ru]$_S$ sase-ru.
      b. First cycle
          (i) Subject Marking: John Mary [Mary *ga* ik-ru]$_S$ sase-ru.
      c. Second cycle
          (i) Equi-NP Deletion: John Mary [ϕ ik-ru]$_S$ sase-ru.
          (ii) Aux Deletion: John Mary [ik-ϕ]$_S$ sase-ru.
          (iii) Verb Raising: John Mary ik-sase-ru.

[12] I am indebted to James McCawley (personal communication) for this observation.

(iv) Subject Marking: John *ga* Mary ik-sase-ru.
(v)   Object Marking: John ga Mary *o* ik-sase-ru.

Note that in the case of *o* causative, Equi-NP Deletion, and not Agentive-*Ni* Attachment, applies. At the time of application of Object Marking, *Mary*, which used to be in the indirect object position of *sase* in the deep structure, has come to occupy the position of the first NP to the left of *ik-sase-ru* 'make go'. Since *sase* is [−stative], *o* is attached to *Mary*.

Now let us examine what happens when the constituent sentence of the causative deep structure is of the transitive construction. There is no reason why the two deep structures of (45a) and (45b), corresponding to (40a) and (40b), respectively, should not be possible.

(45) a. *Ni* causative   b. *O* causative

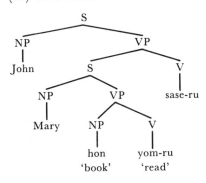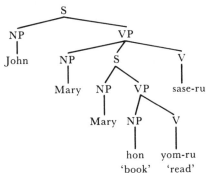

Let us first follow the step-by-step derivation of (45a):

(46) *Ni* causative (transitive construction)
    a. Deep structure: John [Mary hon yom-ru]ₛ sase-ru.
    b. First cycle
      (i) Subject and
          Object Marking: John [Mary *ga* hon *o* yom-ru]ₛ
          sase-ru.
    c. Second cycle
      (i) Agentive-*Ni*
          Attachment: John [Mary ga *ni* hon o yom-ru]ₛ
          sase-ru.

(ii) Aux Deletion: John [Mary ga ni hon o yom-ϕ]$_S$
                             sase-ru.

(iii) Verb Raising: John Mary ga ni hon o yom-sase-ru.

(iv) Subject Marking: John *ga* Mary ga ni hon o yom-
                             sase-ru.

(v)   Object Marking: John ga Mary ga ni hon o *o* yom-
                             sase-ru.

(vi) *Ga/O* Deletion: John ga Mary ϕ ni hon
                             ϕ o yom-sase-ru.

Note that *hon o* at (46c-iv) is the first unmarked NP to the left of *sase*. Since *sase* is [−stative], *o* is added to *hon o* by Object Marking.

Now, the following shows the step-by-step derivation of (45b):

(47) *O* causative (transitive construction)

   a. Deep structure: John Mary [Mary hon yom-ru]$_S$
                              sase-ru.

   b. First cycle

      (i) Subject and
           Object Marking: John Mary [Mary *ga* hon *o* yom-ru]$_S$
                              sase-ru.

   c. Second cycle

      (i)   Equi-NP Deletion: John Mary [ϕ hon o yom-ru]$_S$
                              sase-ru.

      (ii) Aux Deletion: John Mary [hon o yom-ϕ]$_S$ sase-ru.

      (iii) Verb Raising: John Mary hon o yom-sase-ru.

      (iv) Indirect
            Object Marking: John Mary *ni* hon o yom-sase-ru.

      (v)   Subject Marking: John *ga* Mary ni hon o yom-sase-ru.

      (vi) Object Marking: John ga Mary ni hon o *o* yom-
                              sase-ru.

      (vii) *Ga/O* Deletion: John ga Mary ni hon ϕ o yom-
                              sase-ru.

Note that in (47) the indirect object *Mary* does not become an NP closest to the verb because *hon o* is. Thus, *Mary* remains as the second unmarked NP to the left of the verb and therefore receives the particle *ni* because of Indirect Object Marking. The situation was different when the constituent clause was of the intransitive construction. Recall that in (44c-v) *Mary* receives *o* in spite of the fact that it started as the indirect object in the deep structure because it has come to occupy the position of the first unmarked NP to the left of the verb.

In the preceding, we have seen that both the *ni* causative deep structure of (45a) and the *o* causative deep structure of (45b) have resulted in the same surface sentence:

(48) John ga Mary *ni* hon *o* yom-sase-ru.
     'John lets/makes Mary read books.'

This is due to the working of Agentive-*Ni* Attachment, Equi-NP Deletion, Indirect Object Marking, and Object Marking. To repeat, when the constituent clause of the causative constructions is intransitive, the following things happen. In the case of *ni* causative, *ni* is attached to the subject of the constituent clause. On the other hand, in the case of *o* causative, the subject of the constituent clause gets deleted by Equi-NP Deletion. Thus, the indirect object becomes the first unmarked NP to the left of the main verb *sase*. Hence, it receives *o* by Object Marking. When the constituent clause of the causative construction is transitive, the following things happen. In the case of *ni* causative, it is the same as for the intransitive construction. The subject of the constituent clause is marked with *ni*. The object of the constituent clause receives *o* because it is the first unmarked NP to the left of the verb. On the other hand, in the case of *o* causative, the subject of the constituent clause gets deleted by Equi-NP Deletion under identity with the indirect object. Thus, the indirect object becomes the second unmarked NP to the left of the verb. Therefore, it receives *ni* by Indirect Object Marking.

7. Pure Passive Formation
It is assumed that the pure passives are derived from the simplex deep structure corresponding to the active sentences.[13] For example,

(49) Mary ga John ni koros-(r)are-ta.
                   by kill-passive-ed
     'Mary was killed by John.'

---

[13] See Chapter 25, "The Reflexive Pronoun and the Passive and Causative Constructions," for justification of deriving pure passives from simplex deep structures corresponding to active sentences.

Sentence (49) is derived from the deep structure corresponding to

(50) a. [John]$_{NP}$[Mary]$_{NP}$[koros-ta]$_V$.
     'John killed Mary.'

Pure Passive Formation applies to (50a), yielding

(50) b. [Mary]$_{NP}$John *ni* (*yotte*) koros-rare-ta.
     'Mary was killed by John.'

Note that it is possible to mark the agent with *ni yotte* only for pure passives.[14] Agentive *ni* of adversity passives cannot be replaced by *ni yotte*, as can be seen in the following:

(51) a. *John ga ame *ni yotte* hur-(r)are-ta.
                      rain   by   fall
        'John was rained on.'

     b. John ga ame *ni* hur-(r)are-ta.

(52) a. *John wa musuko *ni yotte* sin-(r)are-ta.
                 son   die
        'John suffered from his son's dying.'

     b. John wa musuko *ni* sin-(r)are-ta.

This phenomenon gives an additional support to the proposed analysis in which pure passives and adversity passives are derived through two different processes (namely, the former through Pure Passive Formation applied to the simplex deep structures, and the latter through Agentive-*Ni* Attachment and other transformations applied to the complex deep structures).

Some of the verbs that take a dative object can undergo Pure Passive Formation, and others cannot.[15] Observe the following examples:

(53) a. John ga Mary *ni* katta.
                      to won
         'John has beaten Mary.'

     b. *Mary ga John ni kat-(r)are-ta.
                      by
        'Mary has been beaten by John.'

---

[14] I am indebted to James McCawley (personal communication) for this observation.
[15] I am indebted to Noriko Akatsuka (personal communication) for this observation.

(54) a. John ga Mary *ni* atta.
                         to met
          'John met with Mary.'

    b. *Mary ga John ni aw-(r)are-ta.
                         by
          'Mary was met with by John.'

(55) a. John ga Mary *ni* soodansita.
                         to consulted
          'John consulted Mary.'

    b. Mary ga John *ni* soodans-(r)are-ta.
                         by
          'Mary was consulted by John.'

(56) a. John ga Mary *ni* uinkusita.
                         to winked
          'John winked at Mary.'

    b. Mary ga John *ni* uinkus-(r)are-ta.
                         by
          'Mary was winked at by John.'

It seems that these verbs must be marked individually in the lexicon with respect to whether or not they can undergo Pure Passive Formation.

The passive of the causative sentence always means 'be forced to', and never 'be let to'. Observe the following sentences:

(57) a. John ga Mary *o* ik-(s)ase-ru.
                         go-cau e
          'John makes Mary go.'

    b. Mary ga John ni ik-(s)ase-rare-ru.
                         by go-cause passive
          'Mary is made to go by John.'

(58) a. John ga Mary *ni* hon o yom-(s)ase-ru.
                         book   read-cause
          'John lets/makes Mary read books.'

    b. Mary ga John ni hon o yom-(s)ase-rare-ru.
                         by book   read-cause-passive
          'Mary is made by John to read books.'

Thus, *sase* for the *let* causative should be marked in the lexicon as a verb that cannot undergo Pure Passive Formation, and *sase* for the *make* causative as one that can undergo the transformation.

Pure Passive Formation must follow Equi-NP Deletion. Otherwise, the Equi-NP Deletion, when it applies to the *o* causative construction, would have to delete the subject of the constituent clause under identity with the indirect object in case Pure Passive Formation has not applied, and under identity with the subject in case the transformation has applied, thus resulting in the complication of the conditions for deletion. Pure Passive Formation, in turn, must precede Subject Marking because the subject of passive sentences is marked with *ga*. It seems that Indirect Object Marking must precede Pure Passive Formation. Observe the following sentences:

(59) [John]$_{NP}$[Mary]$_{NP}$[kunsyoo]$_{NP}$ atae-ta.
                       medal   give-past
      'John gave Mary a medal.'

If *Mary* becomes the subject of the passive sentence, everything goes smoothly, as already shown. Thus, we have the following:

(60) a. Pure Passive
              Formation: Mary John ni kunsyoo atae-rare-ta.
                                              by medal   give-passive-past
      b. Subject Marking: Mary *ga* John ni kunsyoo atae-rare-ta.
      c. Object Marking: Mary ga John ni kunsyoo *o* atae-rare-ta.

Now, assume that *kunsyoo* 'medal' becomes the subject of the passive sentence, and that Indirect Object Marking follows Pure Passive Formation.

(61) a. Pure Passive
              Formation: Kunksyoo John ni (yotte) Mary
                                    medal   by
                                    atae-rare-ta.[16]
                                    give-passive-past

[16] The agent in the pure passive is represented in formal style by *ni yotte*, as has been noted before.

(i) Kunsyoo ga John *ni yotte* Mary ni atae-rare-ta.
              by   give-passive-ed
   'A medal was given to Mary by John.'

The use of *ni* in place of *ni yotte* would result in an extremely awkward sentence because of the repetition of NP-*ni*.

b. Subject Marking: Kunsyoo *ga* John ni (yotte) Mary
                         atae-rare-ta.

c. Object Marking: *Kunsyoo ga John ni (yotte) Mary *o*
                         atae-rare-ta.

Since *Mary* is the first unmarked NP to the left of *rare* in (61b) and since *rare* is [−stative], *Mary* should receive *o* by Object Marking. However, (61c) is totally ungrammatical. The indirect object marker *ni* must be attached to *Mary*.

On the other hand, if it is assumed that Indirect Object Marking precedes Pure Passive Formation, there is no such difficulty.

(62) a. Indirect Object
        Marking: John Mary *ni* kunsyoo atae-ta.
                              to medal   give-past

     b. Pure Passive
        Formation: Kunsyoo John ni (yotte) Mary ni
                                              by
                         atae-rare-ta.
                         give-passive

     c. Subject Marking: Kunsyoo *ga* John ni (yotte) Mary ni
                          atae-rare-ta.

     d. Object Marking: (does not apply)

8. Summary of Transformations

The transformations discussed in this section are given here by way of a summary.

1. *Agentive-Ni Attachment:*
   Mark the subject of the constituent clause with *ni*.

2. *Equi-NP Deletion:*
   Delete the subject of the constituent clause under identity with the object (or the subject, depending upon individual verbs) of the matrix sentence.

3. *Aux Deletion:*
   Delete the tense auxiliary of the constituent clause that is not dominated by the NP node.

4. *Verb Raising:*

Attach the tenseless verb of the constituent clause to the left of the matrix verb. (Note: The VP node and the S node of the constituent clauses are deleted by the tree-pruning convention.)

5. *Indirect Object Marking:*

Attach *ni* to the second of three unmarked NP's. (Note: An NP is unmarked if it is not followed by any particle or if it is followed only by *o* or *ga*.)

6. *Pure Passive Formation:*

Place the direct object or dative object NP in subject position, and place the original subject NP after it with *ni* (*yotte*) attached.

7. *Subject Marking:*

Attach *ga* to the subject NP.

8. *Object Marking:*

If the matrix verb is [−stative], attach *o* to the first unmarked nonsubject NP to the left of the verb. If the matrix verb is [+stative], attach *ga* to the first unmarked nonsubject NP to the left of the verb. In the latter case, the transformation is optional if the object is already followed by *o*.

9. *Ga/Ni Conversion:*

Attach *ni* to the first NP-*ga* of the *NP-ga NP-ga Verbal* construction.

10. *Ga/O Deletion:*

Delete *ga* and *o* if they are followed by some other particle.

28[†]

The Position of Locatives in Existential Sentences

1. Introduction

The term "existential sentence" will be used to refer to sentences such as (1a) and (1b), which state the existence of certain indefinite objects in some place.

(1) a. There are two books on the table.

    b. Two books are on the table.

The objective of this chapter is to show that in Japanese, and in many other languages including English, the basic word order of existential sentences is that of (2), where NP_{indef} denotes the "things that exist," and not that of (3).

(2) $LOCATIVE + NP_{indef} + V_{exist}$ (for S + O + V languages)

    $LOCATIVE + V_{exist} + NP_{indef}$ (for S + V + O languages)

(3) $NP_{indef} + LOCATIVE + V_{exist}$ (for S + O + V languages)

    $NP_{indef} + V_{exist} + LOCATIVE$ (for S + V + O languages)

I do not mean to claim that the LOCATIVE precedes the NP_{indef} in the deep structure. This may or may not be the case. What I shall claim is that, at some stage in the derivation of sentences, which might well be the deep structure level, at which nonexistential sentences have the subject in the sentence-initial position, existential sentences have the locative preceding the subject. I shall first present five arguments for this word order in Japanese (Section 2) and then proceed to English (Section 3) and other languages (Section 4).

2. Existential Sentences in Japanese

Japanese has a fairly extensive Scrambling Rule. For example, (4a) can also be realized as (4b) through (4f).

(4) a. John ga   Mary o   Cambridge de mita.
      nominative accusative   in saw
      particle   particle
      'John saw Mary in Cambridge.'

    b. John ga Cambridge de Mary o mita.

†This chapter is mainly for linguists.

      c. Mary o John ga Cambridge de mita.

      d. Mary o Cambridge de John ga mita.

      e. Cambridge de John ga Mary o mita.

      f. Cambridge de Mary o John ga mita.

The same holds true for existential sentences.

(5) a. Teiburu no ue ni koppu ga aru.
       table   's top on cup   exist

    b. Koppu ga teiburu no ue ni aru.
       cup   table   's top on exist

     'There are cups on the table.'

Both (5a) and (5b) are grammatical. Note that the nominative particle *ga* is used for marking the "things that exist" in these sentences. I shall henceforth use "Subject" to refer to the NP_{indef} of existential sentences. What I am going to show in this section is that (5a) is the word order more basic to existential sentences, and (5b) is the result of the application of the Scrambling Rule.

Because of the freedom of its word order, it is extremely difficult to argue for or against a given word order in Japanese. In the ensuing sections, my arguments will often take the following form:

With respect to certain grammatical features, existential sentences with the word order $L(ocative)$ + $S(ubject)$ behave similarly to nonexistential sentences with the word order $S(ubject)$ + $O(bject)$, and existential sentences with the word order S + L behave similarly to nonexistential sentences with the word order O + S. Since there is overwhelming evidence that S + O + V is the basic word order for nonexistential sentences,[1] L + S + $Exist$ is the basic word order for existential sentences.

---

[1] First, as will be described in Section 2.1, the S + O word order occurs 17 times more frequently than the O + S word order. Second, the object becomes a reflexive pronoun when it is coreferential with the subject, but the subject never becomes reflexivized under coreferentiality with the object:

(i)   John ga *zibun* o hometa.
             self   praised
    'John praised himself.'

(ii) *Zibun* ga John o hometa.
      self   praised
    '(Lit.) Himself praised John.'

2.1 Relative Frequencies of Occurrences

Statistically speaking, the ratio of frequencies of occurrences between the $S + O + V$ pattern and the $O + S + V$ pattern in Japanese is 17 to 1. On the other hand, the ratio between the $L + S + Exist$ pattern and the

---

On the assumption that Reflexivization does not operate backward in a simplex sentence, for which there is strong evidence in the language, the ungrammaticality of (ii) indicates that the subject precedes the object at the time of application of Reflexivization. On the other hand, in the following, example (iii), although of dubious acceptability, is far better than (iv), which is totally ungrammatical:

(iii) ??*Zibun* o John ga hometa.
      self   praised
      '(Lit.) Himself, John praised.'

(iv) *John o *zibun* ga hometa.
      '(Lit.) John, himself praised.'

The acceptability of (iii) can be accounted for by the same principle that Postal (1971) has proposed. Namely, *zibun* (*o*), although it is coreferential with *John*, can be preposed (although it would result in a sentence of low acceptability), crossing over *John*, because it is not a pronominal virgin (that is, because it has already been reflexivized). Example (iv) is ungrammatical because *John* (*o*), which is a pronominal virgin, has been preposed, crossing over *zibun*, with which it is coreferential, and because Reflexivization, which should have been applied before this preposing rule, is applied after it.

    Third, some $S + O$ sentences resist word order inversion. Observe the following sentences:

(v) John ga *eiga*   *ga* suki   da.
             movies   fond-of is
     'John likes movies.'

(vi) *Eiga*   *ga* John ga suki   da.
     movies   fond-of is
     '(Lit.) Movies, John likes.'

(vii) John ga *eigo*   *ga* wakaru.
              English   understand
     'John understands English.'

(viii) *Eigo*   *ga* John ga wakaru.
     English   understand.
     '(Lit.) English, John understands.'

When verbs, adjectives, and nominal adjectives are stative, *ga* is used for marking their objects if they are transitive. This is why *ga* appears after *eiga* and *eigo* in (v) and (vii), respectively. As (vi) and (viii) show, object noun phrases "NP + *ga*" for such verbals cannot precede subject noun phrases. On the other hand, there are no $O + S$ sentences that cannot be paraphrased as $S + O$ sentences. (For details on *ga* for object marking, see Chapter 4 of this book.)

$S + L + Exist$ pattern is 3.5 to 1.[2] Although the latter figure is not as convincing as the former, it shows that the preferred word order for existential sentences in Japanese is $L + S + Exist$.[3]

2.2 Word Order Constraints

There are many existential sentences that sound very natural with their locatives at the sentence-initial position but awkward or ungrammatical with them placed after the subjects. For example,

(6) a. Sya-nai   ni inemuri o site-iru zyookyaku ga atta.
        train-inside in nap   doing-is passenger   was
        'There were passengers on the train who were dozing.'

    b. ??Inemuri o site iru zyookyaku ga sya-nai ni atta.[4]
        '(Lit.) Passengers who were dozing were on the train.'

---

[2] These figures are based on a large-scale statistical study of sentence structures conducted by the National Language Research Institute, Tokyo, Japan. I am indebted to Akira Mikami for pointing it out to me. In fact, I owe this whole chapter to him because, at the time when I had a mere conjecture, based on Section 2.5, that locatives must precede subjects in existential sentences in Japanese, he, whose linguistic insight I trust, told me that he had firmly believed that this must be more or less a language universal and thus gave me encouragement for pursuing my analysis. Semantic arguments for hypothesizing that the basic word order of existential sentences in Japanese is that of $L + S + Exist$ are given in Mikami (1969).

[3] Relative frequency of occurrences in itself does not constitute a strong argument for a given word order as representing the deep structure order. Bach (1970), for example, argues that despite the overwhelming frequency of SOV sentences in surface structures in Amharic, Amharic is not an SOV language, but is an SVO language in the underlying structure. On the other hand, no one has claimed that Japanese is an SVO language because there is no justification for hypothesizing a rule that obligatorily transforms the assumed SVO word order into the SOV surface order. I think that it can be claimed that the predominant word order in the surface sentence represents the underlying word order unless there are compelling reasons for not assuming so.

[4] *Aru* 'be'/*atta* 'was' ordinarily require an inanimate subject. When the subject is animate, *iru*/*ita* is used instead. For example,

(i)   Boku no ie   wa Boston ni { *aru* / is / *iru }.
      I   's house   in
      'My house is in Boston.'

(ii) *John wa Boston ni { *aru / *iru* }.
      'John is in Boston.'

Therefore, it is not possible to interpret (6b) as a nonexistential sentence with a definite (anaphoric) subject meaning '*the* passengers who were dozing were on the train' because the sentence in this interpretation would require *ita* 'were' in the place of *atta*.

(7) a. Yama   ni ki   ga aru.
        mountain   tree   exist
        'There are trees on the mountain.'

   b. ??Ki ga yama ni aru.[5]
       '(Lit.) Trees are on the mountain.'

(8) a. Itinen   ni 365-niti (ga) aru.
        one-year in   day   are
        'There are 365 days in a year.'

   b. ?*365-niti (ga) itinen ni aru.
       '(Lit.) *365 days are in a year.'

(9) a. Mukasi, aru tokoro ni oziisan   to   obaasan   ga arimasita.
        long-ago a   place in old-man and old-woman   were
        'Long, long ago, there were in a certain place an old man and
        an old woman.'

   b. *Mukasi, oziisan to obaasan ga aru tokoro ni arimasita.
       '(Lit.) Long, long ago, an old man and an old woman were in
       a certain place.'

On the other hand, I have not been able to find any existential sentences
that are natural with the *Subject + Locative* word order but are awkward
or ungrammatical with the *Locative + Subject* word order.

2.3 Theme and Contrast
Wa, which is ordinarily called a thematic particle, has two functions:
(i) to mark the theme of a sentence, (ii) to mark an element that is contrasted with some other element, either present or understood, in the sentence (cf. Chapter 2). For example, *wa* in (10) marks *ningen* 'man' as the
theme of the sentence.

(10) Ningen *wa* kangaeru asi   da.
     man   think   reed is
     'Man is a reed that thinks.'

---

[5] Sentence (7b) would be acceptable as an answer to "What is on the mountain?" but
not as a statement in isolation.

The theme of a sentence must be either generic or anaphoric. Therefore, note the following:

(11) a. *Ame *wa* hutte-iru.
      rain   falling-is
      '(Lit.) The rain is falling.'

    b. *Oozei no hito   *wa* party ni kita.
       many   people   to came
       '*Speaking of many people, they came to the party.'

These examples are ungrammatical in isolation because *ame* 'rain' and *oozei no hito* 'many people' in these sentences are neither generic nor anaphoric.[6] On the other hand, if these indefinite noun phrases are contrasted with some other noun phrases, we have grammatical sentences.

(12) a. Ame *wa* hutte iru ga, yuki *wa* hutte-inai.
      rain   falling is but snow   falling-is-not
      'It is raining, but it is not snowing.'

    b. Oozei no hito   *wa* party ni kita ga, omosiroi   hito   *wa*
       many   people   to came but interesting people
       konakatta.
       did-not-come
       'Many people came to the party, but interesting people didn't.'

Now, when the *subject* noun phrase is followed by *wa*, if it is either generic or anaphoric, both the thematic and the contrastive interpretations result. For example,

(13) a. John ga Tokyo ni itta.
                      to went
      'John went to Tokyo.'

---

[6] *Ame* 'rain' in (11a) cannot receive the generic interpretation because what is falling now is not generic rain, but must be specific rain. Similarly, *oozei no hito* in (11b) cannot receive the 'many people in general' interpretation because of the specific nature of its predicate. On the other hand, the following example is a perfectly grammatical sentence because *ame* can be taken as a generic noun phrase here since its predicate can represent a generic action:

(i) Ame *wa* sora kara huru.
    rain   sky from fall
    'The rain falls from the sky.'

   b. John *wa* Tokyo ni itta.
      (i) Theme: 'Speaking of John, he went to Tokyo.'
      (ii) Contrast: 'As for John, he went to Tokyo (but as for the other people, . . .).'

(14) a. John ga Tokyo kara kita.
                      from came
      'John came from Tokyo.'

   b. John *wa* Tokyo kara kita.
      (i) Theme: 'Speaking of John, he came from Tokyo.'
      (ii) Contrast: 'As for John, he came from Tokyo (but as for the other people, . . .).'

On the other hand, if a *nonsubject* noun phrase is followed by *wa*, ordinarily only the contrastive interpretation results.

(13) c. Tokyo ni *wa*, John ga itta.
                  to   went
      (i) Contrast: '(Lit.) As for to Tokyo, John went (there).'

(14) c. Tokyo kara *wa* John ga kita.[7]
                  from   came
      (i) Contrast: '(Lit.) As for from Tokyo, John came (from there).'

   With regard to existential sentences, when locatives are followed by *wa*, we get both the thematic and contrastive interpretations.

(15) a. Sono teiburu no ue ni koppu ga atta.
         the table   's top on cup   existed
      'There were cups on the table.'

   b. Sono teiburu no ue ni *wa* koppu ga atta. (thematic/contrastive)

(16) a. Yama   no ue ni zinzya ga atta.
         mountain 's top on shrine   existed
      'There was a shrine on top of the mountain.'

   b. Yama no ue ni *wa* zinzya ga atta. (thematic/contrastive)

---

[7] The particle *kara* 'from' is never deleted when it immediately precedes *wa*. The particle *ni* for locatives may optionally be deleted before *wa*. The particles *ga* and *o* must be deleted before *wa*. Sentences (13b) and (14b) are derived from

John *ga wa* . . .

by the obligatory deletion of *ga*.

On the other hand, when the subject noun phrases of existential sentences are thematized, we get only the contrastive interpretation.

(15) c. Koppu *wa* sono teiburu no ue ni atta. (contrastive)
        cup   the table   's top on existed

(16) c. Zinzya *wa* yama   no ue ni atta. (contrastive)[8]
        shrine   mountain 's top on existed

This may simply be because the subject of existential sentences is neither generic nor anaphoric, but is indefinite. However, the ambiguity of (15b) and (16b) can be best accounted for if we assume that the locative is the sentence-initial element in existential sentences, and that the addition of *wa* to the sentence-initial element in a sentence results in the thematic/contrastive interpretation, while the addition of *wa* to noninitial elements results in the contrastive interpretation only.

2.4 Order of Quantifiers

It has long been observed that the order of quantifiers in surface sentences in English corresponds more or less to the order of quantifications in the

[8] Sentences (15c) and (16c), in appropriate contexts, have another reading: '*The* cup was on the table' and '*The* shrine was on top of the mountain', respectively. In these interpretations, they are no longer existential sentences, and, as expected, they can receive both the thematic and the contrastive interpretations. For example, (16c) preceded by (i) receives the thematic interpretation.

(i) Watakusi wa mai-asa   mura no zinzya ni oinori ni itta.
    I   every-morning village 's shrine to praying for went
    'I went to a shrine of the village every morning for praying.'

However, if it is preceded by (ii), it receives the contrastive interpretation.

(ii) Mura ni wa zinzya to otera   ga atta.
     village in   shrine and temple   were
     'There was a shrine and a temple in the village.'

In the context of (i), it is more natural to start (16c) with *sono zinzya* '*the* shrine', while *sono* cannot be used before *zinzya* when (16c) follows (ii). On the other hand, it is not possible to interpret *koppu* and *zinzya* of (15b) and (16b) as '*the* cup' and '*the* shrine', respectively, because in that interpretation they should be preceded by determiners such as *sono* 'the' and *kono* 'this'. This phenomenon shows that, in spite of the generally held view that Japanese lacks articles and that nouns can be used freely both as singular and plural and as definite and indefinite without overt grammatical markers, there are cases where determiners such as *sono* 'the', *kono* 'this', *ano* 'that', and *aru* 'certain' are obligatory. At present, it is not clear when these determiners must, can, or may not be used.

corresponding expressions of predicate calculus.[9] For example, to many speakers of English, sentence (17) means (18a), and not (18b).

(17) Every girl likes some candies.

(18) a. $(\forall x)\ (\exists y)\ \text{LIKE}(x,y)$
          'For every girl, there are some candies that she likes.'
      b. $(\exists y)\ (\forall x)\ \text{LIKE}(x,y)$
          'There are some candies that every girl likes.'

On the other hand, to the majority of the same speakers, sentence (19) means (18b), and not (18a).

(19) Some candies are liked by every girl.

The same rule applies to Japanese, as is shown here:

(20) a. *Daremo*   ga *dareka*   o aisite-iru.
          everyone   someone   loving-is
          'Everyone likes someone.' (Cf. 18a.)
      b. *Dareka*   ga *daremo*   ni aisarete-iru.
          someone   everyone   by being-loved-is
          'Someone is liked by everyone.' (Cf. 18b.)

Sentence (20b) is in the passive voice. Note that *dareka ga* 'someone' in this sentence is the subject of the passive sentence, and, as a passive sentence, (20b) has the basic word order of the subject preceding other elements of the sentence. In (20a), someone that Person A likes may be different from someone that Person B likes, who, in turn, may be different from someone that Person C likes. On the other hand, in (20b), the same person is liked by A, B, C, ... I shall use the expressions "different someone" and "the same someone" to distinguish these two interpretations.

---

[9] For example, see Bohnert and Becker (1966). Lakoff (1971) has attempted to account for the interpretation of quantifiers by what he calls derivational constraints on quantifiers. They are as follows:

If quantifier Q1 is in a higher S in the deep structure than quantifier Q2, either (i) the same must hold true for the surface structure or (ii) if Q1 and Q2 appear in the same simplex S in the surface structure, Q1 must precede Q2.

I shall show in Section 3.3 that neither in the framework of the Interpretive Hypothesis (Jackendoff, 1969) nor in the framework of the Derivational Constraints (Lakoff, 1971) do these principles of quantifier interpretation work even for nonexistential sentences.

I came upon the idea of using the interpretation of quantifiers as an argument for the basic word order of Japanese existential sentences through reading Kuroda (1969).

Observe, further, the following examples:

(21) a. *Yonin* no syoonen ga *sannin* no syoozyo o okasita
       four   boy   three   girl   sexually-molested
       koto   ga aru.
       experience   have
       'Four boys have the experience of sexually molesting three girls.'

    b. *Sannin* no syoozyo ga *yonin* no syoonen ni okasareta
       three   girl   four   boy   by molest-passive-ed
       koto ga aru.
       'Three girls have the experience of being molested by four boys.'

I shall examine, among others,[10] the following three logically possible interpretations of these sentences:

(22) a. Each of the same four boys has sexually molested each of the same three girls. (4 boys and 3 girls involved)

    b. Each of the same four boys has sexually molested three (possibly) different girls. (4 boys, and minimum 3, maximum 12 girls involved)

    c. Each of the three girls has been sexually molested by four (possibly) different boys. (minimum 4, maximum 12 boys, and 3 girls involved)

Sentence (21a) means either (22a) or (22b), but it cannot mean (22c). On the other hand, (21b) means either (22a) or (22c), but it cannot mean (22b). From the preceding, we can tentatively hypothesize that if a simple sentence contains two quantifiers Q1 and Q2 in that order, Q2 receives the interpretation "for each member of (the same) Q1, different Q2."[11]

A different result obtains when the word order of noun phrases containing quantifiers is changed because of scrambling. Observe, first, the following sentence, which is derived by preposing *sannin no syoozyo o* 'three girls' of (21a):

[10] One plausible interpretation of these sentences is that a group of four boys has sexually molested a group of three girls. In this interpretation, it is not necessarily the case that each of the four boys has molested each of the three girls. Since this interpretation does not play a role in distinguishing between the basic word order and the scrambled word order, I shall exclude it from further consideration.

[11] According to the preceding hypothesis, (22a), which is a possible interpretation both for (21a) and for (21b), is a special case (the minimum case) of (22b) and (22c).

(23) *Sannin* no syoozyo o, *yonin* no syoonen ga okasita   koto ga aru.
      three   girl   four   boy   molested
      '(Lit.) Three girls, four boys have the experience of sexually molest-
      ing.'

This sentence means neither (22b) nor (22c). It can mean only (22a). Namely, the sentence can be used only when there are only three girls and four boys involved. Similarly, compare the following two sentences:

(24) a. Syutuzyoosya no uti no *sannin* ga, *nizyup-pako* no manzyuu o
        participant   among three   20-boxes   pastries
        tabeta.
        ate
        'Each of three of the participants ate 20 boxes of pastries.'
   b. *Nizyup-pako* no manzyuu o, syutuzyoosya no uti no *sannin* ga
        tabeta.
        'Three of the participants altogether ate 20 boxes of pastries.'

In (24a), a total of 60 boxes of pastries were consumed, while in (24b), a total of 20 boxes were consumed.

From these observations, we can hypothesize the following rules for interpreting quantifiers in simple sentences:

(25) Rule 1. The quantifier Q that appears as the leftmost quantifier either before scrambling (namely, in the structure representing the basic word order) or in the surface sentence receives the "same Q" interpretation.

     Rule 2. The quantifier Q2 that appears to the right of another quantifier Q1 in the surface sentence receives the "different Q2 for each member of Q1" interpretation unless already marked otherwise by Rule 1.

According to this hypothesis, *yonin no syoonen* 'four boys' in (23) receives the "same four" interpretation (Rule 1) because it used to be the leftmost quantifier in the structure representing the basic word order, as shown in (21a). At the same time, *sannin no syoozyo* 'three girls' of the same sentence receives the "same three" interpretation because it appears as the leftmost quantifier in the surface sentence (Rule 1).

The difference in meaning between the following pairs of sentences can be accounted for by the same rules:

(26) a. *Minna* ga *nanika*   o tabeta.
      all   something   ate
      'All ate something.' (different something)

    b. *Nanika* o, *minna* ga tabeta.
      'All ate something.' (the same something)

(27) a. *Minna* ga *dokoka*   ni itta.
      all   somewhere   went
      'All went somewhere.' (to different places)

    b. *Dokoka* ni, *minna* ga itta.
      'All went somewhere.' (to the same place)

(28) a. *Minna* ga *dareka*   ni aisarete iru.
      all   someone by loved   are
      'All are loved by someone.' (by different persons)

    b. *Dareka* ni, *minna* ga aisarete iru.
      'All are loved by someone.' (by the same person)[12]

Now, we are ready to examine the word order of existential sentences on the basis of the preceding hypothesis. Observe the following sentences:

(29) a. *Dono* ike   ni mo *san-syurui* no sakana ga ita.
      every pond in   three-kind   fish   were
      'In every pond were three kinds of fish.' (three different kinds)

---

[12] Observe the following examples:

(i) *Dareka* ga *minna* o mimamotte iru.
   someone   all   watching is
   'Someone is watching all.' (the same someone)

(ii) *Minna* o, *dareka* ga mimamotte iru.
    'Someone is watching all.' (the same someone)

These two sentences are synonymous, contrary to the pattern that we have been observing between sentences that represent the basic word order and those that obtain after scrambling. However, the synonymity of (i) and (ii) is also what Rules 1 and 2 predict. According to these rules, (i) and (ii) should receive interpretations (iii) and (iv), respectively.

(iii) The same someone is watching different all.

(iv) The same someone is watching the same all.

Since 'all' is coextensive with the set of people under discussion, there is no semantic difference between 'different all' and 'the same all'. Hence, (iii) and (iv) are synonymous.

b. *San-syurui* no sakana ga *dono* ike ni mo ita.
'Three kinds of fish were in every pond.' (the same three kinds)

Assume, first, that (29b) represents the basic word order. The meaning of (29b) is consistent with Rules 1 and 2. In (29a), *san-syurui* 'three kinds' should receive the 'same three kinds' interpretation because Rule 1 says that the quantifier that is the leftmost quantifier before scrambling receives the "same Q" interpretation. The actual meaning of (29a) is inconsistent with this prediction. Assume, next, that (29a) represents the basic word order. Then, the meaning of *san-syurui* 'three kinds' of (29a) is consistent with what Rules 1 and 2 predict. Namely, it receives the 'different three kinds' interpretation because it is the right-hand quantifier and it is not marked otherwise by Rule 1. The meaning of (29b) is also as Rules 1 and 2 predict because *san-syurui* in this sentence is the leftmost quantifier in the surface representation, and thus Rule 1 assigns the 'same three kinds' interpretation to this quantifier.

Similarly, observe the following sentence pairs:

(30) a. *Dono* syasin ni mo, *hitori*   no otoko ga ututte   ita.
        every picture in   one-person   man   photographed was
        'In every picture appeared a man (photographed).' (a different person for each picture)

     b. *Hitori* no otoko ga *dono* syasin ni mo ututte ita.
        'A man appeared (photographed) in every picture.' (the same person)

(31) a. *Dono* heya ni mo *dareka*   ga ita.
        every room in   someone   was
        'In every room was someone.' (a different person for each room)

     b. *Dareka* ga *dono* heya ni mo ita.
        'Someone was in every room.' (the same person, as in a horror movie)[13]

We have observed that the same two rules for quantifier interpretation that we hypothesized for nonexistential sentences on the assumption that $S + O + V$ represents the basic word order also apply to existential sentences if we assume that $L + S + Exist$ represents their basic word order. On the other hand, if we assumed that the basic word order of existential

---

[13] Thus, (31b), if it is used in the sense of (31a), is extremely awkward.

sentences was that of $S + L + Exist$, we would have to set up a completely new set of quantifier interpretation rules just for existential sentences, and, furthermore, we would have to prevent Rules 1 and 2 from applying to existential sentences.[14]

2.5 Subjectivization

Japanese has a productive process, which I shall call Subjectivization (cf. Chapter 3), that has thus far escaped the attention of transformational grammarians. Observe the following sentence:

(32) Bunmeikoku   no dansei no heikinzyumyoo   ga mizikai.
      civilized-countries's male 's average-life-span   is-short
      'It is the average life-span of males of civilized countries that is short.'

Incidentally, *ga* for subject marking assumes the "*A* and only *A*" connotation when the predicate represents a state or a generic/habitual action. English translation 'It is *A* that...' is used to represent this "exhaustive listing" connotation. Subjectivization changes the leftmost "noun phrase + *no*" to "noun phrase + *ga*" and makes it a new subject of the sentence. As is shown in the following, Subjectivization is an iterative process and can apply to its own output. Note, in the following, that it is only the leftmost "noun phrase + *ga*" that assumes the "*A* and only *A*" connotation:

(33) a. Apply Subjectivization to *bunmeikoku no dansei no* of (32):
          Bunmeikoku   no dansei ga heikinzyumyoo ga mizikai.
          civilized-countries 's male   average-life-span is-short
          'It is males of civilized countries that (their) average life-span is short.'

      b. Apply Subjectivization to *bunmeikoku no* of (33a):
          Bunmeikoku   ga dansei ga heikinzyumyoo ga mizikai.
          civilized-countries   male   average-life-span   is-short
          'It is civilized countries that males—their average life-span is short (in).'

[14] I suspect that there are a great many idiolectal variations in quantifier interpretations, and, accordingly, different sets of quantifier interpretation rules will be required. What I am predicting here is that, for each such idiolect, the same set of rules applies to both nonexistential and existential sentences if we assume $S + O + V$ and $L + S + Exist$ to be their respective basic word order.

If Subjectivization is applied to *bunmeikoku no* of (32), we obtain

(33) c. Bunmeikoku   *ga* dansei no heikinzyumyoo   ga mizikai.
       civilized-countries   male 's average-life-span   is-short
       'It is the civilized countries that males' average life-span is short
       (in).'

Similarly,

(34) a. John no otoosan ga sinda.
          's father   died
        (i) 'It is John's father that has died.'
        (ii) 'John's father has died.'

     b. John *ga* otoosan ga sinda.
        (i) 'It is John whose father has died.'
        (ii) 'John—(his) father has died.'

(35) a. Yama   no ki   ga kirei   da.
       mountain 's tree   pretty is
        (i) 'It is trees of mountains that are pretty.'
        (ii) '(Look!) The trees of the mountain are pretty.'

     b. Yama *ga* ki ga kirei da.
        (i) 'It is mountains that the trees are pretty (in).'
        (ii) '(Look!) That mountain—the trees are pretty.'

Examples (34) and (35) show that the newly formed subject is not restricted to the "*A* and only *A*" interpretation. It can receive a neutral-
description interpretation if an appropriate predicate, which can represent
a temporary state or a nonhabitual action, follows. In the preceding (i)
represents the "*A* and only *A*" interpretation, and (ii) the neutral
description.

Although it is not clear what types of "noun phrase + *no*" can undergo
Subjectivization, it is easy to show that only a sentence-initial "noun
phrase + *no*" before scrambling can be subjectivized.

(36) a. *John no* kodomo ga sensei   ni sikarareta.
            's child   teacher by was-scolded
       'John's child was scolded by the teacher.'

     b. *John ga* kodomo ga sensei ni sikarareta.
       'It was John whose child was scolded by the teacher.'

(37) a.   Sensei   ga *John no* kodomo o sikatta.
          teacher   's child   scolded
          'The teacher scolded John's child.'

   b.   *John no* kodomo o sensei ga sikatta.

   c.   *John ga sensei ga kodomo o sikatta.
        *John ga, kodomo o sensei ga sikatta.
        'It was John whose child the teacher scolded.'

In these examples, (36b) is grammatical because *John no* in (36a) is in sentence-initial position, while (37c) is ungrammatical because *John no* in (37a) is not in sentence-initial position. Incidentally, the scope of the application of Subjectivization is much smaller than that of Thematization, as is witnessed by (38).

(38) a.   (Boku wa) *John no* otooto   o yoku sitte-iru.
          I   's brother   well know
          '(I) know John's brother well.'

   b.   *John ga otooto o yoku sitte-iru.
        'It is John whose brother (I) know well.'

   c.   *John wa* otooto o yoku sitte-iru.
        'As for John, (I) know (his) brother well.'

Now, Subjectivization applies to the "noun phrase + *no*" at the head of locatives of existential sentences and to the "noun phrase + *ni*" of such locatives. Observe the following sentences:

(39) a.   *New York no koogai   ni* yoi   zyuutakuti   ga aru.
                        's suburbs in good residential-area   are
          'In the suburbs of New York, there are good residential areas.'

   b.   *New York ga* koogai ni yoi zyuutakuti ga aru.

   c.   *New York no koogai ga* yoi zyuutakuti ga aru.

   d.   *New York* ⎰ *ni* ⎱ koosookentiku   ga takusan tatte-iru.
                   ⎱ *ga* ⎰ high-rise-building   many   standing-exist
          'There are many high-rise buildings standing in New York.'

Example (39a) is an existential sentence whose locative is modified by a "noun phrase + *no*." Subjectivization can be applied either to *New York no*, yielding (39b), or to the entire locative *New York no koogai ni* 'in New

York's suburbs', yielding (39c). Sentence (39d) is another example of Subjectivization applied to the locative of an existential sentence. Contrast the preceding with

(40) a. John ga *New York no koogai   ni* sunde-iru.
                          's suburbs in living-is
          'John lives in the suburbs of New York.'

     b. *New York no koogai ni* John ga sunde-iru.

     c. *New York *ga* koogai ni John ga sunde-iru.

     d. *New York no koogai *ga* John ga sunde-iru.

(41) a. John ga *asoko   ni* tatte-iru.
                       that-place in standing-is
          'John is standing there.'

     b. *Asoko ni* John ga tatte-iru.
          '(Lit.) There, John is standing.'

     c. **Asoko ga* John ga tatte-iru.[15]
             (i) 'It is there that John is standing.'
            (ii) 'Look, there, John is standing.'

New York no koogai ni and *asoko ni* of (40) and (41) are locatives, and they appear in nonexistential sentences. Examples (40c), (40d), and (41c), with *New York ga*, *New York no koogai ga*, and *asoko ga*, respectively, are ungrammatical. It might be argued that (40c) and (40d) are ungrammatical for a semantic reason. Note that what (39d), with *New York ga*, means is that out of all the possible places, it is only in New York that high-rise buildings are standing. More specifically, (39d) means that it is

---

[15] Perlmutter has pointed out to me that a similar phenomenon can be observed in English. For example,

(i) a. New York has many high-rise buildings in it.
   b. New York has many rich people living in it.

The preceding sentences are grammatical, but the following are not:

(ii) a. *New York has my house in it.
   b. *New York has my cousins living in it.

I do not know whether one can find, for this English phenomenon, an explanation deeper than merely stating that only indefinite nouns can appear after "have" in this construction. For the Japanese construction under discussion, it is possible to find a deeper explanation, which is given in this section.

only New York that has the characteristic of many high-rise buildings standing there. On the other hand, it is not easy to impose a similar reading on (40c) and (40d). It does not make much sense to say that, out of all the possible places, it is only New York that John lives in the suburb of (or it is only the suburb of New York that John lives in), or that it is only New York that has the characteristic of John living in the suburb there (or it is only New York's suburb that has the characteristic of John living there). However, the ungrammaticality of (41c) cannot be totally accounted for in the same fashion. Remember that the previously cited example (35b) is ambiguous, meaning both 'It is mountains that the trees are pretty (in)' and 'Look! That mountain—its trees are pretty'. Sentence (35b) in its second interpretation does not mean 'It is only that mountain that has the characteristic that the trees are pretty'. It is a neutral, purely descriptive statement. This interpretation is possible, as has been mentioned before, because *kirei da* 'is pretty' can represent not only a permanent state but also a temporary state. Now, let us examine (41). *Tatte-iru* represents a temporary state. Therefore, there is no semantic reason why (41c) cannot receive the interpretation 'Look! There, John is standing'. The explanation for the ungrammaticality of (40c) and (41c), therefore, seems to lie in the fact that *New York ni* and *asoko ni* in these sentences are not sentence-initial noun phrases with *ni* before the scrambling of word order.

Directional "noun phrase + *ni*" behaves the same way as the place phrases in (40) and (41). Observe the following examples:

(42) a. Gakusei ga oozei *New York ni* itta.
         student   many   to went
         '((Lit.) Students went many to New York.) Many students went to New York.'

   b. *New York ni* gakusei ga oozei itta.
       '(Lit.) To New York, students went many.'

   c. **New York ga* gakusei ga oozei itta.
       '(Lit.) It was New York that students went many.'

This phenomenon can be accounted for most economically by assuming that only sentence-initial noun phrases with *ni* or *no* (namely, sentence-initial noun phrases that are not already the subject) can be subjectivized and that the locative for existential sentences is a sentence-initial constituent and the locative for nonexistential sentences is not a sentence-initial constituent.

3. Existential Sentences in English

In the previous section, I gave five arguments for regarding $Locative + NP_{indef} + V_{exist}$ as representing the basic word order for existential sentences of Japanese. In this section I shall give several arguments for regarding $Locative + V_{exist} + NP_{indef}$ as the basic word order for existential sentences of English.

3.1. Word Order Constraints

English has at least two ways of representing existential statements:

(43) a. There are two books on the table.

b. Two books are on the table.

The mere fact that there is *there* in (43a) suggests that the locative *on the table* used to be in the sentence-initial position before it was postposed to the end of the sentence.

Now, there are many sentences that are acceptable using the pattern of (43a) but awkward or unacceptable using that of (43b).

(44) a. There is still some room in the house.

b. *Some room is still in the house.

(45) a. There is space in the margin.

b. *Space is in the margin.[16]

(46) a. There is a policeman here.

b. ??A policeman is here.

(47) a. There is a bird in the tree.

b. ??A bird is in the tree.[17]

[16] I am indebted to Ruth Fowler (personal communication) for (44) and (45).
[17] It has been pointed out by John Haig that (46b) is acceptable in certain contexts, for example, when announcing an unexpected caller, as in:

(i) Dad, a policeman's here.

(Continued overleaf)

On the other hand, when definite subject phrases are involved, the pattern of (43b) is acceptable, but that of (43a) is unacceptable.

(48) a. *There are *the* two books on the table.

  b. *The* two books are on the table.

This phenomenon can be accounted for if we assume that existential sentences have locatives in the sentence-initial position: *Locative* + V_{exist} + NP_{indef} (for example, *On the table are two books*). A transformation, which I shall call Locative Postposing, will move locatives to the sentence-final position, leaving a trace in the form of *there* in their original position. On the other hand, nonexistential sentences, such as (48b), do not have locatives in the sentence-initial position, but have subjects sentence-initially (that is, *NP* + *Be* + *Locative*) so that Locative Postposing does not apply to them. Hence, (48a) is unacceptable. According to this analysis, the unacceptability of (48a) is related to the unacceptability, in standard English, of (49b).

(49) a. On the table are two books.

  b. *On the table are *the* two books.[18]

Specifically, (43a) is acceptable because its source, (49a), is acceptable, while (48a) is unacceptable because its source, (49b), is unacceptable.

Similarly, (47b) would be a natural answer to (ii) or when used as an exclamation.

(ii) I heard a noise. What's in the tree?

In both of these instances, it should be noted that the subjects, that is, *a policeman* and *a bird*, receive an emphatic stress. This seems to indicate that the *S* + *Be* + *L* word order is used to emphasize the subject and therefore is the marked word order for this construction. Both (46b) and (47b) have the tone of a child's English.

  Bruce Fraser (personal communication) has pointed out to me that the pattern of (46b) and (47b) is also acceptable when one is listing a number of items, as in

(iii) A man is here, a woman is there, and three boys are in the swimming pool.

[18] It has been pointed out to me by John Haig that, although (49b) is not fully acceptable as it is, sentence (i) is fully acceptable.

(i) On the table were the two books which I'd been searching for.

It seems that the *the* of (i) is due, not to anaphoricity, but to definitivization by Relativization, as discussed in Perlmutter (1971b). Only in such cases can apparently definite noun phrases appear in *there* sentences also. For example,

(ii) There were *the two books which I'd been searching for* on the table.

(iii) In England there was never *the problem that there was in America*.

Locatives that are postposed by the Locative Postposing transformation can be placed in the sentence-initial position by the Adverb Preposing rule:

(50) a. *On the table*, there were two books.

　　 b. *In the room*, there were many students.

Note that *there* is retained untouched in these sentences.

3.2. Order of Quantifier Interpretation

In Section 2.4 I mentioned that the order of quantifiers in surface sentences in English corresponds more or less to the order of quantifications in the corresponding expressions of predicate calculus. For example, to many speakers of English, sentence (17) means (18a), and not (18b).

(17) Every girl likes some candies.

(18) a. $(\forall x)\ (\exists y)\ \mathrm{LIKE}(x,y)$
　　　　'For every girl, there are some candies that she likes.'

　　 b. $(\exists y)\ (\forall x)\ \mathrm{LIKE}(x,y)$
　　　　'There are some candies that every girl likes.'

On the other hand, sentence (19) means (18b), and not (18a).[19]

(19) Some candies are liked by every girl.

Kuroda (1969) has observed in a different context that existential sentences in English are counterexamples to this linear interpretation of quantifiers.[20] For example, observe the following sentence:

(51) There are sŏme girls in *every* class.

Let x stand for 'girl', and y for 'class', and $\mathrm{EXIST}(x,y)$ for 'x is in y'. Then, (51) means (52b), and not (52a).

(52) a. $(\exists x)\ (\forall y)\ \mathrm{EXIST}(x,y)$
　　　　'There are some girls who exist in (belong to) every class.'

　　 b. $(\forall y)\ (\exists x)\ \mathrm{EXIST}(x,y)$
　　　　'For every class, there are some girls who are in the class.'

---

[19] There are wide dialectal variations in the interpretation of (17) and (19). In some dialects, each sentence has both interpretations. In the discussions that follow, I shall be using only those dialects in which (17) and (19) are unambiguous and mean only (18a) and (18b), respectively.

[20] As far as I know, the first mention of this phenomenon was given by Kuroda in his unpublished paper (1964).

Before discussing how this phenomenon can be accounted for, let us examine more carefully whether or not the principle of linear interpretation really holds in general for nonexistential sentences in English. First, observe the following sentences:

(53) a. *Many* girls like *all* movie stars.

b. *Every* rule has *some* exceptions.

c. *All* students here take *many* courses.

d. *Some* students here take *all* the courses.

(54) a. *Many* people go to the rest room *every* hour.

b. *Many* people eat at the Occult Club *every* day.

c. I read *many* books *every* day.

d. They assigned *some* girls to *all* the dormitories.

e. I meet *many* people at *all* the linguistic meetings.

Note that all the sentences in (53) are unambiguous, while those in (54) are ambiguous. For example, (53a) can mean only that there are many girls who like all movie stars, and not that, for each of the movie stars, there are many girls who like him/her. On the other hand, (54a) means either that there are many people who go to the rest room every hour, or that every hour the number of people who go to the rest room is large. In other words, the sentences of (53) follow the principle of linear interpretation of quantifiers, and those of (54) appear not to.

Sentences (53) and (54) seem to indicate that the linear interpretation of quantifiers applies when quantifiers are attached to the subject and the object of a sentence, but not when one of the quantifiers is attached to a time or place adverb. This does not mean that all sentences with two quantifiers Q1 and Q2 are ambiguous if one of the two quantifiers is attached to a time or place adverb. They are potentially ambiguous, but if semantic anomalies result for either of the two interpretations, they become unambiguous. Observe the following sentences:

(55) a. *Many* old people are required to take an eye examination test for a driver's license *every* year.

b. *Many* old people are required to take an eye examination test for a driver's license *every* day.

If one does not know that a driver's license is valid for, say, two years, one can interpret (55a) in two ways: (i) there are *many* old people who are required to take an eye examination test for a driver's license *every* year; and (ii) *every* year there are many old people who are required to take an eye examination test for a driver's license. On the other hand, since everyone knows that a driver's license does not have to be renewed every day, sentence (55b) is unambiguous and receives only the "every-many" interpretation. Similarly, note these examples:

(56) a. *Many* people come to Japan *every* day.

b. *Many* people die *every* day.

c. The boys caught *many* fish in *every* pond.

d. *Many* explosions occur *every* day.

These sentences are unambiguous because (i) the same people do not come to Japan every day, (ii) the same people cannot die repeatedly, (iii) one cannot catch the same fish in every pond,[21] and (iv) the same explosions cannot occur every day, respectively. On the other hand, (57) can receive only the "all-every" interpretation because it is not the case, under the current practice, that all driver's licenses have the same starting date.[22]

(57) *All* driver's licenses are to be renewed *every* two years.

One explanation why sentences such as those in (54) can receive bi-directional quantifier interpretations is that time or place adverbs can be either within a major clause or outside it in a higher sentence in the underlying structure. For example, (58) can be derived from both (59a) and (59b).

(58) Many people come to Japan every year.

(59) a.   b.

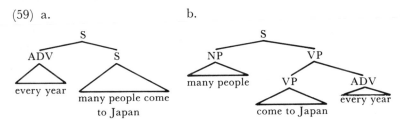

---

[21] *Many fish* here should not be interpreted as meaning 'many kinds of fish'. In that interpretation, example (56c) would be ambiguous.

[22] Of course, if the licensing regulations were changed so that each one is valid only from January 1 of an even-numbered year through January 1 of the next even numbered year, then (57) would become ambiguous.

In the preceding, I have assumed, merely for ease of exposition, that quantifiers appear as constituents of noun phrases in the deep structure. Structure (59a) corresponds to the interpretation of (58) as 'Every year there are many people who come to Japan', and (59b) to the interpretation of (58) as 'There are many people (who come to Japan every year)'. Structure (59a) can undergo a transformation that lowers the adverb and places it at the end of the sentence, yielding (58). On the other hand, the adverb of (59b) cannot undergo an Adverb-Preposing transformation. Or, to put it more accurately, if the adverb of (59b) is forcibly preposed, the sentence ends up meaning (59a). Note that the following sentence means unambiguously that every year there are many people who come to Japan, and does not have the meaning corresponding to that of (59b):

(60) Every year, many people come to Japan.

On the other hand, it is not possible to assign a deep structure similar to that of (59a) to the sentences of (53). For example, (53a) cannot be derived from the deep structure of (61a), which is ill-formed. This will account for the unambiguity of the sentences of (53).

(61) a.					b.

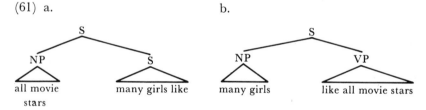

I have shown that *every year* of (59a) can be postposed to the end of the sentence, crossing over *many people*, without changing the order of interpretation of the two quantifiers. I have also stated that *every year* of (59b) cannot be preposed to the beginning of the sentence, crossing over *many people*, without changing the order of quantifier interpretation. What has been hypothesized here is the following: "Quantifiers A and B in that order in a given phrase marker retain the same order of interpretation '$A - B$' if A is postposed, crossing over B by some transformation, but undergo reversal in the order of quantifier interpretation if B is preposed, crossing over A." This hypothesis might look contradictory at first glance, but it seems to be a fact of English. Consider the following sentences:

(62) a. *Every* girl gave *many* boys welcoming kisses.

b. *Many* boys were given welcoming kisses by *every* girl.

c. Welcoming kisses were given *many* boys by *every* girl.

Speakers of the dialect in which (62a) receives only the "every-many" interpretation and (62b) only the "many-every" interpretation ordinarily see (62c) as synonymous with (62a). They also accept the (62b) interpretation for (62c), but this interpretation is marginal and secondary to the first one. Note that in (62c), as well as in (62b), the order of the two quantifiers has been reversed from that in (62a). Therefore, the reason that (62c) is synonymous with (62a) in its first reading must lie, not in a linear order of the two quantifiers, but in how the new order has been obtained. In passivizing (62a) to produce (62c), *welcoming kisses* has been preposed to the beginning of the sentence. However, this preposing has not involved in itself the reversing of the two quantifiers. *Every girl* is postposed to the end of the sentence, accompanied by *by*, crossing over *many boys*. Note that it is not the case that *many boys* has been preposed, crossing over *every girl*. This seems to be why (62c), in its first and dominant interpretation, is synonymous with (62a). In contrast, observe how (62b) is derived. *Many boys* has been preposed to the sentence-initial position crossing over *every girl*, which in turn has been postposed to the end of the sentence.[23] Thus, the change in the order of interpretations of the two quantifiers is obligatory according to the proposed hypothesis, and this is exactly what happens between (62a) and (62b).

(63) a. *Many* detectives interrogated *every* suspect.

b. *Every* suspect was interrogated by *many* detectives.

c. The interrogation of *every* suspect by *many* detectives took a long time.

In the preceding, (63a) means that a group of many detectives interrogated every suspect. On the other hand, (63b) means that every suspect was interrogated by a large number of detectives, but not necessarily the same

[23] This analysis is based on the hypothesis that Passivization preposes the original object NP to the subject position before the original subject is postposed to the end of the sentence and adjoined to *by*.

group of detectives for every suspect. Namely, (63a) has the "many-every" interpretation, and (63b), the "every-many" interpretation. Now, (63c), in spite of the fact that *every* precedes *many*, seems to have the "many-every" interpretation. Its dominant reading is that the interrogation by the same group of many detectives of every suspect took a long time. Therefore, (63c) is more directly related to (63a) than to (63b). It must be the case that *the interrogation of every suspect by many detectives* of (63c) is due to the postposing of *many detectives* of (63a) crossing over *every suspect*, and not to the nominalization of (63b).

The following set of examples gives a fuller view of what is happening in the derived nominal construction:

(64) a. *Many* artists portrayed *every* cabinet member.
      b. *Every* cabinet member was portrayed by *many* artists.
      c. *Many* artists' portraits of *every* cabinet member are hanging in the gallery.
      d. The portraits of *every* cabinet member by *many* artists are hanging in the gallery.
      e. *Every* cabinet member's portraits by *many* artists are hanging in the gallery.

In the dialect of English that I have been discussing, (64a) means that each of many artists portrayed every cabinet member. Sentence (64b) means that, for every cabinet member, there are many artists (probably different sets of artists) who portrayed him.[24] In other words, (64b) has the "every-many" interpretation, as expected. Sentence (64c) parallels (64a) in that it has the "many-every" interpretation. On the other hand, (64d), which has been formed by postposing the agent noun phrase, still has the "many-every" interpretation as the predominant reading in spite of the fact that the order of the two quantifiers has been reversed. One gets the "every-many" interpretation only as marginal and secondary reading. In (64e), *every cabinet member* has been preposed to the initial position in the noun phrase,[25] but has not crossed over *many*. Example (64e)

---

[24] In fact, there is a third meaning, which is "illogical," for both (64a) and (64b). It says that every cabinet member was portrayed, and many artists were involved, but it is not necessarily the case that each artist portrayed every cabinet member, or that each cabinet member was portrayed by many artists. Similar interpretations can be assigned to many sentences involving two or more quantifiers. However, I shall not be concerned with this interpretation in the rest of my discussion.

[25] The derivation of (64e) from (64c) via (64d) is due to Chomsky (1970).

is still ambiguous between the two interpretations, although the "every-many" interpretation is the dominant one for this sentence. This seems to be due to the fact that the postposing of the agent for (64d) as well as the preposing of the object, with an apostrophe accompanying it, has the net effect of preposing the second quantifier, crossing over the first one. The fact that (64b) has unambiguously the "every-many" interpretation while (64d) is ambiguous seems to indicate that these two sentences are derived through two different steps: namely, the former by a single transformation, that is, Passivization, applied to (64a), and the latter by two transformations, that is, Agent Postposing and Object Preposing applied to (64c). Agent Postposing is a left-to-right-movement trans-formation, and therefore (64d) retains the original meaning of (64c).

In summary, the following set of instructions seems to account for the interpretation of quantifiers:

(65) Given that command relationships between two quantifiers are symmetrical.[26]

    a. Assign symbol Q1 to the first quantifier, and Q2 to the second quantifier, in the deep structure. The symbols Q1 and Q2 indicate the order of quantifier interpretation.

    b. If the first quantifier is postposed, crossing over the second quantifier, retain the same symbols for the dominant reading. Switch the symbols for the secondary reading. For example, if the deep structure contains two quantifiers, A and B, in that order, and if A is postposed to the right of B, the following readings result:

        (i) Dominant reading: B ... A
                         Q2   Q1

        (ii) Secondary reading: B ... A
                         Q1   Q2

    c. If a quantifier with symbol Q2 is preposed over a quantifier with symbol Q1, switch the symbols. For example, if the given phrase marker contains

      A ... B
      Q1   Q2

---

[26] A commands B if the first S node higher than A dominates B. Command relationships of A and B are *symmetrical* if and only if A commands B *and* B commands A.

and if *B* is preposed over *A*, the following reading results:

$$B \ldots A^{27,\,28}$$

Q1   Q2

[27] I have avoided presenting here the principle of quantifier interpretation either in the framework of the Interpretive Hypothesis (see Jackendoff, 1969), or of Derivational Constraints (see Lakoff, 1971). It is not easy, although it is possible, to represent this principle in either of the two approaches. In both approaches, the outputs of transformations are examined, but not how transformations have moved elements in the trees. On the other hand, what is important in the interpretation of quantifiers seems to be whether one quantifier has crossed over another while moving to the left or to the right.

The proposed set of instructions, if it is taken to be a real procedure, within the theory of grammar, for interpreting quantifiers, has one unpleasant effect: it allows two derivations for (58) in its "many-every" interpretation. Namely, it can be derived from (59b) directly or from (59a) by the postposing of *every year* to the end of the sentence. In the latter derivation, since *every* is postposed, crossing over *many*, the "many-every" interpretation results as a secondary reading because of (65b). Similarly, there are two derivations of (60). Namely, it can be derived from (59a) directly or from (59b) by application of Adverb Preposing. In the latter process, *every* is preposed over *many*, and therefore, because of (65c), the order of quantifier interpretation is reversed, and the "every-many" interpretation results. I do not see at present any easy way out of this problem of false ambiguity.

[28] Kuroda (1971) has observed that the subject-object construction displays peculiarities that are not shared by other constructions with respect to the interpretation of Japanese quantifierlike particles *mo* 'also', *dake* 'only', and *sae* 'even'. For example, (i) is a grammatical and meaningful sentence.

(i) John *sae*   ga *Syntactic Structures dake* o yonda.
         even   only read
'Even John read only *Syntactic Structures*.'

On the other hand, example (ii), which is formed by inverting the word order of the subject and the object, slips away from any clear semantic interpretation.

(ii) *Syntactic Structures dake* o John *sae* ga yonda.
'Only *Syntactic Structures*, even John read.'

He, however, notes that the same does not hold for constructions not involving the subject-object relationship. For example,

(iii) John wa nitiyoobi ni *dake* 20D-102 goo situ de *sae*   *S.S.* o yonda.
              Sunday   on only   No. room in even   read
'Only on Sundays John read *S.S.* even in Room 20D-102.'

(iv) John wa 20D-102 goo situ   de *sae*   nitiyoobi ni *dake S.S.* o yonda.
             No. room in even Sunday   on only   read
'Even in Room 20D-102 John read *S.S.* only on Sundays.'

He argues that (iii) and (iv) are not synonymous, and the semantic order of *sae* and *dake* is identical to their linear (word) order in (iii) and (iv). He states that it would follow that word order has different grammatical significance with respect to the syntactic subject and object, on the one hand, and with respect to time and place adverbials, on the other hand.

Let us now see how this set of instructions for quantifier interpretation works for constructions that we have not discussed before. First, observe the following sentences:

(66) a. They provided *all* detectives in the police force with the names of
             Q1
   many campus radicals.
   Q2

   b. They provided, with the names of *many* campus radicals, *all*
                           Q2   Q1
                           Q1   Q2
   detectives in the police force.

Sentence (66a) is unambiguous because it is not plausible to hypothesize ungrammatical deep structures such as (67).

(67)

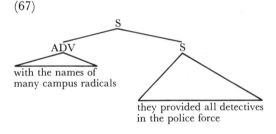

Kuroda's observation just given applies to (i) and (ii), which involve *sae* and *dake*, in that order, but not to sentences involving some other combinations of quantifierlike particles. For example,

(v) John *dake* ga *S.S.* o *mo* yonda.
       only   also read
   'Only John read *S.S.* also.'
(vi) *S.S.* o *mo* John *dake* ga yonda.
      also   only read
   '*S.S.* also, only John read it.'

Both (v) and (vi) are meaningful. Sentence (v) is unambiguous, and it means that it was only John who read *S.S.* as well as many other books. However, to me, (vi) is ambiguous. Its first interpretation is that there are many books that only John read, and *S.S.* also is among those that only he read. Its second interpretation, which is marginal, is identical to that of (v). In note 33, I shall discuss briefly the interpretation of Japanese quantifiers when one of them is attached to a time or place adverbial.

Although I do not agree with this particular analysis of Kuroda's of Japanese quantifier-like particles, his observation has made me aware of the possibility of this asymmetry between the subject-object construction and other constructions and has led me to an observation of English presented in (65).

Sentence (66b) is derived by applying to (66a) Complex NP Shift, which is a transformation that postposes a complex noun phrase to the end of a sentence. As predicted by (65b), sentence (66b), in its dominant reading, is synonymous with (66a).[29]

Next, observe the following sentences:

(68) a. He talked to *many* girls about *every* instructor.

  b. He talked about *every* instructor to *many* girls.

The fact that the primary reading of (68b) is identical with that of (68a) suggests that (68b) is derived from (68a)[30] by postposing "*to* + NP,"

[29] I am indebted to Edward Witten for suggesting to me the use of the Complex NP Shift transformation as a possible test for the proposed hypothesis of quantifier interpretation. Complex NP Shift can be informally represented (with irrelevant details ignored) as follows:

Structural Description: $X - NP - Y$
$$1 \quad 2 \quad\;\; 3 \Rightarrow$$
Structural Change: $1 - 0 - [3 + 2]$
where 2 is a complex NP

It cannot be formulated as a transformation that preposes what follows the complex NP to the left of it (namely, as $1 - [3 + 2] - 0$), because what follows the complex NP may be of variable syntactic types. For example,

(i)   a. They have many books on linguistics *available*.

  b. They have *available* many books on linguistics.

(ii) a. I met a man with a dog *in the park*.

  b. I met *in the park* a man with a dog.

(iii) a. They elected the man *president of the company*.

  b. They elected *president of the company* the man who . . .

(iv) a. They regard sleeping and eating *as vice*.

  b. They regard *as vice* sleeping and eating.

Moreover, what follows the complex NP may not be a single constituent:

(v)   a. They elected the man [*president*] [*at the last meeting*].

  b. They elected [*president*] [*at the last meeting*] the man who . . .

See Ross (1967, Chapter 3) for more detailed discussions on this transformation.

[30] It is proved that (68a) represents the basic word order, and (68b) the derived word order. Observe the following:

(i)   John talked to Mary about *herself*.

(ii) *John talked about Mary to *herself*.

The unacceptability of (ii) above is due to the violation of the Crossover Constraint. See Lakoff (1968) for details.

crossing over "*about* + NP," and it is not the case that it is derived by preposing "*about* + NP."

Next, consider the following sentences:

(69) a. *Every* girl likes *many* boys.
         Q1   Q2

    b. *Many* boys, *every* girl likes.
         Q1   Q2

Example (69b) has been formed by applying a transformation called Yiddish Movement (abbreviated as Y Movement)[31] to (69a). Here, Q2 has been preposed over Q1, and therefore the markers must be switched. Thus the proposed hypothesis predicts that the same many boys are liked by every girl. This is the correct and only interpretation of (69b). Similarly,

(70) a. *Every* girl likes *many* boys.
         Q1   Q2

    b. *Many* boys are liked by *every* girl.
         Q1   Q2

    c. By *every* girl, *many* boys are liked.
         Q1   Q2

In forming (70b) from (70a), the second quantifier has been preposed over the first one. Therefore (65c) applies, and the markers are switched. Consequently it is predicted that (70b) receives the "many-every" interpretation. In forming (70c), *every*, which has a new marker, Q2, assigned to it

---

[31] Y Movement transforms the following (a) sentences to the corresponding (b) sentences:

(i)   a. I like *Harry*.
      b. *Harry*, I like.
(ii) a. I think you hate *Harry*.
      b. *Harry*, I think you hate.
(iii) a. I bought a book *for Harry*.
      b. *For Harry*, I bought a book.

In some dialects of English, Y Movement can apply to *fond of* in (iv-a) to yield (iv-b).

(iv) a. John isn't *fond of Harry*.
      b. *Fond of Harry*, John isn't.

in (70b), has been preposed over *many* with Q1, and therefore the markers must be switched again. For this reason (65) predicts that (70c) has the "every-many" interpretation. Although (70c) is extremely awkward, the "every-many" interpretation is the only one that the sentence can have.[32]

Let us now return to existential sentences. First, observe the following:

(71) *Many* students are in *all* the courses that I am offering this year.

It seems that (71) is ambiguous. It can mean either that there are many students who are in all the courses that I am offering this year, or that all the courses that I am offering this year have many students. According to the proposed hypothesis, this ambiguity is due to two different deep structures which are shown in (72).

[32] Lakoff (1971) has tried to show that Y Movement comes after a cutoff point for derivational constraints on quantifiers. His argument is based on the synonymity of the following sentences:

(i)   Sarah Weinstein is*n't* fond of *many* boys.

(ii) Fond of *many* boys, Sarah Weinstein is*n't*.

Since he regards quantifiers and negatives as belonging to the same class of "logical predicates," and since he generalizes his derivational constraints of quantifiers so that they apply to both quantifiers and negatives, his argument can be extended to the synonymity of

(iii) *Every* girl is fond of *many* boys.

(iv) Fond of *many* boys, *every* girl is.

He claims that since (iii) and (iv) are synonymous in spite of the fact that the order of quantifiers has been reversed, the derivational constraints on interpretation of quantifiers and negatives do not apply to the output of Y Movement. However, observe

(v)   *Many* boys, Sarah Weinstein is*n't* fond of.

(vi) *Many* boys, *every* girl is fond of.

Sentence (v) is not synonymous with (i), and (vi) is not synonymous with (iii). This shows that Y Movement is subject to the derivational constraints of quantifiers. (Edward Witten has independently arrived at the same observation.) It seems that (ii) and (iv) are synonymous with (i) and (iii), respectively, because *many boys* is embedded in a larger phrase *fond of X*. This must be due to the same reason that makes (vii) and (viii) synonymous.

(vii) *Every* girl wants to believe that *many* boys like her.

(viii) That *many* boys like her, *every* girl wants to believe.

Namely, if quantifier A is in a matrix sentence, and quantifier B is in an embedded structure, however the concept of "embedded structure" is to be defined, the order of quantifier interpretation is always that of "$A-B$" regardless of whether A precedes B or not.

(72) a.

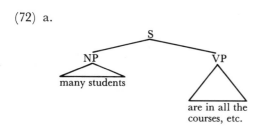

b.

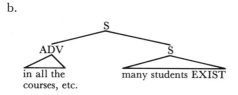

In the diagram, (72a) corresponds to the first interpretation, and (72b) to the second interpretation of (71). Now, compare (71) with (73).

(73) There are *many* students in *all* the courses that I am offering this year.

The first and dominant interpretation of this sentence is that of "all-many," or that of (72b). It has as a marginal interpretation that of "many-all." This seems to indicate that the underlying structure for (73) is not (72a) but a structure similar to that of (72b). Otherwise, it should be as easy to detect the second meaning in (73) as in (71).

Let us tentatively assume that (73) is derived from the underlying structure corresponding to:

(74) In *all* the courses are *many* students.
        Q1   Q2

Locative Postposing is applied to the structure of (74), yielding (75):

(75) There are *many* students in *all* the courses.
                Q2   Q1

Although (75) has the reversed order of the two quantifiers, the "all-many" interpretation is retained because *all* has been postposed over *many*, and not the other way around. Now, *in all the courses* can be preposed by an adverb-moving transformation, yielding

(76) In *all* the courses, there are *many* students.
        Q1   Q2

Note that *all* and *many* are still accompanied by symbols Q1 and Q2, respectively, in spite of the preposing of *many* over *all*, because (65c) does not apply since *all* of (75) has the symbol Q1. In other words, if a constituent containing quantifier A is postposed, crossing over quantifier B, and is preposed back, again across B, no change in interpretation of the two quantifiers results.

In obtaining (75) from (74), the hypothesis of (65) predicts that there will be a secondary meaning of "many-all." From this point of view, it is rather strange that (75) does not seem to have any secondary meaning. However, for some *there* sentences, it is possible to detect, with some effort, the predicted secondary reading.

(77) There is only *one* kind of fish in *every* pond.

The first reading of this sentence is that in every pond there is only one kind of fish: for example, in Pond A, only goldfish, in Pond B, only guppies. However, it is also possible to read (77) as meaning that every pond has, for example, goldfish, and nothing else. In this interpretation, the sentence is very awkward. One would more often say

(78) Only one kind of fish is in all the ponds.[33]

[33] It will not be amiss here to reexamine the quantifier interpretation in Japanese in the light of the observations presented here for English. In Japanese, also, sentence (i) is ambiguous.

(i) *Takusan* no hito   ga *mainen*   nihon ni kuru.
    many   people every-year Japan to come
    'Many people come to Japan every year.'

It seems that (i) is derived from two underlying structures, one with *mainen* 'every year' in the sentence-initial position, the other with it in the sentence-medial position. To accommodate this phenomenon, it is necessary to modify Rules 1 and 2 given in (25) in the following manner:

(ii) Rule 1. If a simple sentence contains two quantifiers Q1 and Q2 in that order in the basic word order representation, assign to Q1 the "same Q1" interpretation, and to Q2 the "different Q2 for each member of Q1" interpretation.

   Rule 2. If Q1–Q2 reverses its word order because of the preposing of Q1, assign "the same Q2, the same Q1" interpretation.

   Rule 3. If Q1–Q2 reverses its word order because of the postposing of Q2, retain the interpretations that obtained before word order changes.

In the preceding, I have assumed that Japanese has, in addition to the Scrambling Rule, which I presume to be a preposing transformation, a rule that postposes sentential adverbs (for example, *mainen* 'every year' that appears at the beginning of a sentence in its basic word order representation).

Note the similarity between the rules just given for Japanese and those given in (65) for English.

I have shown earlier that time adverbs, as well as place adverbs, can appear in a higher-order sentence in the deep structure. It seems that time adverbs must appear in a higher-order S in the deep structure of existential sentences. Observe the following pair of sentences:

(79) a. *Many* people are here *every* morning.

b. There are *many* people here *every* morning.

Sentence (79a) is ambiguous with respect to whether it means that every morning there are many people here, or that there are many people [who are here every morning]. On the other hand, (79b) is unambiguous. It can mean only that every morning there are many people here. The deep structure for (79b) seems to be that shown in (80).

(80)

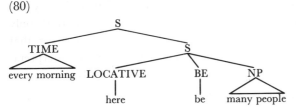

Similarly, (81) is hypothesized to have the underlying structure shown in (82).

(81) There are *many* explosions in the city *every* day.[34]

(82)

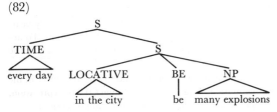

Note that, in this analysis, the locative in an existential sentence is regarded as an element in a simplex S, that is, as the first member of the $L + V + S$ phrase marker, while the time adverb is regarded as an element in a higher-order sentence. There are three reasons for this particular analysis. First, the locative in existential sentences, when it is postposed,

---

[34] The fact that (81), with quantifier *every* attached not to a locative but to a time adverb, is also a counterexample to the linear interpretation of quantifiers has been observed by Lakoff (personal communication).

leaves *there* as its trace, whereas the time adverb does not. This seems to indicate that only the locative occupies a subjectlike position in a sentence.[35] Note that only the subject position *requires* a placeholder when its original filler is moved.

(83) a.   *That John is a genius* is certain.
        It is certain that John is a genius.
        *Is certain that John is a genius.

    b.   *John* is a genius.
        John, *he* is a genius.
        *John, is a genius.

    c. John likes *Mary*.
        Mary, John likes *her*.
        Mary, John likes.

    d. I plan to go to Japan *next year*.
        *Next year, I plan to go to Japan *then*.
        Next year, I plan to go to Japan.

    e. I plan to go *to Japan*.
        *To Japan, I plan to go *there*.
        To Japan, I plan to go.
        Japan, I plan to go to.
        Japan, I plan to go *there*.

Second, sentences with the $L + Be + S$ pattern are possible, whereas those with the $TIME + Be + S$ pattern are not possible in general.

(84) a.   On the table are books.

    b. *In the morning are many explosions.

Third, the deep structure of (82) predicts correctly the *normal* word order of time and place adverbs in surface structures. Consider the following sentences:

(85) a. There was an explosion [*in the city*] [*in the morning*]. (natural)

    b. There was an explosion [*in the morning*] [*in the city*].[36] (awkward)

[35] See O. Jespersen (1954) for the subjectlike behavior of *there*.
[36] David Perlmutter (personal communication) has given me two arguments for the "place-time" word order in general. First, sentence (i) is grammatical, but not (ii).
(i)   He lived *there then*.
(ii) *He lived *then there*.

3.3 Advantages of the Proposed Analysis

I have presented three arguments for deriving *there*-existential sentences of English from the underlying $L + V + S$ pattern. They are

(86) a. The presence of *there* in the sentence-initial position suggests that there used to be a locative in that position.

   b. There are existential sentences that cannot be paraphrased in the $S + V + L$ pattern, but there are no $S + V + L$ sentences with indefinite subjects that cannot be paraphrased as *there* sentences.

   c. *There*-existential sentences usually allow only the "Q2 – Q1" interpretation of quantifiers, while ordinary $S + V + L$ patterns allow both the "Q1 – Q2" (dominant) and "Q2 – Q1" (secondary) interpretation.

In conventional analysis,[37] *there*-existential sentences are derived from $S + Be + L$ sentences by applying *There* Insertion, a transformation that inserts *there* in the sentence-initial position and reverses the order of the subject and the *be* verb. This transformation will apply to the phrase marker corresponding to (87a) and will produce the one corresponding to (87b).

(87) a. Two books are on the table.

   b. There are two books on the table.

Such an analysis, however, cannot account for the fact that *there*, and not, say, *it*, is inserted. Furthermore, it cannot account for the difference of meaning between (88a) and (88b).

(88) a. *Many* girls are in *every* class.
   $(\exists_m x) (\forall y) \text{ EXIST}(x, y),$
   $(\forall y) (\exists_m x) \text{ EXIST}(x, y)$

   b. There are *many* girls in *every* class.
   $(\forall y) (\exists_m x) \text{ EXIST}(x, y)$

Second, sentence (iii) means unambiguously that he worked in 40th to 49th streets (in New York) in the years 1950 to 1959, and it does not mean that he worked in the years 1940 to 1949 in 50th to 59th streets.

(iii) He worked *in the forties in the fifties.*

[37] For example, see Ross (1967).

In this example, $\exists_m x$ is to be read as "there are many x." According to this analysis, *There* Insertion applies to the phrase marker of (88a) and produces (88b). Therefore (88b) should be synonymous with (88a), particularly because the two quantifiers retain the same word order in the two sentences.

It has been proposed that sentences such as (89) are derived from the underlying structures corresponding to those such as (90).

(89) There is someone waiting for you downstairs.

(90) Someone is waiting for you downstairs.

Indeed, application of *There* Insertion to (90) would result in (89). However, such an analysis would multiply the difficulty that the *There* Insertion analysis presents with regard to the interpretation of quantifiers. Observe the following sentences:

(91) a. *Many* detectives are interrogating *every* suspect in the interrogation room.

    b. There are *many* detectives interrogating *every* suspect in the interrogation room.

Note that (91b) is synonymous with (91a). Both sentences mean that there are many detectives in the interrogation room such that they are interrogating every suspect, and not that for every suspect there are many detectives interrogating him. In (88) we observed that *There* Insertion rejects the "Quantifier 1 – Quantifier 2" interpretation of the corresponding $S + V + L$ sentence. Now, in (91) we have observed that *There* Insertion retains the "Quantifier 1 – Quantifier 2" interpretation of the corresponding $S + V + O$ sentence. In other words, (88b) is a counterexample to the so-called principle of linear interpretation of quantifiers, while (91b) is not. One would need a peculiar rule stating that quantifiers A and B in that order in a sentence are to be interpreted in the order $B - A$ if the sentence undergoes *There* Insertion, except when the sentence is of the progressive construction. Obviously, such a rule of interpretation lacks generalization.

According to my analysis, in which the locative appears in the sentence-initial position in existential sentences and is later postposed, (88b) and (91b) are derived from (92), where INTERROGATE (x, y) stands for "x is interrogating y."

(92) a. In *every* class are *many* girls.

     $(\forall y)\ (\exists_m x)\ \text{EXIST}\ (x, y)$

    b. In the interrogation room are *many* detectives who are interrogating *every* suspect.

     $(\exists_m x)\ (\forall y)\ \text{INTERROGATE}\ (x, y)$

For (92a), *every* is postposed over *many* in the Locative-Postposing transformation, and therefore the order of interpretation of the two quantifiers does not change. Consequently (88b) receives the "every-many" interpretation, thus producing a counterexample to the so-called linear interpretation principle if it were to apply to the surface structure. On the other hand, although *in the interrogation room* of (92b) is moved to the end of the sentence, yielding (93), the order of *many* and *every* has not been affected at all.

(93) *There* are many detectives who are interrogating every suspect in the interrogation room.

Relative Clause Extraposition and Relative Clause Reduction, both of which are optional rules, can apply to (93), yielding

(94) a. There are many detectives interrogating every suspect in the interrogation room. (= 91b)

    b. There are many detectives in the interrogation room who are interrogating every suspect.

    c. There are many detectives in the interrogation room interrogating every suspect.

    The proposed analysis gives a natural explanation for why *there* appears sentence-initially, and not *it* or some other grammatical formative. It is that the postposed locative leaves its copy in the original position in the form of locative pronoun *there* just as the postposed (that is extraposed) sentential complement leaves its copy in the form of [+abstract] pronoun *it*, as in

(95) a. [*That John likes Mary*] [+NP, +singular, +abstract] is obvious.

     [*It*] [+NP, +singular, +abstract, +pronominal] is obvious that John likes Mary.

    b. (*On the table*) [+locative] is a book.

     [*There*] [+locative, +pronominal] is a book on the table.

3.4 Drawbacks

The proposed locative-postposing analysis of existential sentences for English is far from being conclusive. I shall list in this section some of the problems that must be solved. Tentative solutions to some of these problems are suggested in Section 4. First, there are *there* sentences that lack locatives. Observe the following:

(96) a. There are *there* sentences that lack locatives.

      b. There will be no more money left.

      c. There are two more weeks of school.[38]

For some of these sentences, especially for (96c), it is not easy to supply implicit locatives. At present I do not have any solution other than to suggest an ad hoc hypothesis of the presence of dummy item LOCATIVE, with no semantic content, and to consider the (96) sentences to be derived from the underlying structures corresponding to

(97) a. LOCATIVE are *there* sentences that lack locatives.

      b. LOCATIVE will be no more money that is left.

      c. LOCATIVE are two more weeks of school.

Second, there is a class of existential sentences in which noncopulative verbs precede the subjects.

(98) a. There *exist* people in this world who do not have enough to eat.

      b. There *arose* revolts everywhere in the country.

      c. There *ensued* a disaster.

(99) a. There *lived* an old man and an old woman in the mountain.

      b. There *dwelt* an old hermit in the mountain.

      c. There *comes* a time when one has to make up one's mind.

The sentences in (99) have some poetic flavor about them. Note that the verbs in (98) and (99) all have included in them the meaning of either "be in existence" or "come to existence." The interpretation of quantifiers in the preceding sentences follows the same rule as that in ordinary existential *there* sentences. For example, sentence (100) means that in each mountain, there were many hermits.

---

[38] This example is due to Ruth Fowler (personal communication).

(100) There dwelt many hermits in each mountain.

Therefore this sentence, according to the proposed analysis, should be derived from

(101) In each mountain dwelt many hermits.

However, *dwell* happens to be an intransitive verb that requires a locative following it. Therefore, if (101) were to represent the deep structure word order, this selectional restriction would have to be stated twice—once for the locative following *dwell*, and the second time for the locative preceding the verb, as in (101).[39]

Third, the proposed analysis of quantifiers predicts that (102) would be unambiguous because (103) is unacceptable, and therefore its only reading would be that of "many-each."

(102)   *Many* Orientals reside in *each* South American country.

(103) *In each South American country reside many Orientals.

However, (102) is ambiguous, and its primary reading is that of "each-many." Furthermore, the proposed analysis of locative-postposing for existential *there* sentences predicts that (104) is unacceptable because its source, (103), is unacceptable.

(104) There reside many Orientals in each South American country.

However, (104) is acceptable, and it means what (103) would mean if it were acceptable. I have no explanation for this phenomenon at present.
Fourth, observe the following sentence:

(105) There are many records kept of all transactions.

This sentence means that for each of the transactions under discussion, many records are kept, and it cannot imply

(106) ?There are many records [which are kept of all transactions].

I have no solution to this problem at present.[40] What is curious about this sentence is that its ordinary active and passive versions, given in (107),

---

[39] I am indebted to William Watt (personal communication) for this observation.
[40] This counterexample is due to Edward Witten. The same applies to *there* sentences involving the passive construction of idiomatic expressions such as *make mention of*, *take note of*, *find fault with*.

do not seem to follow the principles of quantifier interpretation: both sentences mean that, of all transactions, there are many records kept.

(107) a. They keep *many* records of *all* transactions.

b. *Many* records are kept of *all* transactions.

That is, the reverse of the expected order of interpretation applies here.[41] Deriving (105) directly from (107b) via *There* Insertion might appear to be a better solution. The same analysis would account for the synonymity of (108a) and (108b) without the need for hypothesizing the relative clause construction, given in (109).

(108) a. *Many* suspects were examined by *all* detectives.

b. There were *many* suspects examined by *all* detectives.

(109) There were *many* suspects who were examined by *all* detectives.

However, the same problem of inconsistency in *There* Insertion that was brought up in Section 3.3 would result. Namely, *There* Insertion changes the order of quantifier interpretation for the $NP + Be + X$ if X is a locative but does not change the interpretation order if X is a present or past participle.

There are at least two more problems that neither the *There* Insertion analysis nor the proposed locative-postposing analysis can solve. The first involves *there* sentences representing inalienable possession. For example,

(110) a. This table has a marble top *to it*.

b. There is a marble top *to this table*.

(111) a. This problem has no clues *to it*.

b. There are no clues *to this problem*.

Quantifiers in these *there* sentences behave in the same manner as those in existential *there* sentences. For example, in (112) the first reading that one gets is that of "all-many/some."

(112) a. There are *many* solutions to *all* these problems.

b. There is *some* solution to *all* family problems.

[41] In fact, the same applies to other "NP$_1$ of NP$_2$" constructions. For example,

(i) *Many* sections of *every* chapter in this book are poorly written.

(ii) He knows *many* friends of *every* VIP in the city.

Namely, (112a) ordinarily means that, for each of these problems, there are many solutions; it does not mean that there are many solutions that apply to each of these problems. The proposed analysis leaves unsolved the problem of how to derive these *there* sentences.

There is also a problem of number agreement. Observe the following sentences:

(113) a. There *seems* to be a *book* on the table.

b. There *seem* to be *some books* on the table.

These sentences are derived in the following manner according to the *There* Insertion analysis:

(114) Deep structure: It [{ a book / books } be on the table] seem.

First cycle:

a. Number Agreement: It [{ a book is / books are } on the table] seem.

b. *There* Insertion: It [there { is a book / are books } on the table]

seem.

Second cycle:

c. *For-To* Complementizer: It [for there to be { a book / books } on the

table] seem.

d. *It* Replacement: There seem for to be { a book / books }

on the table.

e. Number Agreement: (No way to assign the correct number on "seem")

The situation is more or less the same for the locative-postposing analysis. The only solution I can think of at present is to hypothesize a cyclical Number-Copying Rule that copies the number of the subject to the sentence-initial locative. According to this hypothesis, we would have

(115) a. (On the table)$_{singular}$ be a book.

b. (On the table)$_{plural}$ be books.

Then application of Locative Postposing would yield

(116) a. $[\text{There}]_{\text{singular}}$ be a book on the table.

      b. $[\text{There}]_{\text{plural}}$ be books on the table.

4. Existential Sentences in Other Languages

In Section 2, I presented what I think is conclusive evidence for $L + S + V$ as the basic word order for existential sentences in Japanese. In Section 3, I gave not-so-conclusive evidence for $L + V + S$ as the basic word order for existential sentences in English. The preferred word order for existential sentences in many other languages is that of $L + S$. In Russian, for example, sentences (117) and (118) are not synonymous.

(117) Na stole kniga.
       on table book

(118) Kniga na stole.
       book   on table

Sentences (117) and (118) mean (119a) and (119b), respectively.

(119) a. There is a book on the table.
      b. The book is on the table.

In French, (119a) and (119b) are realized as (120a) and (121b), respectively.

(120) a. Il *y* a un livre sur la table.
         'There is a book on the table.'
      b. *Un livre est sur la table.

(121) a. *Il y a ce livre sur la table.
         '*There is the book on the table.'
      b. Ce livre est sur la table.

As is shown in the foregoing, the $S + L$ word order can be used only for nonexistential sentences, and the *il y a* construction, with the locative adverb *y*, can be used only for existential sentences.

In Chinese, also, $L + S$ is used for (119a) and $S + L$ for (119b):

(122) a. Chuo¹ tzu shang   yu³ i²   pên³ shu¹.
       table   on-top-of exist one copy book
       'There is a book on the table.'

     b. Nei⁴ pên³ shu¹ tsai⁴   chuo¹ tzu shang.
       that copy book be-located table   on-top-of
       'That book is on the table.'

Note that two different verbs, yu^3 and $tsai^4$, are used depending upon whether existential sentences are involved or not.[42]

Turkish is another language that seems to render support to the proposed analysis of existential sentences. According to Underhill (1972),[43] indefinite noun phrases in Turkish are postposed to the position immediately to the left of the verb. For example, corresponding to (123), in which all the noun phrases are definite, we have the sentences of (124), among others.

(123) adam su-yu   oğlan-a at-tï.
      man water-3sg boy-to threw
      'The man threw the water at the boy.'

(124) a. adam oğlan-a su   at-tï.
       man boy   water threw
       'The man threw water (indef.) at the boy.'

---

[42] Alongside (122a), the following locative-first pattern is also possible:

(i) Yu³ i¹   pên³ shu¹ tsai⁴   chuo¹ tzu shang.
    exist one copy book be-located table   on-top-of
    '(Lit.) There is a book being located on the table.'

It is interesting to note that yu^3 'to exist' is used for the matrix sentence, and $tsai^4$ for the embedded construction. This shows that the semantic subject of $tsai^4$ is definite, while that of yu^3 is indefinite.

    In Chinese, it seems that the appearance of locatives in the sentence-initial position is limited to those cases where the subjects are indefinite. For example, (ii) is a natural sentence, but (iii) is highly marked.

(ii) T'a *tsai⁴ shu¹*   *tien⁴ li* mai³   .lê i¹ pên³ shu¹.
     he in   bookstore inside bought one   copy book
     'He bought a book in the bookstore.'

(iii) *Tsai⁴ shu¹ tien⁴ li*, t'a mai³ .lê i¹ pên³ shu¹.
     'In the bookstore, he bought a book.'

[43] I have also profited greatly from discussions with Engin Sezer of the phenomenon reported in this section.

b. su-yu oğlan-a bir adam at-tɨ.
 water boy   a   man   threw
 'A man (indef.) threw the water at the boy.'

c. oğlan-a bir adam su   at-tɨ.
 boy   a   man water threw
 'A man (indef.) threw water (indef.) at the boy.'

Now, observe the following two sentences:

(125) a. šarap masa-nɨn üst-ün-de dir.
      wine table's   top-3sg-on is
      'The wine is on (top of) the table.'

   b. masa-nɨn üst-ün-de šarap var.
      table's   top   wine is
      'On (top of) the table is wine. There is wine on the table.'

Note that (125b), which is an existential sentence, has the *Locative +
Subject + Exist* word order, while (125a), which is not an existential sentence because the subject is definite, has the *Subject + Locative + Exist*
word order.

Now, Turkish uses two participles, subject participle (SP) and object
participle (OP), in forming the relative clause construction. Underhill's
analysis shows that the subject participle is used when the noun phrase to
be relativized is the leftmost subject NP or the leftmost genitive NP in the
embedded clause, and that the OP is used otherwise. For example,

(126) a. [*adam* su-yu oğlan-a at-tɨ] adam
        man water boy   threw man
       '[the man threw the water at the boy] man' (Cf. 123.)

   b. suyu oğlan-a at-*an*   adam
      water boy   throw-SP man
      'the man who threw the water at the boy'

(127) a. [adam *su*-yu oğlan-a at-ti] su
        man water boy   threw water
       '[the man threw the water at the boy] water'

   b. adam-ɨn oğlan-a at-*tɨğ-ɨ*   su
      man- 's boy   throw-OP-3sg water
      'the water that the man threw at the boy'

(128) a. [*su*-yu oğlan-a bir adam at-tɨ] su
          water boy   a   man   threw water
          '[a man threw the water at the boy] water' (Cf. 124b.)

   b. *oğlan-a bir adam at-*an*   su
       boy   a   man   threw-SP water
       'the water that a man threw at the boy'

   c. oğlan-a bir adam-ɨn at-*tɨğ-ɨ*   su
       boy   a   man-gen throw-OP-3sg water
       'the water that a man threw at the boy'

(129) a. [adam-ɨn oğl-u   mekteb-e gid-er] adam
          man- 's son-3sg school-to go-es   man
          '[the man's son goes to school] man'

   b. oğl-u mekteb-e gid-*en* adam
       son   school   go-SP   man
       'the man whose son goes to school'

In (126a), *adam* 'the man', which is to be relativized, is the leftmost subject NP in the embedded clause. Therefore, the subject participle -*an*
appears in the corresponding relative clause construction given in (126b).
In (127a), on the other hand, *su-yu* 'the water', which is to be relativized,
is not the leftmost NP in the embedded clause. Therefore, the object
participle -*tɨğ*- appears in (127b). Note that the subject of the relative
clause with OP is marked with genitive suffix -*ɨn*. Example (128a) has
su-yu as the leftmost NP in the embedded sentence. However, it is neither
a subject NP nor a genitive NP. Therefore, the use of the SP would result
in an ungrammatical sentence, as shown in (128b). In (129a), *adam* 'the
man', which is to be relativized, is the leftmost genitive NP, and therefore
the SP is used in the corresponding relative clause construction.

   The leftmost genitive NP does not have to be the modifier of the subject
NP, as in (129). Compare the following two relative clause constructions:

(130) a. [dana-lar bostan-ɨn ič-in-e   gir-iyor] bostan
          calf-s   garden-'s inside-3sg-to enter-ing garden
          '[*the* calves are entering into (the inside of) the garden] garden'

   b. dana-lar-ɨn ič-in-e gir-*dig*-i   bostan .
       calves-'s   inside enter-OP-3sg garden
       'the garden into which *the* calves are entering'

(131) a. [bostan-ɨn ič-in-e dana-lar gir-iyor] bostan
          garden-'s inside calf   enter-ing garden
          '[calves (indef.) are entering into the garden] garden'

     b. ič-in-e dana-lar gir-*en*   bostan
       inside calves   enter-SP garden
       'the garden into which calves (indef.) are entering'

In (130a), *dana-lar* 'the calves' is definite; therefore the place phrase that contains *bostan-ɨn* does not appear in the leftmost position in the embedded sentence. Consequently the OP appears in the relative clause construction of (130b). On the other hand, in (131), *dana-lar* 'calves' is indefinite, and so the place phrase appears sentence-initially. This time *bostan-ɨn* 'the garden's' is the leftmost genitive NP, and therefore the SP appears in (131b).

Concerning the examples of (125), Turkish noun phrases corresponding to '*the table that the wine is on (top of)*' and '*the table that there is wine on*' are (132) and (133), respectively.

(132) a. üst-ün-de šarab-ɨn ol-duğ-u   masa
         top   wine 's be-OP-3sg table
         'the table that *the* wine is on'

     b. šarab-ɨn üst-ün-de ol-*duğ*-u masa

(133) a. üst-ün-de šarap ol-*an* masa
         top   wine be-SP table
         'the table that there is wine on'

     b. *šarap üst-ün-de ol-*an* masa

Note that the OP appears in (132), confirming the basic word order of *Subject + Locative + Exist* when the subject is definite, while the SP appears in (133), confirming the basic word order *Locative + Subject + Exist* when the subject is indefinite.[44]

In Turkish, as has been shown in the examples given in (124), the appearance, in the sentence-initial position, of locatives is not peculiar to existential sentences, but is a part of the general principle in the language

---

[44] The appearance of *üst-ün-de* in the initial position in the relative clause in (132a) must be due to a later application of a scrambling rule. Note that in the case of (133), which involves an existential sentence, the *üst-ün-de* must appear in the clause-initial position, as is predicted by the basic word order of existential sentences.

for reordering noun phrases in such a way that indefinite noun phrases appear after definite noun phrases. Relativization with the use of subject and object participles relies upon the "basic" word order obtained after this reordering has taken place. In contrast, languages such as Japanese and English have the basic word order more functionally oriented, namely, that of *Subject + Object* except for existential sentences, whose basic word order has been claimed to be that of *Locative + Subject*.

In Spanish,[45] *hay* 'there is/are' is used to introduce existential sentences. For example,

(134) *Hay* vacas en el Japón.
           cows in
       'There are cows in Japan.'

Hay is a crystallized verbal expression, uninflected with respect to grammatical number, which, etymologically speaking, consists of *ha* (third person singular present of *haber* 'to have')[46] and *y* (locative proform). Thus, it corresponds to the French *(il) y a*. Now, observe the following sentence:

(135) Jorge dice que no hay vacas en el Japón,
           says that   cows

       pero a mi me   parece que $\left\{ \begin{matrix} las \\ them \\ *ellas \\ they \end{matrix} \right\}$ hay.
       but to me to-me seems

       'George says that there are no cows in Japan, but it seems to me that there are (them).'

Note that the accusative pronoun *las*, and not the nominative pronoun *ellas*, appears before *hay*. This otherwise mysterious phenomenon seems to be explainable if we assume that the existential sentence has the basic word order *Locative + NP_{indef}*, and that the locative occupies a subject-like position, and the indefinite NP an objectlike position, in the sentence.

I have given supporting evidence from Russian, French, Chinese, Turkish, and Spanish for my hypothesis that the basic word order of

[45] The observation that follows is due to Perlmutter (personal communication). I have also profited greatly from discussions on the same subject with Colette Craig and Paolo Valesio.

[46] *Haber* in modern Spanish is used only as an auxiliary verb and is not used as a transitive verb meaning "to have (something)."

existential sentences is that of *Locative + Subject*. The list can be extended to include languages such as Korean, modern Greek, Dutch, Arabic, and so on. Why, then, is it that in so many languages locatives seem to appear before subjects in existential sentences? This seems to be due to the fact that there is a strong tendency in a continuous discourse to start sentences with old information, that is, with something already known, and to introduce new information toward the end of the sentence. In most existential sentences, locatives are definite, and subjects are, by definition, indefinite. Therefore, the natural word order is locative before subject. Thus, it might not be unreasonable to assume that existential sentences have, after all, the $S + L$ word order in the "deep" underlying structure, the level that is deeper than what is usually referred to as the deep structure level, and that the locatives are preposed very early in the derivation of sentences because of this general tendency.[47] By assuming this, some of the difficulties for the locative-postposing analysis discussed in Section 3.4 can be solved. Namely, selectional restrictions apply to this "deep" underlying level. What is not clear is why this initial preposing of definite (already-known) information seems to apply more or less obligatorily only to the locatives of existential sentences.

As an additional piece of evidence for this analysis, observe the following:

(136) a. ?A bird is in the tree.

     b.   In the tree is a bird.

     c.   There is a bird in the tree.

(137) a.   A bird is in a tree.

     b. ??In a tree is a bird.

     c. ?There is a bird in a tree.

(138) a.   The bird is in a tree.

     b. *In a tree is the bird.

     c. *There is the bird in a tree.

Example (136a) is an existential sentence with a definite locative at the end. The sentence is rather awkward, presumably because the definite locative, which should have been preposed by the initial Definite-Locative-Preposing Rule, is still in its original position. Hence, (136b), which is the

---

[47] I am indebted to William Watt (personal communication) for this insightful observation.

form derived from application of the Definite-Locative-Preposing Rule, is a more natural sentence than (136a). Example (136c), which, according to the proposed analysis, is produced by Locative Postposing, is an even more natural sentence. On the other hand, at least for some speakers of English, (137b) is less natural than (137a). This seems to be due to the fact that the locative of this sentence is indefinite and does not have to undergo this initial Definite-Locative-Preposing Rule. Now, observe (138b). This sentence has been formed from (138a), which is not an existential sentence, by preposing an indefinite locative across the definite subject. Note that this sentence is totally unacceptable in standard English. Consequently, the *there* sentence derived from it is also unacceptable. The foregoing examples seem to indicate that the locative preposing is a natural phenomenon for existential sentences when locatives are definite.

It seems that, while definite locatives thus preposed to the sentence-initial position early in the derivation (probably precyclically) are allowed to remain in that position all through the derivation in languages such as Japanese, Korean, Chinese, and Russian, they have come to be postposed back to the sentence-final position in languages such as English and French, because of the structural pressure of the languages for conforming to the $S + V$ pattern. Derived sentences in English and French, namely, *There are* . . . and *Il y a* . . . patterns, indeed, display the $S + V$ pattern.[48]

[48] Perlmutter (1971a) has proposed that the grammars of French and English contain the following surface structure constraint: "Any sentence other than an Imperative in which there is an S that does not contain a subject in the surface structure is ungrammatical." This constraint accounts for the ungrammaticality of sentences in (i) and (ii), and the obligatory presence of *grammatical subjects* in (iii), (iv), and (v), given here.

(i) *Wh*-Question Movement of the subject of a subordinate clause introduced by *que* and *that*:
{ *Qui a-t-il dit que s'est évanoui?
{ *Who did he say that fainted?
      Compare: { À qui a-t-il dit que Nicole a donné l'argent?
               { Who did he say that Nicole gave the money to?

(ii) Relativization of the subject of a subordinate clause introduced by *que* and *that*:
{ *la speakerine qu'il a dit que s'est évanouie
{ *the announcer that he said that fainted
      Compare: { la personne à qui il a dit que Nicole a donné l'argent
               { the person whom he said that Nicole gave the money to

(iii) *Il/ce* and *it* for Extraposition:
{ *Il* est évident que l'impérialisme suédois est à bout de souffle.
{ *It* is evident that Swedish imperialism is on its last legs.

(Continued overleaf)

The proposed analysis has the unpleasant effect that it must allow the postposed locatives to be preposed again:

(139) a. "Deep" underlying
structure   A BOOK IS ON THE TABLE.

b. Early structure: (Prepose the locative using the general principle of "old information" first.)
On the table is a book.

c. Apply Locative
Postposing: There is a book *on the table*.

d. Apply Adverb
Preposing: *On the table*, there is a book.

This back-and-forth movement of locatives in the derivation is unusual, to say the least, and is not shared by derivations of other patterns of English. However, there is no a priori reason for rejecting it outright. It might be that this is a fact about the language, especially since the word orders corresponding to (139a) and (139b) are acceptable in some of the surface existential sentences, and since (139c) and (139d) are acceptable for all existential sentences.

(iv)   Impersonal constructions:
{ *Il* pleut.
{ *It's* raining.

(v)   *Il/there* for existential sentences:
{ *Il* y a un livre sur la table.
{ *There* is a book on the table.

References

Akatsuka, N. (1970) "Some Aspects of Japanese Pronominalization," unpublished paper, University of Illinois, Urbana, Ill.

Alfonso, A. (1966) *Japanese Sentence Patterns*, Sophia University, Tokyo.

Bach, E. (1970) "Is Amharic an SOV Language?" *Journal of Ethiopian Studies*, Vol. 8, pp. 9–20.

Bach, E. (1971) "Questions," *Linguistic Inquiry*, Vol. 2, No. 2, pp. 153–166.

Bohnert, H. G., and P. O. Becker (1966) "Automatic English-to-Logic Translation in a Simplified Model," unpublished paper, IBM Thomas J. Watson Research Center, Yorktown Heights, New York.

Chomsky, N. (1961) "On the Notion 'Rule of Grammar,'" *Proceedings of the Twelfth Symposium in Applied Mathematics*, Vol. 12, pp. 6–24, American Mathematical Society, Providence, Rhode Island.

Chomsky, N. (1970) "Remarks on Nominalization," in R. A. Jacobs and P. S. Rosenbaum, eds., *Readings in English Transformational Grammar*, pp. 184–221, Ginn and Co., Waltham, Mass.

Greenberg, J. H. (1963) "Some Universals of Grammar with Particular Reference to the Order of Meaningful Elements," in J. H. Greenberg, ed., *Universals of Language*, pp. 73–113, The MIT Press, Cambridge, Mass.

Hattori, S. (1968) "*Kore, Sore, Are* and *This, That*," in S. Hattori, *A Study in the Basic Vocabulary of English*, pp. 71–80, Sanseido, Tokyo.

Howard, I. (1969) "A Semantic-Syntactic Analysis of the Japanese Passive," *Journal-Newsletter of the Association of Japanese Teachers*, Vol. 6, No. 1, pp. 40–46.

Inoue, K. (1966) "Nihongo no Zyosi (Japanese Particles)," presented at the International Seminar in Linguistic Theories, Tokyo Institute for Advanced Studies of Language.

Inoue, M. (1971) "Notes on Japanese Subject Complements," unpublished paper, University of California at San Diego, Calif.

Jackendoff, R. S. (1969) "Some Rules for English Semantic Interpretation," unpublished Ph.D. dissertation, MIT, Cambridge, Mass.

Jespersen, O. (reprint 1954) *A Modern English Grammar on Historical Principles*, Vol. 5, George Allen and Unwin, London.

Jorden, E. (1962) *Beginning Japanese*, Parts I and II, Yale University Press, New Haven, Conn.

Josephs, L. (1971) "Selected Problems in the Analysis of Embedded Sentences in Japanese," unpublished Ph.D. dissertation, Harvard University, Cambridge, Mass.

Kiparsky, P., and C. Kiparsky (1971) "Fact," in M. Bierwisch and K. P. Heidolph, eds., *Recent Developments in Linguistics*, Mouton and Co., The Hague.

Kruisinga, E., and P. S. Erades (1911) *An English Grammar*, Vol. 1, Part 2, P. Noordhoff N.V., Groningen.

Kuno, S. (1967–1968) "*And* to *To, Ni, Ya* (*And* and *To, Ni, Ya*)," *Kotoba no Uchu*, December 1967, January and February 1968, Tokyo.

Kuno, S. (1970) "Some Properties of Non-Referential Noun Phrases," in R. Jakobson and S. Kawamoto, eds., *Studies in General and Oriental Linguistics, Presented to Shiro Hattori*, pp. 348–373, The TEC Co., Tokyo.

Kuroda, S.-Y. (1964) "Six Miscellaneous Remarks on English Passivization," unpublished paper, MIT, Cambridge, Mass.

Kuroda, S.-Y. (1965a) "Generative Grammatical Studies in the Japanese Language," unpublished Ph.D. dissertation, MIT, Cambridge, Mass.

Kuroda, S.-Y. (1965b) "Causative Forms in Japanese," *Foundations of Language*, Vol. 1, pp. 20–40.

Kuroda, S.-Y. (1965c) "*Ga, O*, oyobi *Ni* ni tuite (Concerning *Ga, O*, and *Ni*)," *Kokugogaku*, No. 63, pp. 75–85.

Kuroda, S.-Y. (1969) "Remarks on the Notion of Subject with Reference to Words like *Also, Even*, or *Only*, Illustrating Certain Manners in Which Formal Systems Are Employed as Auxiliary Devices in Linguistic Description," Part I, *Annual Bulletin*, Vol. 3, pp. 111–130, Logopedics and Phoniatrics Research Institute, Tokyo University.

Kuroda, S.-Y. (1971) "Remarks on the Notion of Subject with Reference to Words Like *Also, Even*, or *Only*," Part II, *Annual Bulletin*, Vol. 4, pp. 127–152, Logopedics and Phoniatrics Research Institute, Tokyo University.

Kuroda, S.-Y. (forthcoming) "Where Epistemology, Style and Grammar Meet—A Case Study from Japanese," to appear in S. Anderson and P. Kiparsky, eds., *Studies Presented to Morris Halle*, Holt, Rinehart and Winston, New York.

Lakoff, G. (1968) "Pronouns and References," unpublished paper, Harvard University, Cambridge, Mass.

Lakoff, G. (1970) *Irregularity in Syntax*, Holt, Rinehart and Winston, New York.

Lakoff, G. (1971) "On Generative Semantics," in D. D. Steinberg and L. A. Jakobovits, eds., *Semantics—An Interdisciplinary Reader in Philosophy, Linguistics, Anthropology and Psychology*, pp. 232–296, Cambridge University Press, Cambridge, England.

Lakoff, G., and S. Peters (1969) "Phrasal Conjunction and Symmetric Predicates," in D. A. Reibel and S. A. Schane, eds., *Modern Studies in English*, pp. 113–142, Prentice-Hall, Englewood Cliffs, N.J.

Martin, S. E. (1962) *Essential Japanese—An Introduction to the Standard Colloquial Language*, Charles E. Tuttle Co., Rutland, Vt., and Tokyo, Japan, 1954[1], 1956[2], 1962[3].

Mikami, A. (1960) *Zoo wa Hana ga Nagai*, Kurosio Syuppan, Tokyo.

Mikami, A. (1963) *Nihongo no Koobun (Japanese Syntax)*, Kurosio Syuppan, Tokyo.

Mikami, A. (1969) "Sonzaibun no Mondai (Problems of Existential Sentences)," *Ōtani-Zyosidaigaku Kiyoo*, Vol. 3, pp. 38–48.

Mikami, A. (1970) *Bunpoo Syooron Syuu (Essays on Grammar)*, Kurosio Syuppan, Tokyo.

Miller, R. A. (1967) *The Japanese Language*, University of Chicago Press, Chicago.

Muraki, M. (1970) "Presupposition, Pseudo-Clefting and Thematization," unpublished Ph.D. dissertation, University of Texas, Austin.

Nakau, M. (1971) *Sentential Complementation in Japanese*, unpublished Ph.D. dissertation, MIT, Cambridge, Mass.

Perlmutter, D. M. (1971a) *Deep and Surface Structure Constraints in Syntax*, Holt, Rinehart and Winston, New York.

Perlmutter, D. M. (1971b) "On the Article in English," in M. Bierwisch and K. F. Heidolph, eds., *Recent Developments in Linguistics*, Mouton and Co., The Hague.

Postal, P. (1971) *Cross-over Phenomena*, Holt, Rinehart and Winston, New York.

Ross, J. H. (1967) *Constraints on Variables in Syntax*, unpublished Ph.D. dissertation, MIT, Cambridge, Mass.

Ross, J. H. (1969a) "A Proposed Rule of Tree-Pruning," in D. Reibel and S. Schane, eds., *Modern Studies in English*, pp. 288–299, Prentice-Hall, Englewood Cliffs, N.J.

Ross, J. H. (1969b) "On the Cyclic Nature of English Pronominalization," in D. A. Reibel and S. Schane, eds., *Modern Studies in English*, pp. 187–200, Prentice-Hall, Englewood Cliffs, N.J.

Ross, J. H. (1971) "Gapping and the Order of Constituents," in M. Bierwisch and K. F. Heidolph, eds., *Recent Developments in Linguistics*, Mouton and Co., The Hague.

Sakai, M. (1970) "Igi-Tokutyoo Kizyutu no Kokoromi (An Attempt to Describe Sememic Features)," *Sciences of Language*, No. 1, pp. 31–53, Tokyo.

Shibatani, M. (1971) "Three Reasons for Not Deriving 'Kill' from 'Cause to Die' in Japanese," presented at the Summer Linguistics Conference, University of California, Santa Cruz, July 16–17, 1971.

Tamura, S. (1969) "Nihongo no Tadoosi no Kibookei, Kanookei to Zyosi (Desiderative and Potential Forms of Transitive Verbs and Particles in Japanese)," *Waseda Daigaku Gogaku Kyooiku Kenkyuzyo Kiyoo*, No. 8.

Tokieda, M. (1941) *Kokugo-gaku Genron (Principles of Japanese Language Study)*, Iwanami, Tokyo.

Tokieda, M. (1950) *Nihon Bunpoo (Japanese Grammar)*, Part I, *Koogo-hen (Colloquial Japanese)*, Iwanami, Tokyo.

Underhill, R. (1972) "Turkish Participles," *Linguistic Inquiry*, Vol. 3, No. 1, pp. 87–99.

Index